MANAGING PROJECTS
A Systems Approach

MANAGING PROJECTS
A Systems Approach

Daniel D. Roman

Professor Emeritus
The George Washington University
Washington, DC

Elsevier
New York • Amsterdam • Oxford

658.404
R 75 m

Elsevier Science Publishing Co., Inc.
52 Vanderbilt Avenue, New York, New York 10017

Sole distributors outside the United States and Canada:
Elsevier Science Publishers B.V.
P.O. Box 211, 1000 AE Amsterdam, The Netherlands

© 1986 by Elsevier Science Publishing Co., Inc.
Chapters 3 and 7 copyright by J. Davidson Frame

This book has been registered with the Copyright Clearance Center, Inc.
For further information, please contact the Copyright Clearance Center,
Salem, Massachusetts

Library of Congress Cataloging in Publication Data

Roman, Daniel D. Managing projects.
Includes bibliography and index.
    1. Industrial project management
    I. Title.
HD69.P75R65 1986 658.4'04 85-13566
ISBN 0-444-00966-3

Current printing (last digit):
10 9 8 7 6 5 4 3 2 1

Manufactured in the United States of America

to Roz

UNIVERSITY LIBRARIES
CARNEGIE-MELLON UNIVERSITY
PITTSBURGH, PENNSYLVANIA 15213

Contents

Preface

A distinct evolutionary change is in process in technologically developed countries. There is a definite decline in the number of people employed in the mass production industries. More and more activities represent thinking and creative effort. To support the aforementioned, there is a trend to organize people into small entrepreneurially oriented groups. These groups are usually projectized and objectively directed rather than functionally oriented. Functionalism is the more normal approach in traditional mechanistic organizations. Projectization of activities is often a logical approach to organization in organic operations where production is not cycled, the work is frequently customized, and the effort may involve creative inputs.

From all indications, project management is rapidly growing in importance. Since projects represent a noncycled activity and are an ad hoc organizational arrangement, the management of such activity transcends and is far more sophisticated than management processes employed in cycled activities. This book starts from the traditional management base but emphasizes management within the project operational structure.

It is envisioned that this book can serve as a reference guide for professional project managers. The thrust of the book is concept rather than technique. Ideas are presented that hopefully will provide insight and possible direction into project operations which heretofore have been either neglected or sparsely treated in the literature. It is also envisioned that this book, by the nature of its comprehensive treatment of project management, can be a valuable textbook for the classroom.

There is an inclination, when thinking of project management, to narrow the range of project activity to research and development. Projects can be initiated to cover many situations requiring special skills and concentrations in a large variety of operational environments. Projects and project management are universal concepts and transcend geographical boundaries. Evidence of the intensified interest in project management is the proliferation of courses and seminars addressing the subject. Such courses vary in scope and intensity from short one-day to one-week seminars to instructional courses offered for university credit.

The bulk of the literature and most of the formal and informal educational approaches to project management emphasize only one phase of project management: operations. Invariably the emphasis is on technique rather than concept. Technique is, of course, important, but concept is more important, especially since the operational range of projects is so extensive. To set forth techniques that have universal application is unrealistic. Techniques have to be adapted, modified, or innovated to fit the specific project management situation. Project management requires ingenuity and constant managerial improvisation.

This book does not concentrate on just the operational phase of a project; instead, it looks at the total life cycle of a project. There is a logical organization pattern from conceptual to formative to operational and, finally, the termination phase of the project life cycle. Each phase in the life cycle of a project has distinct operational characteristics. There are interaction and dependency in the four phases as the project evolved from concept to completion or termination. Accordingly, as mentioned, the book is divided into four sections, each of which deals with the activities that can normally be expected in the particular phase of the project life cycle. There are, however, some topics that overlap and could organizationally fit in more than one section or life cycle phase. In dealing with such topics, the author placed them sequentially where they seemed most appropriate.

Much of the material in this book has been developed and tested in project management seminars taught between 1980 and 1984 at the George Washington University. The author also has had over 30 years of operational experience in project management. Managing technologically complex projects is involved and challenging and requires a broad knowledge base; this conclusion has been reinforced by the experience in teaching project management.

The author is endebted to and wishes to acknowledge the contributions made by J. Davidson Frame, who did the chapters on project selection methodologies (Chapter 3) and planning and control techniques (Chapter 7), Max Weiner, who wrote the chapter on the legal considerations involved in project management (Chapter 11), and Richard Armour for his contribution of the chapter covering the use of the computer in project management (Chapter 8). In addition, the author wishes to thank the many professionals who participated in the project management seminars for their ideas, stimulation, and confirmation relative to the need for a comprehensive exposition dealing with the subject of project management.

Finally, the author would like to thank his wife, Roz, for her unfailing dedication and enthusiasm in typing the manuscript. Much of her effort was reflected in early morning typing sessions before she started her normal job activities.

Dan Roman

MANAGING
PROJECTS
A Systems Approach

CHAPTER ONE

Introduction

Introduction to Project Management

Mechanistic and Organic Organizations

Managing projects involves many operational variations that are not present in more routine activities. Project management is a departure from management in cycled activities where risk and accomplishment can, with some degree of probability, be anticipated. Often in cycled activity the organization is mechanistic, reflecting a reasonably stable market and a reasonably stable technology. In this operational milieu production is standardized and distribution channels are known and established. There is a predictable environment, change is relatively slow, and functional obligations, including authority and responsibility relations, are well defined.[1]

Project management, on the other hand, is more normally found in organic organizations. Organic organizations are adaptive, generally exist in a volatile technological and/or market environment, and are subject to frequent change. Such an operational setting usually reflects the need for a high degree of technical, professional, conceptual, and managerial skill. Decision making is often decentralized and operational latitude significantly expanded from the mechanistic organization.[2]

Technical decisions in organic organizations normally are more complex than decisions in mechanistic organizations. Often there is limited or no explicit technical precedence for guidance. By the same token, managerial decisions in such situations also are quite involved and are usually made with little or no previous explicit experience to provide direction.

The Project: A Frame of Reference

Projects are formed to achieve objectives; they are ad hoc organizational arrangements that normally have a start and completion schedule. In some instances, however, such as in seeking a cure in medical research, the project end date may be indeterminate. The project may have a comparatively simple objective, which can be accomplished by one or a few specialists, or it may be an intricate undertaking, calling for a collection of diverse or allied skills. Depending on the technical challenge, a project may entail one or several tasks, involve a few or many people, span one or several functions, cover a short period or many years, and cost an inconsequential sum or millions of dollars.

Barndt and colleagues reinforce the aforementioned:

> A project organization is established for a limited period of time, generally to accomplish one specific purpose—to bring a new idea or project from its conceptual stage through development and cause its full implementation.[3]

Archibald further elaborates:

> Projects are intended to produce certain specified results at a particular point in time and within an established budget. They cut across organizational lines. They are unique endeavors, not completely repetitious of any previous effort.
>
> A project may be viewed as the entire process required to produce a new product, new plant, new system, or other specified results. The product to be created often receives more attention than the process by which it is created, but both the product and the process—the project—require effective management.[4]

For illustrative purposes, some objectives of projects can be to develop hardware, verify by testing, carry out feasibility studies, or investigate technical problems. Other objectives can also exist that lend themselves to project organization. The project can solve a narrow problem or advance the state of the art. It can involve many or a few knowns, or unknowns, constants, or combinations of these.

Distinctions Between Cycled and Noncycled Activities

Cycled Activities

Perhaps a better understanding of project management can be derived from a comparative look at operations that normally follow a cycled pattern and uncycled operations which lend themselves to projectization.

In most product- or process-directed activities, there is a sequence of events that can be established from the beginning of the cycle to the end. The sequence normally will have little or no variation, except where product modifications are incorporated to enhance marketability. The start, operational, and stop phases are generally predictable and repeated.

Operational objectives usually are quite explicit, reflecting commitment to a product or group of products. Any significant departure from the product cycle would require operational deviation. A major or significant deviation could become a separate project activity, the results of which could ultimately be incorporated into the production cycle.

Where there is a repetitious cycle, the end product, except for cosmetic marketable differences, is standardized. Generally, in cycled activities, a reasonably predictable consumption pattern is established; production is normally in anticipation of demand. In cycled, or mechanistic, organizations, planning, scheduling, and control factors can be developed and programmed, based on predictable repetitive activities.

There are also different operational pressures in cycled and noncycled activities. Constant change is a fact of life in uncycled operations. The types of people who gravitate to operational environments, where there is constant flux, are stimulated and thrive in such situations. For these people a more predictable or cycled operational environment would tend to be boring and would afford little or no professional challenge. People who affiliate with organizations where there are more predictable operational cycles would probably, in many instances, be constantly frustrated and unhappy by the ever-present change and the inability to predict or identify with a tangible end product.

Skill levels can be high in both cycled and uncycled activities. In most cycled activities the ratio of professional skill to the total operational work force would generally be less than in uncycled situations. Skills or professions in cycled mechanistic organizations are usually segregated so that the emphasis or concentration is on functional performance or contribution. In uncycled operations skills are entwined to enhance total objective accomplishment rather than immediately concentrated on a functional segment. In essence, the emphasis shifts from function-directed activity to objective-directed activity.

In cycled situations the operational environment can vary from a moderate to a tightly closed system. There is, based on the inherent constraints of the system, limited latitude for operational variations and innovations.

Cost estimating, cost control, product pricing, and market penetration and share can be determined or forecast with various degrees of certainty, depending on the nature of the end product. There usually is some past experience that can be used to calculate potential costs, to anticipate and provide for possible contingencies, and to control operating costs. The existing competition and the organization's market position also provide guidance for comparative value and quality analysis and contribute to the determination of pricing policies. Most products are evolutionary variations of existing products. Therefore, excluding those instances where the product is radically unique or new, there is also some degree of anticipation of consumer acceptance based on past experience.

Noncycled Activities

There are several demarcation points between cycled and noncycled activities. These differences are often so distinctive that organizing along project lines is intimated in order to provide emphasis, direction, and specific responsibility for accomplishment.

Noncycled activities, by definition, are not repetitive. It would, however, be unusual if there were absolutely no past experience related to the activity. The applicability of past experience to a new undertaking can range from some degree of parallelism to a completely new situation. Precedence may or may not be important in determining a project's direction. While the undertaking is a significant departure from past practices, it follows that there will be little or no past experience to help in anticipating cost, schedules, and potential technical accomplishment.

Noncycled activities may involve considerable technological change, which, in turn, can have rippling organizational impacts. The operational environment, depending on the nature of the technology, can become extremely volatile. Human skill inventory requirements are constantly changing in amount, degree, and types of specialities. In a multiproject organization projects phase in and out, and human and material resources can be drastically affected by the extent of need and the variation of human and material specialization required to meet operational commitments. Balancing resources and maintaining a responsive technical capability are critical managerial problems.

Often in noncycled activities the end product is in response to a specific demand rather than in anticipation of demand. Where the product is customized, there may be difficulty in determining a true or fair value. The difficulty may be compounded where the end product is so different that related products or services do not exist for comparative analysis. If the end product is tangible and of material substance but new, determination of value involves considerable subjectivity. Subjectivity is more intensified in value determination where the end product is knowledge. How and when can knowledge be applied? What is it worth?

Organizations may be committed to many noncycled activities that may entail diverse projects. There is the difficulty in selecting projects that are compatible with present and future organizational objectives. Objectives in a dynamic operational setting can shift because of technological influences that are uncontrollable by the organization. Project selection also, as previously indicated, involves balancing and utilizing existing resources and accommodation and anticipation of future needs and resource development.

Measurement and evaluation of product and human performance are also difficult in a noncycled environment. What constitutes a reasonable performance standard where there is no comparative precedence? How can standards be determined? Can a price tag or quantitative evaluation be placed on knowledge generated? There may also be difficulties in evaluation attached to the uncertainties of initial product performance. Even though projects, at the time of authorization, have performance specifications and time and cost constraints, it is not unusual to subsequently find deviations from the original concept.

Projects are usually launched under enthusiastic conditions. Often the level of ultimate accomplishment is less than original perceptions because of unforeseen problems, undue optimism, or time and resource constraints that act as developmental constraints.

There can be instances where the project was authorized because the degree of potential technical difficulties was minimized. At times management is either naïve or acts naïve in not actually recognizing potential difficulties in achieving project objectives. Where there are more unknowns than knowns involved and the state of the art is being pushed, there is a reasonable probability that original technical, time, and cost objectives will subsequently have to be adjusted.

In some instances technical goals are quite explicit and are contractually required. Failure to meet contractual obligations can organizationally be disastrous. In other instances the technical goals can be so tenuous that, rather than contractually committing the project to tight specifications and unpredictable technical performance, the project is undertaken on a best-effort basis. In such situations the parties to the contract may agree on some technical approach and negotiate terms that exclude or minimize specific performance.

Projects involve three dimensions: time, cost, and performance. Performance, or accomplishment, within a stipulated time frame to a determined objective is usually a paramount consideration. Cost is also critical, but, depending on the urgency of the project operations, cost may be subordinated to technical accomplishment within established time constraints.

A project involving any high degree of technical and marketing uncertainty is a high-risk venture. As a generalization, the longer a project extends into the future, the more intense the risk. Risk factors include failure to achieve technical objectives. Or the technical objectives can be achieved at a disproportionate cost, which limits, or maybe even eliminates, the potential market. The longer into the future, the greater the probability that there may be competitive forces or interceding technological breakthroughs that obviate the original premises of the project. Additional risk associated with time can come about due to sociological, cultural, or economic changes that affect the need, acceptance, or marketability of the project and product.

Projects also involve many managerial problems that usually are not found in operations in cycled activities. For instance, the end product of a project frequently reflects knowledge, creativity, and innovation. Which people should be assigned to the project? By its nature, the human productive element of the project will require some, or many, special skills. Not only must the skills ingredient be properly proportioned, but also the professionals possessing those skills must be blended to achieve harmonious and positive synergistic results.

The project, by its organizational form, is not a completely self-contained operational entity. The resources to accomplish the immediate technical objectives probably will be localized; however, a project may require functional support from a variety of sources that are not under the direct control of the project manager. The project manager is in effect forced to subcontract out many project-related activities, some of which may be extremely critical to the ultimate project success. Subcontracting such activities can involve extensive coordination. There are problems associated with guaranteed, or even acceptable, performance—getting schedule commitments where there may be competition for functional support with other projects and controlling financial resources. Usually the functional support areas cannot or will not actively respond and commit resources until budget authorization is released. The release of funds curtails controls.

The Project Organizational Form: A Response to Need

Evolving to Need

The concept of organizing human and physical resources into projects is not new. Several examples of project organization (e.g., building the pyramids) can be traced to antiquity. However, project management as a distinct organizational concept did not come into sharp focus until World War II, when there was an urgency to produce, and deliver, sophisticated hardware and solve complex war-related operational problems within severe time constraints.

Traditional organizational methods were not sufficiently responsive to operational requirements. Traditional organizations tend to be mechanistic, product directed, and functionally oriented. Many of the problems arising out of the World War II crisis were extremely urgent and required innovative solutions and organizational methods responsive to operational objectives. In project organization intense focus is on objectives; the physical and human resources are coordinated so that ideally functional affiliations are subordinated to project objectives. The emphasis shifts to team activity and the integration of skills.

Small Organizations

Variations of project organization have become increasingly important during the latter part of the 20th century. Selective organization of specialized resources into small or relatively small close-knit, objective-directed teams can enhance the prospects for innovative solutions to involved problems. In support of the aforementioned, several landmark studies have substantiated the impressive amount of technical innovation fostered by small organizations.[5]

Small organizations are often characterized by the lack of established vested interests; red tape is minimal, response to operational needs is quick, and operational flexibility is generally good. Top management in small organizations frequently is actively involved in projects; in such an environment there is a reasonable probability that the management style will be informal, encouraging give and take, and communication quick, sensitive, and applicable.

The negative aspects revolve around the inclination for decisions to be technically dominated to the exclusion of relevant and important management factors. Enthusiasm regarding the technical prospects can all but obliterate critically needed managerial decisions. Resources are invariably very tight in small organizations, and failure to properly use these limited resources can be catastrophic. Technical objectives can be achieved, but the end product may not have a market or the costs can be so high that the market will not support the product sufficiently to make an adequate return on investment. Market failure is more frequent than failure to achieve technical objectives. What is important and challenging is to retain the operational characteristics normally found in small organizations and complement these with good management practices. In essence, both technical and managerial accomplishment, including market awareness, is essential for a successful project.

Large Organizations

Large organizations operating in a dynamic technological environment are increasingly becoming sensitive to possible organizational methods that can encourage innovation. As a consequence, there appears to be a growing trend to group people into relatively small project teams. Projects may represent professionally and technologically compatible teams that are directed to functional development or may be composed of people with diversified professional skills organized to achieve objectives which extend beyond functional development.

Projects

Project Objectives and Types of Projects

Often there is a misconception of project operations. The adaptability of the project organizational form may have too narrow a connotation. There is a tendency to think "project," where, for example, the design and development of hardware for new products are being engineered. Project organization can be an effective device to achieve a variety of objectives under many different operational environments. This section will look at some project objectives, including the types of projects, the elements of a project, and the phases in the project life cycle.

The following are illustrations of some areas where projects can be used:

1. To experiment and seek new knowledge[6]
2. To do feasibility studies as to technical potential, market prospects, time constraints, and costs preliminary to all-out commitment of resources
3. To develop new products
4. To improve existing products
5. To reduce costs
6. To improve production processes
7. To find new uses for existing products[7]
8. To find potential uses for by-products or waste products generated by present production
9. To analyze and study competitors' products[8]
10. To embark on major construction projects
11. To provide a technical service to functional departments in the organization
12. To facilitate investment in developmental projects[9]
13. To inaugurate socially directed activities[10]
14. To improve functionalism in such fields as marketing, finance, personnel, production, and engineering
15. To develop educational programs within the established as well as specialized programs within or outside the system, in response to particular organizational needs
16. To anticipate and accomplish personal objectives, including such diverse activities as social functions, personal development, travel, and home maintenance

Of course, the preceding list is not all inclusive. Its intent was to give some idea of the enormous range of activities that can be encompassed.

Elements of a Project

As mentioned previously, projects can be simple undertakings with relatively few phases, or they can be technically and managerially complex, incorporating many and diverse resources. An example of a simple project may be yard work in the spring. The work may involve one or a few persons, some relatively unsophisticated tools, and limited and standard materials. In such a comparatively simple project, there probably will be little formal planning. Nevertheless, in order to accomplish the objectives, using a minimum amount of time and energy, the project manager, who is also the project performer in this instance, should identify the desired end results, the tools and materials required, the sequence of operations, and allow for time and weather constraints.

In a simple project, as just described, there are many relevant elements that should be considered to facilitate accomplishment. Not all elements are applicable to all projects, but, surprisingly so, most of the project elements are present and should be accommodated even in the simplest of situations. The elements of a project[11] are as follows:

Tasks
   Needs, purpose
   Selling concept (internal/external)
   Possible solutions
   Value of the end product
   Time constraints
   Costs (cost/benefit analysis)
   Authorization

Method
   Technical objectives
   Technical alternatives
   The plan
   Project organization
   Implementation, operations
   Control functions, feedback

Resources
   Human: skill inventory and availability
   Facilities
   Equipment
   Materials
   Information
   Time
   Capital

Project environment
   Stakeholders
   Management
   The customer
   Functional support
   The project team
   Legal/social environment

Project Life Cycle

Most of the project management courses and project management literature concentrate on techniques applicable to the operational phase of the project life cycle. Project management and the project manager are involved in critical activities that precede, and follow, the operational phase. Each phase of the project life cycle entails distinct activities and skills. Failure to properly address the issues involved in the successive phases of the project life cycle can jeopardize the ultimate success of the project, and may even mitigate against initial authorization.

Different phases in the project life cycle can be identified. The project may evolve through the idea, structural, process or functional, and conclusion phases. Archibald classifies the life cycle phases as progressing from concept to definition to design to development to application and, finally, to postcompletion.[12] Karger and Murdock identify the four phases of the project life cycle as being (1) the conceptual phase, (2) the formative phase, (3) the operational phase, and (4) the termination phase.[13] Figure 1-1 indicates a partial but representative list of actions that must be considered during the phases of the project life cycle. Each project phase has special management considerations and represents different operational problems and functional involvement.

The project life cycle phases set forth by Karger and Murdock are considered relevant, understandable, and generally applicable to most projects. Therefore their classification will be adapted and used as a reference frame in the succeeding chapters of this book.

Figure 1-1. The project life cycle.

Go* (proceed)	Phase 1	Idea
		Market analysis
		Demand pull/technology push
		Technical feasibility
No go* (abort)	Phase 2	Structural
		Management
		Competition
Go*		Opportunity costs
		External factors/economics/regulations
		Resources
		Proposal preparation
No go*	Phase 3	Process or functional
		Planning
Go*		Detailed work breakdown
		Schedules/priorities
		Operations
	Phase 4	Conclusion
		Project completion
		Termination for convenience
		Termination for default
		Project evaluation

*Decision points.

Philosophy and Organization of This Book

Philosophy

In industrially developed countries, the United States particularly, there has been a dramatic and relatively rapid transition from productive to service- and information-oriented societies. The number of people, as a percentage of the total population of the United States, employed on the farms and in the production of material goods has rapidly diminished since the beginning of the 20th century. It has been estimated that manufacturing will provide approximately 10% of the jobs at the start of the 21st century, and agricultural jobs will supply somewhere between 3 and 4% of the total employment opportunity.[14] The implications are that somewhere in the neighborhood of 85% of the working force will be engaged in activities and occupations that will deviate, in part or totally, from traditionally cycled activities.

Noncycled activities will become increasingly a part of the economic scene. Often noncycled activities are adaptive to projectization. The project, as a vehicle to accomplish organizational objectives, will probably become a more pronounced operational form. More organizations will undoubtedly either voluntarily opt for or be, by necessity, operationally pushed into this method. There are two important points that should be made relative to project organization. First, project management, by its structural and conceptual bases, is a complex and managerially sophisticated procedure. Second, project management methods are bound to evolve and vary in response to the dynamic operational environments in which they are peculiarly adaptable.

Project management builds on traditional management theory and practice. It also transcends such practices. Successful management of projects often requires imagination and innovation applied to individual situations. Among the purposes of this book is to provide perspective. The emphasis is on the conceptual rather than the mechanical.

It is thought that perspective can be encouraged by a holistic view of the various elements involved in project management. In the past, as mentioned earlier in this chapter, educational aspects of project management have primarily been technique directed toward operational problems. Also, the general management philosophies expanded have frequently been nothing more than reinforcement of traditional management theory. It is recognized that the same processes (i.e., conceptualization, planning, organizing, and managing human and material resources) and control procedures that exist in more mundane managerial settings also exist in project management. However, it is iterated that project management is an operational phenomenon in which processes, which are employed in more prosaic activities, will often fail unless modified or adapted in order to be responsive to this unique operational environment.

The attempt is to depart in significant degrees from the general run of project management literature. An objective of this book is to identify and address the relevant aspects of the project that must be accommodated and managed in each phase of the project life cycle. There will also be an attempt to call attention to important external and internal factors that can substantively affect a project; these factors may not be considered or may be minimized owing to the tendency to concentrate on the immediate technical obligations of the project.

Organization

Beyond the introductory chapter, the book is divided into four major sections to reflect the phases of the project life cycle.

The first section of the book examines some of the conceptual aspects of the project. Included in this section will be distinctions between project management in various operational environments, as well as a look at some of the external and internal factors that can prove to ultimately be controlling, insofar as project authorization is concerned. Project selection will also be covered in this section. In addition, this section will discuss proposal preparation, including external and internal proposals, as well as solicited and unsolicited proposals.

The second section of the book examines some of the elements associated with the formative phases of the project. In this section such topics as organizational methods to facilitate accomplishment, planning aspects, including work breakdown methods, and planning and control techniques applicable to project management will be covered, as well as the use of the computer in project management.

The third section of the book is devoted to project operations. In this section concentration will be focused on managing the project to achieve its technical, managerial, and economic objectives. This section addresses financial management, project controls, the use of the computer, patents, and trade secrets, and an awareness of human factors and productivity.

The fourth and final section will emphasize the issues involved in project termination. Such topics as evaluation and determination of accomplishment, causes for termination, termination procedures, and a project termination audit procedure will be covered. The role of the project manager will also be discussed.

Endnotes Chapter One

1. H. L. Tosi and S. J. Caroll, *Management*, 2nd ed., New York, Wiley, 1982, p. 56.
2. *Ibid.*
3. S. E. Barndt, J. C. Larsen, and P. J. Ruppert, "Organizational Climate Changes in the Project Life Cycle," *International Journal of Research Management*, Vol. 20, No. 5, p. 33, 1977.

4. R. D. Archibald, *Managing High-Technology Programs and Projects,* New York, Wiley, 1976, p. 19.

5. J. Jewkes, D. Sawers, and R. Stitlerman, *The Sources of Invention,* 2nd ed., New York, Macmillan, 1979; A. C. Cooper, "Small Companies Can Pioneer New Products," *Harvard Business Review,* Sept./Oct. 1966; James R. Bright, *Research, Development and Technological Innovation,* Homewood, IL, Richard D. Irwin, 1964; Donald A. Schor, *Technology and Change,* New York, Delacorte, 1967; Sumner Meyers and Donald G. Marquis, *Successful Industrial Innovations,* Washington, DC, National Science Foundation, 1969; Daniel Hamberg, *R & D Essays on the Economics of Research and Development,* New York, Random House, 1966.

6. The range of such project possibilities is enormous. Representative of such activities are medical research, physics, materials, and so on.

7. "Losing Its Flash: As Polaroid Matures, Some Lament a Decline in Creative Excitement," *Wall Street Journal,* May 10, 1983, pp. 1 and 19.

8. The Japanese have been uniquely adept in this area. The Soviets are also active in using this approach as a quick means of transferring technology.

9. A good example is some of the projects undertaken by the World Bank. Representative are Mario Kamenetzsky, "Choice and Design of Technologies for Investment Projects," unpublished paper, *World Bank,* August 1982, and "Participation of Local Professionals and Technicians in Projects Financed by the World Bank," *World Bank,* S & T Report No. 14.

10. Social projects can involve activities dealing with public health, welfare, ecological objectives, planned parenthood, saving endangered species, and so on.

11. Adapted and modified from Foreningen Project Plan, Danish Project Management Society, *Organizing Export Projects,* Hans Mikkelsen (ed.), p. 14.

12. Archibald, *op. cit.,* p. 20.

13. D. W. Karger and R. G. Murdock, *Managing Engineering and Research,* New York, Industrial Press, 1963, p. 299.

14. M. L. Cetron, "Getting Ready for the Jobs of the Future," *Futurist,* p. 15, June 1983.

The Project Conceptual Phase

CHAPTER TWO

Conceptual Aspect of Project Selection

Operational Objectives

Determining Feasibility

Organizations are formed and activities are generally initiated under optimistic conditions. The organization may be a distinct new entity, it may be an addition to and part of an existing organization, or it may be split off from an established organization and assume a separate identity, even though retaining an affiliation with the parent organization. Ideas develop into concepts and concepts can be translated into objectives. Prospects for the attainment of objectives may vary from a high probability for success to remote chances for achievement. If any magnitude of effort is involved, it is reasonable practice to make a comprehensive analysis of the technical and economic feasibility of the proposed operational objectives.

The model depicted in Figure 2-1 indicates the organizational operational life cycle moving from the inception or conceptual phases, steps 1 through 3, to the formative phases, steps 4 and 5, to the operational phases, steps 6 and 7, and to the termination phase, when the cycle has been completed, step 8.

As indicated, step 1 starts with the idea and instigates the subsequent phases in the cycle. In step 2 research is undertaken that is critical to the ultimate decision to proceed or not to proceed, which is made in step 3. In the second phase the general operational environment is explored as to past, current, and future prospects. If the prospective area of activity is already established, what are the future prospects? What are the prospects for a new entrant into the field? What are the technological pros-

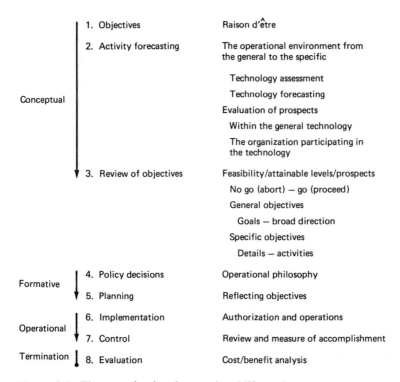

Figure 2-1. The organizational operational life cycle.

pects? Legal impacts? Competition? If the area represents a new techno-logical frontier, what markets can be developed? What developments might be anticipated that could improve the technological prospects or obviate the technology and render it obsolete? These are very important considerations in order to avoid involvement that subsequently can prove to be costly and embarrassing owing to new technological developments which neutralize or even negate past effort.[1] Another factor to be consid-ered in step 2 is technology assessment or environmental impact. Future prospects may be diminished if accomplishment of the objectives affects the environment and leads to legal or regulatory problems.

Step 3 is a review of the original objectives following the in-depth research covered in step 2. After the additional information becomes available and is interpreted, the original organizational concept may be abandoned owing to prospective technical, marketing, or legal problems; the original organizational concept may appear valid in light of the addi-tional supporting information; or the decision may be to proceed after making modifications to the original operational objectives based on the added input in step 2. If the decision is to continue, the organization should have general objectives to provide operational guidance and specific objectives on how to accomplish and implement its goals.

Steps 4 through 8 assume an operational organization. These phases may be repeated or modified, depending on the nature of operations and assuming organizational continuity. The project life cycle also parallels the steps indicated in Figure 2-1. Project selection is closely related to steps 1 through 3 of the model.

Project Selection and Operational Objectives

Project selection should support operational objectives. The project selection process involves many operational facets. It is a decision process relating to future activities, including areas of current and prospective technical concentration. In the selection process management is making a resource allocation decision, ordaining the extent as well as direction of the commitment. The nature of the projects selected and the acquisition and maintenance of the resources required to support the projects will determine the breadth and depth of the operation.

The decision to proceed on a project, the authorization, may be external to the organization and represent a legal contract. Project activity may also start as a consequence of internal authorization. Internal approval of projects will not have the same legal connotations as externally approved projects, but there still is an inferred liability for performance accomplishment between the project leader and the authorizing source within the organization. The project may also be subject to modification of original objectives, depending on the unknowns and uncertainties involved when the project is started. If the project objectives involve significant technological development, it is possible that internal or external factors can subsequently affect the original project premises. Additional information or unforeseen technical, economic, sociological, or political changes can affect the successful conclusion of any project.

Management must provide for periodic evaluation and review as follow-ups to the initial selection process. Projects may not be achieving objectives or may become incompatible with operational goals, or projects authorized that were at one time compatible with operational goals may no longer be feasible since operational goals have been reviewed and subsequently changed. In a volatile technological environment it is imperative to frequently review operational objectives and, if indicated, be responsive to changing environmental requirements. In light of the aforementioned, newly proposed projects may offer better prospects than some projects that are in process. Terminating existing projects short of completion represents a separate and serious avenue of managerial decision making and will be discussed in a later chapter.

The balance of this chapter will discuss how organizational objectives differ between government and profit and nonprofit organizations, the operational environmental factors that can affect project selection, the qualitative and quantitative factors involved in project selection, and some possible suggestions to encourage new ideas leading to viable projects.

Operational Objectives and the Selection Process in Different Economic Sectors

Motivational Factors for Project Selection Vary by Economic Sector

The operational environments of for-profit organizations may be very similar or considerably different. In each of these environments there are fundamental missions and, at times, distinct operational idiosyncracies. However, despite operational differences, there are overriding considerations: The projects selected and authorized should have a reasonable probability of accomplishing their objectives and should be compatible with the organization's mission.

In this section some of the influential factors that affect project selection in each of the three sectors will be discussed. The motivational factors for project selection, as indicated, will vary by sector, with different orders of priorities in the different sectors. In some instances the critical motivational factor for selection may exist in one sector, such as need in the government or profit in the private sector, and may not be an element for consideration in another sector, for example, profit in the government.

The priorities that impinge on the selection of projects within the different economic sectors are determined by the sector mission requirements. Once the project is selected and moves from the conceptual stage to the formative, operational, and terminal phases, management of the project will depend on many factors. The possible range of managerial alternatives is so vast, depending on the nature of the project, its objectives, and its operational setting, that a universal managerial template is impossible. Nevertheless, there is some commonality in project management processes. For instance, generally, as part of the selection process, proposals are generated to indicate the technical scope of the work, potential contribution or benefits anticipated from the project, time frames or periods of performance, cost expenditures, and, if applicable, profit expectations. As part of the project process there are other common elements, such as organization, planning, cost management, operational control, managing the human element, and project evaluation.

The project manager is invariably involved with the aforementioned activities. He or she must respond to such activities, consistent with the organizational objectives and any unique operational aspects resulting from the nature of the immediate project. An effective project manager will frequently innovate managerially, as well as technically, to accomplish project objectives.

The Government Sector

It is difficult to generalize when discussing government and military operations. The "government" encompasses many organizational units. Even though each governmental unit is operationally directed by its mission responsibilities, there is considerable latitude in operational procedure between the various governmental agencies. Therefore, in essence, the government represents many sources and many different procedures rather than a single, uniform operational source.

The government has political as well as cultural, economic, social, and educational obligations. Most of the government's involvement in establishing technological goals is in consonance with the general welfare. In our private enterprise society a pattern has emerged whereby the federal government supplies most of the money and private industry does most of the work. The government maintains relatively little in-house operational capability. Project management in the government is often synthesis, coordination, and contract administration.

In the government and the military, projects develop from ideas in response to need. When the problem is apparent, a project may suggest itself almost spontaneously as the means of satisfying the need. In some instances, however, problems are not obvious, and a project is not initiated until ideas are generated and proposals offered. These may come from an individual or group within the organization or from outside organizations seeking applications compatible with their technical capabilities.

Project selection in the government can also be greatly influenced by political considerations. Politicians respond to public pressures, and such pressures often are the forerunners of funding authorizations. Funding levels are influential considerations in project authorizations. If the federal agency is well funded, projects of questionable validity may be initiated because the field or fields of investigation are politically defensible. If public sentiment is unfavorable, other areas may not be funded and may be neglected, even though prospective projects in these fields have an excellent probability for success.

Project authorization may be relatively simple to obtain if the proposed project falls within the mission objectives of the sponsoring agency, can be financed with funds already allocated or appropriated for the fulfillment of these objectives, and involves no momentous or controversial technology. On the other hand, authorization can involve great complexities when mission requirements are not clearly established or proponents of different technical approaches argue on behalf of their causes.[2] The funds required may also be beyond the available resources of the administering agency or they may be contingent on congressional investigation and approval of the project.

The government does not look at a potential project in the same way a commercial organization does. It does no market analysis and has little or no concern with commercial application and none directly with profit.[3] The compelling force is the identification and justification of the need relative to the cost and potential value of the project, in line with the organization's mission.

By way of summary, certain characteristics of project selection by the government can be identified. Some of the more relevant factors can be outlined as follows:

1. Government projects are subject to an extensive range of technological sophistication, depending on the mission objectives of the authorizing agency.

2. The determination and authorization of a program are based on need and on mission requirements.

3. Need, time, and performance are primary considerations.

4. Cost and value are secondary but important factors, and there is little or no concern with immediate commercial applications.
   a. Market forecasts are not made.
   b. A government R&D project involves only one buyer and usually ultimately one prime seller.
   c. The government is not directly concerned with product profitability.
   d. There are often limitations on the contractor's profit.[4]

5. Often the technical concepts involved or hardware delivered is subject to rapid obsolescence, especially in areas where the technology is new or evolving.

6. Project selection may be closely allied to source selection.
   a. Relatively little in-house work is done by the government.
   b. Sponsoring agencies and services may call for certification of vendors.

7. The government frequently shifts specifications.
   a. Changes occur in the nature, scope, and cost of the project owing to technological developments or changing mission requirements.
   b. Contracts frequently undergo modification to reflect changes indicated in (a).
   c. Generally, the longer the project is operable, the greater the probability that there will be technological and contractual adjustments.

8. On their side, contractors often make overoptimistic presentations.
   a. They tend to run over original time and cost estimates to complete the project.

   b. They frequently request modifications of original performance
      specifications.[5]

The Private Sector

The criteria used for project selection in the private profit sector of the
economy are significantly different from those applied by government
organizations. In private industry the ultimate determining factor,
whether the firm deals with the government/military complex or operates
around a commercial product line, is the potential contribution to organizational objectives. This often can be translated as anticipated profit and a
means to enable organizational continuity. However, to base project selection only on immediate profit aspirations is to ignore many important
contributory factors related to operational, financial, production, technical, market, and facilities aspects of the total organization. The decision
process must evaluate all these considerations before a conclusion is
reached to embark on a project or reject it.

Project selection can be strongly influenced by operational factors that
may or may not provide short-run prospects for profit. The organization
may operate in a comparatively stable technological environment or it
may be part of an extremely volatile technological milieu in which constant operational change is the norm. The total organization may consist
of a few or many projects. Projects constantly phase in and phase out.
Those being introduced do not necessarily balance those being terminated
in resource requirements or contribution to organizational objectives. The
firm operating in a volatile technological environment is susceptible to
severe operational fluctuations that compound the difficulty of managing
and maintaining the organizational balance. A proposed project may not
offer great profit potential, but it could contribute to operational stability
and provide the means to maintain or upgrade the technical organization.

Undertaking many comparatively small and short-lived projects
presents operational problems, such as reassigning personnel and physical resources. Management costs on a small project are at times disproportionate to its contribution and accomplishments. Another operational
consideration is the cost of working up a proposal when the anticipated
project has little chance of acceptance, is incompatible with long-term
operational objectives, or is outside the realm of actual or desired competence. There are, however, situations where small or short-lived projects
can be justified. The small project may be a prelude to a much larger
undertaking; it may be a feasibility study to provide information as to
potential new areas and indicate a need to reappraise operational objectives; it may serve as an educational vehicle for the people assigned to the
project; and it may, as mentioned, provide a fill-in to maintain the technical organization during slack periods.

Project selection must also consider the time from inception to marketability of the end product of the project. Generally, the longer the project

extends into the future, the greater the technological and financial risk due to unforeseen changes. Again, the firm must determine its operational niche. Is it in a technologically revolutionary or evolutionary environment? What are the competitive forces? What is management's operational philosophy? Is it a follower, a leader, or has it carved out a small but special segment of an industry or technology? Many a firm has found that to enhance the prospects for organizational survival it has been necessary to establish itself in a small, selective, but important part of a larger technology. No better example can be advanced than companies developing specialized computer software.

Many quantitative formulas have been developed to factor in the different essential project elements in order to improve the probability for successful project selection. Quantitative project selection methodologies are covered in the next chapter. Profit potential would, under normal operational conditions, be the determining force for project selection. Profit potential can be calculated from prospective volume or market acceptance (if a product is ultimately involved), the probability of technical success, R&D and production costs, and the anticipated selling price. Risk and uncertainty, which must be factored into any profit formula, are difficult to evaluate if technological frontiers are being pushed. The longer the project extends into the future, the more difficult it becomes to forecast the impact of economic or political conditions, technological advances, and competitive products. Estimations of technical achievement and costs can be reasonably accurate, but profitability can be miscalculated owing to inopportune timing or failure to correctly anticipate need and demand in the introduction of a product.

Most quantitative formulas for project selection are financially oriented. In these formulas return on investment is the predominant consideration, but the use of this standard to the exclusion of other relevant factors can distort the selection process; it fails to portray accurately other actual contributions of a project besides estimated profitability. Another possible limitation of the return on investment method is that unless a project is completely isolated from all other operations, it may be difficult to determine its true cost and hence its contribution to organizational profits. Costs may not be properly charged or may not reflect subsequent benefits passed on to later projects.

There are additional financial considerations in project selection. They involve use of plant and equipment, depreciation, direct and indirect project charges, any new capital outlay requirements, overhead allocation, opportunity costs, the cost and availability of funds, and cash flow.

Other important factors in project selection that may not be directly operational or financial involve the organization's public image and how a project or a new product might contribute to it. Indeed, how does an organization achieve a public image? In all probability, it reflects the reputation of the enterprise built upon its technological leadership, pioneering products, quality of products, market sensitivity, and responsiveness to the public welfare as a good citizen of the community.

In some situations financial inducements in project selection can be secondary to the opportunity to provide a public service. The public goodwill generated by embarking on a project can be priceless. Also, it is well at times to contemplate project selection negatively. What might happen if the project is not undertaken? The reverse approach can provide interesting insights into operational factors that would not be apparent from the positive approach.

In the preceding paragraphs many factors that bear upon project selection in industry have been identified. In summary, some of the more pertinent characteristics are listed as follows:

1. The need for new products, new skill areas, and potential markets

2. Shorter project decision lines and more immediate sensitivity, and quicker reaction to operational need than in government/military organizations

3. Less individual latitude in resource commitment than in government/military organizations

4. The technical probability of success

5. The potential profitability of the project
   a. As a contribution to organizational objectives
   b. For follow-on projects
   c. For entry into new areas

6. Operational growth and stability
   a. The relationship of the project to existing projects
   b. The development of technical skills
   c. Existing technical skills inventory
   d. Available resources
   e. Alternative opportunities for utilizing the resources

7. Possible diversification to provide stability in the operational base

8. Technical contributions of a project
   a. The development of a proprietary product or unique marketable knowledge

9. The firm's market position and extent of product control

10. The effect of a new project on existing equipment and facilities

11. The firm's public image and prestige
    a. Demonstration of technical leadership through innovation and high-quality products
    b. The value and contribution of a project to society

The Nonprofit Sector

One badly neglected area in management generally and projects management specifically is the nonprofit sector of the national economy. The magnitude of effort in nonprofit activities is quite significant.

According to Internal Revenue Service records, there were approximately 840,000 active nonprofit entities in 1980. Statistically, in 1982 it was estimated that nonprofit organizations generated $90 billion worth of activities, as compared to about $2,500 billion in the profit sectors and $290 billion in the public sectors of the economy. Of added interest is the fact that the nonprofit sector appears to be growing more rapidly than the profit or government sectors. As further indication of nonprofit economic involvement, it was estimated that in 1982, 16 million people were employed in this sector, compared with roughly 60 million in the for-profit sectors and 19 million in the various public sectors.

Projects may be performed by nonprofessionals as well as professionals; however, when thinking "project management," there usually is the connotation of professional activity. It has been estimated that one out of every six professionals is employed by nonprofit organizations. According to Lane, there are five general classifications of nonprofit organizations[6]:

1. Charitable
2. Social
3. Trade associations
4. Government
5. Political

The U.S. government indicates a much broader classification for nonprofit activities. A partial but representative list includes religious organizations; schools; colleges; cultural, historical, other educational, and health services; scientific research; business and professional organizations; farming associations; nautical organizations; employee or membership benefit organizations; sports, athletic, recreational, and social activities; youth organizations (such as the Girl Scouts and Boy Scouts); conservation, environmental, and beautification groups; community affairs; civil rights; and charitable organizations.[7]

The diversity of activities performed under the aegis of nonprofit organizations is considerable. The spectrum ranges from very simple to extremely complex and from vocational to highly professional operational requirements. Projects in nonprofit organizations will reflect, of course, the operational environment and will vary in the selection and implementation processes. In essence, the factors that affect project selection in nonprofits are normally subject to a wide range of considerations and, in some instances, will parallel project selection in for-profit organizations, and at other times and in other organizations will more closely approximate project selection methodologies employed by governmental organizations.

Because of the operational diversities of nonprofits, it is extremely difficult to generalize on factors that are compelling in project selection. Perhaps nonprofit organizational project selection is, in the final analysis, closer to the government than for-profit organizations. The following are some of the elements that could be instrumental in selecting projects in nonprofit organizations:

1. The project should be compatible with the organization's franchise and support its mission(s).
2. The need of its constituency should be a compelling force in the selection of the project.
3. Funding is often erratic and may be subject to severe year-to-year fluctuations that may make long-range projects tenuous.
4. Nonprofit organizations are not directly motivated by profit owing to the nature of their franchise; however, the project may materially affect fund raising and subsequent organizational continuity.
5. Cost/benefit analysis is critical owing to the nature of funding and demand for services.
6. Projects may or may not have prospects for commercialization. In some instances a considerable part of the nonprofit organizations' funding may be derived from separate for-profit corporations.[8]
7. Much of project selection and implementation is motivated by the desire to obtain a favorable image and public goodwill.
8. Generally, the project, as distinct from the government, is performed in-house.
9. Projects are not necessarily undertaken for follow-on activities or operational continuity as is the case in for-profit organizations. Projects should support the organization's mission and help provide continuity insofar as mission requirements might evolve.
10. The project should afford the organization the opportunity to develop technical skills needed to support its mission.
11. The project should, wherever possible, provide the opportunity for people assigned to experience professional growth and development. This is necessary to provide challenge, maintain the technical competence to support the mission, and retain the necessary core of professionals needed by the organization to accomplish its objectives.

Project Screening

Organizational Constraints and Approaches to Project Selection

Most projects that involve significant resource allocation are subject to a screening process before authorization. In some instances the ultimate sponsoring authority is not even aware of a need or potential benefit until attention is directed to that need. Awareness may be precipitated by an unsolicited proposal. In other instances need and potential benefit may have been recognized, but procedure and implementation may be uncertain. In such instances assistance might be requested internally or externally to the organization by soliciting methodological and procedural proposals (requests for proposals).

Other approaches to project selection also exist. An organization may have a capability that it feels is marketable. Finding possible users, ascertaining user interest, and submitting a project proposal is a normal procedure in such situations. Another possibility is that the mission of the organization is relatively definitive in establishing the scope of prospective projects. In other words, project selection is to some degree preordained by the organizational charter. The general range of prospective projects is limited, but selection of specific projects that complement the overall operational objectives is subject to screening.

The preceding paragraphs raise the age-old issue of what comes first, the chicken or the egg? At times operational restrictions act as restraints on project selection; at other times, and in different situations, proposals for potential projects are submitted and such activity triggers a screening or selection process. To paraphrase the chicken-or-egg concept, what comes first, the proposal or the project selection? As indicated, proposals may be developed to support an established range of possible projects, for example, a firm doing business in the construction industry, where it is highly improbable that they would submit proposals for projects outside their area of expertise. In this example prospective projects may further be limited by specialization, such as highway construction or commercial or residential building.

There are other situations where an organization has a diversified inventory of human skills and operational resources that can be adapted to a variety of applications. In cases like this, project selection is not necessarily dictated by the present nature of operations; the project selection process may reflect available resources and internal and external factors.

Too often organizations and project managers suffer from technological myopia. They become locked into a narrow operational area that may be technologically vulnerable or they fail to exploit opportunities which hold promise. In essence, it is very important to recognize the internal and external factors that might limit or extend the type and range of projects which offer beneficial prospects to the organization. In the following sections some external and internal factors are cited. It is suggested that it is important to go beyond the immediate operational environment and look for possible adaptions where there might be promise for growth.

External Factors

In a mechanistic product-oriented organization, special projects may be formed for process improvement, product development, cost reduction, or to solve functional problems. The main operational thrust is product centered and projects are incidental and supportive of the product. Maintenance of the project organization and continuity is not a paramount operational objective.

Organic organizations may be either functionally or technologically concentrated. Usually the total organic organization represents project components that are in various stages of completion. Project managers in this operational environment are responsible for accomplishing the project objectives. The project normally has a finite existence; the project may or may not move into subsequent phases. In the event that the project is terminated because its objectives have been accomplished, the project team can be disbanded or reassigned to other projects. The problem associated with reassignment relates to a need for and compatibility of resources between the completed project and a new project.

The project manager in organic organizations has important responsibilities beyond accomplishing the immediate project objectives. He or she must look beyond the existing commitment in order to provide operational continuity to the organization, effectively utilize resources, maintain and possibly upgrade the technical organization, and—perhaps a selfish but realistic motivation—sustain himself or herself in the role of project manager. The aforementioned adds another dimension to the project manager's job: entrepreneurial responsibilities. The project manager must seek out opportunities and sell capabilities. This may be difficult, because project managers often are more technically than managerially qualified and, as a consequence, may not be aware of potential opportunities for follow-on activities.

If we assume that the organization is dependent on external sources for support, many factors must be weighed and evaluated. There generally is more than one possible operational direction. The organization can concentrate on an established market or clientele, try to expand the market base within a given technology, attempt technology transfer by seeking new applications of its capabilities outside the realm of its current operations, or possibly expand its operations to include two or more of the above options. The directional decision could be affected by external factors; timing could also be critical in determining the direction.

What is being suggested is that selecting a project or being obsessed with an objective can be a disaster if support for the activity is not forthcoming. It is like having a solution and seeking a problem. Realistically, the present scope of operations can be reviewed and prospects for the future can be examined by looking at current and potential capabilities relative to such external forces as need, environmental pressures, economic considerations, legal and moral issues, and social responsibilities. The following is a representative list of the aforementioned that could be considered:

Need
  Associated with demographics
    Regional population distribution
    Population age distribution
    Life expectancy
    Urban/suburban population distribution
    Fertility rate (family size)
    Population growth rate
    Household growth rate
    Household size (singles)
    Mobility
    Minorities
    Illegal aliens
    Composition of the work force
  The government market
    Defense
    Social programs
    Political environment
    Availability of funds
    State/local programs
    Regulation/control
  The private sector
    Need: an existing need or the possibility to cultivate a need
    State of the technology
    Degree of control of the technology
    Potential market and profitability
    Cost
    Time
    The nature of the operational environment growth/static
    Availability of resources

Environmental factors
    Educational level of indigenous population
    Emerging technologies
    Occupational shifts
    The employment market
    Part-time workers
    Retired people
    Leisure activities
    Quality of life
    Ecological considerations

Economic considerations
    State of the economy

Availability of resources
  Types of resources required
  Opportunity utilization
Productivity
General business climate
Availability of capital
  Interest rates
  Inflation
Competition
  Domestic
  International
Type of operational environment
  Monopolistic
  Oligopolistic
  Competitive

Legal and moral issues
  Regulation
  Legal liabilities (consumerism)
    Product liability
  Ethics
    Product testing
    Research methodology
    Impinging on others' research

Social responsibilities
  Environmental dangers or disturbances
  Commercial versus public welfare
  Private versus government support
  Public image

Of course, this list is not all inclusive. It is intended to provide a general guide to stimulate a thought process that might create an awareness of existing but previously unthought of opportunities. Also, since projects are normally one of a kind and vary considerably, it is recognized that evaluation of some or all of the external factors indicated may be far too ambitious in relation to the prospective project.

Internal Factors

In the preceding section it was assumed that the organization is dependent on outside support for its continued existence. If so, it should not be oblivious to those outside forces that might have significant impact. There are also internal factors that could ultimately be controlling relative to the scope of operations and the projects selected.

The organization's managerial philosophy can be the single most critical factor in determining the operational range and nature of projects. Is management aggressive? Passive? Or defensive? Is the management approach to expand slowly, rapidly, or to maintain the organization's current and relative position? Are the decision makers risk takers or risk avoiders? Are they willing to try new things and explore previously unchartered operational areas? An important caveat here is that the project professional's goals should be compatible with management's operational philosophy. A gung-ho project professional will be frustrated in a conservative environment. Conversely, the reticent project professional will probably be ineffectual in a technologically volatile operational environment.

The operational philosophy of management can be reflected in the nature and extent of available resources to the organization. It is also possible to have an aggressive managerial posture but experience operational limitations because of resources. The availability of capital is an obvious factor that can be instrumental in establishing operational boundaries. If money is scarce and interest rates high, there is the probability that the range of project selection will be restricted, and the selection process will no doubt be more conservative than in periods of more readily available funding.

Many projects are dependent on the human element as the prime productive factor. Promising projects may be discarded because the organization's human resources are presently overcommitted or lack the technical know-how to instill management with confidence that the project will be a success. On the other hand, and somewhat contradictorily, the project may be selected because there currently is underutilization of the technical organization, or the project can be a vehicle to upgrade the organization's technical competence.

Resources may involve facilities and equipment. The project selection decision could hinge on the utilization of existing facilities, including overhead and depreciation allocations, the need to upgrade the facilities, and, again, the availability and cost of capital.

Internal constraints to operational latitude could be imposed by the organization's position in an industry or technology. A large organization can benefit by size and hedge by diversifying project activities. A small organization may find itself in a less enviable position where resource constraints prohibit extensive diversification. The organization's position in an industry or technology can be affected by size, available resources, and its policy or philosophy as to whether it is a leader or a follower or has attempted to carve out a specialized and, hopefully, noncompetitive niche within the industry or technology.

Preliminary Considerations: Qualitative and Quantitative

Preliminary Considerations

Figure 2-1 indicated the different phases an organization experiences from its inception through its operational cycle. As indicated, project selection should be compatible with the organization's operational life cycle. The manager's analysis and evaluation must cover such factors as the complexity of the project, the resources involved, the time phase, and the potential contribution to organizational objectives. In the preliminary stages, before final authorization, the project might evolve through such sequences as the idea, discussion and screening with prospective project contributors, and some research and analysis of technical and economic feasibility, including identification of resource requirements, cost, market potential, and extent of confidence in achieving technical objectives. Variations of the aforementioned are possible based on the nature of the organization and the project.

Attention to the various phases of the project life cycle can offer definite help to management in the selection process; a project may look encouraging at one or more stages, but obstacles identified in other stages may be large enough to discourage future expenditures of time, money, and effort. In the selection process management must be cognizant of contribution, competition, and obsolescence, especially where the project involves a lengthy time frame and the technology is dynamic.

There are several elements that might be applicable in considering whether or not to authorize a project. It is suggested that in organizations where sophisticated projects are undertaken, a comprehensive checklist should be developed to provide guidance in project selection. The selection factors could be segregated under quantitative and qualitative elements. Not all elements would be applicable to all projects, and different elements would probably have different weights or values at different times. The benefit of this approach is that management would be alerted to all relevant considerations and the chance that one factor would lead to project selection to the exclusion of other possibly relevant factors would be minimized.

Quantitative Factors

The ideal system would be where all the germane factors could be identified and quantified. Quantification of critical project elements can provide some general indication or probability of project success; however, even though quantification can help by providing some range of probability, it is wise to recognize that total reliance on this approach is tenuous.

The accuracy of the calculations is limited by the validity of the figures used in the computation. Additionally, the relative weights given these figures in assessing probabilities could be distorted by the prejudice or ignorance of the person making the calculations. Also, the evaluation of absolute or relative value is based on the subjective estimate of the person(s) doing the calculations.

Another problem in quantification is cost classification. Quantitative estimates can differ, owing to variations in the methods of handling cost data. Other difficulties include the lack of precedent to use as a base for calculations, the unpredictability of time and performance in instances where the project is technologically complicated, the unforeseeble duration of the benefit period, the impossibility of measuring fallout gains not directly associated with the immediate project, and the inability to place a specific value on the project's contribution, not only to organizational objectives, but also to other functions within the operation.

Aware of the preceding cautions, one might list the following quantitative elements for consideration in project selection:

* Facilities
  New/existing/modernization
  Overhead
  Depreciation
* Investment alternatives
  Opportunity costs
  Cost/benefit analysis
* Return on investment
* Probability of technical success
* Probability of marketing success
* Human resources
  Skills/numbers
* Time
* Cost
* Technical specifications

Again, it is important to recognize that, while the above factors are essential in project selection, exclusive reliance on quantification can convey a misleading indication of both the relative and the absolute value of the overall project. Despite the inherent problems, the quantitative approach can be useful in localizing the factors that can materially affect project selection and improve the probability of successful project selection. More extensive coverage of project selection methodologies follows in the next chapter.

Qualitative Factors

There are many nonquantifiable elements that may be exceedingly important in the project selection process. Managers operating in a sophisticated project environment do not like to have themselves thought of as managers who make decisions by the "seat of their pants." Nevertheless, while quantification can help improve the probability of a good decision, intuition may be, in the final analysis, the most critical ingredient. A list of nonquantifiable factors to be considered in project selection might include the following:

* Philosophy of management
    General operational environment
    Risk-taking or risk-avoiding posture

* Confidence level in the project manager
    Past experience and successes

* Availability of resources
    Present and anticipated commitments
    Need to maintain the technical organization
    Need to update the technical organization

* Compatibility of the project with organizational objectives

* Possibility that the project may be the vehicle to help in moving into new and desirable areas of activity, even though this project does not have the promise for immediate profitability

* Fallout benefits that might accrue to other functions within the organization

* Prospects for an enhanced market position
    New customers
    New products
    Patents
    Extended product line to forestall possible competition

* Evaluation of competitive technology to ascertain whether it represents a threat or provides an opportunity

* Creation of a position of technical leadership (the professional image)

* Training of technical personnel in new skills or techniques, avoiding organizational obsolescence

Use of Both Quantitative and Qualitative Factors

There is no one foolproof method for project selection. A great deal of subjectivity or intuition, as mentioned, is often involved in project selection. Total reliance on either quantitative or qualitative factors can impact unfavorably on project selection analysis. More often than not, quantitative project selection methods are ignored or given only cursory attention by management. Management reluctance to use a valuable supplemental tool can frequently be attributed to the model builder's enamorment with technique and the subsequent undue complexity of the selection model, or the manager may have an outright distrust or suspicion of quantitative methods and feel uncomfortable or defensive about relying on such techniques. Realistically, most managers are only casually acquainted with the use of quantitative methods in decision processes. Simple models, better management education, and recognition of advantages, as well as limitations to quantification, would enhance the use of mathematical techniques.

The project selection decision process could conceivably be improved were management to rely on both quantitative and qualitative factors. A synthesis of the best features of both systems is recommended.

Encouraging New Ideas

The Need for a Broad Perspective

Selecting projects that contribute to the organization's objectives is obviously important. In some instances the selection of projects is almost within a predetermined range of choice; at other times opportunities may be squandered owing to force of habit or ignorance relative to exploring new avenues to productively utilize an organization's resources.

In the preceding sections of this chapter several controlling factors relative to project selection were indicated. Projects should be compatible with operational objectives. Project selection is influenced by the operational objectives in the different economic sectors. There may be situations where an organization operating within one economic sector can crossover and perform work for or within another economic sector. Rigid adherence to economic sector boundaries may not be advisable. It is possible that project people can be locked into their immediate economic sector because of unawareness of the possibilities of expanded activities and the benefits of technology transfer. Timing and operational philosophy can also be critical elements in the selection process. The entrepreneurial project manager must constantly be alert to the need for maintaining his or her technical organization, including economic and professional progress. Such awareness would involve meaningful analyses of factors that are external as well as internal to the organization. The external environment could present opportunities that previously had not been considered. It is also possible that projects that at first blush appear to be winners when considered within the immediate confines of the internal operational environment may, in fact, have little chance for success because of noncontrollable external forces.

Additional perspective can be gleaned by setting up a checklist of all the factors that can affect the project. Enthusiasm over the technical or prospective marketing prospects resulting from a project can obscure many other factors that could ultimately affect the success or failure of the undertaking. A list of the quantifiable factors, as well as nonquantifiable but nevertheless important considerations, could assist in providing a reasonably objective approach to project selection.

Sources

At times, as indicated, project selection is dictated by the nature of the activity; at other times projects can be initiated as a result of aggressive and expanded approaches to identify opportunities. Project selection often requires a coordinated effort. Normally most ideas for products originate in the R&D and marketing divisions, but the source of ideas is by no means limited to these two areas. In a survey of how 25 manufacturers located ideas for new products, Larson found that they came from executives' wives, salespersons, customers, government inquiries, employees, advertising agencies, inventors, the R&D organization, and brokers, among others.[9]

It is not uncommon to conduct research looking for specific ideas or applications and find something out of direct context that can be modified and productively employed. People responsible for project activities, especially project selection, must constantly be alert for opportunities, even though such opportunities may not be within the normal sphere of operations. In the preceding paragraph Larson's research showed that usable ideas may be generated from outside the normal channel of idea sources. Other idea sources could emanate as a result of attending professional meetings. Papers presented at such meetings or informal discussions with colleagues could be stimulating. A variety of professional journals might also provide clues as to opportunities. The government is another extremely valuable source of information. Information on government activity and funding is forthcoming from congressional appropriations and the political environment. Also, establishing personal communication with key government people in the various agencies to see how the agency is organized and what activities they might be interested in to support the agency's mission is another potentially fertile field.

Finally, there must be internal stimulation and encouragement to generate innovation. The need for a receptive operational environment cannot be overemphasized. Besides the many obvious and not so obvious sources for project ideas, it is suggested that, whenever possible, the organization should do the following:

1. Set aside seed money to be used to investigate promising activities and encourage professionals to champion new projects
2. Organizationally establish a neutral screening committee to evaluate such prospective projects
3. Provide the project champion some entrepreneurial inducements or incentives to encourage new projects

Endnotes Chapter Two

1. To cite one relevant example, the conversion of a former Paris abattoir into one of the world's biggest science museums. In the mid-1970s there was a multimillion dollar investment of public funds in a multistory abattoir on the northern side of Paris. The structure was rendered obsolete before it became operable by the development of new technology in meat processing and transportation. To convert the present structure into the proposed science museum, it is estimated $330 million will be required, plus a further $190 million to furnish the contents and an additional $90 million a year for operational costs. ("France's Monumental Science Museum," *Science*, 1983 (Aug. 26) Vol. 221, No. 4613, p. 836.)

2. This frequently happens in the selection of weapon systems, especially where there are competing alternative systems. The TFX (F111) aircraft is a representative example.

3. A caveat here is that, while the government is not concerned with a profit accruing to itself directly as a result of the project, there is concern and awareness of project profitability to the contractor(s) actually doing the project work on behalf of the government.

4. The various contractual forms are discussed in a subsequent chapter. Depending on the nature of the project and the degree of risk involved, the theory is to establish an equitable contractual arrangement to provide the contractor profit incentive and still avoid excessive costs and profiteering.

5. Modified from D. Roman, *Science, Technology and Innovation: A Systems Approach*, Columbus, Grid Publishing, 1980, pp. 299–300.

6. Marc J. Lane, *Legal Handbook for NonProfit Organizations* (1980 AMACOM).

7. U.S. Government Printing Office: 1981-0-381-544.

8. A few examples are Hughes, Battelle, and The Ford Foundation.

9. Gustav E. Larson, "Locating Ideas for New Products," in *Product Strategy and Management*, T. L. Berg and A. Schuchman (eds.), New York, Holt, Rinehart and Winston, 1963, p. 420.

CHAPTER THREE

Project Selection Methodologies*

Projects and Needs

Projects do not arise in a vacuum. They are a response to perceived needs. Consider the following examples of how some typical projects originate:

After looking around at his work environment, an office manager determines that his staff is working in an environment that is not much different from what existed in the 19th century. The trouble with such an environment is that it results in low worker productivity. Consequently, the office manager sets up a project to automate the office.

It is brought to the attention of the lab chief of a ceramics company that a new ceramic developed by the lab has extraordinary heat resistance characteristics. After discussing the new discovery with her staff, the lab chief decides to set up a project to explore its commercial possibilities.

Top management in the Department of the Army concludes that hand-held guided missile systems present a threat to American tanks in the field. Consequently, a decision is made to fund a multimillion dollar project to explore possible ways to meet this threat.

In each of these cases needs were identified and projects were initiated in order to address them. In the first case there was a need to bring an office into the 20th century, in the second a need to exploit a new product

---

* This chapter was written by J. Davidson Frame, Department of Management Science, George Washington University, Washington, DC 20052. Copyright 1985 J.D. Frame.

commercially, and in the third a need to protect tanks in the field. Clearly, the first step in the birth of a project is awareness that a particular need must be filled. Once the need has been identified, then the details of selecting, planning, and executing a project can be addressed.

Of course, the actual process of identifying, defining, and articulating needs can be quite complex. At the heart of the complexity is the fact that users often have little more than a vague idea of what their needs are. If a project is initiated on the basis of vaguely defined needs, it is likely to run into trouble at some point. This is well recognized in the automatic data processing area, where a major cause of project failure is the vague definition of needs. If the system designer's perception of the user's needs does not correspond to the user's own perceptions of these needs (and this is a common occurrence), the resulting product may be underutilized, misused, or not used at all! Consequently, a very significant step in system development projects is defining user needs. This generally entails having systems analysts and users getting together and spending large amounts of time ascertaining just what the user needs are.

Needs can arise within the project-performing organization or in the environment surrounding the organization. This is illustrated in Figure 3-1.

Figure 3-1. Need origins with respect to the organization.

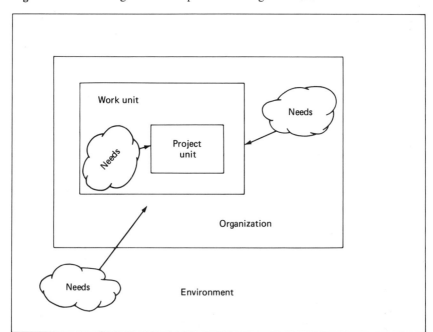

Top-Down Versus Grass Roots Project Selection

Who makes the project selection decisions? The answer to this question varies from organization to organization and often even within a given organization. Sometimes decisions are made from above and sometimes from below. We call project selection from above top-down selection, and from below grass roots selection.

Top-Down Selection

With top-down selection, projects are selected by individuals who do not have direct responsibility for carrying out the project. With very important projects the selection decision will be made at the highest reaches of management. For example, top management at Northrop made the decision to develop—without government support—a fighter aircraft for export. Because this project involved hundreds of millions of dollars of outlays and would have a dramatic impact on all corporate operations, the final project decision could only be made by the most senior managers with corporate-wide responsibilities.

With more mundane projects top-down selection involves decision making at, say, the divisional level. Here managers focus their attention on divisional objectives. These may include such items as increasing new product development, utilizing technical staff more effectively, and taking a longer-term outlook on product development. Project selection decisions are made in the context of these objectives.

Occasionally organizations have projects selected by a central group, possibly located within the marketing department or a designated projects office. Such a setup allows managers to take a "big picture" view of project selection, since decisions can be made from a supradivisional perspective.

Top-down project selection has both its strong points and its weaknesses. Its strengths include the following:

Selected projects are likely to be relevant to organizational goals, because the projects are being selected by the goal setters themselves.

Duplication of effort is likely to be reduced, since higher-level managers are apt to be aware of the broad range of activities being undertaken at the divisional level, if not in the organization as a whole.

Higher management levels are more likely to be committed to the successful execution of the project, insofar as they were involved in its selection.

The top-down approach can be full of pitfalls if the decision makers do not get feedback from people on the operational level regarding the organization's capabilities to carry out given projects. If the decision makers are out of touch with their people, then the following situations might arise:

Operational staff may be asked to undertake projects that they are incapable of carrying out effectively, owing to lack of needed skills, overcommitment to other projects, insufficient hardware, and so on.

Time, cost, and schedule estimates used to make the selection decision may have no basis in reality, leading to selection of a project that will almost certainly face time and cost pressures.

Operational staff may have little commitment to a project, since they played no role in its selection.

Grass Roots Selection

Projects selected by top-down procedures tend to be fairly substantial; however, organizations continuously undertake smaller projects as well, and these projects are selected at the operational level. When project selection occurs at the operational level, it is called grass roots project selection. Consider the following examples of grass roots projects:

A project to establish new hardware requirements for the work unit

A project to automate the office

A project to establish new hiring criteria for acquiring new technical staff

A project to develop software for the work unit's internal management information system

These projects tend to be quite mundane and are necessary for the day-to-day functioning of operating units.

Grass roots project selection may also involve more glamorous projects in project-oriented organizations. In such organizations operating units may be given a budget over which they have considerable control. This is often true of the research departments of large organizations. Here a certain portion of the department budget is set aside for projects that the research staff want to undertake. The researchers themselves play a significant role in choosing the projects on which they work. The reason research staffs are given substantial autonomy in selecting their projects is that their employers hope important new breakthroughs will emerge as a result of their doing work in which they have interest.

Externally Generated Projects

In our discussion up until now we have focused on projects originating within the organization itself. Frequently, however, project opportunities arise outside the organization. Perhaps the most dramatic example of this is projects arising in the government sector, particularly defense- and health-related projects. The whole defense industry—a multibillion dollar undertaking—is based on such projects.

Typically, the project selection decision facing management here is whether or not to bid on such projects. Selection decisions are typically made using the same criteria as for internally generated projects: Do we have the manpower to undertake the project? Will the project help us expand our capabilities? Is our physical plant adequate to accomodate project needs? In addition to these standard questions, one other question looms large in the minds of the decision makers who will make a bid or no bid decision: What is the likelihood that we will be awarded the project if we decide to submit a proposal? This is a very important question, since proposal preparation can be an expensive activity. For smaller projects it may entail a few thousand dollars in salary and materials costs; for large projects it may consume the time of many staff members and cost millions of dollars.

Various factors come into play in determining the likelihood of winning a contract in a competitive procurement. For example, how many other qualified organizations will be submitting proposals? If there are many, then the a priori probability of winning the award is small and it may not be worth the time and expense of preparing a proposal for consideration. Another question that arises is Can we put together a credible proposal? In answering this question, attention focuses on the organization's past experiences, the quality and reputation of the proposed project team, the organization's reputation, the estimated cost for doing the proposed work, and so on.

Still another question that is often raised is this: Is the proposal wired? This question is asked because anyone with experience working on government contracts recognizes that competitive procurements are not always very competitive (i.e., they may be "wired," so that a particular contractor is sure to get the award). Frequently the government office issuing the request for proposals (RFP) has a strong preference for a particular group to undertake the project. In these cases RFPs may be written in such a way that only the desired group has the qualifications to perform the work. If it is suspected that an RFP is wired, it may be a waste of time to prepare and submit a proposal.

Nonconscious Versus Conscious Project Selection

In this book we focus on projects undertaken with some deliberation, but we should recognize that projects are not always undertaken consciously. In our professional and personal lives we are constantly selecting projects to work on without even being aware of it. Circumstances arise that require action. Without giving the matter much thought, we respond in what seems a natural way. Thus when the car breaks down, we call up the

AAA and have the vehicle towed to a local mechanic. In the work place, when a clerk suddenly quits his job, we respond automatically by advertising the opening in the Sunday want ads.

Not only do we not give much conscious thought to considering the range of alternatives open to us, but we probably do not even recognize that what we are dealing with are projects. In the case of the broken-down car our project is to get the car working again. An alternative project we might have selected is to buy a new car. In the case of the clerk vacancy our project is to fill the vacancy with a new clerk. A possible alternative would be to replace the clerk with a computerized filing system.

Nonconscious, Ad Hoc Project Selection

In order to appreciate some of the implications of nonconscious, ad hoc project selection, consider the following brief case study.

The ABC Publishing Company is a major magazine publisher and highly regarded in the industry as a well-managed enterprise. Last year its president, Marylin Jones, became concerned about dwindling profit margins. She suspected that the problem was caused in large part by rising production costs in the printing and binding department. In order to get a better handle on the problem she appointed a committee to explore possible causes of declining profits. The committee was comprised of three individuals: one from the accounting department, one from the editorial department, and one from the printing/binding department. They were given two weeks to study the matter of declining profitability and draw conclusions from their efforts.

After undertaking a comprehensive review of the company's operations, the committee confirmed Mrs. Jones' suspicions. The basic cause of declining profit margins appeared to be rising production costs, especially steep increases in the cost of paper.

Mrs. Jones thanked the committee for doing a good job. She then turned her attention to increasing profits through direct action. An obvious approach to resolving the problem was to pass on the cost of increases directly to advertisers and consumers. But this could be a hazardous move, since it could result in a dramatic loss of revenues as consumers dropped their subscriptions and advertisers reduced their advertising in the company's magazines. In order to address this issue Mrs. Jones hired a consulting firm to determine the effects of passing on cost increases to consumers and advertisers.

During a period of four weeks the firm performed market studies and econometric investigations. At the end of this period the firm submitted a report to Mrs. Jones suggesting that subscription and advertising prices could be increased by 10%, yielding a measurable improvement in profit margins; however, increases beyond 10% would probably result in further declines in profits.

On the basis of this report, Mrs. Jones decided to increase subscription and advertising rates by 10%, but she estimated that this move was insufficient to place profit margins at a high enough level. It was clear to her that to improve its health the company would have to do a better job of controlling costs. Since so much of the cost problems were associated with the printing and binding operations, she assigned the printing/binding operations manager the task of identifying specific areas in the production process where costs could be reduced. At the same time she requested that the accounting department undertake a study to measure the financial effects of having outside contractors print and bind the company's magazines.

This case shows that much of typical business activity contains project management elements in it, even though decision makers may not be especially aware of this fact. At least four projects can be identified in the case study, and they are the four tasks undertaken by the following:

The committee Mrs. Jones established

The consulting company

The printing/binding department

The accounting department

They are projects because they entail clearly defined, limited objectives; they are of limited duration; they involve noncycled activities; and they entail the commitment of time, material, and human resources. There is even what may be termed a metaproject: the overall task Mrs. Jones set herself of implementing policies that would improve profit margins.

What is interesting about the case from the point of view of this chapter is that these projects are being chosen without the principal decision maker being aware that she is in fact engaged in a project selection procedure. That is, Mrs. Jones is engaged in nonconscious, ad hoc project selection. Her choices are logical, one decision flowing logically from another; however, Mrs. Jones never sits back and says, "Okay, I have limited resources to work with and a seemingly infinite number of needs to fill. What projects should I launch that will most effectively utilize the limited resources I have in order to meet my organization's objectives?"

Is this bad? The answer is a qualified no. From a management theory perspective, an unappealing feature of ad hoc project selection is that it is essentially reactive, and not proactive. We may find that our decisions are being controlled by immediate circumstances—that we are not managing circumstances, but rather are being managed by them.

However, it should be recognized that in the real world we all engage regularly in ad hoc project selection. So long as the problems we address are of relatively small size, entail limited resource commitments, and have limited consequences, it is unlikely that the conscious implementation of systematic project selection procedures will be cost effective. If our project is to go to a restaurant, it is probably not worth examining a lengthy list of alternative activities, performing Delphi rounds, initiating peer review proceedings, and so on. However, if the project is to redecorate our house and anticipated dollar costs associated with the effort are $15,000, it would perhaps be wise to systematically review the implications of such a cash outlay, consider alternative uses of the funds, and so forth. Clearly, the larger the stakes of a project, the more important it is to be consciously aware that we are in fact making a project selection decision that may have major implications for us.

In Mrs. Jones' case it would appear that her ad hoc project selection procedures were well suited to the circumstances. Through these procedures she was able to identify a prudent course of action quickly and with a minimal use of scarce resources.

Conscious Project Selection

This book focuses on projects where individuals are conscious of the fact that they are indeed undertaking projects. As a consequence, they are concerned with selecting projects rationally, carefully undertaking planning and control activities, evaluating their efforts, and so on. With conscious project selection, many factors are taken into account before select and do not select decisions are made. The remainder of this chapter will examine some of these factors.

Project Selection Checklist

When giving consideration to selecting a project, it is useful to examine different aspects of the project against a checklist of important items. Too often we are swept off our feet by one or two exciting features of a project and lose sight of some details that may have an important impact upon the project's prospects for success. For example, we may rush into supporting a given project because it opens up a whole new market for us; however, a little reflection may show us that this particular market is saturated, and also that the project will tax our resource base, threatening the health of ongoing efforts.

The most useful checklist that decision makers can create will take into account special considerations germane to the organizational environment in which they work. For example, a checklist put together for in-house projects carried out by a government agency will not contain items regarding the profitability of products resulting from projects; however, it may contain items concerning the impact of the project on the legislature, on government policy, on the next election, and so forth.

The following are some major categories of items that decision makers might want to include in a project selection checklist. Clearly the relevance of these items will vary from organization to organization.

Organizational Capabilities

Before choosing a project, decision makers must decide whether the organization has the capability to carry it out effectively. If the prospective project is very large in relation to these capabilities, a decision may be made to reject the project in order to avoid organizational indigestion, even though the project is very appealing in other respects. In another case a project that is not very exciting might get the go-ahead because it helps to expand the organization's range of expertise.

Some questions pertaining to organizational capabilities that might be raised include the following:

Do we have the expertise to undertake the project?

Do we have sufficient numbers of workers?

Do we have adequate facilities?

Do we have necessary equipment?

Will the project help us expand our capabilities?

What future commitments do we have that might be affected by this project?

Required Resource Commitments

An important matter that always finds its way into project selection decisions is the question of how many resources the project will consume. Many of the items that one would want to consider here can be estimated in a straightforward fashion. Thus labor costs are calculated by estimating the number of person-hours needed to perform project tasks, multiplying this figure by relevant salary figures, and adding this quotient to fringe benefit costs. However, it may also be important to calculate opportunity costs, and this can be a difficult undertaking. Opportunity costs are derived by asking and answering the following question: How much income will we lose by dedicating our scarce resources to this particular project and not to others? By looking at opportunity costs, we may find that a given project—by tying up resources—is in fact costing us far more than we originally anticipated.

Some resource-related questions we might want to consider when building a project selection checklist include the following:

What are labor costs?

What are the costs of materials?

Will we have to expand production capacity in order to carry out the project?

How will the project be funded?

What are the opportunity costs associated with the project?

What future resource commitments will the project place on us?

Benefits Derived from the Project

The ultimate justification for undertaking projects is that they will generate benefits for the organization. Some of the potential benefits can be
obvious (e.g., increased market share); others can be more subtle (e.g.,
the project enables us to employ skilled staff during the slow season).
When estimates of benefits are compared to estimates of cost, we have an
important indicator of the desirability of a project. Clearly, if anticipated
costs outweigh anticipated benefits, the project is not very appealing. On
the other hand, if the benefits of a project exceed expected costs by a
factor of 3, we will give serious consideration to supporting it.

Important questions about benefits that can be included in a project
selection checklist include the following:

Will the project contribute directly to profitability?

Will it expand our expertise?

Will it expand our market?

How much time will pass until benefits are realized?

Will the benefits be substantial or marginal?

How large are the benefits in relation to cost?

How long will the benefits endure?

Are there benefits to be derived from spin-offs generated by the project?

Market Factors

It is a widely recognized fact that a major cause of failure of products
emerging from high-technology projects is the marketplace. Frequently,
new products are developed that have no market, or else products are
explicitly targeted to a specific market but market demand shifts, or competitor's products in the market eclipse the new product. For whatever
reasons, the market can be a perilous place for new products, and to the
extent that organizations undertake projects to develop new products,
they must devote time and resources to understanding the market.

When making project selection decisions, some questions about the
market that should be answered include the following:

Is there a market for the product that results from the project?

Will the project help open up new market opportunities?

Will the project help us maintain our position in existing markets?

Who are our competitors and what threats do they pose?

Level of Risk

All projects have risk associated with them. Some projects, however, are inherently more risky than others. For example, long-term and state-of-the-art projects often entail very high levels of risk; on the other hand, short-term projects involving cosmetic changes in a product tend to be low-risk undertakings.

There are basically two kinds of risk associated with projects: technical risk and commercial risk. Technical risk is a measure of the likelihood that a project can be completed technically in an effective manner. When technical risk is high, there is a substantial probability that technical problems will arise that cannot be resolved in a cost-effective way. Projects are commercially risky when there is a high likelihood that they will not succeed in the marketplace. Technical risk and commercial risk are often independent of each other; that is, one can have a project whose technical risk is high and commercial risk low, or a project with low technical risk and high commercial risk.

When considering risk in project selection, some questions that can be addressed are as follows:

What is the level of technical risk of the proposed project?

What is the level of commercial risk?

Are we a risk-taking organization?

Will selection of this project increase or decrease the risk to our portfolio of projects?

Other Issues

A project selection checklist can address many more issues than have been noted here. For example, any checklist should have at the top questions regarding the fit of the project with organizational objectives and the corporate culture. If a project does not "fit" here, then there is a good chance that it will encounter problems. Also, in view of the difficulties associated with defining needs, questions might be included in the checklist designed to determine whether in fact we really know what needs a proposed project is addressing. If we cannot identify explicit ideas, then perhaps we do not really understand the full nature of the project.

Formal Techniques for Selecting Projects

Over the years various formal techniques have been developed to aid decision makers in making project choices. These techniques vary dramatically in form and substance; however, one thing they have in common is the desire to make objective, unbiased choices of those projects most worthy of support.

It is difficult to say how widely used these approaches are. Organizations that are fundamentally project oriented tend to have rather elaborate project selection procedures, whereas organizations that only occasionally support projects use more informal approaches.

In the remainder of this chapter we briefly discuss some of the more widely used formal project selection procedures.

Project Selection Formulas

A common dream held by organizations involved with project development is to be able to hit upon a quantitative means to select projects. In this scheme of things managers need merely feed some data into a computerized project selection algorithm, run the algorithm, and then look over the output to see whether a given project is worth pursuing.

In order to make this dream reality, many organizations have experimented with project selection formulas. More often than not, these formulas are set up as ratios, where the numerator measures the benefits derived from undertaking a project, and the denominator its costs. A simple example of such a formula is one created by Hart:

$$\text{Project index} = \frac{S \times P \times p \times t}{100C}$$

where S is the peak sales volume, P the net profit on sales (%), p the probability of technical success, t the time discount factor, and C R&D costs.

Consider first the meaning of the numerator. By multiplying peak sales volume (S) by net profit on sales (P), we have some idea of the dollar value of profit associated with the product resulting from a project. However, it is possible that the project will fail technically. Consequently, in order to have an idea of expected profit levels given a certain probability of technical failure, the profit figure resulting from $S \times P$ is multiplied by the probability of the technical success of the project. The resulting figure gives us expected profit, given that the project may fail technically. Finally, a time discount factor t is introduced in order to account for the fact that a dollar earned today is not equal in value to a dollar earned several years from now. In a highly inflationary period the value of t will be chosen so as to dramatically reduce expected profit levels, whereas in noninflationary times the effects of t typically will be negligible. The numerator, then, gives us a measure of the benefits associated with undertaking a project. The denominator measures cost.

Project selection formulas can be far more complex than this. For example, the numerator (benefits) can explicitly take into account such things as the probability of technical success, the probability of commercial success, annual sales (in both physical units and dollars), market share, value of the market, unit costs, expected product life (in years), and salvage value. Similarly, the denominator (costs) can account for a plethora of cost items, such as expenditures for R&D, market research, patent acquisition, market development, start-up losses, and plant and equipment. Complexity increases when dollar figures are discounted for the cost of capital, opportunity costs are factored in, and each of our estimates for the relevant variables is presented as a distribution of possibilities rather than as a simple point estimate.

A project selection formula filled with integral signs and Greek characters is an impressive thing to behold. It certainly looks objective and scientific. Unfortunately, as in many others areas of life, looks can be deceiving here. While a well-formulated project selection formula may in theory be a valid indicator of the worth of projects, in practice, the numbers we plug into the equation are usually highly speculative, subjective values. We simply do not know how many units of a product we will sell. We do not know how long the product will last in the marketplace. We do not know the probabilities of success and failure. Thus we come face to face with the old data processing adage: Garbage in, garbage out. We cannot escape from the fact that the formulas we use are only as good as the data fed into them.

Project selection formulas are most useful when applied to projects that are similar to others carried out in the past by the organization. For example, an engineering firm that has built many cantilever bridges can, on the basis of experience and historical data, make reasonable estimates of such things as project cost variables and the probability of technical success. On the other hand, project selection formulas are all but completely useless when applied to projects that entail blazing new trails. In this case insufficient data exist to make reasonable estimates of variable values in the project selection formula.

Peer Review

A serious problem in selecting projects in an organization is that those who are best qualified to assess its strengths and weaknesses are often its champions. Presumably they would not push for its support if they did not feel their project was worthwhile in the first place. If managers responsible for allocating resources to projects want an unbiased assessment of the project's future, it is unlikely they will find it among the project champions.

Peer review of project proposals is a mechanism often employed in organizations looking for unbiased assessments of the merits of a project. In the peer review system project proposals are sent to leading experts on the subject matter of the project. These experts work outside the organization. Consequently, there are two strong points to the peer review process: First, the organization is receiving an expert assessment of the project, and, second, this assessment is probably more objective than one arising from within the organization.

Peer review can be undertaken in a variety of ways. One common approach is to send the proposal to three or four outside experts who independently review it. After receiving the comments and judgments of the reviewers, the organization decides on whether or not the project deserves support. Another approach is to submit the proposal to a panel of experts who discuss its strengths and weaknesses with each other. As a result of this interaction, the panelists have an opportunity to reflect on the insights of fellow experts.

The peer review system serves as the central project selection mechanism in the major U.S. government science agencies that disperse billions of research funding dollars extramurally. The National Science Foundation (NSF), for example, has NSF program officers send to outside reviewers proposals that have been submitted to the Foundation. The outside reviewers are given guidance on how to evaluate the proposals (e.g., what are its technical merits and how qualified is the principal investigator?). Interestingly, the reviewers are given no remuneration for their effort. They are generally reminded in a cover letter that the effective running of a large scientific funding system requires the voluntary cooperation of those individuals who are members of the scientific community.

In contrast, the National Institutes of Health (NIH) gathers panels of experts who in a day or two jointly review a sheaf of proposals. Because participation in the NIH system requires travel to a central location, as well as eating and hotel expenses, participants receive enough support to cover travel and out-of-pocket expenses.

Government science agencies favor a peer review approach to project selection for a number of reasons. One is that the system appears to be fair. When decisions are based on the opinions of outside reviewers, it is difficult for funding administrators to play favorites with grant applicants. A second reason is that the peer review system is already accepted by the scientific community for assessing scientific merit in other ways. For example, the leading scientific journals do not accept articles for publication until they have been reviewed and accepted by scientific peers.

Although the use of peer review by U.S. government science agencies suggests that the selection of projects is fair, it is by no means self-evident that the system consistently leads to the support of the most worthy projects. In a recent study of the NSF peer review system, researchers found that a substantial portion of proposals reviewed by different teams of experts received different ratings by the different teams. This suggests that there is a significant element of arbitrariness in the selection procedure.

The peer review approach is not appropriate for all situations. For example, a company that develops products with proprietary value may be reluctant to give outside reviewers insight into some of the ideas it has for product development.

Project Scoring Sheets

Many organizations that regularly undertake projects employ project scoring, or evaluation, sheets. These sheets list those criteria considered important in evaluating the merits of proposed projects. Typically, the criteria are grouped into broad categories, such as prospects for technical success and for commercial success. Evaluators are asked to assess a project according to each of these criteria. They offer their opinions by scoring a project for each criterium. Thus a given project may receive high scores on criteria dealing with technical success, and modest scores on commercial criteria.

An example of a project scoring sheet is provided in Table 3-1. As the example shows, different criteria may be weighted differently according to their perceived importance. Thus in the example market factors are weighted more heavily than either technical or financial factors.

There are several positive features to project scoring sheets. First, they require an organization to think through and be explicit about what it wants out of a project. The listing of the criteria on a scoring sheet explicitly reflects the organization's outlook on what is and what is not important. Second, by assigning different weights to the criteria, the organization makes a conscious choice about the relative significance of such things as technical, marketing, and financial factors. Giving nontechnical factors their due weight can be especially important in organizations such as engineering firms, where there is a tendency to evaluate projects primarily on their technical merits. Third, project scoring sheets provide management with a convenient way to sum up the appraisals of several evaluators, since the evaluators assess projects numerically. Comparisons between prospective projects can be made on the basis of the weighted numerical scores.

Table 3-1. Project Scoring Sheet

		Project A		Project B	
Criterium	Weight	Raw score	Weighted score	Raw score	Weighted score
Technical soundness	10	5	50	3	30
Financial soundness	40	3	120	3	120
Marketability	50	2	100	5	250
Total	100		270		400

As with all the other project selection mechanisms discussed in this chapter, scoring sheets have their drawbacks as well as their strengths. Its principal weakness is the same as for project selection formulas; that is, its trappings of objectivity may hide the fact that it is at heart a very subjective procedure. The evaluators are offering their opinions on a project's strengths and weaknesses. Another set of evaluators may have a different collective opinion, with the result that a project that scored highly with one group may not do so well with another.

While project scoring sheets are imperfect instruments for project selection, their widespread employment by organizations active in project management suggests that they serve a useful function. If nothing else, their use forces management to be explicit about what it wants to get out of a project—no small accomplishment.

Adversary Proceedings

With adversary proceedings project champions are asked to make a case for their projects before a panel of judges qualified to assess the merits of the projects. The panel is explicitly charged with the task of poking holes in the project proposals it reviews. The theory here is that a good project should be able to successfully withstand a critical onslaught.

The adversarial approach typically works in the following way: The project champions develop a written proposal describing the project they wish to have supported. The proposal should not only describe the outlines of the project, but point out its special features and weaknesses as well. A time and cost estimate should also be included. This written proposal is submitted to the panel of judges for their review.

At the actual proceedings the project champions make a short presentation designed to sell their project idea. In this presentation they should not only describe the technical features of the proposed project, but show how the project would be beneficial to the organization.

After the presentation the panel asks questions designed to elucidate points that may not have been clear in the presentation. Once these have been answered, the panel critiques the proposal. The project champions are asked to address each of the criticisms, defending their proposal if they can.

Such proceedings often can identify weak project suggestions, particularly those that have not been carefully thought out. It is unlikely that project champions who have not devoted sufficient thought and effort to the development of their proposals will be able to defend them adequately against a penetrating critique.

Even essentially strong project ideas can benefit from adversary proceedings. It is a rare proposal that does not have some weak points, and by identifying them and allowing the project champions to overcome them, fundamentally strong projects can be made even stronger.

One weakness of adversary proceedings is that although they may be effective in telling you what is bad about a project suggestion, they may not be very useful in telling what is good. The adversary procedure can highlight poor project design, insufficient attention to market conditions, or lack of commitment to project success on the part of the project champions; however, it tends to be less effective in identifying whether a particular approach undertaken in a project is good.

Another weakness of the adversary procedure approach to selecting projects is that with its accent on the negative, it may lead to excessively cautious project selection. If the panel has done a good job of critiquing projects and pointing out weaknesses, few projects that entail risk taking will look very appealing. Yet it is often such high-risk projects that lead to the greatest economic returns when they succeed.

A final problem with the adversarial approach is that the success of a project in surviving the proceedings may be due more to the skills of the project champions in making their arguments than to the inherent merits of the project. It should be recognized, however, that it is a basic fact of life that successful projects have a substantial history of salesmanship associated with them, from the moment of their inception right through the time they are put into the marketplace. Inherently good projects do not sell themselves—they require substantial assistance.

Computerized Packages

The introduction of the microcomputer into the work place is having major consequences for managing projects. Computerized packages are rapidly being developed for project management purposes. Most of these are concerned with project scheduling and budgeting. They allow project managers to perform PERT/CPM and Gantt chart analyses (see Chapter 7) readily, without having to depend upon their organization's central computer facilities.

Some general-purpose packages are also useful for managing projects. Most pronounced here are packages that integrate spread sheets, data management systems, and graphics. These packages allow project managers to custom-make computerized planning and control systems for their projects. Significantly, they can do this without being expert computer programmers.

An interesting development that has major implications for project selection is the creation of software packages explicitly designed to help managers make choices. Typically, these systems require the decision maker to make pairwise comparisons between alternative choices (see the package *Expert Choice,* produced by Decision Support Systems, McLean, VA). For example, let us say that Robin Smith can only afford to support one project out of four possibilities: project A, project B, project C, and project D. In using a computerized decision-making system, she might be asked to list those factors that are important in selecting a project. Robin Smith enters costs, payoffs, and the payback period as the most important factors. Then she is asked, What is more important to you, costs or payoffs? Payoffs or the payback period? Costs or the payback period? After she has entered her choices, the computer algorithm determines the rank order of the three factors according to their importance to Ms. Smith. Then Ms. Smith might be asked to take each of the projects and note how strong it is with respect to each of the three factors. After she does this the algorithm rank-orders the four projects according to their desirability. Ms. Smith chooses the one with the highest ranking.

Ultimately the time may arrive when project selection choices can be fully automated. The tool that may make this possible is what is called an expert system. Expert systems entail the application of artificial intelligence to the making of choices. One hypothetical system applied to project selection may work as follows: The computer queries a project selection committee on a number of matters regarding each project in a collection of projects. What is the nature of the project? How many individuals will it employ? How long will it last? Will it enable project staff to gain new expertise? What kind of expertise would this be? After receiving answers to a dozen or so such questions, the package queries internal data banks on various issues, for example, How successful has the organization been in the past with projects of this nature? Will there be an anticipated demand in the marketplace for the expertise being developed on the project? How will this project fit into the larger portfolio of projects being supported by the organization? After weighing the information provided by the selection committee as well as the information in the internal data bank, the algorithm will hit upon the best project for the organization.

Conclusions

As this chapter has shown, projects are selected under a great variety of circumstances. Sometimes selection is undertaken systematically, and sometimes in an ad hoc fashion. Sometimes quantitative techniques serve as the basis for project selection; sometimes qualitative approaches dominate. Sometimes project selection is made in a top–down fashion, whereas on other occasions selection occurs at the grass roots level. Sometimes project selection focuses on projects that arise within the organizations, and sometimes on outside projects.

All this is confusing to people who are new to project management. "Okay, we see that people take many different approaches to selecting projects," they might say, "but tell us, which are the best?" Unfortunately, our answer will provide no succor to project management novices. Our answer is that there is no overall best approach to selecting projects.

How they are selected is situationally determined. Thus for very small projects, following an elaborate project selection procedure is tantamount to killing a mosquito with a shotgun; however, for large, costly projects, formal project selection may be important.

For high-risk, state-of-the-art projects, it is unlikely that employment of a project selection formula will provide meaningful results; however, if the project is to build a bridge, and we have experience in building many bridges, the formula may be appropriate and useful. For projects within the government profitability is not a factor that should play an important role in project selection, but in the private sector it may be the single most important factor.

Perhaps the only real constants that apply across all kinds of projects are the following:

Projects arise out of needs, so be certain that you fully understand what they are. If you have only a vague appreciation of the needs a proposed project will address, think twice before supporting it.

Projects that do not fit in with the organizational culture and are out of line with the organization's objectives will likely run into trouble. Avoid them.

Projects that do not have the support of higher levels of management have two strikes against them. If these are inherently good projects that will benefit the organization, an attempt should be made to interest higher levels of management in their merits. If disinterest persists, you should take this into consideration before going ahead with them.

Remember that your estimates of cost, schedule, and benefits are likely to be off the mark. In most instances these estimates tend to be optimistic, ultimately leading to strong time and cost pressures. Try to factor out overly optimistic elements in your estimates so that projects are not selected on the basis of unrealistic expectations.

Keep in mind the formula

$$\text{Project selection} = \text{future commitment}$$

What this formula tells us is that tomorrow we will have to live with the decisions we make today. Project selection is serious business and should not be taken lightly.

CHAPTER FOUR

Proposals, Proposal Evaluation, and Source Selection

Proposals

Introduction

Project selection and proposal preparation and presentation are closely related activities. A short-lived and simple project may be initiated without the preliminary formality of a proposal. However, more normally, a candidate project may be identified, but authorization to proceed withheld until a proposal is prepared. In some instances the project selection process does not begin until proposals are submitted.

Proposals for projects can vary from a simple statement of intent to a comprehensive and voluminous document covering in considerable detail the various facets of the proposed project. Essentially, a project represents organized activity to accomplish an objective. As indicated in an earlier chapter, there can be a considerable range of effort directed to projectization. The proposal is a structured presentation covering, among other things, the anticipated scope of the project, including such elements as a statement of the problem, the technical factors that are considered relevant, resources required, schedule of effort, potential cost, and related experiences, including qualifications of the people who will be assigned to the project. The proposal elements will be elaborated upon in a subsequent section of this chapter. Succinctly, a proposal should incorporate all relevant aspects of a project that should be considered and evaluated prior to project selection and authorization.

Proposal as Prelude to Project Authorization

A simple personal project may be started either on a whim or after careful thought and deliberation. Resources to accomplish the project may be at hand or have to be acquired. Since such simple and personal projects normally are initiated by individuals, no extraneous authorization is usually required to proceed with the project once the decision has been made. Excluding such situations as the aforementioned, most projects represent activities involving decisions on resource allocation and the coordination of effort. Before authorization decisions are made, the validating authority usually requires a formal statement of intent, expectations, and resource requirements. This is the proposal.

Proposals can result from several situations. A need to accomplish a nonroutine objective can lead to a request for a project plan (proposal). The request may be directed to sources internal to the organization or, if internal capability and capacity do not exist, the request may solicit support from individuals or organizations external to the operation. There are other situations where individuals or organizations have or are developing competence in specific technological areas and submit a proposal eliciting support in order to proceed with the work. In such instances there generally is some community of interest between the soliciting and sponsoring organizations. Sponsorship of such projects would probably be contingent on perceived potential benefits, confidence in technical procedures outlined in the proposal, and managerial competence relative to accomplishing the project objectives. Unsolicited proposals may also be submitted in instances where "we have a solution looking for a problem." The initiating organization may have technical competence and experience that it feels can be applied to solving problems which exist in another organization.

If the organization is aware of a problem and feels the problem is important and should be resolved, it will take an aggressive posture and request support. At other times, as in unsolicited proposals, the organization may not be aware of a problem or a potential need and the initiative for the project comes from a source other than the ultimate authorization or user source. In this latter situation the project sponsor has to be convinced of the possible project benefits, have the resources to direct to the project, and have the authority to implement the proposals.

Proposals may be formulated as a result of the following:

1. Solicited or unsolicited proposal activity.
2. External or internal proposal activity.

The material covered in the subsequent sections of this chapter is not intended to be all-inclusive or the final authority. Different organizations operating in different environments may entail a multitude of procedural variations in proposal activity. Also, authorizing individuals or groups, representing sponsoring organizations, may have idiosyncrasies that must be accommodated if the proposal is to be bought off. While the objectives of subsequent sections of this chapter are to provide guidance, suggestions, and perhaps a procedural checklist, it is strongly emphasized that in the final preparation and presentation of a proposal, close coordination, if possible, be maintained with the sponsor. Specifically, the final proposal should be tailored to a format reflecting proposals that were submitted and subsequently authorized by the sponsoring organization.

Request for Proposal

A request for a proposal (RFP) is a solicitation and may be directed to internal or external sources. Internally, a request for a proposal would probably be directed to a specific individual or group, based on demonstrated, related, or anticipated competence to handle such a project. The internal solicitation may be to solve an urgent or perhaps not so urgent problem, investigate areas that promise future productive activities, or upgrade or maintain technical groups or individuals within the organization during slack periods of activity.

External support may be requested when the potential project involves activity outside the technical capabilities of the organization or in areas where the organization does not want to commit a substantial investment. It is also possible that the project may relate to a current need but has little or no promise for future benefits. Another reason for outside solicitation may reflect opportunity cost analysis, wherein start-up costs would be considerable relative to costs of established organizations. It may be felt that resources could be more productivity directed to other operational areas.

The RFP may be a general solicitation. It may be an open publication of a need in a trade or technical journal. The RFP could also be directed to a certified list of vendors. A selective request could be based on past experience with certain vendors. The solicitation list could be made up of prospective vendors who have qualified for inclusion on such a list as a result of demonstrated technical competence, financial responsibility, availability of applicable facilities, and competent management.

An RFP may also be directed to a single vendor. A sole source procurement has to be carefully considered. The government normally is particularly reluctant to engage in sole source procurements. In a sole source procurement competition is eliminated. There is little or no basis for comparative analysis on the proposed technical procedure, schedule commitment, resource requirements, or anticipated cost. Additionally, if other vendors who feel qualified are excluded, there can be political reverberations with the government and bad public relations in the community in the private sector. As a generalization, sole source procurements are usually avoided, unless the RFP is directed to a source where there are unique abilities available and such a selection can be justified on a technical base and anticipated cost savings.

There are instances where a single source represents the only feasible avenue to accomplish the project. The original RFP may have been directed to several vendors. The project may entail future activities that require incremental authorization and funding. Once a vendor is selected, after competitive evaluations, and work on the project is started, it usually is not practical to request multiple competitive bids for subsequent project increments. The original winning bidder has experience and, hopefully, a level of accomplishment. A new vendor would probably have to start all over again or dissipate many resources in a learning program to come up to the level of the original contractor.

Another situation where an RFP may be sent to a single source is when that source has a patent or technique critical to the project success. There may be a situation where the contractor enjoys a selective competitive position owing to the possession of proprietary information or knowledge essential to the project. Still another possibility for a sole source procurement is where an unsolicited proposal is submitted and subsequently bought.

In most cases the RFP contains essential information for prospective bidders. The complexity of the anticipated project would probably dictate the amount and depth of information contained in the RFP. There are, however, instances where the RFP is actually inadequate. An inadequate RFP could be intentional or unintentional. For instance, the requesting organization may have a problem and does not know how to solve it. Unfortunately, there are times when questionable ethics are involved. The RFP may only be a "fishing expedition" to solicit ideas from knowledgeable people or organizations. The organization originating the RFP can later use the ideas submitted to solve the problems. The RFP was actually issued with absolutely no intent to ultimately authorize a project. In essence, the RFP was a ploy seeking free consulting information. Sad to say, the author has known of such cases and as a result has become cautious about responding to proposals unless there is reasonable certainty of intent and rapport, as well as need, with the initiator of the RFP.

At times the RFP may be inadequate because the issuing organization is not really sure what it actually wants or ultimately expects. The solicitation is really seeking some guidance on the scope of the project and the technical approach. There is a sense of need, but only a vague feeling of the details on how the need can be satisfied and the performance level that might reasonably be expected. If possible, this type of situation should be avoided.

The proposed project should be thought out carefully before an RFP is sent out. The sponsoring organization should be able to give a firm specification as to expected performance requirements. The specifications should be attainable, consistent with need and use, and within reasonable cost limitations. Often there is a tendency to overstate specification requirements relative to the anticipated need. Meeting difficult specifications contributes to cost escalation. Schedule requirements should also be explicitly stated in the RFP. Again, the schedule should reflect need and an appropriate time to develop the project objectives, including accommodation for perceived technical problems that have to be surmounted. Additionally, the RFP should indicate any cost constraints or the type of contracting arrangement into which the contractor is willing to enter. Types of contracting arrangements will be discussed in Chapter 11 covering the legal aspects of project management.

There are some other considerations worth mentioning relative to RFPs. There should be no indication of prejudice or discrimination in soliciting bids other than ability to perform. There should be adequate notice of the need so that qualified bidders will have sufficient time to prepare a proposal. In many instances the soliciting organization should conduct a preliminary bidders' conference before the actual RFP is submitted. At such a conference relevant information as to beneficial expectations on the project should be communicated to prospective bidders. Questions and answers would be forthcoming and prospective vendors could determine whether or not to bid on the project. A decision not to bid could reflect the vendor's lack of confidence in its ability to technically perform, cost and profit expectations, existing or anticipated commitments, the cost of generating the proposal, considering the prospects for successfully winning the project in view of the competition, or inability to meet the proposal submittal deadline.

Coming back to the point made earlier that the proposed project should be thought out carefully before an RFP is issued, if the RFP is poorly conceived and a contract is subsequently granted on the RFP, downstream problems can almost certainly be anticipated. A knowledgeable vendor can "buy in" in such situations. Buying in is bidding on the project at a low price, knowing that the project will undoubtedly have to be reformulated later. Knowing that a contractual redefinition is probable, the vendor will invariably request that procedures for renegotiation of costs be incorporated into the contract to accommodate any changes from the original contract that will subsequently be requested by the contractor. A poorly conceived project may require substantive changes to meet the needs of the sponsoring organization; these changes, which are deviations from the original contract, are almost always expensive and lead to project costs that were not originally planned for. The situation described often results in contractual overruns; however, overruns can be misleading in that the project end product(s) may substantially differ from the end items identified on the original contract.

Even where the RFP is comprehensive and proposals are accordingly submitted, there may be further negotiation on details with the successful bidder. A project source may be selected and project authorization to proceed may be granted, but the finalized contract could reflect negotiations on performance/cost trade-offs, schedule adjustments, reporting requirements, coordination meetings, test specifications, and so on.

External Proposals

Proposals for project work are more normally thought of as being directed outside the organization. External proposals are made in response to the possible authorization of a project from another organization wishing to buy the technical capability of the proposing organization. External proposals can be solicited or unsolicited. The solicited proposal can result, as indicated in the previous section, from an RFP, where an organization has a problem and seeks outside help. The unsolicited proposal represents more of a direct marketing approach.

Often the organization sells its technical capability. The organization may or may not have consumer product identity, or its operational activities may be so diverse that it spans a range of available services from internal and external consultation to establishing technically directed projects to product development. It can also be operationally organized to devote part of its activity to carrying out internally generated projects and part to servicing other organizations. When a distinct technical capability exists, the organization may employ an active marketing function to seek other organizations that can use its services. Preliminary contact with customers may result from marketing activity or through the efforts of project managers.

A considerable part of the project manager's job is to maintain and perpetuate the project organization. The project manager, usually in concert with the marketing department, will try to sell technical capability to prospective customers. A prospective customer might be a new client for the services the project manager has to offer. In most situations, where a new customer is sought, the search for the customer and the preliminary contact is made by marketing. Another possibility is where the project manager has a customer and an existing project that has possibilities for related follow-on work. The project manager can submit an unsolicited proposal for follow-on activity or the customer can issue an RFP for additional effort. There are times when the project manager might try selling project efforts to former clients or, through professional contacts, selectively approach new prospects.

Internal Proposals

Internal proposals come from within the organization. An internal proposal can be solicited or unsolicited. A solicited internal proposal may result from a request by management for an estimate of the magnitude of a project in terms of anticipated technical scope, time, and projected cost.

Management's interest may be to develop a new product, solve a technical problem, investigate a prospective activity, and so forth.

An unsolicited internal proposal may be initiated by an individual or group of people within the organization desiring management's approval and the allocation of resources for the investigation of a special project. This is a relatively common practice in organizations where technological frontiers are being explored. Problems arise relative to granting authorization, in that the unsolicited internal proposal may be submitted by a person or a group already committed to a project. The work on the existing project may suggest some interesting tangents that these people would like to investigate, or it is possible that they have other interests which could result in a project not immediately related to their current project assignment. They may want to move in another direction that is more closely allied with their discipline or interest than their current assignment; many times, in the situation described, the people involved will not even bother submitting an unsolicited proposal but will bootleg the work and charge their time to their assigned project. If they do submit a proposal for internal authorization that subsequently is not approved, they may sulk on their present assignment or still pursue their own technical goals. Handling proposals of this nature constitutes one of the more difficult aspects of project management.

The manager must evaluate the potential benefit of the proposed project to the organization. This can vary according to the timing. For instance, what is the current work load? Would the commencement of the project infringe on work already planned or begun and still considered necessary? What resources are available? Should other effort be extended, put on hold, or be terminated? Does the proposed project have immediate or prospective application? How important is the prospective application to the organization's present or projected operational mission? What generally useful knowledge could accrue to the entire organization? To what extent can the proposed project activity lead to constructive technology transfer that might benefit the organization? Is there a comparative lull in operations that could profitably be filled by this project? Also, what effect on internal morale and technical capability would it have? Finally, the decision to implement or not implement the proposed project might hinge on the reputation of people involved.

There are a few more observations that are considered relevant to internal proposals. Depending on the nature of the project proposed, the proposal can be as simple as a one-page overview or more comprehensive, with explicit technical aspects indicated. In some instances the level of technical detail might exceed the technical detail contained in an external proposal, in that the internal proposal would contain information that would be considered proprietary to the organization. Disclosing excessive detail in an external proposal to a prospective customer might possibly compromise the organization's prospects for ultimately receiving project authorization.

A prospective project is usually championed by an enthusiastic individual or group. In the author's long experience with projects and project organizations, unsolicited internal proposals frequently understate the extent of technical effort involved, overstate the prospective results and benefits, minimize potential resource requirements, and are unduly optimistic relative to a time frame for the accomplishment of the project. Often the tendency to project optimistic results stems from an inherent belief that, if management were informed of the actual anticipated magnitude of the project, there would be a high probability that the project would not be authorized. On the other hand, most seasoned managements are not so naïve as to expect the results promised within the budget limitations requested or the time frame set forth. In practice, if the proposed project does have organizationally beneficial potential, management must evaluate such potential in view of resource expenditures and availability. Management must also factor in the intangibles of prospective success related to the technical and possible economic aspects of the project, the assigned project manager, and the proposed project team. The astounding fact is that management is invariably aware that solicitation is liberally tempered with optimism and yet appears to be surprised and perhaps even indignant when the end results of the project do not measure up to the initial prognostications.

Proposal Coordination

Proposal coordination is a foundation activity. The project's eventual success or failure may be traced to coordination activities entailed in delineating the scope of the project and preparing the proposal. The extent of proposal coordination depends on the nature of the project and the organizational setting. In an organization where there are extensive project operations, proposal coordination would generally involve a representative from the proposal coordination activity, assuming the existence of such a function, and a technically competent person who normally would become the project manager in the event the project were ultimately authorized. Other important actors in proposal preliminaries would be the potential customer and internal legal representation.

When preliminary evaluations are completed and a decision is made to proceed and prepare a proposal, proper coordination should follow. Proposal coordination brings together the various organizational functions that will contribute to the objectives of the project. The proposal coordinator, who probably has had extensive experience covering a variety of projects, should assist the technical person in identifying all the possible activities and functions that will be involved in the project.

Often proposal coordination is flawed from the beginning by failure to bring in people who do not seem to be extensively or primarily involved. Assumptions are often erroneously made that certain people, activities, or functions will subsequently be available and participate in the project. Problems frequently arise because functional representation, advice, and commitment were not solicited in the proposal coordination state. At times the subsequent problems are more psychological than real. By way of explanation, people are usually very sensitive of their operational prerogatives and tend to become obstreperous if they feel they have been excluded in decision processes in which their participation and support are required. They often adopt an attitude that they have relatively little obligation to support the project since their advice and inputs were not sought in the project's formative stage.

It is very important to perhaps overkill by requesting the presence of all prospective project participants at early coordination meetings. Bringing together a variety of skills and experiences has several possible advantages: It can provide additional insights into the project that may not have been considered by the proposal and technical coordinators; it can provide communication to various organizational factions as to prospective activity; it can solicit active participation and commitment; and it can possibly identify other activities or functions which were inadvertently excluded at the outset of project planning.

Errors of omission can and do occur in proposal coordination activities. Frequently the exclusion of factors that should have been considered, or were inadequately treated, can be attributed to time pressures which are often involved in proposal coordination and preparation. With the recognition that time constraints in proposal preparation are more typical than atypical, it is suggested that a proposal coordination plan, including a checklist or sequence of activities, be available in order to minimize the danger of excluding a requisite input. There should also be provisions for review by management before the formal submission of the proposal to the customer. In all probability, even after management review and approval, meetings will be held between the customer and the contractor's personnel before final presentation to further define the project.

Proposal Ingredients

The number and type of project possibilities are infinite. To prescribe a universal proposal preparation model is not only impractical, but also foolhardy. As has already been mentioned several times, a project can be very complex or very simple, long or short in duration, and external or internal. Some or all of the aforementioned factors can be influential in the preparation of a proposal. At best, some suggestions can be advanced that might be applicable or considered in the preparation of a proposal.

Proposal activity is a normal process in the project manager's job. The project manager may have the sole responsibility for the coordination and preparation of the proposal or, as indicated in the previous section, a proposal coordinator may actually assume the responsibility for the final assembly and mechanical presentation of the proposal. In either event consideration and care are important in knowing what and how much information to present.[1]

The proposal should be well written and understandable. It should communicate technical competence. It should avoid technical excesses aimed at impressing the reader. It should also avoid a patronizing tone, which might create a negative reaction. Of utmost importance is the actual text of the proposal. It should be presented in a logical sequence, be easy to read and follow, contain relevant information, be visually attractive, and must be carefully prepared and reviewed to avoid technical and mechanical errors. Such errors can easily be interpreted by a prospective buyer as a reflection of the attitude, care, or quality that might subsequently be employed on the project. Mechanical errors are a significant distraction!

Earlier in this chapter it was mentioned that the format and ingredients of a proposal should be adapted to the idiosyncrasies of the authorization source. This is an important reminder. If possible, either by direct communication or studying previous proposals that have been accepted and approved by the individual or organization, the proposal should be submitted in a format which appears to be favored by the sponsor.

The Cover Letter.   The cover letter can be very influential in the final decision to buy or not to buy a proposal. In an interview with the president of a consulting firm located in the Washington, DC, area, the author was told that in the president's opinion the cover letter was the most important part of the proposal package. The president of this firm maintained that his organization had a high percentage of proposals bought off relative to the number of proposals submitted. Most cover letters are unimaginative and even sterile; usually the text of the actual proposal is somewhat clinical. The cover letter, on the other hand, affords the opportunity to be more personal. The cover letter can attract the reader's attention and convince him or her that the organization is well qualified to perform the project. The cover letter can be an effective selling vehicle. However, care should be exercised in presenting a rationale for accepting the proposal; there may be subtle shadings between being persuasive and being flamboyant.

The cover letter should also indicate the period of proposal validity. It is essential that the proposal have such a date, or else it becomes an open-ended document that can be validated much later when costs have escalated or the proposal submitter has neither resources nor further interest in the project. The cover letter should, in addition, where applicable, include a statement of projected end item commitments, cite the person or persons the customer may contact, and give a brief statement of interest, related experience, qualifications, ability to perform the project, and anticipated project cost.

Executive Summary.   There are times when the person who has the authority to authorize the project does not feel competent to evaluate the proposed technical aspects of the project. It is also possible that the authorizing individual does not have the time to examine and validate the detailed information presented in the proposal. A good, succinct executive summary can spell out the significant aspects of the project so the reader can determine the project's applicability and potential contribution to the organization's mission. If the executive summary is well presented and the project appears to be compatible with organizational needs, the busy executive can be induced to pass the project proposal to qualified people for evaluation.

Technical Section.   This is a very sensitive area. In this section the proposer must convey impressions of understanding the problem and indicate technical competence to solve the problem. If the authorizing body does not feel there is a proper understanding of the technical problems and issues involved, there is a high probability that the proposal will be summarily disqualified. The next issue, assuming that there is mutual recognition of the technical aspects of the proposed project, is to communicate to the sponsor that the technical objectives can be accomplished.

The technical section should indicate the anticipated scope of the project, including the general technical approach planned and a statement of proposed work. If applicable to the project, anticipated performance specifications should be cited. In some instances quality factors have to be included in this section. After discussing the proposed content and approach to the technical section with several project managers, the message from them was very explicit: The sponsor should feel there is ability to perform the project, but avoid details that could compromise the prospects of getting the project authorized. Too much detail can become a negative factor if the sponsor takes exception to the specific approach suggested. If the sponsor is of the opinion that the proposer has the ability and authorizes the project, the specifics can be discussed after a contract has been reached or possible technical avenues can be negotiated later. The important aspect is to indicate the project goals.

Another problem with providing too much detail is that the proposer gives up all future negotiating power. There is nothing left to sell. Worse yet, the RFP could have been only seeking information that could then be used to solve the problem internally. The externally directed proposal should not contain all the necessary data or methodology to solve the problem. The problem solution methodology may be the critical aspect of the project. The actual implementation of the proposed methodology may be relatively simple. As indicated, once the proposed solution is advanced, there may be no longer need for outside support.

The technical section can include a statement of resource requirements. Resource requirements may involve special facilities or equipment. If such facilities or equipment already exist and can be employed, this can give the bidder a competitive advantage. If special and currently nonexistent resources will be required, they should be identified and a statement of planned acquisition and use should be included in the technical section.

Anticipated Benefits. It must be remembered that impetus for the proposal was provided by a perceived need or, where the proposal was unsolicited, a project is suggested to anticipate a requirement or possible operational improvement. Resources that usually are directed to project activity are often relatively scarce and expensive. There is frequent competition for such resources. Management, in the decision process, must evaluate need, options, and potential benefits related to the project. To cite a few examples of some potential benefits, the project may entail effort that advances the state of the art; it may be a feasibility study which could open up avenues of promising opportunities or verify a technical approach or marketing area; it could enable entry into new business areas; it could be beneficial in reducing operational costs and make the organization more profitable and competitive; it can have sociological and psychological implications that can be exploited for positive public relations.

Some possible benefits may be obvious and other benefits, especially where the proposal was unsolicited, may be less obvious. In any event, the advantages that might materialize from the project should be spelled out. In indicating potential benefits, enthusiasm should be tempered by practicality. If too much is promised, a discerning evaluator may be put off as a result of recognizing goals that have a low probability of achievement. Also, promising too much may lead to high expectations and, even if there is significant project accomplishment, such contributions may later be minimized in the light of expectations resulting from overenthusiastic promises.

Schedule. There are many project-related activities that must be planned for and scheduled in order to determine the progress on the project. There are situations resulting from coordination activities and proposal acceptance where parties to the project agree on the technical approach, including deliverable end items, performance specifications, and cost projections, but further negotiations are required to reach mutually agreeable delivery schedules. Schedules on deliverables may be telescoped or extended. The deliverable schedules, once negotiated, represent a contractual obligation. The contractor will, in most projects, require a comprehensive schedule of activities leading to the deliverable end items. The schedule would normally include a reasonable work breakdown, indicating major project items, phases, and tasks. The schedule would also indicate significant accomplishment milestones so the project could be monitored for progress.

Scheduled activities might additionally provide for periodic progress reports. Provision for progress reports is usually made in government contracts. Periodic coordination or liaison meetings can also be scheduled to enable direct interface between the project people and the sponsoring organization. These types of meetings can be especially important where the project is one facet of a larger program encompassing several projects. The sponsoring organization may desire liaison meetings where representatives from the different projects and different organizations can be present, discuss progress and problems and coordinate, where applicable, activities between related projects.

Financial Section. The financial section can vary in detail from sparse to extremely comprehensive. The level of detail involved would reflect the nature of the project, the contracting parties, and the reimbursement type of contract. Where the government is one of the parties, the financial section requirements are usually quite comprehensive.

Representative information often required in the financial section includes a breakdown of projected hours needed to accomplish the project. The projected hour breakdown would include direct and indirect hours to be charged to the project. Often the direct and indirect hour projections are further detailed by identifying specific functions or activities, such as the project management, technical support, and clerical assistance.

In some contracting arrangements an explanation of how costs are derived is required, for example, the costs involved in direct charges by functional support. Indirect labor charges also have to be identified. Requests for how overhead charges are determined are often made where the government sponsors the project. This section should indicate the type of contractual arrangement proposed, such as fixed price or one of several possibilities covering cost plus some fee arrangement. The various types of possible contractual arrangements will be covered more extensively, as mentioned, in Chapter 11 on the legal aspects of project management.

If the project will require liaison meetings, costs should be estimated and included in the proposal for travel and per diem expenses. Also, any other services that might be required to support the project should be identified and costed.

In the event that the sponsor requests a schedule acceleration and overtime might be required, it would be wise to anticipate such effort and make provisions for how overtime might be reimbursed.

Cost information would probably be required where special purchases of equipment might be necessary, tooling developed, or facilities modified to accomplish the project. Outside subcontractors might be employed, and, if so, such costs should be indicated.

Of critical importance is the inclusion of some method of payment. Payment can be incremental, geared to time, based on achieving progress milestones, or contingent on the delivery of project end items. Whatever the facilitating factor agreed upon, it is essential to include how and when payments are to be made. If the sponsor is notoriously slow in payment, the vendor can have a cash flow problem; prospective delays in receiving payment and the attendant costs should be factored into the project price.

Legal Section. A well thought-out project will anticipate possible and probable problems that might arise. Recognition and legal provision for such contingencies can save a great deal of later difficulties, including ruffled feelings and possible litigation. Some of the areas that might be applicable to the project and which should be incorporated into the proposal with qualified legal assistance are cited in the following.

It is impossible on projects where there is practically no precedent to predict that disputes will not arise as a consequence of unforeseeable problems. It goes without saying that harmonious working relationships are very important between the project people and the sponsoring organization. Some mediation or arbitration procedure should be incorporated into the proposal and the ultimate contract. Such procedures can facilitate the resolution of disputes and ensure the continuance of good working relationships.

Some projects are authorized where the technology involved is so volatile that changes in project concepts are to be anticipated, even though such changes cannot be identified when project authorization is granted. The incorporation of procedures to filter changes that affect the original project concept is important to both parties, but more so to the vendor. When the sponsor requests changes, the scope of the project is usually affected and additional costs are incurred. The project team should normally be willing and able to incorporate change requests initiated by the contractor, provided that project costs and price are renegotiated to reflect the added effort required by the change.

There are also instances when a change request may be initiated by the project team as a consequence of new insights gained on the project. In such instances the proposed change would be presented to the customer with an indication of the cost and benefits involved. The customer would then have the option of buying or not buying the change.

One often neglected area in the proposal is provision for termination procedures. Termination procedures can be very simple, when the end product is a report resulting from a feasibility study. Termination procedures can also be legally very complex and cover a considerable period of time, long after the main project work has been completed. Just a few examples of areas where legal provision might be required are the disposition of raw materials, work in process, spare parts, equipment, and facilities. More elaboration will be forthcoming on this subject in the chapters dealing with the legal aspects of project management and project termination.

Some projects may involve effort that ultimately leads to a patentable product or patentable products may be ancillary results from the major project objectives. All sorts of legal issues can arise as a consequence of patentable effort. It is strongly suggested that, when patentable effort might develop from the project, the proposal include provisions covering the rights and obligations of the parties involved.

Often the legal part of the proposal will have the so-called "boiler plate" section. The boiler plate section usually addresses standard procedures, practices, or laws that might affect the project. Inclusion of these standard but applicable sections is very common in government contracts. A few representative examples that might be applicable on some projects are the type of organization (profit or nonprofit), a minority-owned business, a woman-owned business, equal opportunity provisions, set-asides for small business, and affirmative action.

Management.   There may be situations where the contractor has difficulty making a definitive distinction between bidders on the proposed technical approach of the project. The ultimate decision, positive or negative, might hinge on the management of the competing organizations. The management section of the proposal can be very influential. Some of the information that might be considered for inclusion in this section would include the history of the organization and its growth, financial responsibility, and experience. The experience factor could especially be relevant. A proven track record of accomplishment and an impressive list of satisfied clients can often make the difference between having a project authorized or rejected. A contractor could understandably be very reluctant to authorize a large project to a bidder with little or no demonstrated experience. The organization's history of growth can also be influential, indicating ability to survive and compete. The growth rate would also indicate the levels of past activities and the ability to expand operations and perhaps reflect recommendations and possible repeat business from satisfied clients. A statement of financial responsibility can be influential where the project is of long duration and technologically sophisticated and requires considerable resources.

The management section generally includes the résumés of the key people who would be assigned to the project. The résumé of the prospective project manager is particularly important. An indication of the person assigned as project manager and the amount of time he or she would devote to the project is normally included in the proposal. Information on the résumés of other people to be assigned to the project would usually include years of related experience, organizational titles, and educational attainment.

Some Concluding Observations. Organizations may receive many requests for proposals or may be aware of situations where an unsolicited proposal could be submitted in anticipation of a possible project. The organization may decline to bid for a variety of reasons. It may be felt that the prospective project does not fit in with the long-range objective of the organization. It is possible that current commitments have employed available resources and adding more resources to accomplish the prospective project is not economically or technically feasible. It is possible that a decision to not bid is predicated on a feeling that other organizations responding to the RFP have a competitive advantage. The organization may not be technically competent to address the issues set forth in the RFP. There may be financial restrictions indicated in the RFP that would limit profit prospects to the point where there is insufficient economic incentive to bid. Schedule requirements may be set forth in the RFP that are not considered attainable. There can, of course, be other reasons why a proposal is not developed.

Proposal coordination and preparation are usually highly skilled and expensive undertakings. More often than not proposals are prepared under severe time constraints. Large organizations, where there are many active projects at any given time, will probably have a special function directed to proposal coordination and preparation. Invariably, this is an extremely pressured function. People who specialize in this activity are subject to constant stress and vulnerable to career burn-out.

Proposal preparation can be a very expensive activity, especially if there is a high failure rate of submitted proposals to accepted proposals. High-priced people are usually assigned to preparing proposals. Proposal preparation costs are generally charged to overhead. An excessively high overhead rate can compromise the organization's prospects for getting new business.

Despite some of the problems indicated and an awareness that there is a low probability that the proposal will be accepted, the organization may nevertheless submit a proposal. Failure to respond to an RFP may result in being eliminated from the qualified bidders' list. In one situation in which the author was involved the decision to bid was made, even though there was practically no chance that the proposal would be accepted. When the author questioned the decision maker for the rationale to submit a "can't win" proposal, he was informed that the organization had good working relations with the contracting officer who requested the proposal. The submitting organization wanted to retain the goodwill of the contracting officer who did not want to have to justify a sole source procurement. It was felt that the favor would subsequently be returned in the form of future business.

It is very important to know your prospective customer before going through the time and expense of preparing a proposal. Many times initial contracts are made with people who appear to be knowledgeable and have the ability to authorize a project. Often much preliminary time and effort are expended before it is realized that the actual decision process is beyond the authority of that person. Another frequent problem is based on speculation. Activity is generated in anticipation that subsequent funding will be available. Unfortunately, more often than not the funding has not been allocated or other projects are given a higher priority for funding and the effort is wasted. In essence, what is being said is know the contractor. Is the contractor ethical and reliable? Does the contact source have authority to enter into a valid contract and have the funding available for a commitment?

As indicated in this section, there are many relevant factors to consider before commencing proposal activity. As the saying goes, "the operation was a success, but the patient died." The proposal submitted can be an excellent technical effort from all relevant aspects of the projected project. Nevertheless, in spite of the technical attributes of the proposal, some other organization may be authorized the project on an inferior proposal and with seemingly fewer organizational and technical qualifications. Again, it comes back to knowing your prospective customer.

The organization should have some accumulated experience on proposals prepared and submitted. Past experiences can serve as a guide as to the success level of proposals submitted, proposal costs, prospective customers, acceptable formats, and so forth. With such guidance, proposal preparation processes can be improved and a decline to bid decision made when there is a low probability that the proposal will be bought off.

One final thought for this section relates to timing and proposal evaluation, which is covered in the next section. Most organizations' funding projects have a proposal evaluation procedure. The government in particular has published numerous proposal evaluation procedures.[2] At the beginning of the fiscal year, after funding limitations come into focus, evaluation procedures are generally employed to determine which ongoing projects should be continued and which new projects should be authorized. By the middle of the fiscal year most of the funds have been committed and the prospects for a new project to be authorized are dim, unless there is a sudden and an urgent need. Toward the end of the fiscal year a better picture emerges as to the actual use of committed funds and the availability of support for new projects. In the government next year's funding is often, to a large extent, contingent on the current year's expenditures. Leftover funds from the current year compromises the organization's leverage in requesting more or the same amount of funds for the following year. In such a situation there may be a desperate scramble to authorize projects and allocate funds for activities that might not have been considered earlier in the fiscal year. Proposal evaluation procedures at this time tends to get very loose. A wise manager, seeking support for a project, would be well advised to be sensitive to the financial pulse of various organizations that might be prospective customers.

Proposal Evaluation

Proposal Evaluation and Source Selection

Proposal evaluation and source selection are closely related and yet different. A distinction can be made between proposal evaluation and source selection decisions both objectively and puristically. A proposal may be good, but the source questionable; the proposal may be questionable, but the source good. In actual practice, proposal evaluation and source selection often become entwined and are mutually influential.

It is very possible that an unsolicited proposal or a proposal submitted in response to an advertised RFP will reflect considerable merit but subsequently be rejected. The rejection could be predicated on the buyer's lack of confidence in the person or organization submitting the proposal, even though the actual proposal appears to be technically sound. Buyers are often reluctant to commit funds and authorize projects where there may be a doubt in the ability to perform. There are probably psychological blocks related to having to defend a decision to authorize a project where questions as to the source capabilities can subsequently be raised. This creates situations in some fields where it is extremely difficult for newcomers to break into the system.

Conversely, it is possible that the proposal had deficiencies but is bought off primarily because of the individual's or organization's reputation. There are times when alleged neutral proposal evaluation boards, consisting of technically qualified experts, are assembled to make recommendations as to the acceptance or rejection of a proposal. Such boards' recommendations are generally influential but may not be binding on the project authorization organization. This is a relatively common practice in some government agencies. The author has sat on some proposal evaluation boards and is convinced that in many instances the final selection was determined more by confidence in the source than on the merits of the immediate proposal.

It is possible that a good proposal will not be accepted because of questions as to the qualifications of the proposal source; it is also possible that a mediocre proposal might be accepted because the source may have unusual and demonstrated qualifications. Ideally, each individual or organization submitting proposals should have competence and the proposals should be evaluated on the basis of content and proposed activity.

It is also possible that the submitted proposal will not be evaluated; the proposal may be disqualified because it was received past the officially established time and submittal date. The bidder may also have second thoughts about the proposal and send a formal written notice to the contractor to the effect that the bidder wishes to withdraw the proposal. Such a decision may be prompted by several reasons indicated earlier in this chapter. If the proposal has been submitted, the bidder may have second thoughts as to potential profitability or ability to perform, or there may be other intervening obligations that would make performance difficult or impossible. The proposal may be disqualified and not evaluated because the bidder is not considered qualified, or the bidder may be qualified but the proposal will not be considered because eligibility is based on being on a qualified bidders' list and the vendor has not been placed on such a list.

Objectives of Proposal Evaluation

The objectives of proposal evaluation should be clearly stated and understood. Several objectives may be considered and should be addressed to minimize the chance of one factor overriding other pertinent considerations. For instance, the following is stated in Procurement, *Proposal Evaluation and Source Selection,* Army Regulation No. 715-6:

Objectives

  a. The prime objectives of proposal evaluation and source selection are to:
   1. Insure impartial, equitable, and comprehensive evaluation of proposals.
   2. Insure selection of that source whose proposal, as submitted, offers optimum satisfaction of the Government's objectives, including cost, schedule, and performance.
  b. Additional specific objectives are to:
   1. Provide that an individual serving in a major executive position of the DOD will be fully responsible for the source selection decision in a major procurement action.
   2. Insure a balanced appraisal of all factors in the source selection process by appointing an advisory group of senior military and civilian personnel possessing experience in weapons development, knowledge of military requirements and operations, and comprehension of procurement matters.
   3. Apply and fully utilize the professional skills and knowledge of competent military and civilian personnel in the evaluation and assessment of proposals.
   4. Establish consistent procedures to improve the effectiveness of review and approval within the Department of the Army, and to provide for public understanding and acceptance of the Government's decision.[3]

The aforementioned represents a pretty comprehensive statement on objectives and can be modified and adapted as a policy guide for proposal evaluation and source selection. Objectives may also be broadened where the following applies:

> In the Government procure process (DOD and NASA), contracts are not awarded solely on the basis of a company's cost proposal and demonstration of resources to be applied to a contract, coupled with prior accomplishments. Rather, a company's proposal must demonstrate a complete understanding of all technical problems, to the point of describing therein a substantially finished design of a viable version of the system to be furnished, and discussing the merits of the chosen design versus possible alternatives. The associated technical effort, ranging from studies, computer modeling and design calculations to, in many cases, the construction of prototypes, represents the technical effort required for B and P.[4]

It is important to have a statement of objectives. The objectives may vary by organization and the types of projects to be considered. However, recognizing the necessity for accommodation of differences, applicable objectives can provide some standard for evaluation procedures. Different evaluations within the same organization may put emphasis on different factors. Such a practice not only would be inconsistent, but also could create confusion, lead to poor public relations, and perhaps even result in litigation.[5]

Proposal Evaluation Criteria

Criteria considered essential for evaluating a proposal leading to a project can vary to a considerable extent. There are prospective projects where some factors would be very important; on other projects these factors might only be of moderate consequential importance. Again, on some projects many criteria would have to be considered, whereas on other possible projects only a few relevant criteria would be determinate. The importance of criteria for evaluation might also be affected by the organization, its operational environment, and competition. For instance, cost and availability may be critical criteria for evaluating a proposal and a prospective project in the commercial sector, whereas performance and availability criteria may take precedence over cost criteria in some military procurements.

Evaluation criteria could be spelled out in a request for proposal in order to give bidders some indication of the relative importance of the various elements to be addressed:

> Further, only when the request or invitation properly spells out all of the criteria to be used in awarding the contract can all bids be closely compared and the company assured of a cost-effective and legally defensible decision.[6]

Legality may not be an issue in proposal evaluation, especially where there are internally generated or unsolicited proposals. It might be wise to internally develop a comprehensive checklist of criteria that might be considered in evaluating proposals. Some or all of the criteria could be applicable at different times and for different proposals. Also, the relative importance of the criteria would tend to vary to reflect the factors involved in the proposed project. The existence of an extensive criteria checklist would improve the probability that any factors relevant to the project would be considered and not inadvertently overlooked in the final evaluation.

Evaluation criteria normally would encompass four major areas: the proposed technical approach, schedule commitment, cost, and management. These areas could further be elaborated to evaluate such factors as the following:

Past and related technical experience

The technical reputation of the organization

Existing commitments and capacity of the organization

History of meeting scheduled commitments

Financial responsibility

Resources, such as personnel, equipment, and facilities, to perform the project

Price competitiveness and cost relative to anticipated use and value

Management capability and operational planning and control systems

Of course, this list is not all-inclusive; it is merely indicative of criteria that might be considered. More depth and detail of criteria would probably be warranted for technologically involved projects. The criteria suggested are based on the assumption of competitive bidding. Where there is a solicited or unsolicited sole source procurement, additional or other proposal evaluation criteria could be applicable.

In establishing criteria for evaluation, it is important that the evaluator or the evaluation team agree upon criteria that are considered relevant. It is also important that criteria be put in proper perspective. In highly technical projects the technical section of the proposal may be weighted more heavily than other sections; in other instances cost factors may be the controlling criteria.

Proposal Evaluation Procedures

Proposal evaluation procedures are determined by the sponsoring organization. A myriad of evaluation procedures exist and are possible. Generally two elements are present in a proposal evaluation procedure: There is an evaluation team or an evaluator and there is usually some scoring method or model to rate the criteria against a desired norm and/or competitive proposals.

Evaluation may be made by a person who is technically competent to judge the merits of the proposal. When the proposal is technologically complex, a proposal evaluation survey team may be formed. The survey team can be composed of representatives of functional activities that might be affected by the project. In a very complex proposal, subdivisions may take place within functional groups for more in-depth evaluation. Just as an example, the survey team may have representatives from the technical organization and finance, production, marketing, quality control, legal, personnel, procurement, and management departments. Other functional representatives can also be involved. Each member of the survey team should have a specific assignment, some standard, if possible, of evaluation determination, and a time frame in which to make the evaluation. Communicating an evaluation schedule to the survey team is important because there is usually a committed award date for proposals.

Once the various proposal segments are analyzed and evaluated, it probably is a good idea to reassemble the survey team to compare impressions and evaluations. Often it is possible to obtain new insights when viewing a complicated proposal in concert that were not apparent when viewed singly.

Scoring methods or models can also contribute significantly to proposal evaluation. The scoring can reflect the relative importance ascribed to each criterium, give perspective to the component parts of the proposal, and improve the probability that all relevant criteria have been considered. Scoring models, while having the potential for evaluative contribution, also have limitations that should be recognized. The scoring weights are often subjectively determined. The values given the criteria within the range of the scoring weights are generally based on opinion rather than quantitative proof. There is a tendency to become enamored with methodology and make the model too complicated. The more complicated the model, the more difficult it is to comprehend. If comprehension is not easy, there is a definite probability that management will be suspicious of the model's validity, and the model will actually have little or no impact in the evaluation process.

In considering scoring models or methodologies, simplicity is recommended. Criteria can be scored on a 1 to 10 basis, with 10 being best and 1 poorest, or a descriptive range can be employed, using adjectives like *excellent, very good, good, fair, poor,* and *unacceptable.*

There is no universal procedure or method for proposal evaluation. Each proposal and each organization are different. Methodology has to be developed and employed that is relevant to the situation. In considering the development of evaluation methodology, the following might be useful:

> The evaluation process includes an evaluation plan, a solicitation, the actual evaluation, negotiations to clarify, details, and source selection. The evaluation plan is formulated prior to solicitation and serves the following purposes:
>
> To ensure that all efforts are directed toward a common goal.
>
> To collect, organize, and display the performance, schedule and cost requirements by emphasizing pertinent evaluation criteria.
>
> To provide a structure for organizing the evaluation group and scheduling its activities.
>
> To provide a structure for the preparation of the RFP.
>
> To establish a format for discussion at proposal conferences, if held, and later offerer or contractual discussions.
>
> To serve as a guide for the contracting authority in source selection.
>
> To provide procedures and methodology for evaluation purposes.
>
> To provide guidelines for making trade-offs among, and within, the various factors to the performance of the equipment and to the management of the project in relationship to the development, production, operating and support costs, the delivery schedule and quantity, and the qualitative requirements of the procurement.[7]

Endnotes Chapter Four

1. Roger A. Golde and Jules J. Schwartz, "Be Sure You Say Enough When You Write Your R&D Proposals," *Industrial Research and Development*, pp. 136–139, March 1983.

2. A few representative examples of government proposal evaluation procedures: *Project Managers Guide*, Naval Ocean Systems Center, San Diego, CA 92152, Technical Document 108, 1 June 1977, pp. xvi–28 and xvi–29; *Proposal Evaluation and Source Selection*, Headquarters Department of the Army, Washington, DC, 21 September 1970, Army Regulation No. 715-6.

3. *Proposal Evaluation and Source Selection, op. cit.,* p. 1.

4. "A Position Paper on Independent Research and Development and Bid and Proposal Efforts", Aerospace Industries Association of America, Inc., Washington, DC, Electronic Industries Association, Washington, DC, National Security Industrial Association, Washington, DC, March 22, 1974, p. 6.

5. W. E. Buczynski, "A Method for Awarding Major Contracts," *National Purchasing Review*, January–February 1982, pp. 6–9.

6. *Ibid.,* p. 6.

7. *Project Managers Guide, op. cit.,* pp. xvi–28.

Appendix A*

July 20, 1776

Mr. Thomas Jefferson
Continental Congress
Independence Hall
Philadephia, Pennsylvania

Dear Mr. Jefferson:

We have read your "Declaration of Independence" with great interest. Certainly, it represents a considerable undertaking and many of your statements do merit serious consideration. Unfortunately, the Declaration as a whole fails to meet recently adopted specifications for proposals to the Crown, so we must return the document to you for further refinement. The questions that follow might assist you in your process of revision.

1. In your opening paragraph, you use the phrase "the laws of Nature and Nature's God." What are these laws? In what way are they the criteria on which you base your central arguments? Please document with citations from the recent literature.

2. In the same paragraph you refer to the "opinions of mankind." Whose polling data are you using? Without specific evidence, it seems to us, the "opinions of mankind" are a matter of opinion.

3. You hold certain truths to be "self-evident." Could you please elaborate? If they are as evident as you claim, then it should not be difficult for you to locate the appropriate supporting statistics.

4. "Life, liberty, and the pursuit of happiness" seem to be goals of your proposal. These are not measurable goals. If you were to say that "among these is the ability to sustain an average life expectancy in 6 of the 13 colonies of at least 55 years, to enable all newspapers in the colonies to print news without outside interference, and to raise the average income of the colonists by 10% in the next 10 years," these would be measurable goals. Please clarify.

5. You state that "whenever any Form of Government becomes destructive of these ends, it is the Right of the People to alter or to abolish it, and to institute a new Government." Have you weighed this assertion against all the alternatives? Or is it predicted solely on the basic instincts?

6. Your description of the existing situation is quite extensive. Such a long list of grievances should precede the statement of goals, not follow it.

7. Your strategy for achieving your goal is not developed at all. You state that the colonies "ought to be Free and Independent States" and that they are "Absolved from All Allegiance to the British Crown." Who or what must change to achieve this objective? In what way must they change? What resistance must you overcome to achieve the change? What specific steps will you take to overcome

---

* Edward Schwartz, "Letter to Thomas Jefferson from Lord North," reprinted with permission by *Social Policy,* published by Social Policy Corporation, New York *Social Policy,* Vol. 5, No. 2, pp. 10–11, 1974.

the resistance? How long will it take? We have found that a little foresight in these areas helps to prevent careless errors later on.

8. Who among the list of signatories will be responsible for implementing your strategy? Who conceived it? Who provided the theoretical research? Who will constitute the advisory committee? Please submit an organizational chart.

9. You must include an evaluation design. We have been requiring this since Queen Anne's War.

10. What impact will your program have? We have been requiring this since Queen Anne's War.

11. Please submit a PERT diagram, an activity chart, and an itemized budget.

We hope that these comments prove useful in revising your "Declaration of Independence."

Best Wishes,

SECTION II

The Project Formative Phase

CHAPTER FIVE

Project Organization

Introduction

To Facilitate the Accomplishment of Objectives

Organizations are formed to facilitate the accomplishment of objectives. Organization is based on a division of labor and a delineation of activities for administrative purposes. To achieve objectives it is important to identify activities and the functions required to perform these activities. Functions and activities that are not compatible with objectives should be eliminated or nonexistent to begin with. Additionally, organization of human resources is to indicate functional relationships, delineate responsibility and authority, and establish communication networks.

Organizational Dynamics

Organization can involve a variety of operational situations. An organization may be a company, a division of government, a nonprofit group or association, or a military unit. It may also be a subgroup within a larger unit, such as a functional division, a product cost center, or a project. The nature of the operational objectives will bear on how resources are organized. Operational goals and philosophies are subject to various degrees of change; the organization of people and functions, where there is dynamic operational activity, is continuously susceptible to redefinition and regrouping. Another organizationally impacting factor is the orientation of management. A top management bent toward marketing, finance, production, or R&D can skew functions, assignments, and reporting responsibilities to reflect such orientation.

In some operational environments organization may be relatively stable and perhaps evolutionary, whereas in other operational environments change is an ongoing process and constant organizational adjustment is tantamount to survival. Organizations composed of many operational subunits, such as projects, must be sensitive and responsive to ever-shifting operational requirements.

Operational Environment and Organization

The Ideal Organization

Is there an ideal organizational structure? As a generalization, the answer would have to be no. There is no single method of organization that will encourage maximum operational efficiency in all organizations. It is also possible that an organization can effectively achieve its objectives using more than one method to group people and functions into cohesive work units. At times it is possible to achieve operational objectives while appearing to violate more usual organizational methods. What appears to be a theoretically sound approach to organizing human and material resources may ultimately have dismal results. It is important to remember that organization is only a managerial tool or vehicle used to get operational results. Organization is a means to an end, and not an end in itself!

At times results can be achieved despite an organizational mode or climate that is less than ideal. It must be remembered that organizations are made up of people; people with positive motivations can often circumvent many organizational defects. Lack of human motivation or negative attitudes can neutralize or render inoperable what conceptually appears to be a sound organizational structure.

People Factors

It is assumed that people are the critical element in organization. The human element assumes greater importance as the operation moves from mechanistic to organic activities. The mechanics of organizing people, functions, and material can prove to be a sterile exercise, relative to accomplishing operational objectives, unless human motivation is positively stimulated by a receptive and supportive operational climate.

There has been an evolution in the methods used to organize human resources. The evolutionary pace has accelerated in response to rapid changes in the operational environment. Operational pressures have developed as a consequence of the scarcity of highly trained professional resources, the resultant cost, and the need to productively and competitively use these resources.

Prior to World War II there was comparatively little sensitivity to human organization. The general managerial philosophy was that people were being paid to do a job and if an individual's performance was not deemed satisfactory, there was always someone else available to fill the void. This general operational environment started to change in the 1930s with the union movement; it significantly changed during the 1940s. The trend toward an awareness of human organization has accelerated rather than abated since the 1940s. Some factors that have contributed to this trend are a better-educated work force, more thinking and creative jobs vis-à-vis mechanical work, greater worker job protection, increased awareness and responsiveness to human rights, competition for skilled human resources, and the price of these human resources.

The result has been a growing need for and willingness to experiment with different organizational methods. The following section will discuss some environmental changes that have and are currently affecting organizations.

The Changing Operational Environment

There has been a significant shift in the composition of the work force: First, there has been a marked trend toward a youth-oriented work force and, second, there has been increasing emphasis on and subsequent individual opportunity in thinking versus vocational jobs.[1]

The work place has developed a fetish for youth. When people reach the age of 40, their mobility and organizational desirability generally diminish. After the age of 50 inter- and intraorganizational mobility is usually further diminished. The years between 25 and 35 have become very important in establishing a career pattern. Competition between young people often is intense, promotional opportunities for the successful survivors has been rapid, and individual "burn-out" has become commonplace. Organizations have placed a premium on internal human competition and accomplishment. Also recognized is the need to motivate these potential high achievers. An attendant problem has been that these people often wear out physically, intellectually, and emotionally at a relatively early age. It is a serious and growing social problem to find a 35-year-old who has "had it" and has professionally plateaued. The seriousness of such a situation is that this person can reasonably expect to remain in the work force another 30 years.

The second important change in the work force has been the transitional nature of the job market. With the advent of automation and robotization there has been a sharp decline in the demand for factory workers and people with mechanical skills. According to various estimates, by the year 2000 somewhere between 10 and 23% of the gainfully employed people in the United States will be blue-collar workers in jobs requiring physical or mechanical skills.[2] The result is disequilibrium between the supply and demand for workers. People who have mechanical skills have found the transition to the emerging job market difficult and at times even impossible. It is a high-priority social problem to find some means to gainfully and productively employ these people in the transitional period. The problem is compounded because economically displaced workers often do not have transferable job skills.

Many long-established organizations have been slow in responding to the changing operational climate. The result has frequently been a deteriorating market position, diminishing profits, susceptibility to competition, and a loss of prestige. Once an organization's reputation is tarnished, it may take years to regain a favorable public image.

Response to the changing operational environment can be manifested by a defensive reaction or an aggressive approach to seek better ways to achieve objectives. During the recession years of 1981–1982 there still were considerable inflation, high operational costs, and in many industries depressed profits or even significant losses. Managements tend to become lax in controlling operational costs, especially during periods of prosperity, and such laxness contributed to the economic downturn. The economic recovery in 1983 was partly due to the painful but often necessary expediency to look at the human organization. There were severe cutbacks in many organizations. People, functions, and facilities were frequently evaluated as being redundant, noncontributive, or obsolete. As a consequence, productivity and quality were low in many operational situations. The transition period has led to social and economic problems. However, even though there often were severe organizational cutbacks, it was frequently reported in 1983 that productivity, profitability, and competitiveness generally improved. Attendant to the need for improved operational efficiencies, there have been strong indications that managements have learned and have been willing to try new organizational approaches.

Small Work Groups

Bigness has generally been considered to have built-in operational advantages. Bigness can also have negative connotations. In the emerging high-technology operational environment, survival could be dependent upon an organization's ability to innovate—technically, product-wise, and managerially. It is very possible that large organizations, with several decision-making echelons, can stifle the creative individual. Often, response to important decisions is slow and frustrating. In many technological environments this problem has been recognized. The result has been a departure, in some instances, from past organizational practices and the introduction of a relatively new organizational concept. There has been experimentation and reported successes in breaking large organizational units into small, intellectually, technologically, and emotionally compatible teams.[3] This approach has worked well in the computer industry, where large computer firms have spun-off small divisions. "Companies say that small groups, given great freedom, can react better and more quickly to the abrupt changes in electronics technology."[4]

There are indications that the trend to organizing compatible teams will continue inasmuch as there have been several landmark studies that have indicated that small firms have made many significant innovations leading to technological development.[5]

Organizing people into small, manageable teams can encourage interaction, improve communication, and shorten response time. These benefits should be instrumental in leading to a rethinking of how to organize. The favorable results from small work teams, often organized as projects, suggest other organizational possibilities relative to size.[6] Is there an optimum size for organization? Can organizations get so large and cumbersome that innovation becomes improbable? How can large organizations be broken into small objective-directed, compatible groups, which can in turn use the overall resources of the large organization to productive advantage? To what extent is the overall operational environment a positive or negative motivational force? What can or should be done to improve the operational environment in order to stimulate creativity and productivity? How might internal operational excellence be developed and sustained? To what extent can outside contract sources be used to complement internal skills? Where can outside consultants be used to stimulate, educate, and complement the internal organization?

Answers to the preceding questions could provide guidelines to management in formulating an operational policy that subsequently could be the basis for organization. The rationale in presenting the material in the first sections of this chapter has been to give some indication of the complexities involved in organization. Organization should not be for immediate convenience; it should not be a fetish; it should not be done indifferently; it should recognize operational goals; and it should not be skewed to reflect functional prejudice based on management's orientation. The organization of resources should be a carefully considered action by management. In some mechanistic activities the method of organization is almost dictated by the nature of the operation. In organic activities, especially where there are projects, the organizational method becomes more challenging and often requires managerial innovation.

The following section will discuss the evolution of organizational methods and their salient features.

Organizational Methods

Organizational Methods and Mechanics of Implementation

There is often confusion between organizational methods and the mechanics of implementation. There are several organizational methods. Often different variations of these organizational methods are possible and exist simultaneously within the same operation. Organization can be directed and motivated by such operational considerations as function, product, process, geography (decentralization), project, matrix, hybrid, or free form. The mechanics of implementation include accommodation for line–staff relationships and committee formations and assignments.

The Operational Continuum

The organizational method(s) selected would no doubt be influenced by the nature of the organization's operations. The operational spectrum can range from pure research, applied research, exploratory development, advanced development, and production to the selling of technical services. It is also very possible that in large organizations more than one of the aforementioned activities will be in process. In such situations the type of activity may be instrumental in determining the applicable method for organization. A large organization with a diversity of operations may employ many different organizational methods or combinations of methods.

A single-product or single-purpose operation could be organized along functional lines. If the organization evolves, there may be a combination of objectives and/or products and services; different organizational methods or combinations of organizational methods may be developed in response to operational objectives. Not all possible organizational methods will be discussed in the following sections; only those organizational methods generally adaptable to operations amenable to projectization, such as function, project, matrix, hybrid, and free form, are reviewed.

An Organizational Continuum

Perhaps the earliest and most dominant organizational method has been by function; however, there is evidence that project organization existed in antiquity. A good example is the building of the Egyptian pyramids. The project method of organization really did not come into sharp focus or receive a great deal of publicity until World War II.

In the following organizational continuum model (Figure 5-1) functions exist as a pure organizational method, as well as an essential ingredient in other organizational methods that have been devised to facilitate the accomplishment of operational objectives.

Functional Organization

Identification of the functions or activities required to support organizational objectives is fundamental. Regardless of where the organization is on the operational continuum, functional activity must take place to support objectives. Organization by function is the most common organizational method. A function is an action or activity that supports or is part of a larger organization or activity. An organization is a composite of functions that are established to accomplish one or several goals.

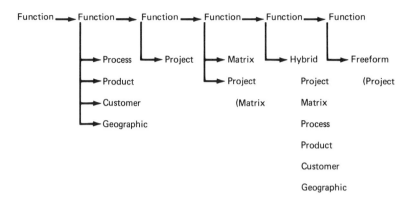

Figure 5-1. The organizational continuum.

There are significant advantages, as well as distinct disadvantages, in functional organization. Organization by function is based on specialization and division of labor. Functional organization can provide operational flexibility by the efficient use of concentrated resources. The grouping of people in an area of functional specialization can encourage the exchange of information and experience and provide operational continuity. A properly staffed function can also provide a broad human resource base.

The functional method has important advantages, but some actual implementations become limiting, especially in project management. Too narrow a functional outlook tends to create little empires within the organization. Overall objectives can become obscured and defense mechanisms developed to promote a particular function into an independent entity instead of part of the entire process. Often in organizations there is a lack of understanding of the contributions made by different functions and their interrelationships. It is also possible that function-directed activity will become self-serving. Too often specialized groups consider themselves competitors with other groups instead of collaborators with them for organization-wide goals and resources.

An operational danger in the functional method of organization is that some functions are more viable than others. Viability can develop owing to the nature of the end product of the organization, management's orientation, or aggressive political maneuvering. There can subsequently be functional polarization where some functions are in a favorable organizational position, whereas other functions become second-class organizational citizens. There may be a failure to recognize that, in order for an organization to be healthy and prosper, the contribution and support of all functions are essential.

Functional maladjustment can throw the organization out of balance, and functional breakdown can ultimately cause the disintegration and collapse of the entire organization. When people view total operations from the narrow perspective of their immediate functional role, they tend to treat the welfare of the overall enterprise as incidental to the local activity with which they are associated. In such situations there is a tendency toward functional isolation and this, in turn, creates communication barriers: Compartmentalization impedes coordination, cooperation, and a proper recognition of the value of other activities.

The possible operational situation depicted is not compatible with project management. Projects are objective directed; functionalism should be subordinated to project objectives. It is possible that a project may have a functional objective and activity to support such a project is kept within the operational sphere of a function; however, where a project involves many functions, functional organization for project accomplishment may place severe restraints on the management of the project.

In functional organization each functional manager is responsible for his or her activity. No one person may be responsible for the total project. Where is the authoritative contact point for the customer or management? Coordination, because of the diffusion of responsibility, is complex, difficult, and may even be impossible, since several organizational jurisdictions are involved, and it may be difficult to motivate people who are organizationally dispersed and only indirectly involved with the project.

The importance of functionalism in organization cannot be minimized. Projects are composed of functional support activities. Functionalism is an organization fundamental. Excluding some higher-echelon managers, people are hired, reputations made, and careers developed on the basis of functional accomplishment. Management must recognize the advantages of functional specialization and at the same time be aware of possible problems associated with functionalism. If there is proper perspective, functionalism can be employed effectively in project management.

Figure 5-2 is an example of a product-centered functional organization, showing line–staff relationships. An important caveat is that the model is representative and not absolute. Many variations of Figure 5-2 are possible reflecting different operational requirements, available resources, internal politics, and management orientation. Depending on the aforementioned, some functions shown as staff activities could be placed in the line, and vice versa.

Project Organization

Project organization combines features of the product and function approaches. In product organization all functions necessary to complete the product are grouped under one jurisdiction. The deviation in project organization is that the project manager usually only has direct control over the immediate technical activities or functions that are crucial to the project. Many other functions may be required, but organizationally and

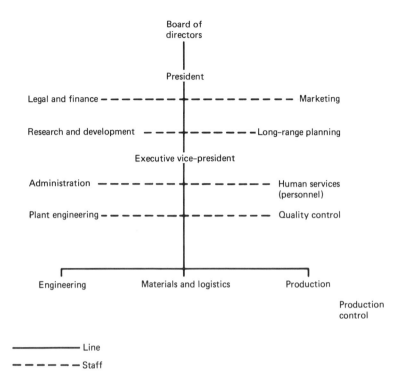

Figure 5-2. The functional organization.

economically it may not be feasible to place these under the direct control of the project manager. In this common situation the project manager is de facto forced to act as a contractor to procure the necessary services to support his or her project. These services may also be required by several other projects.

There are invariably organizational trade-offs in establishing projects. The ultimate organizational resources directed to the project will probably reflect such factors as the nature and scope of the project, operational and contractual priorities, the potential benefits anticipated, the importance of relations with the customer, and the reputation and prestige of the project manager.

Another important consideration relates to the human element. If the project is essentially one requiring productive inputs from people, it then becomes exceedingly important to have the right people assigned to the project. It follows that the project manager will want the best possible people. The best people may have other assignments and may not be available or the project can be so important and the project manager may have enough organizational clout to have these people reassigned to the project.

Management in considering project organizational possibilities must be aware of the extent to which reassignment might disrupt other activities, the skill levels actually required to perform on the project, and any individual and organizational benefits that might subsequently be derived from the assignment of specific personnel. It is a natural inclination for the project manager to want the best people and the greatest organizational visibility for the project. It is also possible that a powerful project manager can have resources diverted to the project that could be better employed elsewhere. Management must constantly be aware of the possibility of underutilization of expensive resources. Management must recognize that each project is a distinct undertaking and must accordingly be evaluated.

It is important to note that several project organizational arrangements are possible. The project may be formed to attack a unique problem. In this situation project organization may involve functional representatives from the various activities affected. It is also possible that the project is formed to resolve a relatively narrow problem that is localized in a specific functional activity. As a consequence, the project team is primarily composed of representatives from that functional activity.

Still another possibility is where a project is initiated that requires resources which are not internally available or economically not justifiable to acquire or assign to the project. In this type of situation much of the required project activity might be contracted out to other organizations.

Another situation, common to organizations having specified divisions of operational competence, is where more than one technically related project is placed under the control of a single project manager. The project manager in such instances may coordinate all technically and managerially related activities of two or more projects and also delegate and concentrate responsibility for individual projects to a project leader.

Management should evaluate the pros and cons of project organization in the light of proposed activity. There are definite advantages in this organizational form, resulting from establishing a focal point of responsibility and obligation for coordination and the high morale and prospective learning opportunities of the people assigned to important projects. There are, on the other hand, potential disadvantages that can, at times, be contradictory to the benefits indicated. For instance, failure to properly communicate with and coordinate activities outside the project manager's domain can lead to confusion, duplication of effort and resources, missed schedules, and unnecessary costs. It is also possible that people assigned to a project for a long period may lose their professional objectivity. There could also be morale problems if the project runs into technical or funding difficulties or is close to termination and the prospects for reassigning personnel are obscure.

Figure 5-3 shows a representative project organization where two or more technically related projects may be managed by one person. There are times when each of the project leaders will require different functional inputs. Also shown in Figure 5-3 are some internal and external activities that may have to be coordinated and which may be essential to the project's ultimate success; these activities are normally not under the direct control of the project manager.

Matrix Organization

Matrix organization[7] has evolved from project organization. Project organization, as discussed in the preceding section, is still practiced in many situations and by many operational entities. However, there often are inherent organizational problems associated with project organization. The development of matrix organization has been an attempt to circumvent some of the organizational problems that occur in project organization and to more effectively utilize resources. It should be recognized that no organizational form is perfect; there are invariably trade-offs. Theoretically, matrix organization eliminates or minimizes some of the problems common in project organization, while at the same time leads to operational problems that are nonexistent or minimal when operations are organized as projects.

In the project method of operation the project manager usually is placed in that position reflecting a high level of technical competence. In project organizations the manager has direct technical responsibility and general managerial obligations. In project organization there can be considerable duplication and perhaps inefficient use of human resources under the jurisdiction of the project manager. The project manager has an inclination to maintain the technical force and, unless there is operational pressure, is loathe to reassign people to other projects. The organization is likely to suffer from operational inflexibilities in project organization because people tend to become very project centered, highly specialized, and relatively organizationally immobile. These problems intensify when there is a multiproject operational base and the attendant constant organizational flux precipitated by the steady phasing in and phasing out of projects. The project organizational method does provide a degree of technical control, but operationally it is costly and cost has often provided the impetus to shift to matrix organization.

The matrix method represents a shift in operational philosophy. In matrix organization the project manager does not directly control all the necessary technical resources. Technical resources are organized functionally and administratively report to a functionally directed manager. The project manager in such an organization buys the technical services needed for the project from the different functional managers who assign functional people to support the project manager.

96

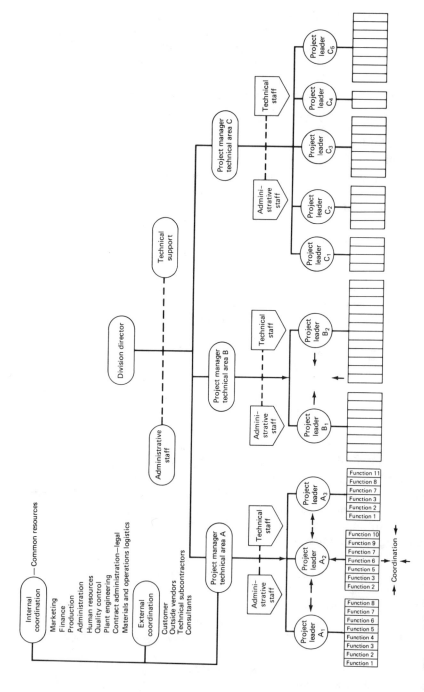

Figure 5-3. Project organization.

In matrix organization the project manager may or may not have related technical qualifications. In matrix organization there is a shift in emphasis to managerial skills. If technical skill or awareness is important, and the project manager's technical ability is limited, the project manager might have to rely on the technical staff or other technically qualified sources for guidance and evaluation. There is an important distinction in the operational mode between project and matrix organization. In project organization the project manager is almost always technically qualified and often relies on staff for managerial support. In matrix organization the project manager may or may not have strong technical credentials, the primary emphasis being on coordination and other managerial skills. In matrix organization the project manager may have to depend on staff for technical support.

The matrix organization represents, as mentioned, operational compromises. Functional people have dual-reporting obligations. This arrangement violates the classic management principles of unity of command and organizational hierarchy. People report administratively to a functional manager and technically to a project manager. This situation can lead to divided loyalties. Frictions can occur, since the project manager has limited personal control and frequently no direct control in selecting people for the project. Differences of opinion can develop between functional managers and project managers as to who should be assigned to a job. Performance evaluation differences between the project manager and the functional manager are also possible, which might subsequently affect individual salary and promotional considerations. Another serious friction point can be the determination of project priorities. The project manager is responsible for the project but can be frustrated because the functional skill requirements are not available or, if so, the caliber of people assigned to the project by the functional manager may not meet standards desired by the project manager. Persuasive project managers, on good terms with functional managers, can succeed in getting the timely assignment of capable people to their projects. Other project managers with less persuasive talents may come up short, even though their projects can be significantly more important.

Figure 5-4 represents one possible version of matrix organization. All functional specialties may not be required by the project manager. Depending on the nature of project requirements, it is possible that two or more functional specialities within a particular area of specialization may be assigned to a project manager. It is also possible that one functional specialist may divide work time between two or more project managers. Still another possibility exists where a functional specialist is assigned part-time to a project manager and the balance of his or her time may be on a functional project, either in support of such a project or as the project manager. In this situation the functional specialist would report both ad-

98

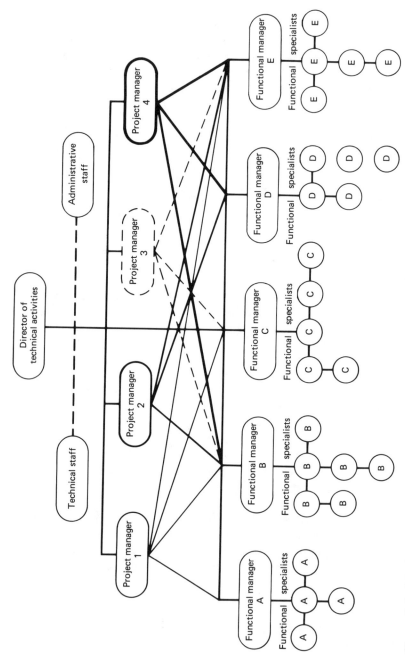

Figure 5-4. Matrix organization.

ministratively and technically to the functional manager. Finally, a project manager may have one or several projects under his or her domain and consequently have a variety of interactions with the different functional managers.

Despite inherent limitations, there are some distinct advantages in the matrix method of organization. Duplication of human resources is minimized. People with similar functional specializations are grouped. This encourages professional exchange and provides more latitude in the utilization and assignment of human resources, and this is an additional important advantage of operational flexibility. The matrix organization is less susceptible to operational disruptions due to the loss of personnel than is the project organization. People have broader operational interests and, hopefully, greater functional skill and awareness. There is less individual and operational vulnerability as a consequence of the phasing in and phasing out of projects. Human resources in this organizational method are more intraorganizationally mobile, since there is usually avoidance of vesting people to specific projects. This is an important benefit, since knowledge and experience can more easily be transferred between projects. Finally, under such an organizational arrangement there should be focus on total operational objectives rather than individual project concentration and identification.

Free-Form Organization

The free-form organization, or perhaps lack of formal organization, is another possible approach to project management. This approach may be applied in situations where there are professionally diverse activities, where the operation is relatively new and it may be too early to make an organizational commitment, where there is not a significant concentration of functional activity, and where by the nature of the operation the encouragement of interdisciplinarity is desirable.

In this method there is no formal or rigid organizational structure. Groups form, expand, contract, and disband in response to operational needs. There are three basic assumptions underlying this approach as a method for achieving operational objectives: (1) a volatile environment of change, (2) a work force dominated by professionals with diverse specializations, and (3) a spirit of selfless dedication to the total operation.

The free-form method can work only under certain conditions and in a select operational environment. Organizations, regardless of operational objectives, invariably make some accommodation for rank or some recognition for service and accomplishment. In some operational settings status provides a strong framework for superior–subordinate relationships. In a professional organization in which career entry is generally contingent on very special educational attainment, and subsequent career progression on accomplishment, the superior–subordinate relationships are likely to be less distinct. In such operational environments colleague authority may be more pervasive.

In the free-form approach there is much operational flexibility. A person can be a member of one group or a member of several groups simultaneously. A person can have a supportive role in one group and be the leader or dominant figure in another. One advantage of this approach that immediately comes to mind is intraorganizational mobility. In project or matrix organization there is a placement problem for the project manager once the project is completed. A formal project manager's title is a connotation of professional attainment and, once the status has been reached, there is a very understandable reluctance to accept other assignments of lesser organizational stature. The free-form approach excludes permanent titles and lasting organizational commitment. Professionals have much more mobility to move to areas where they can be used and where there are opportunities to employ their professional skills and interests. The operational norm is that there is no established hierarchy and assignments reflect potential contribution, rather than largely being motivated by organizational position.

Free-form operations usually result in team formations. For a team to operate effectively, there still must be some directional force to identify objectives and instigate the formation of the teams. Much of the ultimate accomplishment with this type of operational environment depends on human factors. People must respect each other and work well together. A paramount objective is to achieve positive synergism. Individualism must be subordinated to group effort. Good communication is important. Personal dedication, control, discipline, and participation are essential.

The free-form method has significant advantages, as indicated in the preceding paragraph. In addition, this approach can be instrumental in eliminating or minimizing organizational bureaucracy, which has an insidious tendency to grow in most organizations. There is a strong emphasis on individual motivation, coordination, cooperation, and performance, in concert with team activities. The free-form approach encourages contribution and incentive.

Free-form operations are relatively new. Like any other method employed in the use of human resources, there are advantages and disadvantages. Some of the advantages have been discussed, and these potential advantages, in certain situations, can be compelling enough to enable considerations of this operational philosophy. There are also some very real problems that can result from this type of policy. The operational environment must be right. This concept will not and cannot work where there are entrenched interests and strong functional affiliations. There is the human variable and this is a considerable problem; to be successful there must be the immediate subordination of individualism for group objectives. There is the assumption that people will be dedicated, selfless, and perceptive in working to general objectives. There is the further assumption that people will derive enough personal satisfaction from professional participation and contribution to offset the normal strong human desire for individual status and recognition. There are, in addition, such problems as selection and direction of activities. Who decides who goes where and how? There does have to be a focal point for responsibility. There is an old saying that if everyone is assumed to be responsible, the ultimate result is that no one becomes responsible.

There are also, and perhaps most important, management philosophies and attitudes; the receptivity to innovative operational methods; the degree and direction of management guidance; the selection, training, and motivation of people to perform in such an operational environment; and management's confidence in people and its dedication to making such an approach operationally feasible.

Hybrid Organization

There is, as previously stated, no one ideal organizational method that can be applied unilaterally in anticipation of all operational contingencies. The road to the accomplishment of objectives often is possible by means of more than one route. In effect, while organization can facilitate the achievement of goals, the mere organization of resources per se does not guarantee that goals will be achieved.

Proceeding on the assumption that the quantity and quality of resources are available and that the human organization is motivated, organization can be an important means to help achieve objectives. In complex and dynamic operations organization and reorganization are continuing processes. Where change is rapid and there is little operational precedent, managerial innovation is usually essential. Managerial innovation can and should encompass organizational methods that are responsive to operational needs.

There may be operational situations where unique managerial methods have to be employed. There may also be situations where several different operational problems exist and no one organizational method is satisfactory. To achieve objectives in such situations a different organizational approach, structured to the specific situation, may offer the greatest promise, or the best approach may be a combination of established organizational methods. Still it is possible that, because of the diversity of activities, different organizational methods can be applied, as applicable to the different activities. This would be a hybrid case, where an operational entity may be composed of many subgroups. The various subgroups would have distinct operational objectives, which would, in turn, require custom-tailored organizational methods.

Therefore, in a large, technologically complex operation more than one organizational method can often effectively be used. It is possible that such an operation could be organized by the function, product, process, customer, project, free form, or matrix method, or any combination of the aforementioned.

Anticipating Operational Problems

Looking Ahead

Unfortunately, too much management is crisis management. Many problems that confront managements and result in fire drills can be anticipated. Awareness and provision for such contingencies can be factors in better utilization of an organization's resources. Where operations are composed of many project groups of various sizes, objectives, and resource requirements, good management is not only challenging, but essential!

This chapter has emphasized organization relative to project management. The pros and cons of different organizational methods have been discussed. The following section indicates some of the more significant operational problems in the organization and management of projects.

Organizational Problems in Project Management

One of the most difficult managerial problems, where operations are comprised of many projects, is the balancing of resources. Where there are many projects that are technologically homogeneous, the task of balancing resources, resulting from projects phasing in and phasing out, is very difficult. In situations where there are many projects that are technologically heterogeneous, the balancing of resources is infinitely more complex.

Projects may cover different operational landscapes, in terms of the technical difficulties involved, the type of human and material resources required, and the time period of the project's life cycle. The demand for project resources can approximate the demand curve indicated in Figure 5-5.

In Figure 5-5 the demand curve assumes existing or firmly committed projects. It is possible that unforeseen new projects can phase in during the time; existing projects can also unexpectedly be terminated. The people requirement can also be misleading. In routine production activities the skill mix and number of people required can be correlated to production schedules. In the project environment not only are body counts relevant, but proper skill mix is an additional critical element.

Figure 5-5, based on projections, indicates an erratic demand schedule. Project resources generally are scarce and resources expensive. Management is confronted with decisional options. To what extent can and should the technical organization be maintained? Figure 5-6 indicates two options that might be considered.

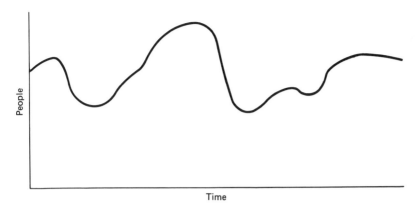

Figure 5-5. Demand for project resources.

In option 1 management may decide to staff up to peak project requirements. Surplus capacity can be used by actively seeking and initiating
new projects. New projects can be instigated internally, through aggressive marketing and the acquisition of new contracts, or to act as a subcontractor to other prime contractors in order to fill the operational void.
Taking this approach could be hazardous. Management must be cognizant
of many external factors. Management would have to be optimistic. However, if successful, this could lead to the building up of the technical
organization.

Option 2 is a more conservative managerial approach. In this situation
the organization is maintained to support the lowest point on the demand
curve. Activity that exceeds capacity is contracted out. It is difficult to
turn down business. The business accepted may put a strain on existing
capabilities. Management must weigh such considerations as to prospects for follow-on activity, the use of specialized resources, the opportunity to educate the technical organization, and other continuing commitments. The operational environment may not be promising and the
resources required by the new projects may be very specialized, with

Figure 5-6. Production and organization options for use of project resources.

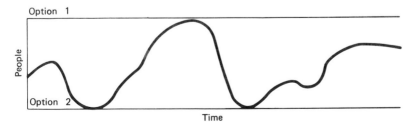

questionable future applicability within the operation. If this is the case, it may be wise not to acquire human and capital resources and go, as indicated, to outside sources for project support.

There are other organizational problems in project management. Many projects require the inputs of highly trained professional people. Unless the project is strictly functional, the chances are that different degrees of interdisciplinarity will be involved. People should be selected and assigned to projects based on technical requirements, the individual's intellectual competence in relation to the technical skill demand, and an awareness of the personal chemistry and compatibility of the people assigned to the project. Functional affiliations organizationally have to be subordinated to project objectives.

Intellectually and emotionally compatible people can be blended into effective project teams. The organizational objectives are to successfully complete the project; minimize cost, red tape, and functional warfare; and effectively communicate and stimulate creativity.

Organizational Objectives

Management should assess the organizational operational environment. Assessment would include, hopefully, evaluation of where the organization has been, where it is, and where management would like it to be in a given time frame.

In the project environment innovation is essential. To stimulate an innovative operational environment the organization should have enthusiasm, free information flow, and flexibility. In addition, there should be a communication of short-, intermediate-, and long-range objectives. Activity should be directed to achieving those objectives. People in the organization should be confident in the operation and its ability to intellectually, physically, and competitively grow. There should be pride in accomplishment and association.

Endnotes Chapter Five

1. "Baby Boomer Push for Power," *Business Week,* July 2, pp. 52–62, 1984.
2. "Faced with Changing Work Force, TRW Pushes to Raise White Collar Productivity," *Wall Street Journal,* Vol. 202, No. 58, Eastern Edition, p. 33, September 22, 1983.
3. A few examples are Apple Computer, Timex, and International Business Machines Corporation (*ibid.*).
4. "Thinking Small," *Wall Street Journal,* Vol. 202, No. 35, Eastern Edition, p. 1, August 19, 1983.
5. J. Jeukes, D. Saivers, and P. Stitlerman, *The Sources of Invention,* 2nd ed., New York, Macmillan, 1969; A. C. Cooper, "Small Companies Can Pioneer New Products," *Harvard Business Review,* Sept./Oct. 1966. James R. Bright, *Research Development and*

Technological Innovation, Homewood, IL, Richard D. Irwin, 1964; Donald A. Schar, *Technology and Change,* New York, Delacorte, 1967; Sumner Meyers and Donald G. Marquis, *Successful Industrial Innovations,* Washington, DC, National Science Foundation, 1969; Daniel Hamberg, *R&D Essays on the Economics of Research and Development,* New York, Random House, 1966.

6. "Small Firms Are Seen as Pivotal to Innovation," *Research and Development,* April, p. 88, 1984.

7. For samples of representative literature on matrix organizations, see Allen R. Janger, *Matrix Organization of Complex Businesses,* a research report from the Conference Board, New York, The Conference Board, Inc., 1979; W. F. Baber, *Organizing the Future—Matrix Models for the Post-Industrial Policy,* University of Alabama Press, 1983. M. F. Wolff, "Managers at Work," *Research Management,* pp. 10–12, November 1982; J. L. Brown and N. McAgnew, "The Balance of Power in a Matrix Structure," *Business Horizons,* pp. 51–54, November/December 1982.

CHAPTER SIX

Project Planning

Overview

Programs and Projects

At times the terms *program* and *project* are used interchangeably. Actually, a distinction can be made in that programs are usually, but not always, relatively long-term operations. A program may consist of several projects of indeterminate duration that support the program. A very complex program requires integration of the constituent projects, including a considerable amount of coordination, and intelligent planning.

A project is more normally thought of as a comparatively short-range activity. The project can be an independent operational entity or part of a larger program. It is also possible that a project will have an indeterminate life span.

To support the aforementioned, Archibald states the following:

Program—A long-term undertaking which is usually made up of more than one project. Sometimes used synomymously with "project."

Project—A complex effort, usually less than 3 years in duration, made up of interrelated tasks performed by various organizations with a well-defined objective, schedule, and budget.

Task—A short-term effort (usually 3 to 6 months) performed by one organization, which may combine with other tasks to form a project.[1]

The emphasis in this chapter is on project activity and more specifically on project planning.

Project Planning: Some Inherent Problems

Organizations in research and development or other highly creative activities revolve primarily around projects. The project in such operational situations is the fundamental productive unit; operating divisions, functions, groups, and individuals are organized to support the project. Except for a quite simple project, the unit will probably not be self-contained. The support requirements frequently cross functional boundaries, and many resources required to complete the project are often used in common with other projects. Considering that a project is usually not totally resource self-reliant there is a positive need for detailed and coordinated planning. Coordinated project planning is necessary for activities under the direct jurisdiction of the project manager and also for activities necessary to the project that are not under the direct control of the project manager.

Planning a project can be an extremely involved process. Project planning extends beyond the immediate technical objectives. Projects often fail because project managers do not adequately recognize or compensate for activities requiring interface beyond the project's technical confines. "Even though a project manager may not be fiscally responsible for certain areas, he is programmatically responsible for these in his total management planning."[2]

As indicated, too often projects fail to achieve objectives because of inadequate planning and failure to properly coordinate functional support requirements. Subsequently, it is possible that bottlenecks may appear either within the immediate project organization or as a result of performance failures in external project support activities. Performance failures that can be attributed to poor planning are frustrating and generally add costs beyond those originally contemplated.

Planning breakdowns can often be attributed to the project manager. The project manager, in many instances, has a technical background and relatively limited managerial experience. Reflecting such experience, the technical aspects of the project under the direct control of the project manager are usually recognized and accommodated for in planning. The difficulties frequently develop in that coordination and planning are inadequate for necessary project activities external to the project.

A suggestion that might improve project planning would be to develop a workable format for a master project plan. Such a proposed format would include procedure and a checklist to ensure that all project participants, external as well as internal, are aware of commitments. The approach suggested would help provide perspective. The author, on numerous occasions, has been privy to situations where projects did not meet objectives as planned because assumptions were made that the required support would be available in the degree and at the time originally planned for.

A comprehensive approach to planning would give an indication of the feasibility of achieving planning objectives. Potential problem areas could be localized. Accordingly, plans could be formulated that would recognize potential contingencies, and alternative or optional courses of action could be set forth.[3]

Objectivity should also be encouraged as part of the comprehensive approach to planning. Project people tend to be optimistic; they are inclined to minimize potential difficulties and assume technical problems will be solved and resources to support their project activities will be available as needed. A comprehensive project plan, as suggested, would foster awareness of possible problems that might develop within the project manager's operational jurisdiction and those problem areas which could occur beyond the immediate control of the project manager. A master project plan would be formulated after considering other projects within the organization that might compete for the use of common resources, make provision(s) to circumvent priorities if they exist, and establish necessary coordination for project support from internal functional areas and from outside contractors.

The discussion to this point has touched on planning aspects that are relatively obvious. A not so obvious by-product of poor project planning is the effect on the morale of the people working on the project. Poor morale can lead to lower productivity and indifferent performance. Bad planning can result in situations where problems have not been anticipated or where the project was poorly conceived and the work scope has to be changed. Dedicated professionals can become demotivated in such situations after they find their effort has been misspent.

A certain amount of doubling back or lost effort is normal and is to be expected on some projects; however, effort that is wasted because of inadequate anticipation and planning reflects questionable management practice. Another demoralizing situation, which is also all too common, is where extra effort is expended in order to accomplish the work planned under a project item, phase, or task only to later find that such effort was wasted because related work segments have been changed or have not been completed as scheduled.

It is not unusual to have communication gaps between the different project participants. Unexpected technical difficulties can be experienced, changes in the project concept can occur, or necessary follow-on resources may not be available and such changes can have a material effect on work in process. Communication breakdowns can occur because the project manager has not properly identified and planned for informational requirements and provided a dissemination system to get the information to the right people at the right time. Communication failures can at times be contrived rather than due to planning omissions. Information can be withheld or distorted because of the reluctance of

project professionals to admit that they are experiencing technical difficulties. Technical professionals more often than not are optimistically
inclined. Because of this inherent nature, they often feel a solution to a
problem is imminent and as a consequence are reluctant to admit they are
encountering difficulties. Good project planning will highlight critical accomplishment points within a precise time frame. If technical objectives
are not accomplished as planned and scheduled, the project manager
should be alerted that problems do exist, notwithstanding the protests of
the people assigned the responsibility of technical performance.

External and Internal Planning Factors

The planning process for good project management of necessity must be
sensitive to many external and internal factors. Some of the external
influences on project planning are the state of the art, competition, customer requirements, community pressures, and social and/or political
considerations.

Advances in the state of the art can have a strong impact on project
plans. Molding the project organization and developing capability take
time and forward planning. Failure to anticipate the level and direction of
technological change that might impact on the project places the operation in a vulnerable position. Unforeseen or unplanned technological developments can make present programs, existing facilities, and even personnel obsolete.

Technology can have a pronounced effect on projects, especially research and development projects and those projects involved in product
development. If product development entails much R&D, reflecting susceptibility to rapid technological change, the product life cycle often is
shorter and the product change greater than in the case with established
consumer goods. Vulnerability to rapid technological change increases
uncertainty and compounds risk because the market can shift more
quickly and more drastically. In such a situation it is possible that the
project or the hardware being developed can be technically sound but
technologically outdated.

If the technology is subject to dramatic change, capital expenditures to
support the technology can be tenuous. Capital expenditures are risky
when the probability of extended or full economic utilization of expensive
equipment or facilities is slight. The development of new materials and
processes can also have a significant influence on planning.

Diversification to hedge against technological miscalculation can be
beneficial and is another dimension to be considered in project planning.
However, diversification, if misdirected, can lead to negative results;
indiscriminate diversification can be as organizationally destructive as
technological vulnerability due to nonprogressive, intense specialization.

Competition also affects planning. It is unusual for a new consumer product to be so drastically different that it promptly and completely outmodes current products. Also, if a manufacturer is contemplating a major product change, competitors usually have some advance indication or information and can take defensive action. Planning in anticipation of completion would allow accommodation for required resource identification and acquisition; operational phase-in; product, process, or procedural innovations and distinctions; and possibly marketing strategies.

In research and development projects a direct comparative analysis of competitors' products or technical activity often is not possible. The predominant form of competition in such an environment is operational capability, built upon anticipating technological developments and planning accordingly. Nevertheless, it is not always possible to anticipate technological breakthroughs by competitors and such accomplishments can radically affect the competitive position of the organization.

If the organization operates in a technologically volatile environment, it is essential for survival to be active and competent at the leading edge of that technology. It is also imperative to be able to translate technological developments to customers' requirements and constantly search out new markets and applications. Frequently customers can use products or services that they may not be aware of. At times a technology or product can be adapted to a need. In other situations the potential customer may not perceive a need until some outside force can indicate the potential beneficial returns that can result from planned change. Again, the technology to implement change may already be in existence and could directly be applied or some modification for use may be needed. In other instances the need can be identified and the technology has to be developed. An aggressive organization will develop technological capability and follow such competence with a well-planned and related marketing program. Passively waiting for requests to bid could compromise the organization's competitive position and reputation. Technological and marketing initiative not only gives the organization an immediate advantage, but also establishes an image that can be marketed in the future.

The community is another external force exerting pressure for intelligent planning. An organization is a citizen of the community within which it operates. The need for good community relations is so obvious that discussion seems superfluous. Projects should be selected that are socialogically and culturally acceptable to the community, as well as economically feasible. Work must be planned diligently to maintain reasonably stable operational continuity. Drastic variations in operational levels are usually accompanied by an erratic economic contribution to the community. Erratic operations can be economically disruptive to the community and have negative repercussions.

Project selection and subsequent planning may also be susceptible to political pressures. At times political factors have a significant bearing on planning for projects dealing with some aspect of science and technology. International tensions may lead to an emphasis on projects directed to defense activities. National concern can focus on sociological problems such as disease, hunger, and ecological disturbances. Where there is strong public interest the chances are that there will be strong political pressures to implement such programs. Public and political interest is usually manifested in the support and funding of related projects.

If there is a major shift in public and political attitudes, it becomes very important for an organization whose operations are sensitive and susceptible to such attitudes to reexamine its operational objectives. The organization may have demonstrated capability in a selected technological area, but if future support appears tenuous, it has to be cognizant of opportunity. Future opportunity could involve a significant redirection of operational emphasis and effort. Planning for transition and adaptation in such a situation is very challenging. Planning would encompass transition and utilization of the human organization and the careful selection and phasing in of projects that would enable an orderly movement compatible with revised operational objectives.

Organizational ownership, as an external factor affecting planning, is not a problem in military, government, or nonprofit organizations, but it becomes a very important consideration in the private sector. Stockholders are interested in profits, progress, growth, and the organization's reputation. If the owners feel that these four desiderata have fallen below their expectations, they can instigate a move for a change in management. Income and growth have become increasingly dependent on technological accomplishment, which in turn can often be related to basic planning premises.[4]

Internal forces must also be recognized in project planning. Some of the internal factors that affect project planning include organizational objectives, available physical and human resources, organization morale, and management. It is iterated that projects frequently fail to achieve objectives because the project manager has too narrow an operational perspective and fails to address influential factors and plan accordingly. Careful planning and considered involvement of the various organizational factions required for project support can well determine the ultimate success or failure of a project.

Twiss states the problem succinctly:

> Project planning and portfolio planning cannot be considered in isolation. The project plan should consist of a detailed programme of work specifying the budgeted cost for each task, the resources needed, and the time scales. These have to be integrated with the requirements of the other projects in the portfolio to ensure that the total demands for each type of resource are kept within the level that is available. Usually, difficulties will be experienced and it will be necessary to change the intended project plans in order to

smooth the total demands upon the resources. Sometimes, this can be achieved by re-phasing the work schedule without affecting the planned completion date, but frequently it is found that the duration of the project must be extended if serious interference between projects is to be avoided.[5]

Planning, unless there is a drastic change in the organization's mission, should be compatible with operational objectives. A dilemma often encountered in organizations susceptible to operational modifications wrought by technological developments is the desirability or urgency to formulate plans for projects involving new or different explorations that are not consistent with the current operational goals or mission. The controlling decision might hinge on a review of the current operational objectives. Are the current goals reasonable and technically and economically feasible? Are the present operational goals incompatible and out of synch with important new technical developments and economic prospects? Will the proposed project lead to new and promising opportunities? Will entering into a technological endeavor alien to proven technological effort compromise the organization technically or financially? Should the proposed project be discarded? Or is there some latitude for planning and initiating a project that represents a deviation from established operational policies?

It is possible that the decision to proceed with or abandon a project will revolve around the availability of resources. The availability of resources is a fundamental internal factor as part of the planning process. Some physical resources are readily procured, whereas others are not so easy to acquire owing to cost and lead time. Plans for activity are even more constrained by the number and skill of available personnel. Generally, good project planning will attempt to achieve an optimum combination and integration of people and physical resources.

Morale is an intangible but important factor influencing project planning. It is reflected by confidence in management and depends in part on the availability of professionally rewarding, interesting projects and adequate resources. Esprit de corps can make it feasible to undertake a program or a project that otherwise would not offer attractive possibilities.

Management, probably the single most critical element in the success or failure of any organization, provides the vision, capability, energy, leadership, and philosophy behind planning. Too often managers mask a complacent attitude with outward but unproductive effort. It takes courage to make commitments and reinforce them with concrete planning and resource allocation. A mediocre or insecure management will be unwilling to assume the obligation and responsibility for planning.[6]

This section has highlighted some of the factors that probably would be applicable in project planning. Intelligent project planning, of necessity, must transcend the immediate technical aspects of the project. Project support, continued and potential follow-on activity, is usually dictated by external and internal influential factors. The project manager who does not plan a project to accommodate these influential factors is courting disaster.

Some Planning Premises

Operational Environment

There may be some similarities between past, present, and anticipated projects, and experience can, to some extent, be beneficial in planning a project. However, there are invariably enough differences between projects to require thought and innovation on the part of the manager in order to properly plan the project. Planning would entail establishing procedures for the accomplishment of the project objectives and accommodation for any relevant internal operational idiosyncracies. No two projects are exactly alike, even though, as indicated, there may be some related experience. Similarities for planning purposes between past and present projects may be neutralized by time.

The passage of time can have a substantial impact on planning a project and minimize the applicability of past experience in planning the present project. For instance, past accomplishment on technologically related projects may be misleading in that different or inexperienced people may be assigned to the current project, or, if the people assigned have some comparable experience, it may be of limited use or applicability owing to technological developments that have transpired from the previous to the present assignment. If interceding technological developments have been substantive, there may have to be a new learning cycle. What might originally appear to be a simple transitional problem, based on anticipated application of past experience, can and often does mushroom and have extensive operational reverberations.

Planning the project consonant with its operational objectives would require identification and allowance for needed resources, determination of critical milestones of accomplishment, informational patterns, and monitoring of progress. Additionally, the manager should factor into the project plan possible contingency actions in the event that subsequent activity dictates the necessity to deviate from the original project plan.

The operational environment can significantly affect project planning. The latitude for operational project planning differs between organizations because of the nature of the projects or products within the organization, the organizational character reflecting managerial attitudes and philosophy, and possible legal restraints. In some organizations the project manager may have broad discretion in planning and considerable freedom to make decisions within the realm of project operations. In other situations the project manager could be moderately or severely restricted in the range of decision making.

Planning can be centralized or decentralized. In organizations where there is strong emphasis on centralized planning, management would be inclined to closely monitor most activity, establish tight program parameters, and distribute individual project segments for implementation to divisions or functions. This approach can be justified on the rationale that there are better management planning and control. It is also possible that if this operational approach is taken, the various support activities may not be aware of the overall project objectives unless there is a very effective communication system. In the described situation there is comparatively little freedom to exercise judgment but misunderstanding and misinterpretation are minimized because assignments are explicit. Success using this approach depends on the types of projects involved, the professional level of the people assigned to the project, and the competence of a centralized management.

In decentralized planning the project manager has much more responsibility for determining the technical and administrative scope of the project and for coordinating the various segments internally and externally. In decentralized planning each organizational division has the responsibility, in concert with the project manager, for planning and implementing its project support obligations. In decentralized planning management divests itself of the detail planning and concentrates on the end product or result.

Another possible approach is where objectives and policy may be centrally determined but planning to achieve goals is decentralized. In this situation management does not delineate functional inputs rigidly, but solicits suggestions and allows leeway for interpretation. Once functional inputs are decided upon, the project manager assembles and coordinates them for compatibility with project objectives.

There are instances where the project manager is limited in planning by customer-imposed constraints. There may be rigid requirements relative to performance specifications, contractual schedules, and/or cost ceilings. Planning may have to be backward from contractually determined obligations rather than from a more normal forward approach that would identify, organize, and integrate project elements in a logical sequence.

The project manager may operationally be constrained by the availability of resources. Planning for resources needed to achieve project objectives is affected by the availability of such resources and the extent of control over the resources delegated to the project manager. Preliminary to actual planning is the need to determine the types and amount of human and physical resources that will be essential to achieve project objectives. Are the resources readily available in-house? Are there other projects that might need the same common resources? When? Are there priorities? If the resources are not directly available to the project, can they be borrowed internally from other projects? Leased? Purchased? If purchased, what problems and lead times are involved?

How human resources are organized internally is another factor that can affect project planning. If the predominant organizational method is by project, it is reasonably safe to assume that the project manager will control and can subsequently plan the use of technical human resources assigned to the project. If the organization is along the matrix method, the project manager will have substantially less control over the human resources required by the project. Depending on the particular situation, the project manager must take this operational fact into account when planning the project. If the organization is functionally oriented and the project is not a pure functional activity or if the project manager does not have direct functional authority, another dimension becomes apparent in planning the project. In this situation the project manager has no direct control over the human resources essential for the accomplishment of the project goals. The project manager acts as a contractor and plans and subcontracts the various project segments to different functional divisions.

The operational environment can aid or retard effective project planning. There is no categorical approach to establish a conducive operational environment. People, projects, and the nature of the operational mission may be the critical aspects of what is a good or bad operational setting. Regardless of the nature of the operational environment, it is important to actively involve the performers in the planning process. The planners and the performers are not always the same people. This is another situation that can lead to planning failures. Planners may lack the ability to evaluate the problems either technically or managerially. Individual work segments may appear feasible but as a composite effort not add up. Planning increments may not be communicated and coordinated so that their feasibility and compatibility can be ascertained, and a serious psychological error may be committed in not actively involving the actual project participants in the planning process. Involving those who will be responsible for doing the work could provide essential insights and would facilitate commitment. Professionals normally resent being "told" how to do their job. They usually have a strong sense of professional pride and want direct inputs into the planning and subsequent operational processes.

Planning Schedules

Scheduling project activities is one of the more critical aspects of project management. Detailed scheduling is logically developed from a project work breakdown analysis including items, phases, and tasks needed to accomplish project objectives. A prelude to the determination of the project work segments would be discernment of the project technical goals and operational or contractual obligations.

Once project obligations are determined, the usual approach is to organize project effort into related work segments. Often the work segments can be reduced to smaller increments of effort such as items, phases, and tasks, as has been indicated. Breaking the work into managerially controllable segments facilitates a reasonable estimate of the magnitude of effort and time required to accomplish the various work segments. A corollary goal is to schedule the work segments so that resources are effectively utilized, down time is minimized or eliminated, and wasted or duplicated effort is avoided.

The approach suggested assumes that all the required resources will be available as scheduled; it represents an ideal situation. In practice, the ideal schedule frequently is not attainable because of unforeseen technical problems or competition for resources. The project manager must be aware of the organization's operational obligations beyond his or her project. Awareness includes knowledge of which other projects have activities that might compete for the resources also essential to the completion of the present project and whether the resources needed will result in a schedule conflict between projects.

The project manager in scheduling project activities really has several concerns. Each project is authorized, whether externally or internally, on the premise that the project will result in some desirable end product. The need for the end product is important to the sponsoring source or else the project probably would not have been authorized in the first place. If authorization includes a stipulated end date, the project manager also has an obligation to finish the project as promised.

Problems can arise in meeting scheduled obligations when the organization is committed to several projects in the same time frame and there are insufficient human and material resources available to accomplish all the projects as scheduled and promised. Often where the aforementioned is the case there is competition between projects for the available resources. Who gets what resources and when can depend on higher managerial authority in establishing project priorities. Some project managers are organizationally adept and ingenious in diverting resources to their project even though other projects have higher priorities for the use of the same resources. This can be good or bad. It can be good because it enables the project manager to accomplish the project objectives as scheduled. It can be bad because more important projects can slip their schedules because resources are unavailable.

From a purely operational position, the project, as mentioned, should be planned and scheduled to accommodate all pertinent activities. Contingencies should be factored into the plan to anticipate unforeseen difficulties. The following gives a few examples of situations where alternative actions might be appropriate. If resources are needed by the project and are not available, can the project work scope be rearranged to productively employ what resources are at the disposal of the project manager? Redeployment of resources might have to be considered in the light of accomplishing technical objectives and avoiding any additional costs. Another possibility is to use substitute resources that can be employed without compromising the project. If internal resources are not available, can the work be contracted out? This is very important, insofar as the project manager should attempt to recognize when schedule conflicts might arise with other projects and what backup sources might be available. If the problem is not anticipated, backup or outside production sources may not have been located or committed and precious time can be lost.

As mentioned, a critical part of the planning and scheduling process is evaluation of what has to be done and in what sequence. The nature of the project may be such that proper sequencing of activities is extremely important to the eventual success of the project. On some projects major work segments can almost be independent accomplishment milestones. In other instances project work segments have to build upon the information and accomplishment of preceding work segments; each successive activity is dependent on what was accomplished in the preceding work segment. This would result in a "goes into" type of schedule where activity A goes into activity B and so on.

Another possibility is where a project has significant work segments that are closely related and mutually dependent; the same project may also have some peripheral activities which are relatively independent. There is a tendency to plan and schedule peripheral activities early in the project life. Early completion of such activities probably has psychological overtones, in that completed work blocks have a connotation of accomplishment. From an efficiency standpoint these activities should not be scheduled and worked upon until they are actually needed. Completing work segments too early can ultimately prove unproductive. First, the project concept or work scope may later change and early completed work can be affected. Work completed may have to be modified, updated, or, worse yet, completely redone. If such a situation were to occur, there would be incremental project costs and no doubt the morale of the people employed on the activity would suffer. Second, even though the preliminary work remains relevant, the results have to sit until utilized at a later date. In this situation capital has been tied up and unproductively used.

There are situations where there can be justification for early completion of some project work segments. A case in point would be where the project manager is aware of future competition from other projects for needed and common resources. If these resources are important to the completion of the project and may not be available later, it can ultimately be cost and operationally effective to use the resources when they are available and in anticipation of future requirements.

There are situations where a project is authorized to resolve an urgent need or problem. If this is the case, *time* might be of the essence. The project manager would probably not have the luxury of optimally planning and scheduling activities sequentially. A "crash" project involves substantial technical risk, a high probability of wasted effort, and greater costs than would be expected if the project could evolve in a more normal approach. Planning, scheduling, and coordination are very difficult in crash projects. Much of the work is planned and scheduled in parallel rather than in sequence. Parallel but related activities proceed on assumptions of forthcoming information and anticipated accomplishment from dependent work segments. If the dependent or related work segments miss their objectives, there is a strong chance that the work attempted in parallel will be negated. In very technically complex projects facing time constraints, backup efforts frequently have to be planned for and scheduled on work segments that are considered critical to the accomplishment of project objectives. There has to be a compelling justification to meet time constraints, because in a crash project there often is considerable redundant effort contributing to cost escalations.

Poor planning is usually reflected in schedule breakdowns and higher than anticipated project costs. Higher costs and the inability to meet schedule obligations could affect contractual obligations, profitability, and customer relations. To minimize the possibilities indicated the project manager not only has to identify and accommodate strategic project work segments, but must also plan how effort will be implemented to realize the accomplishment of the work. The project plan can be simple or very detailed. Developing relevant methodology in project planning in some project situations can be an essential first step. Existing planning techniques can be employed or modified or new techniques developed to facilitate planning and scheduling. One possible technique that can be used is the decision tree.

A decision tree type of plan can be effectively utilized in some situations where potential problems can occur and decisions have to be made. Contingency or optional actions can be identified. Slack can be provided in the schedule to compensate for activities that took longer to accomplish than initially planned. By the same token, the project manager should be aware of activities that can be telescoped or compressed to pick up time lost on other activities. Schedule pads can be effectively utilized early in the program if the project manager has a good feel for what is happening on the project. The effective early use of such pads can buy the project manager important time later in the project.

As has repeatedly been stated in this chapter, good planning can be a material asset in moving a project to its objectives. However, the very nature of projectization involves various degrees of uncertainty. There are times when schedules are not met in spite of reasonable planning premises. In such instances moderate to considerable redefinition of the project work scope may be necessary. Sensitivity to unforeseen problems and quick and appropriate response often can turn a potentially disastrous situation into a minimal inconvenience.

A good project director is a good project manager. Problems and the unexpected are the rule rather than the exception on technically complex projects. The good project manager can anticipate areas where problems may occur and be alerted to instigate contingent activities in the event a change in plans is indicated. To be a good manager one must adopt a thinking approach along with a willingness to be operationally flexible and not be afraid to take calculated risks and use ingenuity in circumventing difficulties. More times than not there is a reasonable and acceptable way to solve a difficult problem if the project manager has an open mind and is receptive to alternatives that normally would not be used but might be applicable in the existing situation.

Cost Effectiveness

Planning cost expenditures is another very important aspect of project management. If the project is a fixed priced contract, the amount of expenditures will ultimately be reflected in a profit or a loss. How costs are calculated and what cost elements are integrated into the proposed project can also positively or detrimentally affect the competitive position and the prospects for getting the project authorized.

There are times when some related effort has taken place on other projects. Such effort can provide a foundation for work on the proposed project and eliminate some costs that competitors have to incur. It is also possible that in planning the project, related experience can be utilized and provided for in estimating and planning for project costs. If related experience can be applied or accomplished and work transferred from one project to another, the actual costs experienced by the recipient project can be less than projected and the surplus can be applied toward profit or used as a hedge against problems that might be encountered later in the project life cycle.

Cost planning should take into consideration the resources needed, the resources available, and the cost options existing relative to employing the resources. Again there is a tendency to use the best and probably most expensive resources when the best and most expensive is not essential to the success of that particular aspect of the project.

Planning for the utilization of equipment and/or facilities often represents significant cost considerations. Expenditures are often planned on the assumption that equipment or instrumentation required to support the project will be purchased. Equipment or instrumentation may not have to be purchased. It could be much cheaper and more cost effective to rent such project tools, purchase test results from other projects already having such equipment, or subcontract work outside the organization to other organizations that have already made a capital expenditure to purchase the needed equipment and are willing and able to provide the required services.

There are situations where a project requires equipment or facilities that are unique to that specific project and which are not immediately or internally available. This leads to a buy or lease decision. The project manager should determine how extensively the equipment or facilities will be used, possible subsequent employment by the project, potential follow-on projects, and other projects in the organization that might be able to utilize the equipment or facilities. In planning for such requirements the project manager should also consider the following: whether the purchase is a capital expenditure or a current project cost; the type of equipment or facilities that will be needed relative to quality, cost, and versatility; and whether it might be possible, if necessary, to buy used rather than new equipment.

It is not unusual in large project organizations to purchase equipment without coordination with other projects. The purchased equipment often is too specialized, not really needed, or too expensive. Better, cheaper, more cost-effective, and more versatile equipment could have been procured with calculated planning or coordination with other ongoing projects. It is also not unusual to find that had the project manager even conducted a cursory search, he or she would have found that similar or adaptable equipment was already readily available within the organization. Capital outlays can also be saved or minimized relative to the building or purchasing of project support facilities by exploring the possible use or modification of existing space.

Taking a Systems Approach

One suggested avenue to project planning would be a systems approach. A very simple systems model is depicted in Figure 6-1. Converted to the very basics, the goals or objectives of the project would be determined by the project manager; this would be the desired output. The next step would be identification of the various components and procedures required to achieve the project objectives; this would be the necessary input. The ultimate success of the project would, to a large extent, be contingent on the conversion process. The ingredients may be present and a reasonable procedure (planning) developed, and still failure can result as a consequence of poor implementation in the conversion process. The cycle should provide for the feedback of project activity and liaison to ascertain whether actual accomplishment has been consummated consistent with planned objectives. Any deviation from planned

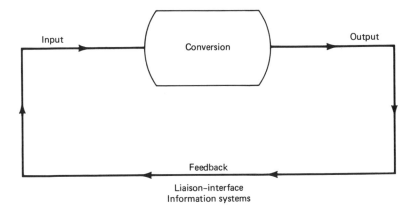

Figure 6-1. A simple system's model.

achievement should result in analysis, possible reevaluation of project objectives, and positive action, if and where required.

Taking a systems approach could provide the project manager with perspective. Resource requirements would come into focus. The inclination for overkill by obligating the project to questionable inputs that are not essential to the desired output would be minimized.

Project Planning Interfaces

Project Constituencies

Plans to meet project technical objectives are obviously a part of project management. In previous sections of this chapter several areas that could positively or negatively affect the outcome of the project were mentioned. The thrust of the preceding sections was primarily on direct project obligations; planning for interface with the different constituencies that might be involved with the project was treated incidentally. This section will look more extensively at the various organizational segments that could impact on the project.

Besides planning for the technical scope of the project and interface with the immediate project organization, the project manager must recognize what other activities, functions, or organizational groups external to the project are necessary for project support. Some of these activities are external to the explicit project organization but are internal to the total operational organization; some essential support activities or control elements, such as the customer, may be external to the organization. These organizational elements are invariably influential to the project. In some instances these constituencies do not have control prerogatives, but their influence is measured by the degree and importance of the support required from their activities. In essence, the project usually cannot operate as a self-contained unit; the project manager normally is in the position where he or she must plan for and integrate operations and activities that transcend the immediate technical organization.

It is easy for the project manager to get caught up with the technical aspects of the project and give inadequate attention to the external support activities. It often is very difficult for the technically oriented project manager to disassociate himself or herself from the technical phases of the project and develop extensive and effective interface with necessary external support forces. Once the technical aspects of the project have been planned, the project manager should divorce himself or herself from hands-on technical involvement. The technical work should be delegated, wherever possible, to competent professionals. The primary role of the project manager is that of a coordinator.

As a coordinator, the project manager has to plan and integrate the resources under his or her jurisdiction. This involves communicating technical and managerial objectives to the project organization and welding the project team into an efficient and cohesive unit. Externally, the project manager may have to plan coordination with the customer, management, internal organizational support operations, and outside contractors and consultants. Additional coordination may be essential to maintain liaison with informational sources where state of the art developments are critical to the project.

Project Organization

A significant part of the planning to accomplish the technical objectives of the project is the assembly and motivation of the project team. The project manager should have enough confidence in his or her colleagues to solicit their advice as well as active support on the project. The project manager must plan to both involve and commit the people assigned to the project.

Internal and external project failures often can be traced to communication breakdowns. It is very important to establish communication networks that provide essential information. Such informational networks must consider timeliness, accuracy, and relevance of information. Informational patterns or networks are also essential to provide the required informational flow internal to the project and from the project to external support activities, and progress and appropriate developments from external operations to affected internal activities. Project objectives should be carefully communicated to and understood by all people actively associated with the project. If objectives are changed or not being achieved, it is essential that this information be promptly communicated to the affected parties.

Communication can be enhanced by the propitious use of liaison meetings. Liaison meetings can be internal to the project, internal to the organization, or with organizational elements external to the organization. How frequently such meetings should be held and the participants in these meetings have to be determined on an individual project basis. The benefits of liaison meetings result from establishing contact points on related technical matters that can enhance working relationships, provide a review of progress, and localize problems. Often problems are recognized or anticipated or solutions forthcoming when involved people report activities in concert. An ancillary benefit from productive coordination meetings is the usually positive effect on morale.

The Customer

The customer can be an outside contractor, an internal functional division requesting support, or management that either initiates a project or approves an unsolicited internal proposal. Liaison planning with the customer can be either intensive or casual.

On some projects, such as in construction, very close proximity to the customer is usually necessary. Frequent liaison meetings may be indicated and planned for in situations where the project is only one phase in a multiproject program. Extensive planning in this type of situation can be absolutely essential in order to mesh the various project activities into a coordinated program.

Another operational possibility is where the current project represents only one step in a prospective multistep program. In this situation projects may be authorized sequentially rather than simultaneously. If this is the case, the project manager has to maintain close contact with the customer to ascertain future plans, or intended direction, and any other follow-on project authorization that might reasonably be expected.

If the project entails internal functional support, coordination has to be planned to ensure that project objectives are interpreted correctly and are compatible with the results anticipated. Planning would include making provisions for the feedback of information on technical accomplishment, any possible problems, cost and budget status, and schedules.

Planning for interface with management would be required in any of the possible situations described. The level of coordination with management could be a factor of the perceived importance of the project where the customer is external to the organization. Planning for interface with management on internally authorized projects would probably be determined by management's interest and direct involvement with the project. Management interface could range from periodic written reports and briefings to extensive and frequent coordination meetings and reviews of decision points.

Internal Organization

One of the more difficult project planning areas is where internal support is required from activities or functions that are outside the direct control of the project manager. Such support requirements may be incidental or they may be extensive and extremely relevant to the ultimate project success. This problem is more pronounced in matrix organization than where the pure project organizational form is used. Planning and implementation where direct control does not exist and the support required is critical to the project can really call forth a great deal of managerial ingenuity from the project leader.

The project manager has to plan where and when functional support will be required. The project manager has to coordinate functional inputs with his or her project people and also coordinate between different functional groups where there is no direct operational control. If special resources will be needed to support the project, the project manager has to be cognizant of functional commitment to other operations or projects.

Planning for and scheduling support from the internal organization may require revision of what is considered an ideal project operational plan. Revisions to the project plan may be very realistic, especially if the project has a relatively low priority for the use of common resources. In line with the aforementioned, it is usual practice for the project manager to submit a project plan to the support function. The plan would include a statement of the project's technical objectives, a budget, and a schedule. Hopefully there will be good working relations between the project and the functional organization. If so, a meaningful and reliable commitment can be obtained by the project manager. By the same token, the project manager should plan for periodic meetings or progress reports to the different support areas to keep them informed that the committed support requirements are still valid. If there is a change in the project concept that could affect the technical direction, cost, or schedule of any support activity, such information should be anticipated if possible, but in any event transmitted quickly. Poor coordination can lead to costly waste of effort and impair future working relationships.

Outside Contractors

Planning for the use of outside contractors and provision for subsequent liaison is another very important facet of project planning. The normal inclination is to try and do everything in-house and avoid going to outside sources for support. It may be impractical to plan the entire project on the basis that all necessary inputs can be accomplished locally. In planning the project, the project manager should carefully ascertain what work has to be performed down to the item, phase, and task levels and determine what support is needed and when and where it can come from. If support requirements are nonexistent or may not be available as needed within the current organizational structure, it may be far more cost effective to go outside to experienced contractors than to develop in-house capability. This decision would be even more positive if the capability developed had little prospective future use in the organization.

Internal capability may exist but may not be available in the quantity or quality or at the time needed. Often the project manager or higher managerial authority is reluctant to make commitments for external project support in the hope that internal support will be forthcoming when needed. This is definitely one area where the project manager should anticipate potential problems and have a contingency plan, including the possibility of contracting for outside services. Waiting until the 11th hour can have bad repercussions: It may take time to locate a qualified contractor, qualified contractors may already have prior obligations to other organizations, there may be a long lead time in acquiring the needed service, a premium price may have to be paid because there is no time to shop around, or the contractor will exact a bonus for short notice support.

On some projects and within some organizations project activity outside the organization is a normal way of operating. The policy of the organization may be to maintain minimal in-house capability in the expectation that the project manager will, as an essential part of his or her job responsibility, perform as a contractor and subcontract different project components to outside specialists. In such an operational situation the major thrust of the project manager's job may shift from immediate technical responsibility to that of coordinating the work segments that have been subcontracted. The project manager will still have overall technical responsibility and must have technical competence to select qualified subcontractors and evaluate their work. However, as indicated, the project manager's dominant activity will be the planning and coordination of the subcontractor's work. Planning a technologically complex project where several contributors are involved is an exercise demanding considerable skill.

Some of the planning considerations where there are extensive external operations include the following: the need for and frequency of liaison meetings; the operational areas that should be represented at such meetings; the discussion of technical progress, problems, and possible project changes; awareness of schedules; evaluation of accomplishment relative to expenditures; and any quality standards applicable.

External support on some projects may be a relatively inconsequential percentage of the total project package. The time and effort for coordination may not approximate the situation indicated in the preceding paragraph, but coordination is nevertheless important because one seemingly small work segment can impact on several other activities.

Technology and Competition

Professional growth and career perpetuation are generally closely related. It is possible that past successes can lead to complacency. Complacency can result in technical and professional obsolence in organizations; a further result can be the loss of a favorable competitive position. Unfortunately, individuals and organizations are often oblivious of a deteriorating competitive position until there is tangible evidence that survival is contingent on taking corrective action. Such action is not always possible, but if the individual or organization can be steered back on the proper technological course, it is usually an emotionally painful and expensive experience.

Planning for applicable technological change is very important. This is one planning area that can easily be neglected, in that the project manager's time and effort are normally consumed by the immediate responsibilities of successfully completing the project. Despite the inclination to address current obligations, there are many technical environments and projects where success can be jeopardized by insensitivity to evolving developments: There may be instances where new developments are rapid and influential in the field; there may be a change in the direction of the technology, in that present and previously unexplored opportunities are available; or the field may be diminishing in importance and is being superseded by recent technological developments.

Attainment of the position of project manager carries a connotation of professional competence. A professionally competent project manager would have an obligation to his or her people and organization to know what technological developments are occurring or imminent and to translate such knowledge into action programs. Some technologies, projects, and organizations exist in a technologically volatile environment. In other instances the operation is in a more stable or evolutionary technological environment. Regardless of the dynamics of the involved technology, the project manager should plan for information and exposure to new developments, current applications, prospective applications or opportunities (technology transfer), and a knowledge of what technologically competitive organizations are doing. However, it should be cautioned that just because the competition is doing something, this does not mean that it is right for every organization. Rather than attempt to emulate the competition that has an established market position, it might be a better tactic to exploit the technology by a unique adaptation or modification and technologically position the organization where it would have a distinct competitive edge. It is also possible that the competition has miscalculated the market and/or the direction of the technology is actually heading in the wrong direction.

The organization's operational philosophy would also be a factor in dealing with technology and competition. Is the organization technologically aggressive or passive? Is the organization a technological leader or a follower? A technological risk taker? There is a strong probability that the nature of the organization would reflect the type of people promoted to or recruited for project managers. The extent of the project manager's technological aggressiveness would probably mirror the organization's operational philosophy.

The Project Master Plan: Components

Planning the Project

Logically, the project plan should be adapted from and closely follow the proposal. More often than not there are significant deviations from the proposed project to the actual project plan. Where the proposal results in contractual commitments there are inviolate agreements that provide a framework for subsequent project planning. Examples of contractual commitments are cost, specifications, deliverables, and schedules.

Ideally, the proposal, with a few changes reflecting internal operational procedures, should, as indicated, become the master project plan. Procedural and planning changes occur for several reasons. There may be a shift in available resources between the time the project was proposed and the time it actually was authorized. The availability of human and physical resources can have a material impact on planning the project. Proposals are often prepared in a time-pressured situation. Between the preparation and presentation of the proposal and the authorization of the project, people may upon reflection decide that there are better methods or procedures than those proposed in order to accomplish the project objectives. It is also possible that additional information will surface that can affect the implementation of the project. Another possibility could relate to strategy in submitting the proposal whereby the intent was to convey confidence without being too explicit in order to retain a competitive edge.

Unless the project is extremely simple in concept and of short duration, there should be a comprehensive project plan before any important activity is authorized or started. Archibald suggests that a written project summary plan be prepared by the project manager covering the following areas:

Project scope

Project objectives, including cost, specifications, etc.

Applicable procedures

Contractual obligations

End items

Schedules

Resource requirements
Major contributors
Potential problems
Financial restraints
Risk areas[7]

    A more comprehensive approach is also offered for large, technologically complex projects. The suggested approach can serve as a guide or model as to methodology to improve project planning. The procedure covers five separate sequences: (1) preliminary coordination, (2) the work plan, (3) the budget, (4) schedules, and (5) status reporting:

1. Preliminary coordination
   a. Assemble responsible representatives from all required supporting operations.
   b. Define, describe, and identify factors that must be planned for to accomplish the project.
   c. Establish technical objectives, areas of performance responsibility, schedule and budget commitments, and profit target goals and communicate committed project obligations.
   d. Secure detailed planning from functional groups supporting the project.
   e. Coordinate the project components into a composite project plan.
   f. Obtain approval of the project plan from the participating functions, the project leader, and management.
   g. Issue, implement, and maintain the plan.
2. The work plan
   a. Project title and identification number.
   b. Delineation of the work:
      1. Technical description of the work to be performed
      2. Major areas of responsibility and support:
         a. Engineering
         b. Manufacturing
         c. Procurement/logistics
         d. Quality control
         e. Personnel
         f. Finance/contracts administration
         g. Other
   c. Project work item schedule.
   d. Authorization for the project:
      1. By the customer
      2. Economic and technical justification
      3. Constraints and obligations

3. The budget
   a. Budget allocation to major work items, phases, and tasks.
4. Schedules
   a. Project schedules should include milestones and deliverable end items.
   b. Coordinate critical schedule elements with the master schedule, which should show all end item requirements on all active projects. This would prevent or minimize schedule conflicts where there may be future competition for common resources.
   c. Provide for schedule revision. If it becomes necessary to process a schedule change, the final internal authorization for it should come from management. After management approval the change would be incorporated into the master schedule and communicated to the organization, stating the following:
      1. Nature of the change
      2. Reason for the change
      3. Effect of the change on cost, schedule, technical requirements, etc.
      4. Date of the change
      5. Change approval
5. Status reporting (To complete the planning cycle and establish a system so that executives will be able to manage by the exception principle, actual versus planned accomplishment must be reported periodically. This is really a control device. On most active projects it is desirable to report the status weekly.)
   a. Schedule status
      1. Scheduled and actual or forecast completion dates
      2. Explanation of deviation(s), if any
   b. Budget status
      1. Total project funding
      2. Expenditures to date of report
      3. Current estimated cost to complete
      4. Anticipated profit or loss
      5. Explanation of deviation, if any, from planned expenditure projection.

Properly conceived and implemented, the project plan should establish an operational frame of reference regarding the project's resource requirements, technical objectives, important accomplishment points, and management, including designating spheres of responsibility and authority.

In a creative professional environment the execution and implementation of planning should normally be left to the individual(s) responsible for performing the activity. After individual inputs have been received, it is necessary to assemble the separate components to determine if the sum of the parts equals or exceeds total objectives. It is possible that individual interpretation of obligations will not be compatible with the project objectives. Negative synergism can occur even though positive synergism is a very desired goal.

One relatively common problem in planning is that projects are often planned individualistically. Planning assumptions may be made. There may be direct coordination between technically related projects, but too often there is inadequate composite planning. The availability of a composite plan showing all projects and present and anticipated obligations would provide organizational perspective. A composite plan could indicate that even though after coordination between technically related projects, present or downstream commitments, which are not readily apparent, may mitigate against the project meeting its goals.

Any proposed planning model is merely a guide to be used as a point of departure. Various organizations would tailor planning to specific operational requirements. It is easy to fall into tendencies of excesses. Care should be exercised to avoid intimidating administrative detail that can be distracting and cost contributive without comparable beneficial returns. Only those factors that are strategic to the project's success should be planned for in detail and monitored. Extensive elaboration can stifle individual interpretation, make coordination difficult, and affect morale by curtailing the responsibility and authority of professionals assigned to the project. The design of the plan should delineate significant work components and leave details to be amplified by the various operating strata.

There can be a very fine line between what is too much planning and what is inadequate or insufficient planning. In actual practice the degree of planning is situational. The level of detail would depend on the project. A technologically complex project involving extensive support outside the immediate jurisdiction of the project manager would require more planning for coordinated effort and perhaps greater detail to enable closer control. The people assigned to a project would also determine the extent of planning detail considered necessary. Experienced and senior people with a proven record of accomplishment could be turned relatively free to plan their activities in support of the project. Less experienced people would need more planning guidance and would probably be given less interpretive latitude. Besides the variables mentioned, the operational philosophy of the project manager would affect the degree of project planning and individual involvement. The operational philosophy of the project manager, as to planning, can range from a very informal general approach, where only broad objectives are highlighted and planned for, to close attention to a myriad of details.

The following section will elaborate on some of the areas where in-depth project planning is usually advisable.

In-Depth Project Planning

Preliminary Coordination.   Before embarking on coordination activities, the project manager should be able to determine what specific people and resources will be needed at a reasonably accurate predetermined point of time. Calling coordination meetings without having substantive information and specific requests for participation is a wasteful exercise.

The purpose of preliminary coordination meetings is to communicate project objectives and identify required resources. In addition, it should be ascertained whether the essential resources will be available when needed and develop the composition of the project team. In some instances management authorization for the release of resources to the project would be prerequisite to subsequent, more detailed project planning. To avoid embarrassment, the project manager should do relevant in-depth planning before requesting the release of resources. If resources are authorized by management and are diverted from other productive occupations and then are not properly employed, the potential repercussions are apparent.

Preliminary coordination planning should indicate the skills needed, the skill levels necessary to achieve project objectives, and when such skills will be required. This type of preliminary planning would also apply to the utilization of facilities and equipment.

Work Plan.   The project work breakdown is fundamental and one of the most important activities in project management. This is basic planning. Practically all major project activity flows from the work breakdown plan. The following would be indicative of contingent activities or events: personnel requirements, facilities and equipment needs, the technical approach, statement of specifications, quality control and reliability factors (if applicable), test procedures, maintainability, materials standards, controlling procedures such as value analysis/value engineering, design to cost, change control, make-or-buy decisions, work and change authorizations, including the release of paperwork into the system, and so on.

As defined in the Goddard Space Flight Center *Handbook for Preparation and Implementation of Work Breakdown Structures,*

(1) *Work Breakdown Structure.* The WBS is a basic management technique which presents systematically subdivided blocks of work (program, project, contract, etc.) down to the point which represents the lowest level of controlled effort (i.e. the lowest level at which the project office plans to maintain routine surveillance). It is a product-oriented family tree composed of hardware, software, services, and other work tasks. It results from systems engineering and management planning processes and completely defines the program/project. A WBS displays and defines the products to be developed and relates the tasks to be accomplished to each other and to the end product. Blocks of related and consistent work effort form a branch of the structure.[8]

Archibald describes the project work breakdown structure as follows:

> The PBS is a graphic portrayal of the project, exploding it in a level-by-level
> fashion down to the degree of detail needed for effective planning and
> control. It must include all deliverable end items (consumable goods, ma-
> chinery, equipment, facilities, services, manuals, reports, and so on) and
> includes the major functional tasks that must be performed to conceive,
> design, fabricate, assemble, test, and deliver the end items.[9]

Kerzner further elaborates:

> The Work Breakdown Structure acts as a vehicle for breaking the work
> down into smaller elements, thus providing a greater probability that every
> major and minor activity will be accounted for. Although a variety of Work
> Breakdown Structures exist, the most common is the five-level indentured
> structure shown below:

Level	Description
1	Total Program
2	Project
3	Task
4	Subtask
5	Work Package[10]

Some Illustrations of a Work Breakdown

Figures 6-2 through 6-9 are some illustrations of WBS.[11] Figure 6-2 is a
sample of representative work preliminarily identified as required to support project objectives. In all probability, individual work items would be
assigned to different project people who would, in turn, develop elabora-
tions of activities necessary to accomplish item work objectives.

Figures 6-3 to 6-9 demonstrate that what initially appears to be a simple
project, building a birdhouse, ultimately involves considerable planning,
including many decision points and several in-depth planning levels. Figure 6-3 identifies the basic project objectives, to build a birdhouse, and an
awareness that subsequent activities must be accommodated. Levels 1
and 2 are at least required to support the fundamental project objectives.
Figure 6-4 identifies the major level-1 component elements of the birdhouse. Figure 6-5 represents an additional work breakdown, including
activity levels needed to complete the project component elements. Figure 6-6 is a possible further elaboration of the work breakdown of one of
the project item components. Figures 6-7 and 6-8 show the evolutionary
aspects, activities, and work segments involved in a comprehensive work
breakdown. In Figure 6-8, the question is also raised as to what might be
missing in order to complete the project successfully. Figure 6-9 indicates
that even though major work phases of the birdhouse have been planned
and completed, the project may not be a success unless supplementary

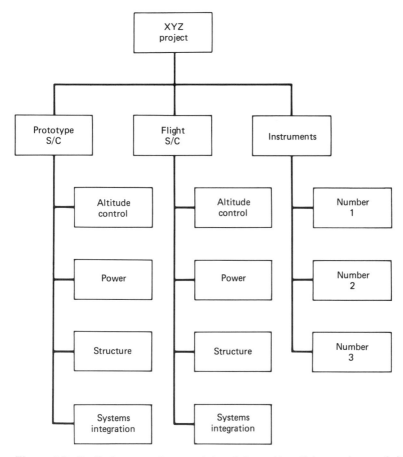

Figure 6-2. Preliminary project work breakdown identifying major work items.

Figure 6-3. Basic project objectives—building a birdhouse.

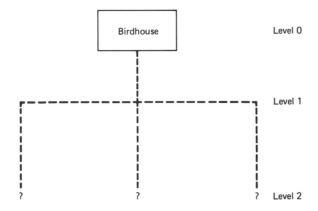

134

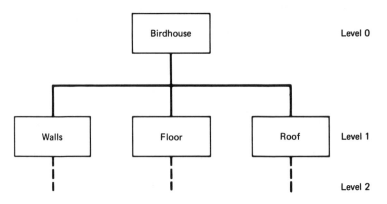

Figure 6-4. Identification of major project level-1 component elements.

Figure 6-5. Additional work breakdown levels and activities needed to complete the project component elements.

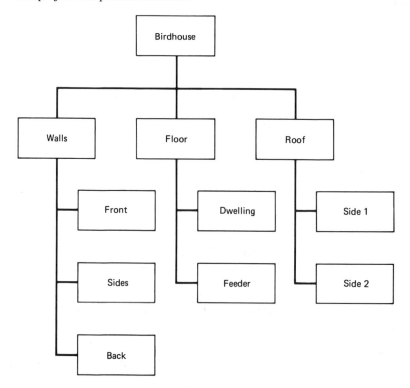

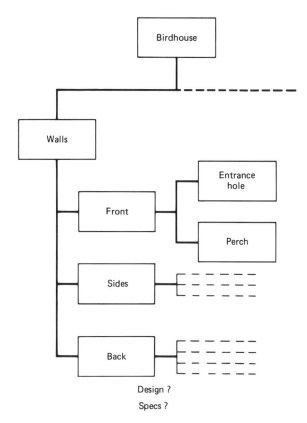

Figure 6-6. Possible further elaboration of work breakdown of a project component.

but important factors are accounted for in order that the project objectives be achieved.

Building a birdhouse would appear to be a very simple project. With the WBS approach the various factors that must be considered come into focus. What initially seems mundane expands into a significant activity. As Figures 6-3 through 6-9 indicate, WBS helps identify the many elements involved in building a birdhouse, some of which could easily be ignored at first. Failure to recognize the different phases and activities could slow the project down, lead to excessive costs and frustrations, and in the worst possible situation cause the project to fail to achieve its objectives.

Planning and Scheduling Based on WBS

Make sure you plan a process/cycle for making plan changes for schedules, WBS, design, test plans, materials and parts plans, and so on.

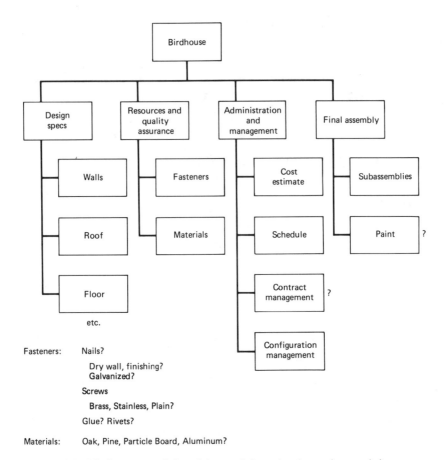

Figure 6-7. Birdhouse work breakdown elaboration by major work items.

The WBS in the birdhouse example illustrates that seemingly straightforward projects should be planned in detail to avoid downstream difficulties. Some of the birdhouse project elements depicted are reasonably obvious, some are not so obvious, and some of the illustrations failed to address other possible issues that could affect the project outcome. For example, where should the birdhouse be located? Are predators a consideration? Will there be competition for the birdhouse between the desired occupants and other birds? Will special provisions have to be made for feeding arrangements? Are there seasonal factors in attracting the occupants for whom the birdhouse was designed and built?

Scheduling generally follows planning. Comprehensive and intelligent planning should be inducive to reasonably reliable schedules. Following are some pertinent considerations in deriving initial schedules: (1) are based on the WBS; (2) should be flow (PERT; see Chapter 7) dia-

137

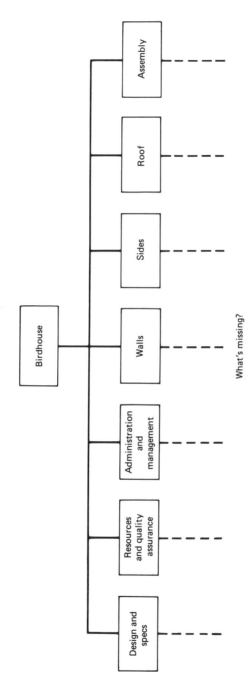

Figure 6-8. Some activities and work segments in planning a comprehensive work breakdown.

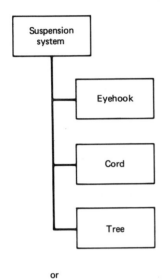

or

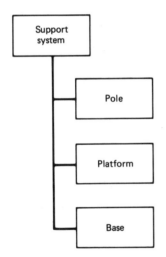

Figure 6-9. Supplementary considerations in achieving project objectives.

grammed; (3) should be *ideal* (no risk, first cut); (4) should *not* include time estimates (first cut); (5) should be coordinated with *all* key players; (6) should include paper, end items, and facilities; (7) should include approval and administration and procurement cycles; (8) should include time estimates from best sources; (9) should compute the critical path; and (10), if the end date is beyond the "drop dead" date, should look at *low*-risk solutions, then *medium*-risk solutions, and so on.

It is difficult to envision a successful project involving any magnitude of effort without the benefit of a comprehensive WBS. The WBS breaks down the various project activities into manageable and definable work packages. It helps identify potential problem areas, enables delegation, assigns responsibility for project support, and is an important communication tool to monitor and control project progress and accomplishment.

Budget. Budgeting project funds and cost management are infinitely simplified when there is a good WBS. Indiscriminate or inadequately planned commissioning of lump sums can result in waste, omissions, and possible overruns because the extent of effort required to support the project was miscalculated.

Breaking the work into small and distinct segments encourages closer scrutiny, tighter control, and better cost and budget management. When a work segment is overrunning or underrunning its projected costs, such information should immediately flag the project manager's attention. The project manager should determine the seriousness of the problem and the possible repercussions, cost- and accomplishment-wise, to other segments of the project. Detailed planning in this area would quickly make one aware of problems, locate the difficulties and, hopefully, the cause of the problem(s), and instigate corrective action before valuable resources are unproductively used up.

In-depth budget planning can also facilitate make-or-buy decisions. It is a rare project that is so rich in resources that trade-off decisions are not required. Once the total scope of the project comes into focus from the WBS, the project manager is in a position to estimate the cost of the various work segments and determine the best and possibly cheapest way to achieve the work objectives. In some instances it may be more feasible to contract the work outside the project or outside the organization. Such a decision may be tenuous unless the project manager has explored alternatives and has confidence in the information used in making a decision.

More on Schedules. Meeting scheduled obligations as already indicated often requires in-depth planning. Lead times to procure internal services, outside support, facilities, and equipment can vary. What might be expected from past experience in the way of lead time can be misleading owing to changed conditions or prior commitments.

Deliverables may entail inputs from several organizational factions, as well as outside contractors. Detailed planning in meeting schedules follows a process similar to that indicated in the preceding section on budgets, in that if a work element is not accomplished on time or as projected, there may be ramifications affecting other scheduled activities. This is especially the case where work cannot proceed on a project segment until there is successful completion of a preceding and related work element.

In-depth scheduling could be based on "goes into" work elements. Often before a project end item is delivered it builds up incrementally from inputs contributed by several different operations. A prelude to the delivery of the end item might be the attainment of significant project milestones. If these are properly established and positioned, the project manager has another useful tool with which to determine the progress of the project.

Status. WBS provides the foundation for project management. The critical components of the project are identified and the necessary detailed activities to achieve the major project components are isolated. Planning in relevant detail is a first step to good project management. The plan by itself is a passive instrument. Once activity is initiated, some measure of accomplishment as to time, cost, and performance must be correlated to the plan.

Status reporting is informational feedback. Quick, accurate, and relevant status reporting facilitates control. A well-designed and well-implemented informational system enables the project manager to take prompt and corrective action before the project gets in inescapable trouble. Information, per se, in the computer age is normally no problem. The problem is obtaining relevant information in time to initiate corrective action. Too often there is much nonessential information in the system, which leads to static; this can be more diversionary than applicable. Consequently, the project manager should determine what information is necessary to evaluate the progress on the project and plan for strategic status reports that are timely, applicable, and action directed.

Endnotes Chapter Six

1. R. D. Archibald, *Managing High Technology Programs and Projects*, New York, Wiley, 1976, p. 18.

2. *Handbook for Preparation and Implementation of Work Breakdown Structures*, Goddard Space Flight Center, GHB 7120.1, August 1971, p. 19.

3. See H. Kerzner, *Project Management. A Systems Approach to Planning, Scheduling and Controlling*, New York, Van Nostrand Reinhold, 1979, p. 158.

4. D. Roman, *Science, Technology, and Innovation: A Systems Approach*, Columbus, Grid Publishing, 1980, pp. 226–227.

5. B. C. Twiss, *Managing Technological Innovation*, London, Longman, 1974, p. 188.

6. Roman, *op. cit.*, pp. 227–228.

7. Archibald, *op. cit.*, p. 136; also see Kerzner, *op. cit.*, pp. 286–287.

8. *Handbook for Preparation and Implementation of Work Breakdown Structures, op. cit.*, pp. 2–3.

9. Archibald, *op. cit.*, p. 141.

10. Kerzner, *op. cit.*, p. 288.

11. These illustrations were developed by James Zerega, Goddard Space Center, and presented at a Project Management Seminar at the George Washington University, Spring Semester, 1983.

CHAPTER SEVEN

Planning and Control Techniques*

Introduction

Planning

Two fundamental tasks of management are planning and control. This is as true in a project management environment as in other environments.

Planning entails spelling out what is to be done in order to meet the project objectives. Various resources must be consumed in order to meet these objectives. Basically, these resources fall into the following four categories:

Time

Money

People

Materials

Project plans must be concerned with the effective utilization of such resources over the life of the project. The time resource is dealt with by creating *schedules* of activities. Money planning is largely handled through *budgets*. Human resource planning entails assigning people to the project, using tools such as human resource matrices and manpower loading charts. Material resource planning may be closely tied to the budget process when it entails the procurement of new materials, or else it may focus on the allocation of physical resources to different tasks over the life of the project.

* This chapter was written by J. Davidson Frame, Department of Management Science, George Washington University, Washington, DC 20052. Copyright, 1985 J. D. Frame.

Control

Control entails seeing that project tasks are carried out according to plan. A major purpose of control is to avoid large deviations from the plan. Clearly, when the plan is not being met, the project is out of control. Because control focuses so strongly on the plan, it too is concerned with the allocation of time, money, human, and material resources.

Over the years project managers, operations research specialists, academicians, and others have developed many techniques to help project staffs in their planning and control activities. Some of these techniques are very sophisticated, and some quite rudimentary. With the meteoric rise of the so-called personal computer, we find new user-friendly ways to plan and control projects and we can anticipate an enormous proliferation of software in the future for project management applications.

In this chapter we will focus only on the most common of the many planning and control techniques that have been developed. Included here are work breakdown structures, Gantt charts, PERT/CPM charts, human resource matrices, and variance analyses of project budgets. Our purpose here is to introduce the reader to some of the most frequently used planning and control tools, not to engage in a detailed exegesis of planning and control methodologies.

Work Breakdown Structure

Preparation of the Work Breakdown Structure

In general, one of the first things we do when we plan something (e.g., a vacation, a trip to the market) is to create a list of the things we wish to do. In project management we call such a list a work breakdown structure (WBS). The WBS not only specifies the tasks we wish to undertake in our project, but their estimated durations as well. If, in addition, the WBS contains information on the cost of each task, it is called a costed WBS. Finally, for each task it is usually useful to provide the name of the individual responsible for its completion.

An example of a simple WBS is given in Table 7-1. This example shows some of the tasks that need to be undertaken in making preparations for a picnic. Two people are involved in the task: George and Martha. All together, preparations entail a total of 44 minutes of effort, plus 20 minutes of driving time to the picnic site.

The question naturally arises: How detailed should our WBS be? The answer depends heavily upon the nature of the problem being addressed. If we are building a submarine for the government, we must develop a very detailed WBS, because this is a very complex project where all tasks must be clearly specified. On the other hand, if we are planning to paint our house—an uncomplicated project—we can simply specify the broad

Table 7-1. Work Breakdown Structure for Preparing a Picnic

Task	Duration (min)	Responsible
1. Start		
2. Make ice tea	15	George
3. Prepare sandwiches	10	Martha
4. Prepare fruit	2	Martha
5. Gather blankets	2	George
6. Prepare basket	2	Martha
7. Gather sports gear	3	Martha
8. Load car	4	George
9. Get gas	6	George
10. Drive to picnic grounds	20	Martha

outlines of the tasks needed to be undertaken: paint the portico, the back porch, the front siding, window trim, and so on.

Even in undertaking a simple project, we may find that we must put together a rather detailed WBS. In the house painting example this might arise if we have a team of three people involved in the effort. In order to avoid confusion and make certain that each worker knows precisely what he or she is to do, we might assign specific windows to individual workers, the left pillar of the portico to one worker, the right to another, and so forth.

Table 7-2 shows how we can make the WBS presented in Table 7-1 more detailed. Here each of the broad activities is broken down into smaller parts.

Composing a good WBS is an important undertaking because it serves as the kernel of the planning and control effort. At a minimum, a WBS is a checklist that permits the project manager to keep track of what has been accomplished and what remains to be done. Beyond this, the WBS provides the basic data needed to construct more sophisticated planning and control tools, such as Gantt charts and PERT networks.

Gantt Charts

A Graphical Work Breakdown Structure

Gantt charts are simply bar charts that graphically portray the duration of the different tasks specified in the WBS. Thus a Gantt chart is nothing more than a graphical WBS. A Gantt chart based on the WBS of Table 7-1 is shown in Figure 7-1.

Gantt charts are probably the most commonly used scheduling tool. Their popularity lies in the fact that they are easy to develop, are easy to

Table 7-2. Detailed Work Breakdown Structure for Preparing a Picnic

Task	Duration (min)	Responsible
1. Start		
2. Make ice tea		George
Boil water	8	
Steep tea	5	
Add ice	2	
3. Prepare sandwiches		Martha
Peanut butter and jelly	4	
Ham and Swiss cheese	6	
4. Prepare fruit	2	Martha
5. Gather blankets	2	George
6. Prepare basket		Martha
Collect silverware	1	
Pack sandwiches	$\frac{1}{2}$	
Pack fruit	$\frac{1}{2}$	
7. Gather sports gear		Martha
Baseball	1	
Frisbee	1	
Badminton set	1	
8. Load car	4	George
9. Get gas	6	George
10. Drive to picnic grounds	20	Martha

Figure 7-1. Gantt chart for preparing a picnic.

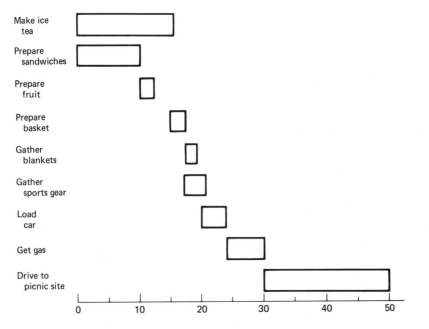

use, and provide project management staff with a quick, comprehensive overview of the project plan.

Large amounts of information can be included in Gantt charts. By color-coding the bars, for example, one can tag who is responsible for the given activities: for example, red bars for Martha and blue bars for George. In addition, by including different symbols in the Gantt chart—upright triangles, upside-down triangles, circles, circles with dots, and so on—one can depict many things, such as the scheduled start date, the actual start date, the scheduled termination date, the actual termination date, critical technical milestones, and budgetary milestones. Incidentally, when Gantt charts contain milestone information, they are sometimes called milestone charts.

A number of computer packages exist that offer sophisticated Gantt chart formats. The trouble with high levels of sophistication is that if the chart becomes too complex, it undermines the principal strength of Gantt charts—their simplicity.

Gantt charts are particularly useful in controlling projects. They show at a glance whether the project schedule is being met or whether it is slipping. Figure 7-2 shows a situation where there is slippage. In task 1, for example, the task began late, lasted the scheduled duration, and ended late.

Figure 7-2. Using the Gantt chart for project control.

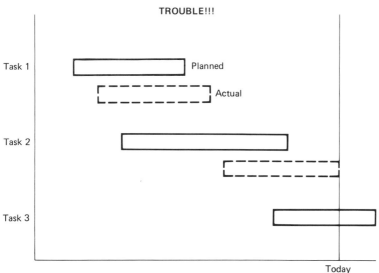

PERT/CPM Approaches

Procedural Relationships

In scheduling project tasks, we often find that a given task cannot begin until other tasks have been completed. In our picnic example we cannot steep the tea until after the water for the tea has been boiled. When we face such situations, we are dealing with precedence relationships.

In project management we show the precedence relationships of different tasks by drawing networks of activities. In these network diagrams we connect tasks with each other in such a way that the dependency relationships of the tasks to each other are clearly portrayed. Flow charts are one way of doing this. With a flow chart activities are laid out on paper in the sequence in which they occur. They are boxed and connected with each other with lines. The flow typically goes from the top of the page to the bottom or from left to right.

Three decades ago networking approaches to scheduling projects were developed that are widely used today in the construction and engineering fields. These approaches are generically referred to as PERT and/or CPM networks. The acronym *PERT* stands for Program Evaluation and Review Technique and was developed in the late 1950s in conjunction with the Polaris missile program; *CPM* stands for Critical Path Method and was developed by the DuPont Company at about the same time as PERT. Over the years many variations of the original PERT and CPM have emerged. In this chapter we will not look at the fine distinctions between the various approaches, but will simply focus on the most basic characteristics of PERT/CPM systems.

A Basic Flow Chart Diagram

What PERT/CPM networks do is incorporate scheduling information into a basic flow chart diagram. This is illustrated in Figure 7-3. Here the tasks portrayed in our original illustrative WBS (Table 7-1) are placed into boxes, the boxes are laid out according to the sequence in which they occur, and their relationships with each other are shown with lines. In each box that portrays a task the amount of time it takes to complete the task is given in the upper right-hand corner. Making ice tea, for example, takes 15 minutes.

An important concept necessary in understanding PERT/CPM networks is that of the critical path. The critical path in a network is the path that takes the longest time to complete. In Figure 7-3 consider the two paths that take you from "Start" to "Prepare basket." The upper path, "Make ice tea," takes 15 minutes to complete, while the lower path, which is composed of two tasks ("Prepare sandwiches" and "Prepare fruit") can be completed in 12 minutes. Given the way the network is drawn, the shortest time that can elapse between "Start" and "Prepare

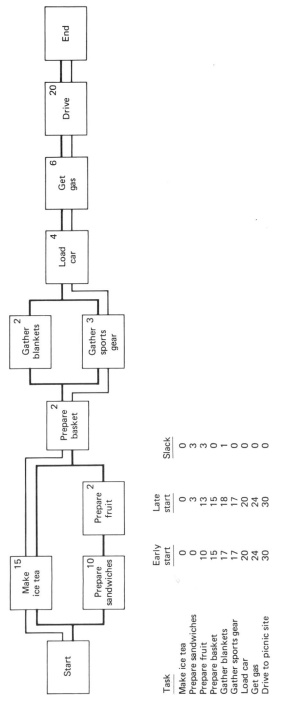

Task	Early start	Late start	Slack
Make ice tea	0	0	0
Prepare sandwiches	0	3	3
Prepare fruit	10	13	3
Prepare basket	15	15	0
Gather blankets	17	18	1
Gather sports gear	17	17	0
Load car	20	20	0
Get gas	24	24	0
Drive to picnic site	30	30	0

Figure 7-3. PERT/CPM diagram: precedence diagram for preparing a picnic.

basket'' is 15 minutes. This means that the lower path has 3 minutes of slack built into it. Since the critical path is always the one that takes the longest to complete, the critical path has no slack at all. In fact, if there is schedule slippage along the critical path, the slippage will be reflected in the project as a whole. It is this feature of the critical path—its inflexibility with regard to slippage of schedule—that gives it its name. Because activities off the critical path have some slack associated with them, they can tolerate some slippage in schedule.

In Figure 7-3 the critical path for the project is portrayed by the double line. To find out how long the project takes to complete, one need merely add together the times it takes to accomplish each of the tasks on the critical path. In our example the time needed to accomplish the whole project is 50 minutes (15 + 2 + 3 + 4 + 6 + 20 minutes).

Because noncritical tasks have slack associated with them, there is some flexibility in scheduling their start times. As we have seen, the lower path has 3 minutes of slack. Consequently, we need not begin to prepare the sandwiches until 3 minutes into the project. If we begin sandwich preparation at the 3-minute mark, we can still complete the project in the allotted time. However, if we begin sandwich preparation at the 4-minute mark, we will cause the project schedule to slip by 1 minute.

Earliest and Latest Start Times

Calculating the earliest and latest start times for projects is easy to do. To calculate earliest start times we begin at the left and work our way to the right. First, we calculate the earliest start times for tasks on the critical path. "Make ice tea" starts at time 0, "Prepare basket" at time 15, "Gather sports gear" at time 17, "Load car" at time 20, "Get gas" at time 24, and "Drive to picnic site" at time 30. After earliest start times for critical tasks have been calculated, we turn to calculating earliest start times for noncritical tasks. Again we move from left to right. "Prepare sandwiches" can begin at time 0, "Prepare fruit" at time 10, and "Gather blankets" at time 17.

To calculate latest start times we work from right to left. Here we subtract the amount of time it takes to perform a task from the total. Once again, we first concentrate on the critical path. Since the project takes 50 minutes to complete, the latest time to start "Drive to picnic site" is at time 30 (i.e., 50 − 20), to start "Get gas" is at time 24, to start "Load car" is at time 20, to start "Gather sports gear" is at time 17, to start "Prepare basket" is at time 15, and to start "Make ice tea" is at time 0. Note that the latest start times are identical to the earliest start times. This is always the case with tasks on the critical path.

To calculate latest start times for noncritical tasks, we also work leftward. Consider the noncritical task "Gather blankets." The activity that occurs after "Gather blankets" is the critical task "Load car," which we have determined should start no later than at time 20. Since "Gather blankets'' consumes 2 minutes of time, its latest start time is at time 18 (i.e., 20 − 2). With similar logic, the latest start time for ''Prepare fruit'' is at time 13, and that for ''Prepare sandwiches'' is at time 3.

Information on the earliest and latest start times for our sample project is provided in Figure 7-3. Note that once these times have been calculated, slack time is easily determined. It is simply the difference between the latest start time and the earliest start time. For critical tasks this value is always zero.

Resources Affecting Network Configuration

The actual configuration of a PERT/CPM network is heavily dependent upon the amount of resources that can be devoted to the project. For example, the more people we have available, the more parallel activities we are capable of conducting. In our example of preparing for a picnic, we find that if George and Martha had three helpers, five activities could be conducted concurrently. One individual could be making the ice tea, another preparing the sandwiches, a third preparing the fruit, a fourth gathering blankets, and a fifth gathering the sports gear. Given these circumstances, we would have a different PERT/CPM network than the one portrayed in Figure 7-2.

The Arrow Diagram or Activity-on-Arrow Network

The kind of PERT/CPM network we have built here is called either a precedence diagram network, or an activity-in-node network. Another popular approach is the arrow diagram, or activity-on-arrow network. This second approach is illustrated in Figure 7-4. Unlike the precedence diagram approach, which puts tasks into boxes, the activity-on-arrow approach places the tasks on the arrows that connect *events* (the circled numbers in Figure 7-4). Events represent either the beginning or the end of a task. Thus in Figure 7-4 event 4 represents both the end of task 3–4 (''Prepare fruit'') and the beginning of task 4–5 (''Prepare basket'').

With the activity-on-arrow approach we sometimes have occasion to create dummy tasks (or dummy activities). Task 7–6 in Figure 7-6 is such a dummy task. Dummy tasks are tasks that consume no resources. In this case we create a dummy task because to get from event 5 to event 6 we wish to undertake two tasks, ''Gather blankets'' and ''Gather sports gear.'' Both of these tasks cannot be described as 5–6, since this would lead to confusion as to whether 5–6 represented ''Gather blankets'' or ''Gather sports gear.'' Consequently, one of the tasks (''Gather blankets'') is arbitrarily given the assignation 5–7, to distinguish it from 5–6. To do so, however, requires the creation of dummy task 7–6.

Which approach is superior, precedence diagrams or activity-on-arrow digrams? Answer: Whichever approach you feel most comfortable with. The project management literature is filled with discussions of the relative

150

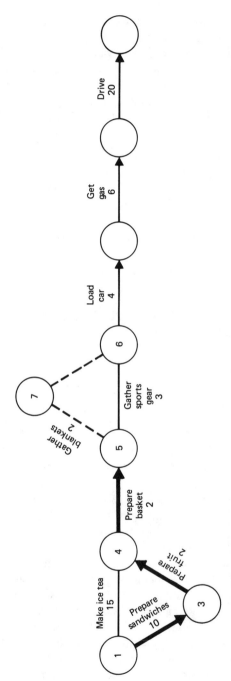

Figure 7-4. PERT/CPM diagram: activity-on-arrow diagram for preparing a picnic.

merits of one approach over the other; however, the advantages of one approach over the other are marginal. With the proliferation of computerized PERT/CPM packages, the project manager will likely learn to live with the approach used by whatever package he or she is required to use.

Statistical Features of PERT

Probabilistic Estimates for Completion

One of the features of PERT that distinguishes it from other network approaches is that it enables project staff to make probabilistic estimates about the likelihood of finishing individual tasks—or the project as a whole—within a specified period of time. To use this feature it is necessary to assume that the time it takes to complete a task is distributed according to a unimodal beta distribution. Given this assumption, one can calculate the *expected* time it takes to complete a task [$t(e)$] by plugging in values for a, b, and m into the following equation, where a is an optimistic estimate of how long it takes to complete a task, b is a pessimistic estimate, and m is the most likely value:

$$t(e) = \frac{a + 4m + b}{6}$$

The standard deviation σ for the beta distribution is calculated as follows:

$$\sigma = \frac{b - a}{6}$$

When putting together the PERT network, one uses the expected time values [$t(e)$] to calculate the earliest start time for a task, the earliest finish time, the latest start time, and the latest finish time. By estimating the standard deviation of all the activities taken together on the critical path and assuming a normal distribution for the time it takes to complete the critical path activities, one can make probabilistic estimates regarding the likelihood that a project can be completed in a given period of time. To see how this can be done, the reader should refer to a basic work on PERT analysis.

Some Limitations

It should be quickly noted that this probabilistic feature of PERT is rarely used outside of construction and straightforward engineering areas. Basically, this probabilistic feature has three problems associated with it: First, it adds to the complexity of performing PERT analysis. The typical project manager has trouble enough making one estimate for the time it will take to complete a task; making three estimates may be asking too much!

Second, unless a project manager has access to good historical data on how long it takes to complete particular tasks, all three of the time estimates will entail sheer guesswork. Under such circumstances it is ridiculous to assume that the PERT model will be able to provide reasonable probabilistic estimates on the amount of time needed to complete the project.

Third, it is not at all obvious that the basic statistical assumptions of the probabilistic PERT model hold for the given circumstances we face. For example, how do we know whether the beta distribution and normal distribution assumptions are valid? If they are not valid, what are the implications for our estimates of completion times?

PERT/CPM for Project Control

Schedule Control

On large, complex projects PERT/CPM analysis can play an important role in project control. As various tasks are undertaken and completed, information on their start dates, duration, and finish dates is entered into the PERT/CPM system to determine the extent to which the project is being carried out according to plan. The PERT/CPM network can be especially useful in allowing project staff to identify the impact of schedule slippages on the course of the project. Analysis of a particular slip may require rescheduling of the entire project. Certain critical tasks may have to be "crashed," while others may have to be dropped entirely. When the PERT/CPM network is closely tied to financial data, the PERT/CPM analysis can also give project staff insights into the impact of slippages on the cost of the project.

Strengths and Weaknesses of PERT/CPM Networks

Strengths

PERT/CPM approaches to planning and controlling project tasks arose in response to a need to better manage complex projects. They are most heavily employed in construction projects and other complex engineering projects. PERT/CPM networks have a number of clear-cut strengths associated with them, including the following:

1. They require project staff to think out consciously and carefully the sequencing and duration of project tasks. To set up a PERT/CPM network, project tasks need to be explicitly identified, their interrelationships must be specified, and determinations must be made of their duration. Clearly a project that has been carefully PERTed is likely to be a well-

planned project. Risk of unplanned surprises is lower in such a project than one with casual, ad hoc planning.

2. In low-risk projects they can provide staff with accurate estimates of when tasks will be accomplished and at what costs. Projects such as constructing houses in a development or building small bridges are reasonably low-risk projects, since they have been done over and over again and engineers have a good idea of what each of the tasks in such projects entails. In these circumstances PERT/CPM networks are capable of giving project staff highly accurate information on project duration and cost, since the data elements put into the networks are not wild hunches but, rather, solid, experience-based estimates.

3. They can serve as an invaluable control tool in complex low-risk projects. Complex low-risk projects that have hundreds or thousands of tasks can easily get out of control without good management practices, simply because there is so much information of which to keep track. PERT/CPM networks excel in such situations. Through periodic updates they force project staff to consciously look at each of the myriad tasks with a view to determining whether or not they are being accomplished according to plan. When there are deviations from the plan, PERT/CPM can provide project staff with a good idea of the implications of the deviations.

Weaknesses

Despite these strengths, PERT/CPM approaches are infrequently used outside of construction and engineering projects. One study shows that in a target group of project managers who were knowledgeable about PERT/CPM, fewer than half used the approach in managing projects. In another study it was found that roughly 5% of project managers in the automatic data processing area used PERT/CPM networks in their projects. Results such as these cause us to question the applicability and/or utility of PERT/CPM approaches, particularly for projects that are not heavily related to engineering. When we look into this matter, we find a number of weaknesses in PERT/CPM approaches:

1. In inherently amorphous, "blue sky," high-risk projects, task-related estimates tend to be very rough, so that PERT/CPM networks based on them give correspondingly rough scheduling and cost information. Thus PERT/CPM approaches are virtually useless in basic research projects, where scientists are not even certain what tasks need to be undertaken, to say nothing of their duration and costs. Similarly, the utility of PERT/CPM is questionable in many state of the art system design and software projects, where system requirements frequently shift and are unstable until the later stages of the project.

2. PERT/CPM networks may provide project staff with a misleading sense of precision, particularly when—as in the case of formal PERT—

the network offers probabilities of completing the project in a given time frame. When any decision support system generates hard numbers as output, there is a tendency to forget the possible weaknesses of the data base on which these numbers are based. On low-risk projects that have a substantial experience base this is not a serious problem. The underlying data base is likely to be good. However, on higher-risk projects PERT/CPM outputs may provide project staff with a false sense of security (or possibly a false sense of crisis!) that results in poor decisions.

3. PERT/CPM approaches may be unwieldy for smaller projects. Maintenance of a PERT/CPM system for a project can mean a lot of work for project staff. Organizations that use PERT/CPM typically have a staff dedicated full-time to running a computerized network system. As a project progresses, the PERT/CPM system must be continuously updated. With each update new PERT/CPM charts are cranked out, and new tabular cost and schedule reports generated. It often is not long before the project manager finds himself drowning in a sea of paper. With large, complex projects the generation of a superabundance of paper is one of the prices managers have learned to pay if they wish to keep control over their projects. With smaller projects formal planning and control approaches are not always necessary—they may be a hindrance, in fact, when they detract project staff from doing productive project work.

Assigning Personnel to Tasks

The Human Resource Matrix

People lie at the heart of the project. With complex projects, coordinating the activities of many people can be a major undertaking. Even with smaller projects, assigning people to different tasks may become difficult, particularly when each individual may be working on a number of different projects in a given time interval, as is common in matrix organizations. Clearly the project manager must devote a fair amount of effort to coordinating staff activities. Basic data on manpower requirements can be gleaned from the work breakdown structure.

One approach to linking people to specific tasks is the human resource matrix, depicted in Table 7-3. Here we have three tasks associated with a project and three people assigned to work on these tasks. The matrix shows that both Bob and David work on multiple tasks, while Cheryl works on only one. It also shows who has primary responsibility for each task: Bob is task leader on task A, Cheryl on task B, and David on task C.

While the human resource matrix gives us a good idea of who will be working on what tasks, it tells us nothing of how the workers' time will be

Table 7-3. Human Resource Matrix[a]

Task	Bob	Cheryl	David
A	P		S
B	S	P	S
C			P

[a] P, primary responsibility; S, secondary responsibility.

distributed among the different tasks. This information is contained in the personnel task assignment chart, a Gantt chart pictured in Figure 7-5. Here we see that Cheryl will work continuously on task B, while Bob will work first on task A, then B, and so on, and David will cycle his time on tasks A, B, and C in sequence.

Often, in planning the project, it is useful to know how many people are slated to work on the project on a month-by-month (or day-by-day or week-by-week) basis. Such information is contained in what is called a manpower loading chart, portrayed in Figure 7-6. The basic silhouette of the manpower loading chart reflects times of activity and inactivity in the project. Figure 7-6 shows us that in months 1–3 the project is relatively dormant, but that in months 4 and 5 it will employ a fair number of people. This suggests that the project manager should be braced for a major increase in management challenges and responsibilities after the third month.

Figure 7-5. Personnel task assignments.

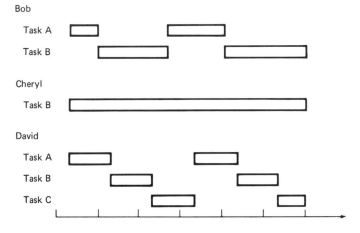

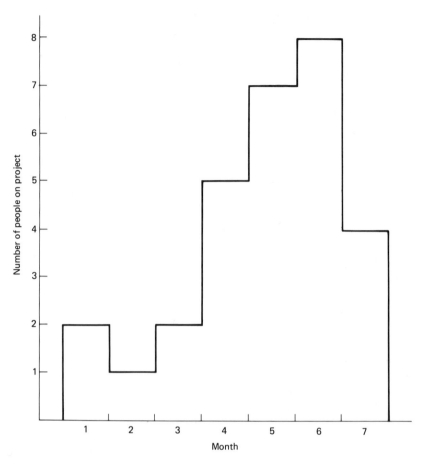

Figure 7-6. Manpower loading chart.

Project Budgeting

Custom Budgeting

A major responsibility of the project manager is developing and adhering to a budget for the project. Often he or she will be rated a success or failure as a project manager according to whether the project comes in under budget, on budget, or over budget. Overshooting the budget can have serious consequences for both the project manager and the organization in which he or she works. Consider that if the project is funded through a contract, a cost overrun may lead to litigation, penalties, and financial losses for the performing organization. If it is funded internally, an overrun may lead to a serious drain of organizational resources.

In view of the importance of budgeting, it is not surprising to find that most organizations focus much of their management attention on the budget. Consequently most organizations have well-developed budgeting techniques that are custom-made for the organization's particular environment and operating style. In this section we will briefly outline some of the basic principles that are common to most organizational approaches to project budgeting.

Component Costs

Projects costs are typically made up of four components: direct labor costs, overhead, fringe benefits, and auxiliary costs. *Direct labor costs* are determined by multiplying the worker's hourly (or monthly) wage by the amount of time that he or she is expected to spend on the project. In most service projects direct labor costs are the largest single component of project cost.

Overhead costs are the typical expenses incurred in maintaining the environment in which the workers function. Included here are the costs of paperclips, other office supplies, the electric bill, rent, and—frequently—secretarial expenses. It should be noted that what might be treated as an overhead expense in one organization may be given different treatment in another. Consider that in an organization that does not typically use secretarial services, secretarial expenses might be included as a direct labor expense. Overhead costs tend to be relatively fixed in relation to direct labor costs. For example, if labor costs increase by 50%, overhead costs similarly tend to increase by 50%.

Fringe benefits are nonsalary benefits derived by the worker from the organization. They include the employer's contribution to the worker's Social Security payments. Depending on the organization, they may also include employer contributions to the worker's health insurance, life insurance, profit sharing plan, stock options, bonuses, university tuition, and so on. Fringe benefit expenses are clearly directly proportional to direct labor costs.

Auxiliary expenses are project-specific expenses that the organization does not incur with any obvious regularity. Project travel expenses, purchases of special equipment, computer time, and report reproduction costs are typical items in this category.

Estimating a budget for a project is closely tied to estimating the amount of labor needed to carry out project tasks. Overhead costs and fringe benefit expenses are linked to direct labor costs, so that if we know what the direct labor costs are, we can readily estimate total project costs, where auxiliary costs have been netted out. If we know what auxiliary costs will be, we have a good estimate of total project costs.

Table 7-4 illustrates a typical estimating procedure for a company whose overhead averages out to be 65% of direct labor costs and whose

Table 7-4. Estimating Project Expenses

Project manager (500 hours at $19 per hour)	$9,500	
Analysts (1,000 hours at $14 per hour)	$14,000	
Technicians (200 hours at $10 per hour)	$2,000	
Total labor		$35,500
Overhead (65% of labor)	$23,075	
Total labor plus overhead		$58,575
Fringes (25% of labor plus overhead)	$14,644	
Subtotal		$73,219
Transportation (4 trips at $60 per trip)	$2,400	
Microcomputers (2 microcomputers at $3,500 each)	$7,000	
Printing and reproduction	$1,000	
Total project expenses		$83,619

fringe benefits average out to be 25% of direct labor costs plus overhead expenses. These overhead and fringe benefit figures are determined by accountants and/or auditors who calculate them from data in the organization's accounting records.

Table 7-4 shows that in the case of our hypothetical company, direct labor, overhead, and fringe benefit expenses are $73,219. This figure turns out to be 2.06 times greater than direct labor costs alone. Thus, in estimating project costs, a project manager can reasonably guess that project costs (excluding auxiliary expenses) will be somewhat more than twice as great as labor costs. Of course, in making the final estimate of total costs, the project manager must include auxiliary costs, which may or may not be substantial, depending on the specific nature of the project.

An unfortunate reality of project management is that as the project is carried out, there is an ever-looming threat that project costs will be exceeded. To cope with this threat it is common practice among project managers to build some "fat" into their cost estimates. One frequently used procedure is to make as realistic an estimate as possible of project costs and then to multiply this estimate by some "fudge factor" in order to take into account unanticipated problems. Doubling realistic estimates is not uncommon. It is interesting to note, however, that even after introducing a fudge factor into the equation, projects frequently bump up against the upper cost limits, suggesting that Parkinson's law is alive and well in project management. It seems that no matter how much you budget for a project, it will not be enough.

Projection of Project Expenditures

In order to have a good sense of how project expenditures will be made over time, it is often helpful to create a week-by-week (or month-by-month) projection of project expenditures. These expenditures will vary

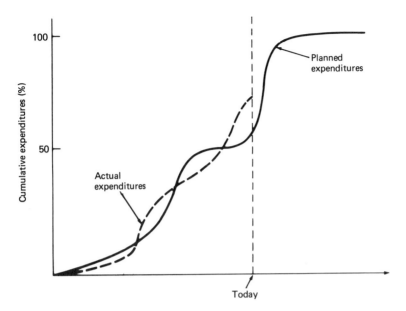

Figure 7-7. Cumulative project expenditures.

from reporting period to reporting period, depending on the level of activity in the project. If one were to plot out these expenditures on a graph, one would be likely to have a jagged chart with peaks and valleys. It is difficult to glance at such charts and make much sense of them because of their irregularities. Consequently, a common practice in making projections of project expenditures is to create a chart of cumulative expenditures. Each month's expenditures are added to the previous month's expenditures, and in this way a smooth nondecreasing curve is generated. These curves are easy to understand at a glance. Figure 7-7 presents such a curve of planned expenditures. It also shows a curve of actual expenditures incurred once the project is underway. It is easy to see from the planned and actual cumulative budget curves those occasions when the project is spending more than planned and those when it is spending less.

Budget Controls

Variances

It is virtually impossible for a project to consume every penny of its budget in exact conformance with the plan. There will always be some deviation from the plan, owing to unanticipated technical developments, personnel shifts, cost changes of procured products, and so on.

In project management these deviations from the plan are called variances. Variances are to be expected. They are not always bad—you can have positive variances (where the project is coming in under budget) as well as negative ones (where the project is over budget). The important thing is not the existence of a variance but, rather, its dimension. In controlling a project budget it is a common practice to determine a threshold level above which variances from the budget should be examined with care. In low-risk, carefully planned projects this threshold level might be quite low; variances of 5–10% of planned expenditures might be flagged and given special attention. In higher-risk, blue sky projects, where project plans are admittedly speculative, higher thresholds may be established, for example, 10–20% of planned expenditures.

Table 7-5 gives an example of how variances can be used in controlling the budget. Table 7-5 portrays a monthly budget report for a small project. The second column of this report, "Amount previously claimed," gives the total value of how much was actually spent on the project (up to, but not including, the month being reported) across the different budget categories (salary, transportation, supplies, etc.). The third column, "Budgeted," shows how much was budgeted for the project for the report month. The fourth column, "Amount claimed this period," gives information on actual expenditures for the report month. The fifth column, "Variance," calculates the difference between budgeted and actual expenditures for the report month; values inside parentheses represent negative variances, and those without parentheses indicate positive variances.

The sixth and seventh columns provide data on budgeted cumulative expenditures (including the reported month) and actual cumulative expenditures (including the reported month), respectively. The last column,

Table 7-5. Financial Controls: Allocation of Monthly Expenditures in Dollars

Expenditure category	Amount previously claimed	Bud- geted	Amount claimed this period	Vari- ance	Cumula- tive total, budgeted	Cumula- tive total, actual	Vari- ance from total
Salary	28,716	1,500	1,716	(216)[a]	30,000	30,432	(432)
Transportation	536	150	0	150	800	536	264
Supply	2,418	300	0	300	4,000	2,418	1,582
Consultants	99	0	0	0	500	99	401
Overhead	17,804	975	1,115	(140)	19,500	18,919	581
Fee	3,965	248	226	22	4,950	4,192	758
Total	53,538	3,173	3,057	116	59,750	56,596	3,154

[a] Amounts in parentheses are negative variances.

"Variance from total," shows the difference between budgeted and actual expenditures. It gives cumulative variances for the project to date.

A quick perusal of Table 7-5 might suggest that things are going pretty well for this project. The total variance for the report month is positive ($116), and the total variance for cumulative expenditures to date is also positive ($3,154), indicating that the project is coming in under budget. However, there are a couple of items in the budget report that warrant closer inspection. Note, for example, the following:

Why is the variance for supplies so large ($1,582 in the last column)?

This positive variance might suggest that project staff have been able to procure supplies at a good price, leading to cost savings for the project. However, it might also suggest that the project schedule is slipping. In this view supply costs are low simply because supplies have not yet been purchased, owing to schedule slippage.

Why has only $99 been expended for consultants when $500 has been budgeted?

On the bright side, cost-conscious project staff may have been able to answer questions through internal resources that otherwise would have required outside expertise. On the negative side, the positive variance for consultant expenditures could be a consequence of schedule slippage.

Is it significant that salary costs have had consistently negative variances (fifth and eighth columns)?

The negative salary variances are small and probably not significant. However, in view of our concerns about schedule slippage, we recognize that it is possible that negative salary variances can become much worse. Furthermore, because salary costs tend to be linked to overhead costs, we may see substantial negative variances for overhead as well.

Cost/Schedule Control System Criteria

This exercise has demonstrated an important lesson in project control; that is, control tools must be considered in relation to each other and not in isolation. By themselves, budget reports (which top management often feels most comfortable in reading) may indicate that all is well with the project, since activities appear to be carried out within budget. However, corresponding schedule reports may show that the project is behind schedule, and that it is simply a matter of time before the budget catches up with the slippage. In recognition of this reality, the U.S. Department of Defense devised an approach to combine budget and schedule information so that they could be looked at in relation to each other. The approach is called the Cost/Schedule Control System Criteria (C/SCSC).

The method of implementation of C/SCSC is too involved to discuss in detail here. Only its rudimentary features will be outlined.

At the heart of C/SCSC are three basic quantities that must be calculated: the budgeted cost of work scheduled (BCWS), the budgeted cost of work performed (BCWP), and the actual cost of work performed (ACWP).

The BCWS is our basic projected budget for undertaking the scheduled activities.

The BCWP takes into account the fact that the work we actually perform may not correspond closely to what we are scheduled to perform. With BCWP we calculate what we would have spent on the project thus far given our actual performance and given our original estimate of what it would cost to carry out the activities we have actually performed.

The ACWP is simply an accounting of what we have actually spent on the project, irrespective of the schedule and planned costs.

With the C/SCSC approach, these three calculations allow us to determine both budget and schedule variances. Budget variances are found by subtracting the ACWP from the BCWP, and schedule variances are calculated by subtracting the BCWP from the BCWS.

Conclusion

The Value of Planning and Control Techniques

Planning and control are two very important management functions. It is difficult to argue against doing a good job in these two areas. However, what is arguable is the extent to which managers should employ sophisticated, elaborate planning and control techniques in carrying out their projects. In this chapter we have only touched on some of the more commonly used techniques, and these represent less than the tip of the iceberg. Operations researchers, for example, have provided us with hundreds of sophisticated approaches that purportedly can make us more effective project managers. The graphical evaluation and review technique (GERT), venture evaluation and review technique (VERT), decision event logical time activity (DELTA), and resource allocation and multiproject scheduling (RAMPS) are only a handful of additional approaches we have not touched on.

After querying more than 200 project managers, we find that outside of the construction industry little use is made not only of the more arcane planning and control techniques, but the more common ones as well. For example, in scheduling projects it appears that most project managers do not go beyond using Gantt charts.

Why is this so? There are a number of answers to this question:

Project managers often have not received training on the use of planning
and control techniques.

Managerial Innovation

Projects are typically headed by individuals who are experts in their field.
Automatic data processing projects are run by automatic data processing
specialists, pharmacy projects by chemists and biologists, legal research
projects by lawyers, and so on. Often people are selected from the ranks
of functional specialists to head projects because of their technical expertise or their demonstrated ability to get things done effectively. Only
rarely do they receive specialized training in managing projects. Their
exposure to many of the planning and control techniques that have
emerged is very light. Consequently, when given project responsibility, they
tend to invent planning and control techniques that seem to be suitable to
their particular circumstances.

The administrative burden of maintaining elaborate planning and control
systems can outweigh the benefits of the systems.

The development and maintenance of sophisticated planning and control systems can demand a substantial amount of staff time. In the development stage detailed plans must be drawn and an elaborate progress
reporting system designed. In the maintenance stage large amounts of
information must be gathered and input into the control system. Once
control reports are generated, the results must be carefully studied. It is
clear that to keep such a system going we might be required to create a
minibureaucracy!

Such elaborate planning and control systems are necessary in large,
complex projects. For example, the only way to keep track of the tens of
thousands of activities necessary to build a nuclear power plant is to
implement sophisticated planning and control procedures. While the administrative burden of these procedures is large in an absolute sense, it
consumes only a small fraction of the total project effort.

With smaller projects the situation may be different. Project staff may
find that they are devoting inordinate amounts of time to jumping through
the hoops required by the planning and control system. Here we may
determine that excessive formal planning and control are detracting from
the effective execution of the project rather than helping it. With smaller
projects planning and control may best be guided by the KISS (keep it
simple, stupid!) principle.

Existing planning and control techniques are not always appropriate to
the specific management requirements of a particular project.

Projects can be undertaken in an overwhelming number of different circumstances: They can be high risk or low risk, long term or short term, state of the art or routine, complex or simple, technical or nontechnical, large or small, technology driven or market driven, performed by the government or carried out by the private sector, contracted out or performed in-house, and so on. Consider that the 8 characteristics just listed can lead to 256 different combinations (2^8 combinations), and that each of these combinations might suggest a different approach to planning and control.

Broad, simple techniques, such as the creation of a work breakdown structure, can apply to all projects, but more specialized approaches (such as the venture evaluation and review technique, or VERT) have narrow applications. Furthermore, a project manager may find that the special circumstances of his or her project may require him or her to tailor-make a new approach to planning and control. To illustrate this point consider the following example.

A project manager in the U.S. Department of Defense (DoD) was given responsibility to head a project to design a new weapons system that ultimately would be manufactured by an outside contractor. From his years of experience in working in the DoD environment, he knew that he would be involved in a fierce battle with other projects competing for limited resources. He decided at the outset that his project plan would be budget driven and that technical considerations would be geared to the DoD budget cycle—typically, projects are carried out the other way around, where the technical plans are first drawn up and then a determination is made as to how the budget cycle fits into the plans. The planning and control system that emerged revolved completely around DoD budget deadlines and meeting their paperwork requirements. Technical milestones were subordinated to these (much to the chagrin of the technical staff, who saw budgetary paperwork requirements as so much bureaucratic busywork). A sophisticated planning and control mechanism evolved that had little relation to existing planning and control packages. The 5-year project was completed only 2 weeks behind schedule! Most competing projects fell by the wayside. In assessing the reasons for the success of his project, the manager gave primary credit to the tailor-made planning and control system that he and his staff developed.

As a final word to this chapter, it should be emphasized that the introduction of the microcomputer into the project management environment will have a dramatic impact on how projects get carried out. Whereas in the past planning and control have been heavily dependent upon centralized computer facilities (e.g., for budgetary data, to carry out PERT/CPM analyses), the microcomputer offers the project staff unprecedented autonomy in carrying out their tasks.

Furthermore, a major emphasis in the development of software for microcomputers is on user friendliness, enabling non-computer professionals to use the computer in sophisticated ways. As user-friendly project management software is developed, it is plausible that sophisticated planning and control techniques that are presently unwieldy will be routinely employed.

CHAPTER EIGHT

Computers in Project Management*

Introduction

Computers in Project Management

Computer-based information systems have been used to aid the management of very large projects since the development of network-based management systems in the late 1950s. Such networking techniques as PERT (Program Evaluation and Review Technique) and CPM (Critical Path Method) were among those project management tools most often implemented in computer-based systems. In the 1960s and early 1970s, when computer costs were still relatively high, most computer vendors provided some form of network-based scheduling software with their systems. When the project manager turned to such systems, it was usually because manual computation of large schedule networks was simply infeasible. With a few exceptions, networking and some associated scheduling and resource allocation techniques were the only computer-based project management tools available. While these systems did perform an otherwise impossible task, they were often controlled by the comptroller or data processing department and were almost exclusively batch oriented, leaving them both physically and organizationally isolated from the user. Computer terminals were a rarity and users were generally required to go to the computer to submit their jobs for processing. If errors were detected, another trip to the computer and another 12- to 24-hour wait for output was the norm. Inputs had to be coded onto worksheets and then

---

* This chapter was submitted by Richard M. Armour, a project management consultant in the Washington, DC, area.

keypunched—all of which cost money and resulted in turnaround times being measured in weeks. Despite these and many other barriers, computer-based project management information systems have come into wide use and provide today's project manager with a wide range of information and services at a surprisingly low cost. This chapter provides a brief discussion of the rapidly evolving management information systems technology from a project management perspective. The following sections address the concepts behind such systems, available features and capabilities, and key factors to successful implementation.[1-3]

Project Management Information Systems

For our discussion the term *project management information system* (PMIS) refers to any computer-based information system providing decision support tools and services primarily to a project manager and his staff. While this is admittedly not a rigorous definition, we shall make some refinements as the concept of PMIS is developed. Information systems common to the corporate environment, such as payroll, accounting, personnel management, and inventory control, may support the project manager, but he or she is not their primary user. These information systems usually fall under the responsibility of specific functional managers. They are often sources of information for the project manager and frequently will require his or her inputs, but they are not "his" systems. The PMIS, on the other hand, is focused on supporting the project management function. A PMIS might include a cost accounting system if that system primarily supported the project manager or his or her staff. The configuration of a PMIS is not necessarily limited to a central mainframe computer. While a PMIS might consist of a set of computer programs (software) and a data base on a central computer, it might also be a separate computer system complete with communications and remote sites. Since the early 1970s the nature of PMIS has changed radically. The rapid advance of information technology coupled with the increasingly complex needs of project management has spawned a new generation of software and hardware products that offer a wide variety of revolutionary functional capabilities and implementation alternatives. In addition to the traditional network-based scheduling techniques these new systems provide a more dynamic and responsive environment and are better prepared to meet the ad hoc information needs of today's project manager.

PMIS Concepts and Experience

Objectives in Applying PMIS

There are numerous statements of objectives for PMIS-type systems in the literature and few criteria for measuring the success of such systems. Archibald and Villoria[4] noted the common objective for management information systems: "to provide the manager at each level with the information needed to make decisions related to his or her responsibilities." Gray[5] provides a slightly more refined objective: "to provide management with timely and meaningful information for decision making." Finally, Goodman and Love[6] articulate what is, perhaps, the most refined objective: "[to ensure] the right information is provided, in the right amount, to the right persons, at the right time." With these objectives in mind we can define criteria by which a project manager can evaluate the effectiveness of a potential or extant PMIS.

Are PMIS Products Used? Do they affect the outcome of the project manager's decision process? Do they enhance the PM's confidence in his or her decisions? Most important, do they improve the quality of these decisions? And can the system answer "what if", "should I", and "what" (e.g., "What cost centers are over budget?", etc.) questions?

Are PMIS Products of High Quality? Are they accurate, current, and timely? Are products based on properly selected, sorted, and summarized data satisfying the manager's essential information requirements? Or, in other words, does the system provide the user with one page of the right information or hundreds of pages of data in which he or she must find the right information? Are PMIS products provided in a form suitable for communication to senior management and customers (e.g., graphics, "key item" reporting, etc.)?

Is the PMIS Cost Competitive? How do PMIS acquisition and operation costs compare to those of other systems and other approaches to developing the required information? What is the relative value of the information and decision support services the system provides?

Many of these questions imply qualitative evaluation on the part of the project manager, especially in evaluating a potential system. These criteria also imply certain capabilities that are critical to the successful implementation of a PMIS. The following sections outline some of the techniques and guidelines for ensuring that those capabilities are considered when implementing a PMIS.

Role of the PMIS

Automated processing systems capabilities and management's requirements for data, information, and intelligence can be viewed as a three-tier setup concept for distinguishing between systems that provide data for operationally oriented applications and those which generate information for management decisions. A number of authors, notably Mandel[7] and Schutt and Ingalls[8], have presented models of the information or knowledge hierarchy that approximate this concept. Although the terminology and delineation of boundaries may vary, the concept is the same: The knowledge requirements of management vary according to the level of decision making being supported, and automated knowledge systems must provide the type of knowledge (data, information, or intelligence) needed at each level. The "data processing" systems at the lower level focus on the performance of clerical tasks that support operational management decisions. These systems are data oriented, tend to handle large volumes of work, and are usually transaction driven. They are not usually designed to respond to inquiries but, rather, to provide a predetermined set of periodic reports on the day-to-day status and application of resources. Examples of "data processing" systems would include payroll, electronic funds transfer, billing, and inventory control applications. The "information" systems at the middle level focus on providing management with the information (data filtered, reorganized, and summarized to meet the manager's specific need) to support tactical decision making. Such "tactical" activities include planning working capital, formulating budgets, making short-term forecasts, administering personnel, and planning production runs. The output of the information systems is less voluminous than that of the data systems and is more tailored to the decision needs of managers. The top, or "strategic," level is only now beginning to make wide use of computer-based systems often termed decision support systems. These systems are structured to address the ad hoc "what if" and "should I" questions of senior managers. They typically support the executive level and are driven by the immediate decision needs of the manager. Such systems are suited to tasks like strategic planning, forecasting analysis, and negotiation planning in an interactive and tailored environment. They allow the manager to define the question at hand instead of forcing on him or her a predefined set of reports and analyses. Decision support systems technology is clearly in its infancy, and advances in expert systems and artificial intelligence are certain to bring rapid growth in decision support systems capabilities in the next few years.

Applying this three-tier approach of knowledge systems to the project management environment requires a review of the trends in the project manager's knowledge, needs, and decision-making processes. The project concept is generally applied to the management of activities when they (1) are a one-time technical effort, (2) are time and cost limited, and (3) involve a complex operation, product, or system development with distinct goals and objectives.[9] These characteristics make the project management arena a dynamic and often unpredictable environment in which to fulfill knowledge requirements. Decision processes and their requirements for information tend to change with each phase of the project life cycle, and completely new requirements may appear, since the project may represent the first time a given task has been attempted.

Many of the manager's knowledge requirements are temporary or ad hoc in nature, may require satisfaction within hours, and may never arise again. Others last through a particular phase of the project life cycle and then disappear. The ever-present complexity of project management's tasks also requires a high level of integration between what are considered by line managers to be separate functional areas. The project manager, especially in matrixed organizations, plays a major role as integrator of resources, schedules, and technical capabilities to achieve the project's objectives. To perform this role, he or she must have access to an integrated and cohesive view of knowledge about the project. And, of course, the manager needs to evaluate the impacts of alternative courses of action on the project from a cost, schedule, and technical perspective before decisions are made (i.e., be able to ask "what if" questions—and get the answers). The PMIS can and should address these needs through the integrated application of state of the art computer hardware and software technologies.

The PMIS cuts across all three levels of the three-tier knowledge concept, but focuses primarily on the information and intelligence levels. The data level functions are typically performed by extant functional systems that may provide interfaces to the PMIS but are not operated in primary support of the project. Even the few data level functions the PMIS might entail are provided to support the effective operation of the higher-level functions that provide the project manager with the required decision support services. This integrated and flexible "function of knowledge" can offer many benefits to the project manager, but there are equally as many pitfalls about which the manager should be concerned.

Potential Benefits of PMIS Implementation

Economy. Doing more with less is probably the most common justification for using computers. In the past only very large repetitive tasks could be economically automated. Today the rapidly expanding capabilities and falling costs of computer technology have made the automation of smaller and more specialized jobs economically feasible. For the project manager PMIS implementation offers both direct and indirect economies. Direct economies can be enjoyed, since automation provides a cost-effective alternative to manual methods for the collection, storage, control, and dissemination of the large volumes of cost, schedule, and technical information characteristic of most projects. Indirect economies are derived by the anticipated improvement in management decisions given the availability of PMIS services to support the project manager. While most automation justifications focus on the direct economies (because they are readily identifiable), the indirect economies are typically much more significant but more difficult to quantify. However, given the low cost of computer technology today, virtually any medium- to large-scale project should realize substantial direct economies from PMIS implementation.

Responsiveness. The speed of computers has long been one of their primary advantages over manual techniques. In the project environment constant revision and change are the norm. The PMIS can provide revised schedules, budgets, and other types of reports within hours versus the days and weeks required with manual methods. Even when the size of an original project data base is small, say, 1,000 activities and associated cost and administrative information, frequent changes to the schedule can easily require thousands of person-hours to evaluate and incorporate. Once automated, such data bases can be quickly revised and reanalyzed.[10]

Improved Management Visibility. Perhaps the most valuable benefit of a PMIS is the enhanced visibility the system provides to project managers at all levels. Through "key item reporting" (i.e., reporting on only those areas or situations in which the manager is interested), exception reporting and other automated interpretive techniques, the PMIS can quickly and accurately perform reviews of information and make rudimentary decisions about what is important and what deserves human attention.[11] The uniformity and legibility of project reports is an often undervalued or overlooked benefit of automation. Typically project staffs are pressed for time and clerical support resources are scarce. Consequently, manually prepared reports may or may not be typewritten and are often provided in inconsistent formats, frequently resulting in errors, omissions, and miscommunications. The PMIS provides a solution to these problems and does not require clerical support every time a report is prepared.[12] The availability of a PMIS capability provides the project manager with an economical, accurate, and responsive tool for asking "what if" types of questions. Managers having such tools available tend to use them, especially if the cost per execution is low and response times are short. The result can be a better-informed manager and, accordingly, better management decisions.[13] Another important aspect of PMIS is the multiproject view of resource data that can detect and identify resource conflicts between various projects and even provide alternative scheduling solutions.[14] In most organizations extant management information systems tend to be functionally oriented (i.e., financial, production, engineering, personnel). The PMIS provides the project manager with an integrated and interrelated view of data derived from all of the pertinent functional areas. This integrated approach to the collection and management of project information allows the project manager to fulfill his or her role as the master schedule coordinator, cost accountant, technical integrator, and resource allocator for the project. The central concept of project management (i.e., put someone in charge of meeting specific time, cost, and performance goals and provide the resources necessary to do the job) requires a project view rather than a functional view of management information. The PMIS capability provides this important perspective and allows the project manager to adequately assess and rank impacts by priority in the overall project in addition to specific functional areas.

Accuracy. Computers are inherently accurate and precise in their manipulation and reporting of information. However, the information that comes out of an automated system is only as good as that which goes in. A great deal of work has been done to improve the end-to-end accuracy of computer-based systems by enhancing their ability to tolerate, detect, and even correct erroneous information. While computers are extremely accurate devices, the old principle of garbage in, garbage out still plagues many state of the art computer systems. Notwithstanding the problems of data input quality, the inherent accuracy of digital electronic technology and the editing, validation, and error-checking techniques now available have substantially increased the accuracy of the PMIS to far outstrip that of manual techniques.[15]

Reduced Clerical Workload. Use of manual project control techniques invariably requires the application of skilled project management specialists and clerical personnel to perform thousands of redundant calculations and track and control the accuracy, currency, and status of massive amounts of data elements while constantly making revisions and changes. The impacts of such a situation on job satisfaction and personnel turnover are obvious and costly. In addition, managers must spend more of their time and energy on the details of performing project planning and control rather than on actually planning and controlling the project. The implementation of PMIS capabilities changes the focus of the manager to managing the project, instead of managing the project management process. The PMIS relieves the manager of the calculations, sorting, selecting, categorizing, and summarizing tasks that take so much time in the manual environment. Using PMIS, the manager is able to quickly assess the impacts of changes, identify trends, forecast the course of the project, and make decisions accordingly.[16,17]

Forced Planning. One synergism derived from the combination in the PMIS of networking and automation is the tendency to force early planning on the part of the project management staff. Many managers view networking as primarily a control tool, but perhaps its most valuable benefit is the ability to document and therefore force planning. When combined with the accuracy and rapid response of automation, networking quickly brings to light gaps and inconsistencies in early plans and highlights areas that deserve management attention. As Matthews[18] points out, "the critical value of networking is [that] it drives the planning process, providing the framework for systematic disciplined planning."

Ability to Manage Complexity. The sophistication, complexity, and sheer size of many projects dictate the use of computers to plan and control the data, actions, resources, schedules, budgets, and performance goals of the project. The trend in defense acquisitions toward more fixed priced contracts, the use of liquidated damages clauses in contracts, and increasing regulatory requirements and constraints all point to more controls and more complexity in project management. For "megaprojects" such as major defense systems developments and nuclear power plant construction, the time frame for managing, planning, and implementing the program may be 10 years or more. The data associated with such efforts is staggering: 500 specifications, 5,000 drawings, 500,000 design documents, 100,000 vendor drawings, and possibly 30 million pieces of paper in all, with most requiring frequent revision. Also consider the dozens of contractors involved and the hundreds of thousands of person-hours usually expended. Automated support of such projects is virtually mandated if the job is to ever get planned, let alone be completed.[19]

Cautions and Pitfalls of PMIS Applications

As discussed above, the technology offers the potential for tremendous benefits to the project management organization that effectively applies PMIS capabilities. However, the literature and experience show that there are a number of serious problems that can severely reduce the effectiveness of a PMIS. The emerging nature of information technology, the complexity of software selection and management, the tendencies of management, and the difficulties of obtaining adequate support are all major problem areas in implementing a PMIS.

Emerging Technology and Marketplace. Just a few years ago not many managers outside the data processing or electrical engineering fields were familiar with computer technology.[20] While the proliferation of computer technology into virtually every part of modern life has substantially reduced the severity of this problem, many managers still misunderstand computer capabilities and are uncomfortable with relying on automated systems for critical management functions. Consequently, there remains a requirement to educate project, functional, and senior managers about current PMIS technology and how it can be employed. Two related factors have aggravated this problem and combined to retard the exploitation of existing PMIS technology: (1) the diverse terminology and often unreliable claims of commercial vendors selling PMIS technology and (2) the lack of substantial amounts of quality literature on the subject of PMIS technology. These difficulties are rapidly disappearing owing to the efforts of organizations such as the Project Management Institute, which has supported several published surveys of available PMIS technology and has contributed to the standardization of PMIS terminology. The "sales pitches" for specific products will always be with us, but as managers have more access to objective and detailed material about PMIS technology, they will be better prepared to analyze their requirements and seek adequate solutions in the marketplace.

Complexity of Software. Software is the essence of every computer-based system's functional capability and has been a problem since the first electronic digital computers were developed in the 1940s. While computer hardware technology has moved at the speed of light in the last few decades, software technology has been moving at the speed of sound. In the past this mismatch in technical advancement has resulted in flexibility and performance problems for many types of computer systems. Inflexible software was unable to satisfy the unique information requirements of individual project managers and it could not be economically modified or upgraded.[21,22] However, today a number of software technology advances, including flexible report writers, fourth-generation nonprocedural languages, and data base management systems, are addressing these long-standing problems by providing the user with fast and economical methods for changing and enhancing PMIS functional capabilities.

Management Tendencies. The responsiveness of a PMIS is a major consideration in determining its effectiveness and acceptance by the end user. Management has often implemented PMIS capabilities with the technical capacity to provide excellent responsiveness, but allowed administrative procedures or organizational placement to severely limit the system's responsiveness to the end users.[23] To the user an unresponsive PMIS is a resource-consuming burden instead of a tool for aiding in the management task. If the user must go through intermediaries to gain access to the PMIS or if availability is limited by physical location, operating hours, or inadequate capacity, then the PMIS will not be effectively employed. Management also tends to improperly use the outputs of the PMIS to place blame for project problems and slips. This use of the system makes middle management reluctant to support the PMIS with the valid and timely data inputs that it must have to operate effectively. In addition, many managers place undue emphasis on the network itself instead of concentrating on the products and analyses that can be derived from the schedule network. Taken alone, the network is not an effective management tool, and this overemphasis reduces the effectiveness of the PMIS capability.[24] Finally, management must establish and maintain a regular and carefully controlled update procedure to keep the network and other elements of the project data base current. Without careful attention to the currency of the data base, the PMIS will quickly become out of date and lose credibility with the managers who must use it. Management's responsibility in PMIS implementation is to become educated on the proper uses of the PMIS, ensure a well-planned implementation effort, emphasize the need for continuous maintenance of the project data bases, and ensure a high level of accessibility for the end users.

Support Services. Any PMIS, whether developed in-house, procured from a vendor, or acquired as a service, requires continuous support services to be effective. Initially such support usually takes the form of user training on the concepts and capabilities of the system. Training should be followed up with up-to-date documentation to include operations manuals, user manuals, tutorials, and system references. In addition, some sort of "hot line" service should be available to answer user questions and provide technical assistance when difficulties arise. The lack of such support has been a problem in many systems (especially those developed in-house) and must be addressed early in the PMIS implementation.[25]

When Should Computers Be Used?

There are many factors that have been proposed as criteria to aid the manager in deciding when to employ computer-based systems. Detailed cost/benefit analysis, the number of activities in the network, the complexity of the network, the duration of the project, and the frequency of reporting requirements are most notable in the literature.[26-28] Drastic reductions in the cost of purchasing and operating computer hardware coupled with the continuous growth in computer performance have nullified most of the economic assumptions upon which these criteria were based. Today the question should perhaps be rephrased from *When* should computers be used? to *How* should computers be used? With the advent of microcomputers in their various forms (home computers, personal computers, intelligent work stations, supermicrocomputers, and even portable computers), substantial PMIS capabilities can be acquired and employed for a few thousand dollars. As shown in the following sections, these advances in computer technology have provided the project manager with a wide range of scale and function in PMIS package. The traditional decision criteria rarely apply except for the smallest of projects. If the project warrants use of PERT or CPM network-based scheduling, then the economic and technical feasibility of PMIS application in some form is virtually assured.

PMIS Technology

Overview of PMIS Functions

The advancing information technology and increased use of project management in new industries outside of construction and defense systems development have encouraged entry of many PMIS products into the market in the last several years. Some of these products are software packages and others are complete sets of hardware, software, and support services. They typically fall into one of two categories: the traditional group of main-frame-based software packages or the new generation of micro/minicomputer-based systems and software packages. Other products are offered as teleprocessing services. However, despite the diversity of products available, most can be viewed as some subset of the PMIS functional architecture shown in Figure 8-1. The functional architecture will serve as the framework for our discussion of the current technology and associated requirements considerations in the following sections. The architecture represents an "ideal" set of PMIS features capable of satisfying the most demanding requirements. There are few, if any, systems that provide all of the features discussed and few project managers who need all these features. However, taken in the aggregate, these features represent a comprehensive definition of the functions that should be considered in implementing a PMIS and the capabilities which are available in the PMIS marketplace. The architecture is functionally oriented and

Figure 8-1. Project management information system architecture.

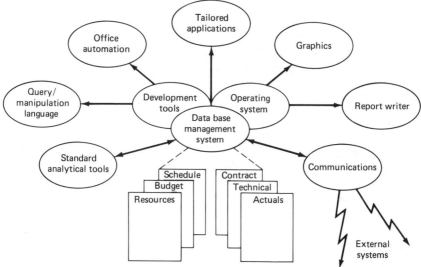

could be implemented on virtually any hardware configuration with the ability to support graphics, communications, and a state of the art operating system. The operating system (O/S), data base management system (DBMS), and the development tools form a set of core functions needed to support the rest of the architecture. Some of the functions such as the query/manipulation language and the report writer are often, but not always, provided as part of a DBMS. They are viewed as distinct functions because they are considered critical to the overall ability of the PMIS to be responsive to ad hoc demands of the project management staff for new or temporary information reporting. Communications, the analytical tools, graphics, and office automation functions are required in many applications and provided by numerous products on the market. The following sections discuss each function in the architecture in terms of features available, desirable characteristics, and issues to consider when reviewing requirements.

Core Functions

The major core functions are shown in Figure 8-2. They include the operating system, the data base management system, and the software development tools as described below.

Figure 8-2. Project management information system basic system functions.

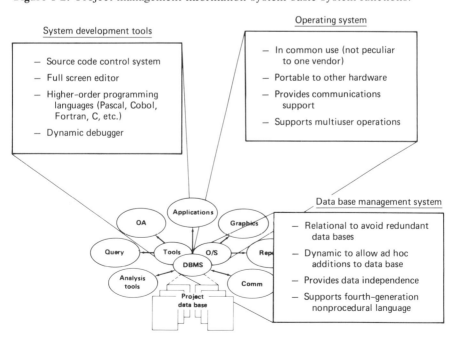

Operating System.   The operating system of a computer performs the housekeeping and control functions necessary to make a computer system run. This operating system software can have a substantial impact on the functional capabilities that can be implemented on the computer system and can severely limit the number of potential applications software packages which may be hosted (installed) on the system. The choice of an operating system is therefore critical and deserves careful consideration. Any operating system chosen to support a PMIS implementation should (1) be relatively standard in the industry, (2) be portable to other vendor's computer systems, (3) provide comprehensive communications support, and (4) support multiple users. Traditionally, the choice of what operating system was to be used in a given application was driven by the computer hardware on which the application was to be hosted, since computer vendors provided only one or in some cases several unique and proprietary operating systems for use with their hardware. However, today many micro- and minicomputer systems vendors offer a choice of operating systems that are becoming de facto standards in the industry. Such "standard" systems include Digital Research's CP/M (Control Program for Microcomputers) and Microsoft Corp's MS-DOS (Microsoft Disk Operating System) for microcomputers and AT&T's UNIX for micro- and minicomputers. The status these systems hold as "standards" makes them quite desirable as a basis for PMIS implementation. In the last few years hundreds of software vendors have sprung up, marketing thousands of very capable software products for these standard operating systems. Applications running under one of these standard O/Ss can be moved (or "ported") to any other computer running the same O/S with very little effort. In the aftermath of the Bell System breakup, the new AT&T has become extremely aggressive in marketing their Bell Laboratories-developed UNIX operation system, which is now available on hundreds of computer models. UNIX offers the user a robust set of built-in functions and a high level of portability, making it an excellent choice for virtually any PMIS application. Communications support is another area where substantial attention should be provided to ensure that the PMIS can interface with the major communications protocols found on most other systems. In most PMIS applications the operating system should also support multiple users and multiple tasks per user; however, in some personal computer-based applications, single user support can be adequate if a local area network or some other easily expandable interface is also available. The operating system is a critical element of the "core" functions of the model PMIS capability and should be given careful consideration when configuring a PMIS.

Data Base Management System.   The DBMS products now available on the market represent a major step in the advance of computer software technology. These packages provide the applications developer and user with many powerful capabilities and substantially reduce the cost and complexity of developing and managing large data base-oriented systems. The DBMS selected as the basis for a PMIS capability should (1) be relational to reduce data redundancy and allow flexibility in ad hoc data query and manipulation, (2) be dynamic to allow quick additions and modifications to the data base structure, (3) provide data independence to free the user and software designer from the details of data management and data base structure, (4) support a fourth-generation nonprocedural data manipulation/query language, (5) provide a high-order language interface to support the development of applications based on the DBMS using common computer languages such as Cobol, Fortran, Pascal, and C, and (6) support transaction logging to provide accountability and recovery capabilities for the data base. Many of these features are available in a number of existing DBMS products and have already been implemented in conjunction with PMIS capabilities. The resulting systems provide a flexible and dynamic data management environment where the user can quickly and easily perform complex queries and manipulations of project data on an ad hoc basis. Such capabilities directly address the system deficiencies that have been major obstacles to the further use of computers in project management and have the potential to radically change the ways in which managers use and interface with project management information systems. The cost of DBMS packages that satisfy these requirements can range from $1,000 to $100,000, depending on the vendor involved, the type of technical support included, and the type of computer on which the DBMS will be operated. The DBMS function is the single most critical element in the entire PMIS structure in assuring that the user has effective yet flexible access to the project data base and that new project management functions can be added to the system without massive changes.[29]

Software Development Tools. For the user planning to conduct any software development a set of software development tools should be considered as part of the PMIS. These tools usually include compilers for the various standard high-order languages, a source code control system to maintain configuration control over the software being developed, various editing and text file manipulation functions to facilitate easy programmer access to the software, and a dynamic debugger to allow for real-time monitoring of the software while it is running. These functions provide a development environment where most of the bookkeeping and clerical work required to manage large developments is automated, freeing the programmer to develop software instead of managing the details of file structures, version numbers, and deficiency tracking. While such functions are standard on some computers, they are not available on many others, so the user must review the need for in-house software development before evaluating PMIS capabilities.

Analytical Tools

For most applications the standard analytical tools (see Figure 8-3) include network scheduling analysis, resource scheduling, cost performance reporting, and in some cases statistical modeling.

Network Analysis.   There are several types of network-based management systems, including PERT and CPM. If networking is a required function (as it usually is), the user should determine which type of networking the PMIS must support. Many systems support activity-based, event-based, and probabilistic networking methodologies. Some systems support only one type. PERT employs optimistic, pessimistic, and most likely durations for each activity to incorporate risk and schedule uncertainty. If the project or projects to be supported involve substantial schedule uncertainty, then PERT or some other risk-oriented networking technique may be required. For more stable and more accurately estimated

Figure 8-3. Project management information system standard analytical tools.

Network-based scheduling

- PERT and CPM methods
- Resource loading allowed
- Multiple starts/finishes
- User-defined calendars
- Expansion capability
- Track progress with actuals
- On-line editing and error checking
- Time/cost trade-off functions

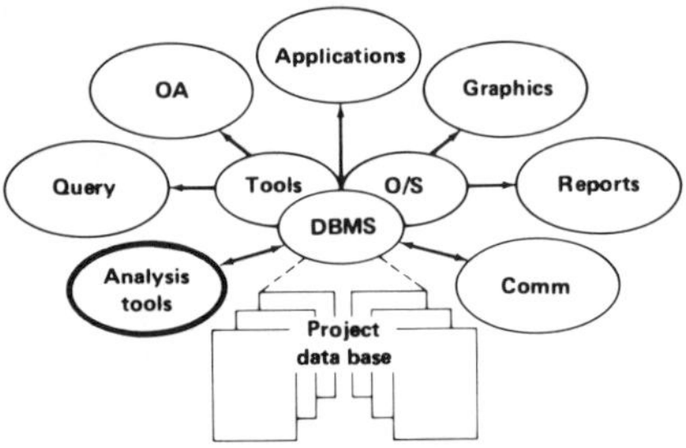

Cost performance reporting

- Budget cost by WBS element
- Interface with network and resources
- Collect actual cost and schedule data
- Roll up costs into WBS levels
- Track BCWS, BCWP, and ACWP
- Compute cost and schedule variances
- Use variance trends to estimate future performance

Resource management

- Resource loading in network
- Flexible resource availability definition
- Time- and resource-limited scheduling
- Scheduling of selected resources
- User-definable scheduling priorities
- Grouped and teamed resources
- Consumable resources and event-driven availability
- Flexible interface for integration with material and equipment control

projects (e.g., construction) CPM arrow or precedence diagramming techniques are appropriate. Both techniques have been used successfully and, despite much discussion of their relative merits, the choice seems to be mostly based on personal preference. However, precedence is mathematically more precise and allows the user to exercise much more control over the relationships between activities in the schedule. Some systems handle both methods, and this feature is clearly desirable if multiple projects (and managers) are to be supported. Beyond the networking technique, the next most critical feature is the maximum capacity (in numbers of activities per network) of each network. The project manager should be extremely conservative (i.e., require much more capacity than is anticipated), since expanding the maximum may be impossible or extremely expensive. It is critical that the networking function support user-defined calendars and provide for specification of multiple starts and finishes. In addition, the network should allow separate starting and completion dates for any activity in the schedule. Event code schemes must also be considered. Many networking packages use sequential or topological event codes that severely limit the user's flexibility in setting up and modifying the network. Random event codes allow almost complete user freedom to assign numbers and, in many cases, letters to each event code. Figures 8-4 and 8-5 are adapted from Webster's *1982 Survey of Project Management Software Packages* and provides an excellent template for preliminary review of PMIS requirements in the areas of network scheduling and resource management. For additional considerations see Archibald and Villoria,[30] Reynaud,[31] and Webster.[32]

Resource Management. The resource allocation and scheduling functions are required if the project manager desires to (1) ensure that critical manpower, equipment, facility, and material resources are not overloaded, (2) have access to summarized manpower and equipment loading for the project, or (3) generate cost estimates based on assigned manpower, material, equipment, and services resources. There are three major elements to most resource scheduling functions: (1) the resource loading information that is usually entered into a schedule network, (2) the resource availability information, and (3) the resource allocation algorithm(s) being used. Primary capacities to be considered include the maximum number of resources per activity and the maximum number of resource types per network. Some PMIS packages allow no more than five resources per activity, which is inadequate for many project situations. There are two fundamental resource scheduling techniques or algorithms in common use: resource-limited scheduling and time-limited scheduling. Most systems provide both. Time-limited scheduling assumes that the late schedule and target completion dates in the network are inviolate and attempts to allocate resources to activities without stretching the schedule beyond the target completion date(s). The result of this type of analysis

182

A. CAPACITY (maximums)
Activities per network _____
Precedence relations/activity _____ ./network _____
Number of characters: /act. ID_____, /event ID_____
/act. desc._____, /event desc. _____

B. INPUT FEATURES
Format: □ free, □ fixed
Device: □ card, □ tape, □ terminal
Data entry modes: □ command driven, □ menu driven,
□ prompting, □ full screen edit,
□ cross system automated transfer
Network generator: □ no, □ yes;
□ Standard subnets on file
□ Network segment replication
Updating: □ total record input, □ data element input
Turnaround documents: □ no, □ yes: how many?-
Accepted data elements: □ % complete,
□ remaining duration, □ revised duration
Dates: □ actual, □ estimated, □ planned
Appended records: □ work list to an activity
Others: □ _____
□ _____

C. EDITING FEATURES (see below*)

	a	b	c	d	e	f
Loop	□	□	□	□	□	□
Hanging event/node:	□	□	□	□	□	□
Repeated event/activity:	□	□	□	□	□	□
Out of range data:	□	□	□	□	□	□
Noncompleted predecessor:	□	□	□	□	□	□

*a, detection; b, identification; c, post to suspense
file; d, reject; e, warn; f, continue processing
How many error types are checked for?_____
Can user specify action to be taken by error type?
□ no, □ yes — □ by run, □ by project,
□ at installation level

D. OUTPUT FEATURES
Data elements per activity:
□ act. ID, □ act. desc, □ event ID, □ event desc.
Start: □ early, □ late, □ directed, □ sched'd, □ actual
Finish: □ early, □ late, □ directed, □ sched'd, □ actual
Slack: □ total, □ free, □ independent
□ Current duration, □ original duration,
□ WBS elem., □ responsibility, □ type of work
□ Location of work
Other: □ _____
□ _____
□ _____
Reports:
Standard, number of _____
User defined: □ no, □ yes
Administrative: □ master file, □ update transactions
Languages: □ English, □ French, □ German,
□ Spanish, □ other _____
By slack: □ increasing, □ decreasing, □ slack path,
□ slippage — □ last run, □ base-line plan
On-line queries: □ standard only, □ custom.
Sort records: max. number of data elements that
can be sorted at one time? _____
Report generator: □ no, □ yes
□ Batch only, □ on-line — □ real time, □ batch
□ Number of — Operators?_____ Conditionals?_____
□ Non-DP staff usage, □ DP staff usage only
Package name _____
Vendor _____

E. NETWORK NOTATION
AOA — Orientation: □ activity, □ event,
(Arrow) Event ID: □ numeric, □ alpha/numeric
AON — Logic: □ followers, □ predecessors
(PDM) Node ID: □ numeric, □ alpha/numeric
Overlap: □ S-S, □ S-F, □ F-S, □ F-F
□ negative amounts
Event/node coding: □ random,
□ sequential (topological)
Multiple — □ starts, □ finishes
Milestones: □ no, □ yes — levels _____
Hammocks: □ no, □ yes — types _____

F. CALENDAR
Span: years
Multiple calendars: □ no, □ yes, number/project
Units: Months Weeks Days Hours — Mixed
Input---- □ □ □ □ □ □
Internal- □ □ □ □ □ □
Output-- □ □ □ □ □ □
Can calendar units be changed within a run? □ no, □ yes
Variable workday definition: □ no, □ yes
Variable workweek definition: □ no, □ yes
Holidays: □ standard, □ user defined
Other days: □ Sat., □ Sun., □ other nonwork

G. PROCESSING FEATURES
Operating mode: □ batch, □ on-line
Interactive: □ full, □ limited; □ help messages
Mixed mode (AOA & AON): □ no, □ yes
Directed/target dates: □ no, □ yes
Starts: □ beginning activities only, □ any
Finishes: □ ending activities only, □ any
Slack calculations: □ total, □ free, □ independent
□ negative
Multiproject calculations: □ no, □ yes
Processing: □ serial, □ parallel, □ user choice
Number of networks per run? _____
Number of interfaces per run?_____
Summary network: □ automatic generation
□ Posted to predesignated activities
Simulation/modeling available: □ no, □ yes
□ Alters temporary file, □ alters master file
Uncertainty recognition: □ no, □ yes
PERT: □ no, □ yes, □ conventional, □ Monte Carlo
Distribution: □ beta, □ other _____
'a' to 'b': □ 99%, □ 95%, □ other
Special features: _____

DCPM: □ no, □ yes
Special features: _____

GERTS: □ no, □ yes
Special features: _____

TIME/COST TRADE-OFF: □ no, □ yes
Cost function: □ linear, □ piecewise linear,
□ curve linear --- □ concave, □ convex, □ both
Algorithm: □ heuristic, □ linear programming,
□ other Analytical Optimum
Special features: _____

Figure 8-4. Network analysis features.

H. GRAPHIC OUTPUT
Network plotting:
  AOA network: □ char. printer, □ pen plotter
    Max. activities/plot?_____, cost/act._____
  AON network: □ char. printer, □ pen plotter
    Max. activities/plot?_____cost act._____
  Translation: □ AOA to AON, □ AON to AOA
  Scale control: □ horiz. (time), □ vert. (spacing)
  Horizontal banding/grouping: □ no, □ yes
  Sheet size: Char. printer_____
              Pen plotter_____
  Pagination: □ Multipanel plots (paste up)
              □ Multisheet plots (stand alone)
              □ Off-sheet interfaces
              □ Manual, □ automated
Gantt chart:
  □ Char. printer, □ pen plotter
  Max. activities/plot?_____, cost/act._____
  Horizontal banding/grouping: □ no, □ yes
Other graphics:
  □ Pie charts
  □ Other _____

I. PERSONNEL TRAINING/EXPERIENCE
   REQUIREMENTS
Minimum prior training/experience required to assure
successful implementation — need not be only one
person.
Education: Degree - High School, some college,
                    bachelors, masters, PhD
           Area   Arts, science, managem't
                  engineer'g, computer sc.
Experience: Computer - Programming course
                       Jr. programmer
                       Sr. programmer
                       Systems software prog'r
       Mgt. systems - Systems course
                      Jr. systems analyst
                      Sr. systems analyst
    Project manager - No previous
                      Some prior
                      Considerable
                      Extensive
            Other - _____
Training
  No charge for_____sessions,_____persons
  Fee basis: $_____/session, $_____/person
Time for a non-DP person, unfamiliar with your
package but with previous networking experience to:
  Achieve useful results?_____weeks. Comments:_____
  _____
  □ Estimated, □ based on actual experience
  Use full capabilities of system?_____weeks.
  Comments: _____
  _____
  _____

M. SPECIAL COMMENTS
Five most important features of package:
1._____
2._____
3._____
4._____
5._____
Five most important improvements to be
implemented in next 2 years:
1. Micro version_____
2._____
3._____
4._____
5._____

J. SOFTWARE
Date package first developed_____
Date of last significant modification_____
Approximate man-years in development _____
Number of clients presently using system _____
Largest known project: number of activities _____
Language: □ Basic, □ Fortran, □ Cobol, □ Pascal
          □ ADA, □ Relational Data Base
                 Language
          □ Other _____
User can add functions/routines: □ no, □ yes
Documentation: Pages   Cost
  User's manual: □ no,□ yes _____ $ _____
  Technical manual: □ no,□ yes _____ $ _____
  Flow diagrams: □ no,□ yes _____ $ _____
Support
  Installation: □ no,□ yes $ _____
  Maintenance: □ no,□ yes $ _____
  Enhancements: □ no,□ yes $ _____
Source code available: □ no, □ yes
  Purchase: □ no, □ yes ··· $ _____
  Lease: □ no, □ yes ··· $ _____

K. HARDWARE
   Type: □ micro, □ mini, □ full scale, □ turnkey H/S
   Implemented on _____

Configuration for network analysis
                                Minimum Maximum
  Number of activities   _____ _____
  Processor memory, bytes   _____ _____
  Random access memory, bytes   _____ _____
  Number of interactive users   _____ _____
  Purchase cost this config.   _____ _____
  Lease cost this config.   _____ _____

L. SERVICE BUREAU PROCESSING   Cost   Basis
   Charges based on
   Number of activities $___   _____
   Connect time $___   _____
   Processor memory/CRUs used $___   _____
   Storage: On-line $___   _____
             Off-line $___   _____
   Charges negotiable: □ no, □ yes
     Fixed charge/period: □ no, □ yes
     Discount for long-term commitment: □ no, □ yes
   Typical cost of using
   Number of Processor time or Other Total cost
   activities resource units   for run
   _____ $ _____ $ ___ $ _____
   1000 $ _____ $ ___ $ _____
   _____ $ _____ $ ___ $ _____
   10000 $ _____ $ ___ $ _____
   _____ $ _____ $ ___ $ _____
   Comments on basis for costing: _____
   _____
   _____

Any comments or special features not otherwise
mentioned: _____
_____
_____
_____
_____
_____
_____
_____
_____

Figure 8-5. Network analysis features.

will be an identification of the resources (in terms of type, amount, and timing) that must be added to keep the project within the target completion date(s). Conversely, resource-limited scheduling assumes that no more resources can be made available and that target completion dates may be slipped if necessary. Typically, the result of this processing is a revised schedule that reflects the earliest possible completion, given available resources. The impact of the scheduling is impressive, as shown by the simplified example in Figure 8-6. The degree of operator control over the scheduling (especially in tailoring the priority scheme to be used) is a critical feature in both approaches. Most medium- to large-scale projects will find both techniques a must at different times during the project life cycle. Other essential features for which the user may find application are split scheduling, resource grouping, and consumable resources. The split scheduling concept is based on the assumption that some activities can be efficiently stopped after they have been started if there is a lack of resources and then restarted when resources are again available. This technique is especially useful when long-duration activities must share resources with shorter but higher-priority activities. Without splitting, the longer activity might never start if no continuous span of available resources could be located by the scheduling algorithm. With splitting, the activity can be started and stopped several times as higher-priority operations demand. Resource grouping allows the user to make sets of resources appear interchangeable to the scheduler. This feature may be used to remove the distinction between minor variations in resource cost or capability (e.g., to specify that engineers grade 1, 2, and 3 may be used wherever a junior engineer is required). This feature also may offer a teaming option that allows for the establishment of teams of resources (typically manpower) which can then be manipulated or scheduled as a single unit. In combination, these features can be used to deal with some very complex scheduling problems. The consumable resource feature is probably most useful to the production manager or construction engineer when large amounts of parts, equipment, or material must be controlled. Consumable resources represent entities that are not only allocated to an activity but actually consumed by it. For example, pouring a foundation may consume cement but only allocate the cement truck and laborers. Many popular packages do not provide consumable resources, so the user should look carefully before committing to a particular vendor's product (see Figure 8-7), which is adapted from Webster's *1982 Survey of Project Management Packages.*[33] See Webster for additional considerations in resource allocation systems.

Cost Performance Reporting. The basic concept behind cost performance reporting (CPR) or similar techniques, such as earned value reporting and performance reporting, is to monitor the progress of the project in

Before resource scheduling

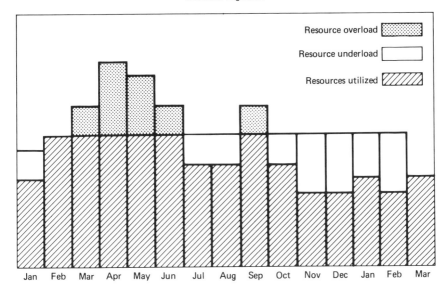

Figure 8-6. Project management information system resource scheduling.

N. Interfaces with: ☐ network analysis, ☐ cost control, ☐ estimating, ☐ materials control, ☐ equipment control

Package name _____
Vendor _____

O. INPUT FEATURES
   Resource types: #/act. ____ #/project _____
      ☐ Homogeneous, ☐ heterogeneous
      ☐ Consumable,   ☐ renewable
      ☐ Crew/team specification
   Resource quantity: ☐ Uniform over act. duration
                      ☐ Specific portion of duration
                      Data field picture (ex., xxx.xx)
                         per activity _____
                         per resource pool _____
   Availability: ☐ predetermined in data file,
      ☐ on-line interactive, ☐ event triggered
   Description: # of characters _____
   Alternate resources: ☐ no, ☐ yes
      Productivity multiplier: ☐ no, ☐ yes
      Application qualified by-activity: ☐ no, ☐ yes
      based on _____
   Costs: ☐ Total amount by activity
          ☐ per unit per period of time

P. PROCESSING FEATURES
   Options: ☐ time constrained, ☐ resource constrained,
            ☐ other _____
   Technique: ☐ Analytical optimum, ☐ heuristic
              ☐ One resource at a time, ☐ all in parallel
   Float allocation: ☐ no, ☐ yes _____
   In process activities assured allocation of
      resources: ☐ always, ☐ optional --- ☐ by activity
   Multiproject scheduling: ☐ no, ☐ yes ---
      ☐ One at a time, ☐ in parallel, ☐ by proj. priority

Q. OUTPUT FEATURES
   Reports: Show resources by activity: ☐ no, ☐ yes
            Sort on resource? ☐ no, ☐ yes
   Resource requirements profile:
      Numerical
      Histogram --- ☐ Char. printer, ☐ pen plotter
         ☐ By single type, ☐ by group of types, ☐ total
         ☐ Unused resources
   Prints total resource time units required: ☐ no, ☐ yes

R. SOFTWARE
   Same terms apply as for network analysis package:
   ☐ yes, ☐ no -- Comments _____

S. HARDWARE
   Same requirements as for network analysis package:
   ☐ yes, ☐ no --- Comments _____

Figure 8-7. Resource schedule features.

terms of work performed against work scheduled and the cost of work performed against the budget for work performed. The CPR functions and data must be integrated into the network schedule and the budget (usually done through the WBS) in order to correlate original cost and schedule estimates with actuals. Figure 8-8 shows a typical report generated by a CPR system. The budgeted cost of work scheduled (BCWS) represents the scheduled expenditure of budgeted resources, while the actual cost of work performed (ACWP) represents what has been expended for the work performed. A third factor, the budgeted cost of work performed (BCWP), shows what expenditures were planned for the work that has been performed. The BCWP also provides the basis for computing cost and schedule variances. Cost variance is a fairly straightforward comparison between the BCWP and the ACWP: A certain amount of work was performed and its actual cost can easily be compared to its planned cost, providing a measure of cost variance from the budget. Schedule variance can be found in much the same way, except that the BCWS and BCWP are used. In this comparison the planned cost of the scheduled work is compared to the planned cost of the work that was performed. The resulting variance shows schedule slippage instead of cost overrun. Trend analysis is then conducted on the cost and schedule variances, and estimated future variances are established. In this way the project manager can discriminate between a project that is simply ahead of schedule and one which is experiencing a major cost overrun. He or she can also project where current trends will lead in terms of overall cost and completion

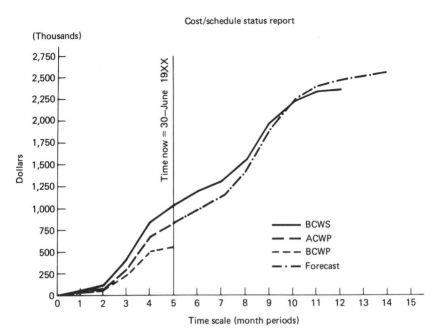

Cost/schedule status report

(Thousands)

Dollars

Time scale (month periods)

Figure 8-8. Sample cost performance report.

dates for the project. A key requirement of the CPR function is the ability to "roll up" the results to various levels in the WBS and to select reported elements by responsible organization, since managers at each level need reports that show how their areas of responsibility are performing individually and in the aggregate. Use of the CPR technique is required on many U.S. Department of Defense contracts and is also frequently used by industry, so the user should be aware of the potential for such a requirement and consider the availability of CPR capabilities for each PMIS.

Communications and External Interfaces

Few projects can be successfully managed without close cooperation between all of the organizations and personnel involved. Whether the involved parties are departments within a company (i.e., accounting, engineering, production), prime contractors and subcontractors, or customers and suppliers, there must be a constant exchange of information if major technical problems, delays, and cost overruns are to be avoided.[34] The project manager must continuously interface with all of the major project participants to both collect and disseminate information. For situations where there is heavy and periodic data exchange between participating parties and the project management staff, there is the potential for direct automation of this exchange through on-line communications or standard exchange media such as magnetic tape. In considering PMIS communication or exchange requirements, the user must (1) determine the major external interfaces (sources and destinations of project information) and (2) identify the most appropriate communications methods (physical and electrical interfaces and protocols) available at each external interface.

External Interfaces. Figure 8-9 illustrates a number of the typical external interfaces for a major product within a large electronics or aerospace firm. The details of the information flows may change from industry to industry, but the concepts remain essentially the same. Project managers are generally concerned with tracking the current performance of the project in terms of cost and schedule. To adequately perform this function, actual cost data must be collected. Since virtually all companies already collect this type of data through computer-based payroll and cost accounting systems, the cost and effort required to manually recollect such massive amounts of data make an automated transfer to the PMIS desirable in many cases. Another area that often reports to the PMIS is

Figure 8-9. Project management information system communications and external interfaces.

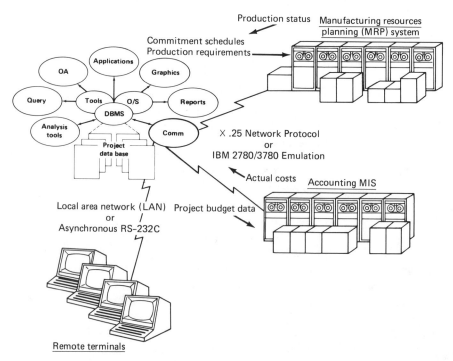

production control. The use of comprehensive computer-based production management or "manufacturing resource planning (MRP)" systems is quickly spreading, and these systems can use PMIS-generated schedules as a basis for initiating detailed production planning, as well as provide rolled-up status information on current production performance in terms of both cost and volume.[35] Automated estimating packages also provide a valuable source of information for the PMIS. Material and labor estimates, along with other projected cost information provided to the PMIS, can be used as a basis for establishing the project budget and assigning overall cost estimates to each element of the work breakdown structure. Other management information system functions often exchange useful information with the PMIS, including accounts payable, accounts receivable, equipment and material control, inventory control, and purchasing. Each project environment is unique and will provide different external interface requirements and opportunities. In some organizations most of the functions mentioned may only exist within the PMIS, while in other environments each may entail a completely separate management information system on a dedicated computer. The point here is that the project manager should consider the communications potential of the PMIS against the extant and potential interface requirements of other systems with which he or she deals.

Communication Methods. In many cases the time and effort required to engineer and initiate the interface will not be justified by the small amounts of data being transferred; however, in other cases the volume of data transfer will virtually dictate an automated exchange of some sort. Automated exchange may involve no more than physically carrying a magnetic tape from one computer installation to another. In other situations the volume and timing sensitivity of the information being transferred may require a continuous computer-to-computer link. Unfortunately, many computer vendors have chosen to ignore accepted standards and implement peculiar communications techniques that are only supported by equipment manufactured by the same vendor and perhaps a few others. There have been, however, some communication methods that have become well accepted and which are available on a wide variety of computer systems. In addition, organizations like the American National Standards Institute and the International Standards Organization have made major advances toward a complete multilevel interface standard for computer-to-computer communications. Portions of that standard have already received widespread acceptance in the industry and are known collectively as the X.25 Network Protocol. Other commonly accepted methods supported by most systems include Serial Asynchronous RS-232C ASCII, IBM 2780/3780 Remote Job Entry (RJE) Emulation (bisynchronous), IBM 3270 Terminal Emulation, and the IBM System Network

Architecture (SNA). Most micro- and minicomputers support asynchronous ASCII-based operations, while most main-frame systems emphasize the use of synchronous or bisynchronous methods. Even when the basic protocols appear to be the same, the user must still carefully review the alternative speeds, handshaking techniques, and protocol options available to ensure that an operational link can be established between the PMIS and the external system.[36] The user who must provide support for many projects and may not be able to identify all of the external interfaces in advance should make sure that the PMIS supports several of the well-accepted synchronous and asynchronous protocols (i.e., RS-232C, IBM 2780/3780, X.25).

User Interfaces

In conjunction with the DBMS discussed above, the PMIS model also includes several functions designed specifically to allow the non-computer specialist/manager to quickly and easily access the project data base, make changes in private data sets, and generate reports with information selected, sorted, and formated to his or her needs. The functions include the query language, the data manipulation language, and the report writer. They are often provided as part of a DBMS, but are discussed separately here because they are critical to the usability of the PMIS by project management rather than information systems personnel. All three functions provide either command language-based or "fill in the form" type interfaces to the user. They are also "nonprocedural." This simply means that the user does not have to write a program in order to get some work done; the user merely specifies through English-like commands what needs to be done—the computer does the rest. For example, if the manager wants to know which project leaders are responsible for software activities more than 10 days behind schedule, he might type into the computer the following:

```
DISPLAY TASK-NO., LEADER-NAME, DAYS-LATE
FROM SCHEDULE
    WHERE DAYS-LATE IS GREATER THAN 10
    SORT BY LEADER-NAME
    END
```

Given that the DBMS has access to a table named "schedule" and that the fields "days-late," "task-no.," and "leader-name" are in the definition for that table, the system will respond with something like this:

Recognized Query!

Task-no.	Leader-name	Days-late
5212	Anderson, John	13
2192	Jones, Mark	13
1254	Smith, Margaret	11
.	.	.
.	.	.
.	.	.

The example above only scratches the surface with regard to the powerful capabilities available through these functions. When relational data base features are also present, the user may link or "join" the information in two or more files or "tables" in the data base to obtain a different view of the data. The relational DBMS model allows the user to dynamically link and select information within the project data base without anticipating the particular query requirement in advance. The query language provides an easy-to-use interface bypassing the computer jargon and detailed control parameters that have been so prevalent in typical computer-based systems. The data manipulation language (DML) available on many systems uses the same syntax and grammar as the query language, avoiding additional training requirements for the user and simplifying the overall system. The DML allows the user to change or delete entries in the data base. Selection criteria, formulas for computing new values based on other fields, constants, or data in linked tables, and the order of execution can be specified. Many systems provide transaction logging and "undo" commands that allow the user to "roll back" the data base to a previous point in time to cancel an erroneous manipulation or access information on the project as it existed at a particular point in the past. Transaction logging is extremely desirable when users have direct access to DML, since the manager can determine who changed what data when and recover the original data base if necessary. A key point to note in considering the importance of the query language and DML is that no programming is required to "set up" for the user's needs. If the desired information is in the data base, then the user can directly enter the query or DML commands and obtain results in real time (i.e., usually within minutes or seconds). The computer specialist intermediary is cut out of the loop, increasing the user's flexibility and control over his or her own data. The report writer is the third element of the user interface and should also support the same syntax and grammar as the query and manipulation functions. The report writer provides the user with a tool for specifying the format, selection criteria, intermediate computations, sorting order, and primary sources for generating reports from the project data base. The report writer automatically handles the mundane functions of page control, page numbering, and data base access and simplifies the user's specification of headings, titles, footnotes, and other common report features. Many report writers specially tailored to support the needs of project management can generate schedule charts on a printer or interface with a graphics package to generate multicolored schedule and management graphics reports. Figure 8-10 shows an example report generated by one of the more capable report writers available and highlights many of the features it supports. The report writer should operate directly from the data base, not require the user to learn another set of syntax and grammar rules, and should be flexible enough to support ad hoc report requirements. When properly integrated (i.e., use a similar syntax and be accessible from the same environment), these three tools can put the real power of the DBMS in the hands of the user, where it must be if the PMIS is to become a responsive knowledge tool for the project manager and staff.

Office Automation

The merger of traditional data processing and administrative support functions is proceeding rapidly. Many computer vendors are already offering integrated systems that provide both data processing and office automation functions in one package. The project management function is information intensive and generally requires substantial office automation support for the preparation and control of the thousands of documents and drawings present in most projects. The PMIS can and should provide some of the basic office automation functions such as word processing, electronic mail, optical scanner input, and executive support services (i.e., suspense lists, "do lists," appointment calendars, file indexes). Other functions normally considered to be included in office automation, such as facsimile transmission, computer-driven copiers, and microfilm storage systems, should be considered by the user, but are not normally available as part of a PMIS. The interfaces to these functions should be reviewed when other external communications requirements are analyzed. Much of the information from which project managers develop the various documents that must be prepared is normally present in the data base and should be accessible to the office automation functions both internal and external to the PMIS. The requirement for mixed text and graphics in reports is becoming more common but is not supported by many existing products. A long-standing problem with integrating text and graphics has been the fact that text printers have not usually been graphics capable and graphics plotters have been relatively slow when printing text and can rarely handle standard fanfold computer paper. However, a new generation of matrix printers with color graphics capability is now on the market that can output high-quality color graphics and high-speed text without manual intervention. These devices should facilitate the development of flexible integrated text–graphics processing packages with direct data base access capabilities, which will be a powerful addition to the PMIS capabilities now available. A well-designed PMIS-based office automation capability can substantially reduce the duplication of data and work that often exists when these functions are separate and cannot communicate. In addition, when all reports (whether text, graphics, or data oriented) are based on the same project data base, the potential for error and conflict is reduced.

Graphics

The well-worn proverb that "a picture is worth a thousand words" may have substantially understated the case. Managers, especially senior decision makers, are very busy. Time is the constraining resource, and any technique that can improve the speed and accuracy of the communication process for the manager is a valuable asset. Graphics (whether text on slides, traditional statistical graphs, or block diagrams) have become the norm in presentations to management, customers, and other groups. Graphic techniques are especially useful in the project management environment, where complexity and massive amounts of data must be continuously reduced and simplified to support decision makers. There are two basic graphics functions shown in Figure 8-11 that are available in the PMIS marketplace: (1) schedule graphics, which includes bar charts, network diagrams, and Gantt charts, and (2) management graphics, which typically includes pie charts, histograms (in a variety of forms), and line graphs.[37] High-quality graphics require not only capable software, but also special peripheral devices (plotters, graphics terminals, graphics printers, etc.) that can generate the output. The use of multicolored graphics (versus black and white) conveys much more information and is usually justified; however, many users have been frustrated by the difficulty and expense of reproducing multicolored charts. A number of multi-color-capable photocopiers are now coming on the market and this problem should be alleviated in the near future. The user should not assume that just because the "system" is graphics or color graphics capable that any or all of the output devices have that capability. The features of each device should be reviewed against the requirements for various types of graphics output to ensure that the appropriate graphics products can be generated. The hardware technology is constantly making advances in the graphics area, so many relatively low-cost input and output options are already available, such as 35-mm slide generation, view graph slide generation, direct computer-generated large screen projection, and ink jet color printing. Costs for these technologies will continue to plummet as capabilities increase, so periodic review of the cost versus benefit of these features is prudent. The user should not overlook the potential of the graphics-capable PMIS to store, manipulate, and generate complete

194

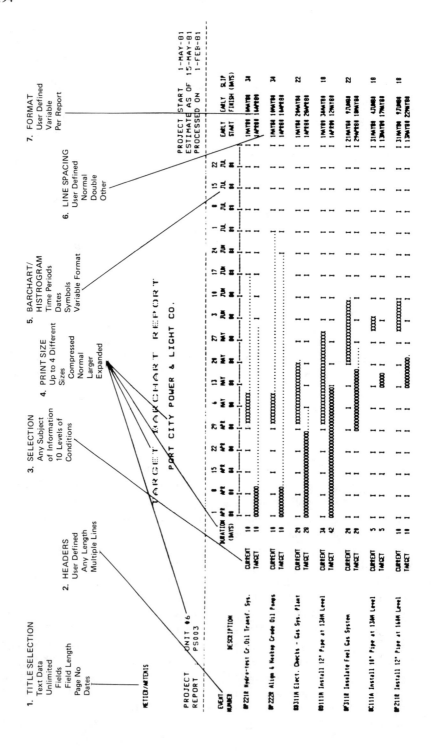

195

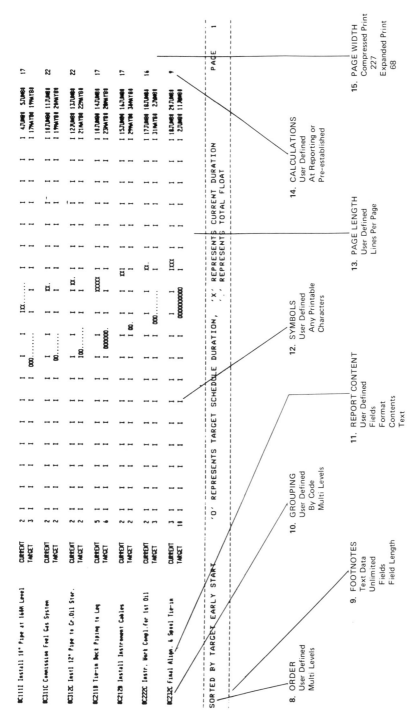

Figure 8-10. Report writer example.

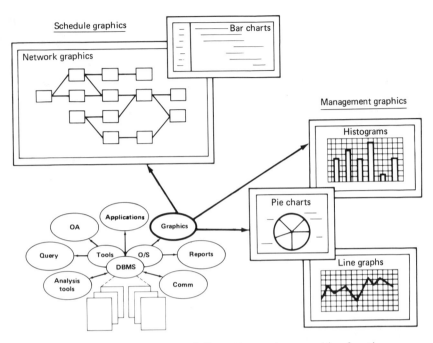

Figure 8-11. Project management information system graphics functions.

presentations in a variety of forms. In fact, in many installations where PMIS graphics have been installed, the use of the system for generation of presentations has been very heavy, eliminating many hundreds of hours of manual graphics development and revision time.

Tailored Applications

No off-the-shelf PMIS can hope to satisfy all of an individual user's requirements. Each organization and type of project involve different objectives and constraints within which project planning and control must operate. The user should assume that additional applications functions will have to be developed or at least existing ones modified. If the PMIS contains many of the user interface and DBMS features described above, the development of new applications using these tools can usually be completed within a matter of weeks or even days. However, if a traditional computer language is used (i.e., Cobol, Fortran, Pascal), the development time would be much longer and the cost much higher. These new applications could address virtually any project function, including project accounting, configuration management, reliability modeling, and production planning modeling. The development of the application involves defining the specific users, available input data (including source), the output information required, the processing that should be performed, and the relationships with the existing project data base. The data table structure can then be defined, data entry options selected, report writer specifications defined, and processing commands written (in DML). For simple applications involving two to four tables, a half dozen reports, and no unusually complex processing, implementation can be completed and tested within 3–4 days by an experienced user. Single-table applications with a couple of reports and ad hoc manipulations can be implemented in several hours (exclusive of data entry time) in many cases. These capabilities free the user to develop (without prohibitive time and cost penalties) new and tailored applications to support his or her unique requirements. For requirements that are permanent in nature, the user may make use of an application generator to automatically create the data entry, query, DML, and report writer commands needed to perform the application function. The generator accepts a functional description of what is to be performed and then converts that description to the commands needed to perform the function. It also develops help screens, menus, and in some cases documentation for the application.[38]

PMIS Function Integration

The real power of the PMIS is integration. In an integrated system any of the user-generated applications can link with and use (even modify if security permission is granted) the other tables in the project data base, including the network schedule, budget, and resources availability. Individual managers may establish applications that aid them in planning and controlling their area of responsibility while still working from the same primary project data base as others in the organization. In the optimum implementation of PMIS, the user can use any tool to access any information in the project data base and has complete flexibility to output the results of his or her work to displays, reports, graphics, or even a new table in the data base.

PMIS Implementation

Importance of Implementation Strategy

The success or failure of any transition to an automated system is dependent on the technology being employed, the support resources made available, the organization absorbing the new system, and the strategy for implementation. A 1983 RAND study on the implementation processes for information technology[39] concluded that the implementation strategy was the single most important factor determining the degree of success realized with a new automated system. The study identified three major elements of implementation that have been consistent factors in successful systems. These successful strategies focus on ensuring that the roles of various players in the organization match their tasks and that their efforts are effectively integrated. Specifically, (1) top management should support the effort but not define the procedures to be used, (2) the technical players should provide expertise and computer resources but not be in charge of implementation, and (3) the users should manage the implementation but must ensure coordination with top management and technical personnel.[40] Notwithstanding these findings, technology, the organization, and the support resources are still critical to successful implementation and must be carefully considered. Project people should have a hand in developing the system so they get the information they need and become committed to successful implementation.

Developing an Acquisition Strategy

The range of possible acquisition strategies for obtaining a PMIS capability is virtually limitless. Some typical approaches include the following:

Develop software and hosting on an existing computer.

Purchase an integrated PMIS, including hardware, software, and support services.

Contract for consulting services that include a PMIS capability and also provide project planning and control expertise and support.

Purchase a microcomputer-based software package and use existing microcomputer systems.

Contract for the development of a customized software package and purchase separate hardware to host the package.

Contract for teleprocessing services that include the required PMIS function(s).

Use a combination of these approaches.

There are obvious advantages and disadvantages to each approach. The user must consider acquisition, development, and support costs; the expected performance characteristics; the risk; and the delivery schedule for each option. Most organizations would be wise to procure (purchase or lease) the core functions and analytical tools off-the-shelf and then use fourth-generation language or application generator tools to develop whatever unique functions are needed. The type of hardware to be used is primarily determined by the technical requirements discussed in the last section and the budgetary and policy constraints of the organization. However, the manager should avoid hosting the PMIS function on a shared user system, since project manager control and system responsiveness (two critical factors for the PMIS) will likely be degraded.

Implementation Life Cycle

The phases of the system life cycle have been defined by many authors in a number of different ways. The details of these definitions vary according to the type of requirement, the selected acquisition strategy, and the type of system being implemented. Typically the life cycle includes requirements analysis, development, and operations and maintenance with a continuous review of performance to identify deficiencies and new requirements. These steps can be expanded in a variety of ways to accommodate the characteristics of individual situations as mentioned above. Martin, in his excellent text on application development without programming,[41] has defined the steps for acquiring an application package. The following list is adapted from Martin, but tailored to the project planning and control function:

List present and anticipated requirements for the application.

Survey all available packages for the application (see Webster[42] for an excellent survey of project management packages).

Examine the documentation of the most promising packages. Ensure that the features discussed in the technology section of this chapter are addressed and match the requirements.

Ensure that the packages are sufficiently "parameterized" (i.e., provide adequate options to support the user's requirements without major modifications).

Ensure that the packages have adequate aids to support future maintenance.

Select a small number of packages for further investigation.

Examine the capability of the vendors to provide long-term support. Ensure that the vendor is financially stable, that support resources are available and responsive, and that costs for these services are reasonable and somewhat predictable.

Contact other users of the package to discuss their experiences. Look for users with requirements similar to the ones under consideration. Also ask about vendor support, documentation, and training quality and responsiveness.

Ensure that each package can be linked to the necessary interfaces (i.e., other MISs) through communications features between computers or compatible data formats within a computer.

Develop a set of sample problems representative of the work to be performed by the package (a bench mark) and run the set with the packages to assess relative performance and ease of operation.

Arrange for end users [project manager(s) and staff] to use the package for a short period to evaluate the user interface.

Make appropriate contractual arrangements and obtain the best buy (i.e., most capable package for the most reasonable cost). Consider contracting issues such as lease versus purchase, whether or not to include training and technical support, and arrangements for future expansion of capacity or functions.

Monitor the operation and use of the package and identify deficiencies and additional requirements.

Installation Strategies

Depending on the acquisition strategy selected, the installation and initial operation of the PMIS (whether it be a package or a complete system) must be carefully planned. A number of options have been identified in management information systems texts[43]: (1) operation of a pilot system, (2) parallel operation of the existing and new systems, (3) gradual phase in/phase out between the systems, and (4) "cold turkey" instant cutover to the new system. Obviously, the installation of a new system is greatly simplified if it is not replacing an existing capability. The manager must consider the normal problems of floor space, terminal placement and wiring, communications service and equipment needs, and power and environmental control equipment whenever new hardware is being installed. Software package installation seems less difficult but still requires adequate free storage capacity, programmed system down time, and the coordinated availability of in-house and vendor personnel. The establishment of communications links can take days or even weeks if the adequate technical planning and coordination are not ensured. Prior to installation of communications service and equipment the manager should obtain the coordinated assistance of the software vendors (both operating system and applications if they are different), the computer hardware vendor, all vendors of communications equipment (i.e., modems, multiplexers), and the servicing common carrier. Recent experience with the new communications environment created by the breakup of AT&T indicates that the user will have to become his own integrator, pulling together the equipment, software, and services of many different vendors into an integrated communications capability. For installations where an existing capability is being replaced, a number of additional issues should also be addressed, including conversion of existing data bases to the new system, the development of new management procedures consistent with the system, and the highlighting to users of the functional differences between the old and new systems.

Documentation

For software packages acquired from a vendor or developed in-house, adequate documentation is as important as the quality of the software itself. The current trend is toward more on-line documentation through the use of extensive help screens and by keeping the text of manuals in the system. In many systems the user may display or print portions of the manual by specifying the command or feature that he or she wishes to have more information on. Tuman[44] has identified four classes of documentation needed for the PMIS as discussed below.

System Documentation. This documentation is the "executive summary" of the system. It describes from a management perspective the major functions provided, the overall data base structure, the primary inputs and outputs, and the interfaces with other information systems. The system documentation should avoid use of computer jargon and emphasize from a project management point of view what the system can and cannot do.

Program Documentation. This form of documentation, often referred to as a programmer's manual, provides detailed information about the actual design of the software and data structures. If the acquiring organization will be supporting the software (i.e., correcting deficiencies and making enhancements), then this type of documentation must be made available and should be carefully reviewed by those who will be responsible for the support of the system.

Operations Documentation. With batch systems and processes this form of documentation was critical to the successful use of the software; however, with on-line systems much less information is required by systems operations personnel, if there are any (many newer minicomputer- and microcomputer-based systems require little or no operations monitoring). In on-line systems the user is often responsible for initiating the few batch processes that must still be performed, such as data base reorganization and recovery from errors; however, some operations functions remain centralized, such as the backup of the data base and the control of access to the system. Consequently, the operations documentation is now usually more of an administrator's manual than anything else.

User Documentation. These manuals provide detailed information about how to access the system, input data, maintain the data base, execute system processing functions, and generate reports. Sample screens, commands, and reports are usually provided. For purchased software this is perhaps the most critical area of documentation, since the user will often be without any other source of information on how to make the software perform a given task. These manuals are often separated into a tutorial format suitable for training and introducing the novice to the system and a reference format organized for quick access to exact technical descriptions on any command or feature. The completeness, readability, and currency of this documentation should be carefully reviewed before installation.

Training

As with documentation, training is also critical to ensure smooth and effective system implementation. Users should be the primary recipients of any training provided. Planning for implementation should include training early in the schedule so that when the system is installed, users are already familiar with its operation and features. Courses can be provided at the user's facility if enough personnel are signed up and adequate classroom space is available; however, vendors usually have excellent training facilities with equipment for hands-on training. In addition, there is the hidden benefit of removing the student from the normal work environment, where he or she is likely to be distracted by the pressing responsibilities of their regular position. User training should avoid the unnecessary use of computer jargon and minimize the complexity of the initial presentations. A subset of basic system features should be introduced first and then used as a basis for introducing the more complex capabilities of the system. Maximum use of hands-on training, graphics, and student handouts should be made to make the student a participant rather than a spectator. When properly used, training can also become an effective marketing tool in converting skeptical users over to the new system. There are other types of training available for most systems, but the first 1- or 2-week user course discussed here is the most critical and probably will be the most used.[45,46]

Technical Support

Even the user with excellent software, complete and current documentation, and adequate training requires additional technical assistance from time to time. For software developed in-house this should be available from the management information system shop or other information system organization. However, for systems obtained from vendors the manager should ensure that adequate technical support can be obtained directly by the user without administrative hassles such as purchase orders or contracts. Many vendors offer a "hot line" service where a technical staff is available to assist users and answer telephone inquiries. Most questions and problems can be solved by this method, but some demand direct intervention or review by vendor technical personnel. In this case a dial-up diagnostic hookup can be quite valuable in allowing rapid solution of complex technical problems and questions without waiting for a service representative to show up. Under this approach the hot line technician calls into the system having difficulty, reviews the problem area, and makes the necessary changes or instructs the user as to what caused the problem. This type of support provides the user with virtually immediate feedback and is often less expensive than the traditional service representative approach. Another important area of technical support is software maintenance. Most package vendors are constantly upgrading and improving their offerings, and the manager should ensure that his or her facility will be able to obtain these upgrades at a reasonable cost. The exact level of support required is certainly dependent on the requirements of each installation; however, there are always some support requirements and they should be identified and provided for early in implementation planning.

Conclusion

Responsible Project Management

The potential for more effective use of existing PMIS capabilities is substantial, especially in light of the powerful off-the-shelf software tools now available. In fact, the technology has now progressed to the point where most of the problems exhibited in past PMIS implementations can be effectively addressed. At the same time increased budgetary constraints and scarce critical resources are forcing much more rigorous control in most project-oriented organizations. The technology is available at a reasonable cost and low risk—it is now incumbent upon project managers and project planning and control specialists to become familiar with the technology and begin applying it in the management of medium- and large-scale projects. Organizations that fail to recognize the opportunities inherent in PMIS technology will place themselves in a position of disadvantage which cannot be afforded in today's increasingly competitive environment.

Endnotes Chapter Eight

1. Cleomir Reynaud, "Computer Systems for Project Control—The Shape of Things to Come," *Applications of Critical Path Techniques,* New York, Elsevier, 1968, p. 349.
2. P. Barneston, "Future Developments in Network Planning by Computer," *Applications of Critical Path Techniques,* New York, Elsevier, 1968, p. 283.
3. Russell D. Archibald and Richard L. Villoria, *Network Based Management Systems (PERT/CPM),* New York, Wiley, 1967, p. 178.
4. *Ibid.,* p. 2.
5. Clifford F. Gray, *Essentials of Project Management,* New York, Petrocelli, 1981, p. 169.
6. Louis J. Goodman and Ralph N. Love, *Project Planning and Management—An Integrated Approach,* New York, Pergamon, 1980, p. 28.
7. Steven L. Mandel, *Computer and Data Processing—Concept and Applications with BASIC,* New York, West Publishing, 1981, pp. 374–380.

8. Harold J. Schutt and Ted Ingalls, "Program Manager's Support System (PMSS)," *1982 Federal Acquisition Research Symposium*, Washington, DC, George Washington University, 1982, p. 11.

9. P. J. Burman, *Precedence Networks for Project Planning and Control*, New York, McGraw-Hill, 1972, p. 181.

10. Thomas T. Samaras and Kim Yensuang, *Computerized Project Management Techniques for Manufacturing and Construction Industries*, Englewood Cliffs, NJ, Prentice-Hall, 1978, p. 7.

11. Archibald and Villoria, *Network-Based Management Systems (PERT/CPM)*, p. 177.

12. *Ibid.*, p. 176.

13. Murray A. Muspratt, "Computers for the Construction Industry," *The Project Management Quarterly*, September, 1983, p. 45.

14. Thomas T. Samaras and Kim Yensuang, *Computerized Project Management Techniques for Manufacturing and Construction Industries*, p. 7.

15. Russell D. Archibald and Richard L. Villoria, *Network-Based Management Systems (PERT/CPM)*, p. 176.

16. Murray A. Muspratt, "Computers for the Construction Industry," p. 7.

17. *Ibid.*, p. 45.

18. Mark D. Matthews, "Standardized Networks—Some Comments on Use in an R&D Organization," *Project Management Quarterly*, September, 1983, p. 34.

19. Muspratt, "Computers for the Construction Industry," p. 45.

20. Archibald and Villoria, *Network-Based Management Systems (PERT/CPM)*, p. 177.

21. *Ibid.*, p. 178.

22. Reynaud, *Computers for Project Control—The Shape of Things to Come*, p. 351.

23. Archibald and Villoria, *Network-Based Management Systems (PERT/CPM)*, p. 174.

24. Reynaud, *Computers for Project Control—The Shape of Things to Come*, p. 351.

25. John Tuman, Jr., "Development and Implementation of Effective Project Management Information and Control Systems," *Project Management Handbook*, New York, Van Nostrand Reinhold, 1983, pp. 524–526.

26. Archibald and Villoria, *Network-Based Management Systems (PERT/CPM)*, p. 174.

27. Charles A. Kirkpatrick and Richard I. Levin, *Planning and Control with PERT/CPM*, New York, McGraw-Hill, 1966, p. 114.

28. Gray, *Essentials of Project Management*, pp. 173–175.

29. Tuman, "Development and Implementation of Successful Project Management," p. 518.

30. Archibald and Villoria, *Network-Based Management Systems (PERT/CPM)*, p. 14.

31. Reynaud, *Computers for Project Control—The Shape of Things to Come*, p. 351.

32. Francis M. Webster, Jr., *1982 Survey of Project Management Software Packages*, Drexel Hill, PA, PMI, 1983.

33. *Ibid.*

34. Goodman and Love, *Project Planning and Management—An Integrated Approach*, pp. 33–35.

35. Harold J. Schutt and Ted Ingalls, "Program Manager's Support System (PMSS)," pp. 33–35.

36. James W. Conrad, *Standards and Protocols for Communication Networks*, Madison, Carnegie Press, 1982.

37. *Ibid.*, p. 7.

38. James Martin, *Application Development Without Programmers*, Englewood Cliffs, NJ, Prentice-Hall, 1982.

39. T. K. Bikson and B. A. Gutek, *Advanced Office Information Technology: An Empirical Study Effort Trip*, Santa Monica, CA, RAND Corporation, 1983.

40. *Ibid.*, p. 158.

41. Martin, *Application Development Without Programmers*, p. 98.

42. Webster, *1982 Survey of Project Management Software Packages*.

43. Tuman, "Development and Implementation of Successful Project Management," p. 523.

44. *Ibid.*, p. 524.

45. Joseph Orlicky, *The Successful Computer System*, New York, McGraw-Hill, 1969, pp. 232–233.

46. Tuman, "Development and Implementation of Successful Project Management," p. 525.

The Project Operational Phase

CHAPTER NINE

Financial Management

Investment

The Project Represents a Financial Investment

Before a project is authorized, there generally is analysis of such relevant factors as need, technical complexity, the probability of accomplishing technical objectives, the prospect for the achievement of technical objectives within the desired time frame, and the anticipated economic as well as technical contribution to the organization's operational goals.

Invariably, organizations have more prospects for projects than available resources to fund all the projects. Often the ultimate decision to go or not to go with a project hinges on the economics of the expected contribution relative to cost and benefit. The prospective project manager in the process of seeking authorization might well be advised to use an entrepreneurial approach in selling the project to a client. Extolling the technical aspects to the exclusion of financial factors can be a serious procedural mistake. Even in government-sponsored projects, where need rather than profit is the primary motivation for authorization, cost relative to anticipated benefit is a critical consideration.

Several different projects may offer substantial promise, but, considering the usual situation where the availability of funds affects the selection process, the final authorization of a project should be based on the most effective use of the available resources. Projects are only independent when there are unlimited resources, and such operational situations are extremely rare. There invariably is competition for physical and material resources, as well as capable project management. As a consequence, project authorization and funding may be contingent on viewing the project as a part of the total project spectrum. It is also possible that a promising project will be discarded because it will require excessive consumption of particular resources that are in short supply and which can compromise the completion of other desirable projects.[1]

Cost Effectiveness

The investment decision on projects often can be related to perceived cost effectiveness. Cost effectiveness is explored by applying economic analysis to resource allocation.[2] It is closely allied to the opportunity cost concept traditionally used in economics. Economic analysis is concerned with objectives rather than objects. According to Hitch and McKean, cost effectiveness relates tangible costs to meaningful endproduct missions or programs instead of to the cost of individual segments. All resources associated with a program or project are evaluated in relation to the benefits anticipated from it.[3]

A program segment may appear defensible when isolated. A composite evaluation of all segments, considered in the light of objectives of a total project program, may prove that the cost of the required resources for the project is disproportionate to the benefits to be derived. By studying cost effectiveness, management can gain insight into the big picture and determine trade-offs that might make it possible to attain objectives at a smaller total cost.

Management frequently must choose among many alternatives that appear desirable. Cost effectiveness provides criteria for a test of preference.[4] An essential step in the analysis is to predict the consequence of alternative actions by putting ratios or relationships into model form; another approach is to distinguish desired combinations or consequences from less desirable ones. Cost-effective criteria are employed to indicate the combination of features in alternative courses of action that will give the maximum return for the resources used. While this is a useful approach, a word of caution must be injected: The criteria are not always hard and fast and often reflect the idiosyncrasies of the individual(s) making the evaluation; comparisons are subject to differing interpretations, based on the relative weights attached to the criteria by the evaluator. Cost effectiveness is also subject to the uncertainties of time.

When these criteria are used as a guide, some definition of maximum effectiveness is required. Maximum effectiveness in one situation may not be the same as in another. There are also intangibles involved that might not be recognized or which cannot be quantitatively valued. In addition, some decision areas are so complex that cost-effectiveness criteria may not have been developed or relevant alternatives employed.

The advantage of using a cost-effective approach in the decision to fund or not to fund a project lies in the fact that it provides a schematic method of evaluating alternative courses of action. It prompts the decision maker to examine the various possibilities available. The concept is less than perfect, because, though cost and gain, as defined, may seem to lend themselves to some degree of measurement, the ultimate analysis may be fallacious if the criteria are erroneously applied or if the concepts of cost and gain involved are inappropriate. Probably the most important cause of this kind of error is the omission of relevant costs from the computation. For the appraisal to be accurate, the costs to be compared must coincide with the full system of costs for each alternative. All costs stemming directly or indirectly from the decision must be covered in the accounting. For example, if a choice is to be made between a missile and an aircraft to accomplish a stipulated mission, the cost information will be misleading if only the manufacturing costs of the competing equipments are compared. It is necessary to include the costs (except those that have already been sunk) of all the auxiliary equipment, the training of personnel, and operations from some appropriate period of time.[5]

Availability of Funds

In the preceding sections the authorization of a project was examined as an investment decision where resources are limited and there are competing projects. As part of the investment decision it was shown that a cost/benefit analysis might be pivotal in the final funding decision. There is, however, one overriding consideration in the investment decision: the availability of funds. Investment prospects for a project may be promising, especially if supported by a favorable cost/benefit analysis; nevertheless, there can be a decision to forgo the project because funds and/or other resources tantamount to project completion are not available. The availability of funds for project support may reflect cash reserves, current obligations, cash flow, the cost of money, and anticipated return on investment, which would consider cost/benefit analysis, opportunity costs, and perhaps whether the project could be treated as a current expense or would require capital investment.

Funding and subsequent authorization may depend on the source of funds. A project may promise beneficial results to the internal organization and also have significant application to an operation that is external to the organization. It may be that while the technology developed by the project is consistent with internal operational objectives, the immediate and possible long-range benefits would be greater for the external organization. To illustrate, the project can be directed to a relatively small part of a larger program where technical support is required. The organization having total program responsibility may not find it feasible to develop an ad hoc technical capability. Funding such support from an outside source could well be more cost effective in the long run. Conversely, the performing organization can develop the technology, but without a committed application, the decision to embark on the project would be highly questionable. In the aforementioned illustration there could be advantages to both organizations, but actual authorization for project go-ahead would depend on external funding.

Undercapitalization appears to be more often the case in operations than overcapitalization. In some rapidly developing technologies survival is largely dependent on keeping abreast, and in some areas ahead of the state of the art, and having some service or product that generates income to enable the continuation of operations. In new technologies, such as gene splicing, fiber optics, and computer software, entry into the field is relatively easy. Most of the entrants have some special skill providing initial incentive for taking an entrepreneurial position. Once in the field, there are pressures to produce marketable products in order to survive. The initial impetus for entry into a technologically dynamic field has to be constantly reviewed in the light of new or imminent changes that could affect the potential market and the structure of the embryonic industry. There are invariably decisions as to which technological direction to move to and what projects to select. Established as well as new organizations are confronted with decisions concerning choice of projects where the market is to some degree indeterminate and the technology undergoing a rapid transition. The decision base is usually constricted by the high cost associated with technological development, limited available funds to support new projects, current obligations, and cash flow.

If funds are internally available and the project prospects for technical and economic success appear bright, the project may be authorized. It is also possible that even if the project does seem to have a good probability for success, it may be passed up or put on hold for future consideration if there are no funds or resources available. Another possible situation is where a project has been funded and is in process, but in the interim between authorization and implementation there are developments that appear to have better prospects. Since funds are limited and competitive projects vie for available resources, it may be decided to abort an ongoing project in favor of initiating a new project that has better prospects for contributing to the organization's goals. It may be a situation where another project that is already in process comes into greater prominence and there is a decision to divert as many resources as possible to a concentrated effort on such a project. Still another alternative might be to reduce the funding of the existing project and stretch it out. Consideration of this alternative could be based on the amount of resources already invested, the possibility of the transferability of knowledge and effort expended on the project to other projects, and the prospects for salvageable benefits if the project is not allowed to continue.

There are instances, especially in emerging technologies, where exciting new projects are suggested but there are no available funds. Rather than pass up opportunities that could have a bearing on the organization's ability to survive, it might be very worthwhile to investigate external funding sources. Capital can be raised by selling stock. Selling stock usually involves the dilution of ownership. Many technically oriented entrepreneurs are extremely reluctant to place themselves in an operational situation where they do not have total control of the technical decisions and direction of the organization. A small slice of large pie may be much better than an insignificant whole pie.

Another possibility is to elicit support from a venture capital organization. This may result in the loss of considerable operational control, but the financial and managerial support might be a mitigating consideration. It may also be possible to seek a bank loan. This approach preserves the equity position, but incurs a fixed obligation that must be met. Banks are normally very reluctant to lend on speculation; they would probably want tangible evidence that a project will be authorized that has sufficient profit prospects to make a loan safe and attractive. The decision to seek a loan and take a leveraged position would depend on the type of project, its prospects for technical and economic success, the cost of borrowing funds, and the anticipated return on the investment.

In the situations cited where outside financing might be considered, several factors would probably have to be weighed: How much investment is involved? What time frame is covered? What is the potential market? How intense is the need? What potential competition is there from similar or related products or services? What is the probability of technical success? What is the relevant experience of the organization? How effective is the management? And perhaps most important, what return on investment can be anticipated?

The decision to fund a project, as has been indicated, may hinge on the evaluation of several pertinent factors. The urgency or relevance of the factors would depend on need or potential utilization, and other decisional elements would vary as to their influence according to the nature of the organization's operational setting or mission. If the project is in a highly sensitive technological area, the direction of the technical effort can be ultracritical. A miscalculation of technological developments or the prospective market can be fatal, even though the project ultimately accomplished the technical goals set forth in the proposal. Technical people can be carried away by the technical prospects suggested by a project and be oblivious to other very important considerations.

Pricing Strategies

Pricing strategy is another essential concern in investment decisions. Pricing strategy can be determined by the type of project, the organization's competitive position, the state of the technology, profit goals, and management. Management determination of pricing strategy might reflect its evaluation of its strength or weakness in the technology or industry, a policy of being a leader or a follower, an imitator or innovator, its ability to control any new product or service generated by the project, and management's willingness or reluctance to take a risk position.

Pricing strategy can, in addition, be affected by the types of projects and the market for those projects. When the government is the purchaser, or a free competitive and comparative market cannot be established owing to the effort covered by the project(s), there may be little or no real price elasticity. Price in such situations can be determined either by requesting competitive bids or by negotiation. Urgency of need and the relative economic and technical strength of the parties can also be instrumental in price determination.

If the project is aimed at developing a commercial project, there can be many factors involved in determining pricing strategies. Product development costs are usually high. Where the product is essentially an evolutionary improvement over an existing product, management would have some indication of consumer acceptance, the availability of competitive products, and cost and revenue experience to determine a pricing strategy. However, when the project is directed to developing what is essentially a new product, pricing strategy becomes far more complex. The commercial producer must consider price elasticity in marketing the product. Other considerations would be affected by recouping costs that might be incurred in research and developmental effort. What are the prospects for the product life cycle? If the product life cycle is indeterminate, the pricing strategy could be to have high initial costs to quickly recoup developmental costs. If the introductory price is high and the market does have a good life expectancy, competition may be encouraged to enter into the field, which could compromise the long-term benefits of the initiating organization.

Another pricing strategy could be to take a long-run position on the gamble that the product resulting from the project will have an extended life expectancy. A low introductory price could discourage competition. Competition could be eliminated or minimized after potential competitors estimate the developmental costs, the current market price, and the fact that there is another organization that has established a foothold in the market and has product identity. A low introductory pricing strategy could be based on an attempt to control the market by, as indicated, discouraging competition. Short-run recouping of costs and profitability would be sacrificed for long-run control and profitability over an extended period of time.

Pricing policies can also be affected by possible product liability. A high potential for product liability could discourage authorization of a project. However, if there is a strong need, the decision to proceed with the project may be forthcoming in spite of inherent product liability risks.

Product liability can be minimized or eliminated in many instances as a result of greater project effort in the developmental phases where explicit attention is directed to neutralizing product-related risks. Added effort and product safeguards would undoubtedly lead to higher product developmental cost and an evaluation would be necessary to determine whether such costs could be factored into the price without destroying the market.

A product may have a potential market, but high or unforeseen developmental costs can lead to a situation where the end product is priced out of the market. Consumers have much competition for expendable dollars. Even though a product may be technologically advanced, consumers will generally go to another product if there is a reasonable substitute of performance and the price differential is significant.

There are situations where a desired pricing strategy can be identified but is discarded. A price might be set that is considered less than ideal because of competitive pressures, the organization's need for new business and an expanded markets, the recognition of the requirement to maintain the technical organization, or the use of price incentives to attract past and present customers into new commitments.

Pricing strategy can also be influenced by considering the desirability of select projects and being aware that a distinct possibility exists where these projects could be authorized to other organizations that have underbid or may underbid a projected price which has been determined on a noncompetitive basis. The bid price for a project can be modified, if the contract is considered important, where all the variable costs will be covered and some allocation is possible from the project to overhead costs.[6] There are other situations where normal or usual pricing strategies could be discarded: to use excess operational capacity, to discourage competition, to get in the first phase of a program where subsequent follow-on projects can reasonably be expected, and where the state of the technology is such that changes, currently not identifiable, can be anticipated that will later impact on the technical and economic scope of the project.

Make or Buy (In-house Capability or Outside Contracting

Pressures to Develop Internal Capabilities

On many projects all or a considerable part of the necessary resources and knowledge requirements are already in place or readily available internally by the time the project is authorized. There are also situations where all or most of the project effort has to be contracted out. This is primarily the case in most governmental project activity. Political pressures dictate that the government does not compete with the private sector. As a consequence, project management in the government often involves determining need, issuing requests for proposals, proposal evaluation, source selection, and contracting the work to a qualified bidder. In essence, project management in the government is often contract administration. Another operational possibility is where some or most, but not all, capabilities exist internally to perform the project. In such instances decisions have to be made as to whether to develop internal capabilities to meet project performance requirements or to subcontract the work to outside sources.

Excluding governmental divisions, there usually are pressures to develop internal capability. Several arguments are often offered to management in favor of internal operational capability. Management must carefully evaluate such arguments to separate validity from self-interest. The inclination is to want to add an activity, function, or capability to an already existing operational unit. Expanding operation capability can be justified under some circumstances; at other times proposed operational expansion can merely be an empire-building ploy. Management has to look at such a proposal relative to urgency of current need, future prospects for continued utilization of such capability, including a continuing commitment, and the implications relative to the total organization of such a commitment.

Arguments are frequently advanced to develop internal capability based on costs. Proponents for internal operational capability usually cite the purchased price versus costs if there was internal performance. Many times comparative costs are unrealistic because the advocates of internal operations fail to include all relevant costs such as overhead and capital expenditures needed to develop the capability, depreciation, and optional uses of resources that might be more productively employed on other projects.

There are also subtle psychological pressures for developing internal capability. Technical professionals often do not feel comfortable accepting inputs from outside sources that may be pivotal to the project's success. The inclination is to develop the data or attendant factors internally. A hands-on approach tends to instill confidence in the validity of information generated. At times this approach is very unrealistic and certainly not cost effective. Outside specialized organizations may have more experience and capability than that which is internally available. What happens, to use a cliché, is a reinventing of the wheel. Unfortunately, the "not invented here" syndrome is all too common and practiced all too frequently.

The make-or-buy decisions generally are difficult, especially where countervailing arguments are advanced by different organizational factions. If make-or-buy decisions are relatively common occurrences rather than isolated incidents, it may be wise to establish a standing committee. A neutral committee can be used to evaluate the benefits and negative aspects associated with developing internal capability or going to external sources for project support. Such a committee or evaluation board could be composed of representatives from the technical organization, as well as from functional support activities as finance, marketing, procurement, quality control, production, legal, contract administration, and so on.

Factors Affecting Make or Buy

At times the decision to make or buy, as has been indicated, is relatively obvious. At other times there are many factors that can be involved in the decision process. It is in these complex situations where a make-or-buy evaluation committee representing various operational segments can aid in the decision process by providing insight and perspective. Following are some factors and questions that might be relevant.

Capacity. What is the existing capacity of the organization? How feasible is it to expand capacity? What are the current commitments to capacity? What are the future prospects that existing capacity will be used?

Future. What is the technology involved? How vulnerable is it to obsolescence? Will an investment provide a hedge against possible future technological developments? To what extent or confidence level can the future, future requirements, and future operational objectives be forecast? Will investment in added capability based on future prospects compromise the organization's ability to survive in the event that such future prospects have been miscalculated?

Effectiveness. How operationally effective will the new activity be? What start-up problems can be anticipated? Will effectiveness be competitive with available external sources? Can resources required for the proposed activity be more effectively employed elsewhere in the organization?

Control. How critical is the work to project success? Is close control vital to achieve technical objectives? Would tight control be difficult or improbable if the work were subcontracted? To what extent is control essential for secrecy purposes to protect proprietary processes or information? Can control be exercised to ensure desirable quality standards? Can control be exerted on the contractor to make sure that the proposed resources are those that are actually used to support the project?

Coordination. How much coordination will be required as a result of letting part of the project activity outside the organization? What coordination problems can be foreseen? Will coordination be a significant cost factor that might neutralize the anticipated benefits from contracting with

outside specialists? To what extent will outside coordination requirements distract from internal project management responsibilities? Is there
a possibility that external coordination activities can be delegated? How
complex is the project? Does the project manager have the skill to coordinate internal and external project work phases?

Capital Investment. What are the capital investment requirements?
The prospects for payback? Capital obsolescence? Continued use? Tax
benefits? Possibility for selling added capability to other projects internally? Is it economically and technically feasible to develop new capability and expand operational ability that can be externally contracted out?
Will the capital expenditure upgrade, modernize, or extend existing operational capabilities? Are funds available for such a capital expenditure
either from internal reserves or as part of the negotiated project cost? Is
the technology involved in the capital investment moving so fast that
better equipment might be available in the near future? In the light of the
aforementioned, would it be feasible to rent or lease rather than buy? Is it
possible to make a capital investment that can be shared with more than
one project and as a result upgrade the purchase? Will the acquisition
have a serious negative impact on the cash flow? How volatile is the
economy? The technology? Would it be wise to at least temporarily
shelve the investment decision until future developments that might affect
such a decision come into sharper focus?

Legal Aspects. Are there any laws that might affect the decision to
contract for external project support? What legal liabilities might be incurred as a result of outside contracting? Will outside contracting possibly
compromise the organization's position relative to product liability?
How? As part of the original contract authorizing the project, were there
stipulated set-asides for contracting to outside sources? Specifically to
small businesses or minority-owned enterprises?[7]

Management Philosophy. It is possible that even after make-or-buy
analysis factors have been evaluated and recommendations based thereon
made that management will take a course opposite from that recommended? The decision to expand operations or remain operationally intact may well be a reflection of how the organization is managed. A
conservative management in a technologically unsettled environment
might opt for a risk-avoiding or risk-minimizing approach. A more aggres-
sively oriented management might be inclined to push the organization in
the direction of perceived opportunities and be willing to take a risk
position. These are times when managerial philosophy may be susceptible
to change because of the nature or state of the technology and the actual
or potential competition.

The make-or-buy decision that often involves more than an immediate commitment may significantly affect future operational capabilities. In some instances buying consulting services, purchasing relatively inexpensive and expendable components, or subcontracting minor blocks of work involves no momentous decisional processes. At other times the decision to make or buy has much farther-reaching implications than the direct support of a specific project and could, as mentioned, materially affect future operational capabilities and direction.

Cash Flow

Available Funds and Commitment

One important view of project management is to look at the project as an entrepreneurial activity. The project manager has to go beyond the obvious responsibility to accomplish the project's technical objectives. The project manager should understand the relationship and the need to synchronize expenditures and revenue. There are situations where the project manager has little or no control of cash flow relative to his or her project. This might be the case where the project is incrementally funded and periodic progress payments are made to reflect work accomplished. There are also situations where, by effectively using capital, it is possible that greater profit can accrue to the project.

If the project requires capital expenditure support, the inclination is to commit for such expenditure(s) as soon as possible after the project is authorized. Commitment or actual expenditure should really be predicated on scheduled need and the lead time required to acquire the capital expenditure. Early commitment and subsequent down time can tie up capital that can be more productively used elsewhere. It is also possible that by correlating actual need to acquisition better, cheaper, or more modern equipment will subsequently become available.

Another cash flow problem can arise because work segments have been assigned and completed but not integrated into the project. Such completed activities are planned to be phased in at a later date when related project phases are scheduled for completion. The situation described parallels work in process in a standard production operation. Work in process ties up capital. A basic objective in production operations is to minimize inventory and work in process. In the project illustration not only has capital been committed to completed but dormant activities, but there is the chance that such work completed will have to be redone or modified later based upon unforeseeable problems or technical changes that occur on the project.

The effective use of funds is an integral part of project management. A competent project manager will understand the financial implications of direct and indirect costs charged to the project, budgeting, expenditures and revenue receipts, and profit objectives.

Cost Estimating

Estimating

Estimating is fundamental to planning. It is a conversion of anticipated effort into resource requirements. An estimate of the costs gives management guidance on the feasibility of the effort and the direction it should take. Furthermore, if the organization is performing the work on a contract basis, an explanation of the component cost elements must be given. Confidence in the accuracy and reliability of cost estimates can be instrumental in determining the avenues to accomplishing a program or a project.

Difficulties in Cost Estimating

Estimating costs can be difficult when there have been technologically complex projects extending over a considerable time period. The estimating and control problems are not the same in research and in development. Sponsored research projects are usually by grant or contract and are generally based on a best effort approach within the work scope defined in the proposal. Cost overruns on research projects have not been a major factor and have not received undue notoriety. There have been situations in which the anticipated level of accomplishment has been optimistic or the time frame for accomplishment has been underestimated in research projects, but, as mentioned, this has not been a great problem and has not been the focus of unfavorable publicity.

Estimating costs and cost management on developmental projects have been quite a different situation. Most of the literature, most of the concern, and most of the cost escalations have been focused in developmental projects. The emphasis, as a consequence, of this section is more on cost estimating in developmental projects than in research projects.

Cost estimating is far more involved than just estimating the direct costs that will be incurred on the project. Whether a project will be authorized or not, its subsequent cost effectiveness or profitability might well hinge on several peripheral factors or approaches to cost estimating. The following discussion will center on some of the cost-estimating problems, the different ways project costs can be handled, some of the cost-estimating methods that can be used, some of the intangibles in cost estimating, the impact of overhead on cost estimating, estimating direct labor costs, estimating to complete the project when work is in process, some of the project cost control problems, and a few possible suggestions for improving cost estimating.

Estimating Problems and Characteristics

When a product or service is standardized, uses standard components, and has an evolutionary production cycle, cost accumulations and future costs can be estimated with reasonable certainty. In such cases it is possible to measure the input–output relationships and periodically review the production process to identify changing cost factors and then use these findings to develop a system of costing for estimating purposes.

Estimating the cost for projects, especially where there is R&D, is complicated by many unknowns or variables such as the lack of precedent, unpredictable technical problems, program changes resulting from new knowledge or shifting requirements, the uncertainty of the time cycle, the optimism of technical people, the human productive variable, inflation, and the possible bias of the estimator.

Previous experience is a limited guideline on projects concerned with development work. The fact that such effort is predicated on exploration is an indication that what was valid in the past may not be applicable in the future. Even when a present project builds on past experience, management can be misled on the size of the present problem owing to the differing ratios of knowns to unknowns.

It is equally hard to anticipate the technical problems that might be encountered when pushing the state of the art. A failure to recognize the extent of technical difficulty at the outset or to foresee the magnitude of problems that were anticipated can also affect estimating by requiring more resources than were planned for. Specifically, there might be an inaccurate work breakdown; the complexity of the technical problems encountered could be miscalculated; relevant work items could be omitted in the original cost estimate and these could become major project cost elements; the wrong estimating techniques could be used in attempting to determine future costs; and the cost estimating may fail to properly assess and compensate for potential risks.

Changes in program objectives or specifications likewise complicate cost estimating. Projects are often undertaken under less than ideal circumstances. Because a need may be apparent and time may be critical, the program may be authorized and initiated without a clear definition of its essential elements or even its total technical scope. Knowledge derived in the course of the project may dictate program changes. Those resulting from technical inputs can obviate much completed effort that originally was considered germane. The added effort that program changes normally entail naturally affects cost estimates.

Allied to changes resulting from new knowledge are changes dictated by shifting requirements. A project that was logical or an approach which was defensible at its inception may later prove inappropriate because of changed social, political, or economic factors, as well as technological considerations. In some situations revised requirements may call for a program modification; in others the change can be so drastic as to make the entire project obsolete.

The time period that might be covered in the project can alter the original estimates in other ways. Programs can extend from months to years, and assumptions made at the beginning of the project will probably be inaccurate for the later phases of the work. Usually the further the program extends from the original estimating base, the less accurate the original estimates of need, performance, and cost are likely to be.

One of the more difficult intangibles to cope with in forecasting project cost is the natural optimism of prospective project managers who have a proclivity for underestimating the time and resources needed as well as the extent of the problem. Realizing that management may defer or refuse authorization to embark on a project if realistic estimates are given, the inclination is to minimize the difficulties and overstate the potential benefits as a means of getting approval for the project. Managers, particularly those in R&D, are usually aware of this built-in optimism when evaluating a potential program. Most often, however, the manager has become too divorced from the technical work to formulate an accurate appraisal of what actually is involved. As a consequence, the manager is forced to make a subjective evaluation to augment the project estimates presented. Besides deciding on the desirability and feasibility of the project proposed, the manager must evaluate the ability of the individual(s) to perform as estimated.

Machine performance can be predicted; people vary in ability, energy, and motivation. The performance of one individual on one technical phase of a project can be predicted, though with reservation; the same person may vary in response to the same stimulus given at different times. But when there are many technical aspects and many people assigned to a project, the difficulty in estimating human performance is herculean. Needless to say, the human productive variable will affect estimates of time and cost as well as performance.

The ability of the estimator is the final ingredient in the accuracy of a project estimate. A proposal is usually generated under extreme time pressure, and the estimator may not be able to examine the many factors associated with it in sufficient depth. The estimator must be technically qualified to identify the resources needed and the amounts required. He or she must factor into the forecasts many of the elements discussed in this section and hedge against unpredictable problems. If the estimator is technically inexperienced or incompetent to evaluate the range of the technical work to be covered or inclined toward optimism or pessimism, the project estimates will reflect this personal bent.

Intangibles

If there is some comparable base for an evaluation, as in the case of similar hardware products, estimating is simplified. The estimator can approximate costs by comparing the product with existing or related products. He or she can also ascertain the value with reasonable accuracy as evidenced by market price and consumer acceptance.

Projects usually are specialized activities. The end product of a project generally entails the formation of knowledge. Unlike hardware, knowledge is not susceptible to standardization, and its value in relation to its estimated or actual cost is not readily determinable. What is knowledge worth? Can the immediate or fallout benefits be measured? Costs are real, but anticipated benefits are often intangible and actual benefits may not be immediately apparent. For instance, it may be that knowledge and insight gained on a project can be carried over to follow-on or unrelated work. The repercussions that contribute to accomplishment on subsequent programs normally cannot be defined with any exactness, are difficult to measure as a benefit related to a cost estimate, and certainly do not lend themselves to any allocation procedure in cost accounting.

A correlation between estimated costs and the value of the physical end product runs the danger of ignoring relevant intangibles. The material product is only the manifestation of knowledge and often represents the least complex phase of the cycle. This is especially true in situations where need and not market return is the motivation for project authorization. The government, the military, and nonprofit organizations often support projects where the determination of direct comparative costs is impossible and value evaluation subjective. Apparent costs often become confused with real costs. The immediate visible end product cost may appear to be badly out of line. However, if knowledge development has been a major intangible associated with the material end product, this can, depending on the knowledge, be a substantive intangible benefit. In some knowledge-generating projects, such as the space program, the fallout benefits have been significant. In many instances where projects are authorized for high-technology developmental work an assessment of the potential benefits are at best subjective. The value of work attempted and performed may not lend itself to a dollar-and-cents appraisal. Actual or estimated cost, on the other hand, is very real and does give the decision maker insight for a course of action. In view of the intangibles involved, the manager is obligated to review subjective elements in concert with readily apparent costs and predictable or immediately anticipated benefits.

Treatment of Costs

Estimates of the costs of a given project or program can be widely disparate owing to individual or organizational variations in methodology and interpretation: The assessment of the technical scope of a project, which affects the estimated program cost, is subject to different concepts, as is the treatment of cost components. By shifting costs between projects or to overhead or by changing the percentage of cost allocation, it is possible to justify some projects financially and to place an undue burden on others. Before much progress can be made in establishing valid input–output relationships, some accurate standard means of ascertaining inputs should be developed.

The difference in methods used for accumulating costs frequently adds to the difficulty of deciding whether to undertake a project. Internally, estimators can make a project appear very promising by assigning or charging related costs to other projects under some subterfuge. Externally, when two or more organizations are bidding on the same project, comparative analysis often is not possible, since cost components and methods are either undefined or unalike. Evaluating and auditing a number of projects for their relative potential effectiveness will have no meaning unless the proposals have a common procedural base.

A case in point was a very large project for which the competition had narrowed to two organizations. Starting with identical specifications, each contractor submitted a program cost estimate. The cost differential in the two estimates was approximately 30%. The proposals were drawn up in such a way that it was impossible for the contracting agency to match the work phases and costs of one bid with those of the other. To analyze the discrepancy more realistically, the contracting agency independently undertook to develop work phases and attendant costs; the agency produced an estimate substantially different from those submitted by the two contractors. What is more, because of variations of interpretation and cost classifications, this estimate defied comparative analysis with either of the two original proposals.[8]

When many organizations are bidding for a contract, some comparative base can be established by breaking the project into small work segments. Taking a large project in its entirety makes step-by-step analysis very difficult. If the contracting organization defines in advance the work phases and items to be accomplished and this information is transmitted to the contractors, a request can be made that bids for project authorization follow the work definition. This approach would encourage segregating each work item and phase and pricing each separately so more valid cost comparisons could be made.

The lack of standardized cost classifications further confuses evaluation of actual costs that might be charged to projects, particularly research and development projects. The usual practices, according to a study made by the National Association of Accountants, are to include R&D expenses as (1) part of the cost of goods sold or (2) a deduction from gross margin. Of the companies that participated in the study, approximately one-third exercised the first practice, and the remainder followed the second. The National Association of Accountants report concluded that the procedure followed by any given company reflected one of three factors: (1) the purpose of the research and the interpretation of that purpose in expense classification, (2) the way in which the R&D function was organized, or (3) the type or nature of R&D activities carried on by the company.[9]

If the organization is involved exclusively in research, total cost accumulation may follow some definite pattern. If it undertakes research, development, and subsequent production, determining where costs or charges should be allocated is more difficult. For instance, what should be charged to R&D as overhead, depreciation on plant, and common use of facilities? Research expenses are also subject to quite a wide fluctuation, depending on how the costs of the operation are accumulated and treated.

The treatment of costs is also problematic when the research department provides technical services to other groups within an organization. How can project R&D costs be allocated to products that are already in existence, but which have been improved by subsequent research and development? Where is the logical cutoff point between research costs and production costs? Should scientific equipment be treated as part of a project expense or should it be capitalized for general use? How should the allocation of common services within the entire organization be handled in relation to the R&D function?

Research and development costs may actually represent a current expense. However, many organizations choose to treat them as a capital expenditure in project selection, basing this on anticipated return on investment.

Another approach to cost identification and treatment has been used on government projects, particularly those projects where military weapons systems have been developed; this is life cycle costing. Life cycle costing goes beyond hardware development and procurement. Life cycle costing looks at the deployment costs associated with the total operational system, including maintenance and support costs. By looking at total cost potential rather than immediate and apparent out-of-pocket costs, a clearer picture of costs that might be incurred over the entire life cycle can be evaluated and possibly compared to competitive or alternate systems. The direct purchase costs may be misleading in that subsequent costs can make the procurement ineffective costwise.

With life cycle costing approach, reasonable visibility is probable and all important cost components of the system will be figured in the system total cost. Many elements constitute the total system life cycle costs. It has been suggested that the different system cost elements may be categorized as follows:

Research and development. Costs primarily associated with the development of a new system or capacity to the point at which it is ready for procurement and operational use.

Investment. Costs beyond the development phase to introduce a new system or capacity into operational use, including installation and checkout.

Operation and support (O&S). Recurring costs of operation, maintenance, and logistics support of the system.[10]

The advantage in establishing system costs under separate categories is to enable planners and decision makers to facilitate evaluation. The costs related to each phase of the system life cycle are subject to different relationships over time and to the number of units to be procured under the system. The investment costs are usually independent of time, but can be directly related to the number of system units to be deployed and to the expected operational life of the system. Research and development and investment costs are considered relatively independent of time and are treated as one-time costs. By contrast, operation and support costs can be long-term costs in systems having the potential for a long life expectancy. The operation and support costs in long-lived systems may account for the major part of the system's total life cycle cost.[11]

This section has only provided a relatively cursory look at how project costs might be approached. There is a wide spectrum of problems involved in treating costs and possible cost classifications. Only a few representative samples have been presented indicating the breadth of the problem.

Cost Methods

Inexorably related to cost treatment and classification is the question of cost method. The four most common methods for analyzing costs are the accounting, engineering, econometric, and parametric approaches.[12]

The accounting method is used primarily as a means of classifying data according to various cost categories. The accountant observes the levels of output from the established categories and then uses these outputs as a basis for estimating and building up basic cost data. In this method little attention is paid to developing hypotheses or to accounting for price changes or other factors that could affect costs.

The engineering approach emphasizes physical relationships, such as pounds of materials used and rated capacity, and converts these into dollars to arrive at an estimate of cost. A good illustration of this approach is an estimation of the cost of an aircraft calculated on the anticipated weight of the vehicle. The engineering method can be useful when there is little or no cost precedent to use for analytical purposes.

In the econometric method a statistical approach combined with economic theory is used to analyze the net effect of output variations on cost. A model of the cost function is constructed, based on historical or cross-sectional data reflecting the static cost curve of economic theory. Since the empirical curve is at best only an average of past relationships, it is not an exact replica of the theoretical cost curves discussed in economic textbooks.[13]

Parametric cost estimating is a relatively new technique. Parametric cost estimating has been defined as "an estimate which predicts cost by means of explanatory variables such as performance characteristics, physical characteristics, and characteristics relevant to the development process as derived from experience on logically related systems."[14]

The four approaches discussed are not exclusive of each other or competitive, but represent possible ways of determining cost. Each method or combination of methods is useful in giving management the information wanted and needed for decision making. A single cost method or a restricted view can create an erroneous impression of the potential value to be derived from any one project. Several approaches generally must be used to provide the organization with all its necessary cost information. The most useful estimates are often those derived from combinations and adjustments of the data.[15]

Spencer and Siegelman distinguish such cost classifications as absolute and alternative cost; direct and indirect; fixed and variable; short and long run; differential or incremental and residual; sunk, shutdown, and abandonment costs; urgent and postponable costs; escapable and inescapable; controllable and uncontrollable; and replacement and original costs.[16]

This brief discussion of cost methods is not intended to be all inclusive. Other factors, tangible and intangible, some intrinsic and some extrinsic, must also be evaluated as cost elements—to name just a few, the cost of capital, the capital structure or available capital within the organization, the cash flow or resources available to the organization, the method of handling the project for tax purposes, the profit prospects or, in nonprofit organizations, the benefits to be expected, and the potential follow-up or technical justifications for undertaking the particular project or program.

Overhead

The project manager can control many of the direct costs related to the project; he or she can also control some of the indirect costs that might be charged to the project. There are also some indirect or overhead costs that are beyond the control of the project manager. The project manager must be acutely aware of overhead costs, controllable and noncontrollable, and how overhead rates can affect the prospects for a new project or the operational range of an existing project.[17]

Overhead rates plus the cost of direct labor dollar inputs can take a prospective project out of a competitive position. If a project has been bid on, and subsequently authorized, based on projected direct labor rates and overhead application, and overhead rates later increase, the project manager will probably encounter financial problems. Increased overhead applied to ongoing projects raises the total project costs. Unforeseen costs of this nature can severely compromise the financial success of the project. The project manager is faced with the task of either redefining the scope of the program, changing the resource mix, or risk a cost overrun. This will be elaborated upon in the section dealing with labor costs.

It is very important for the project manager to understand how overhead rates are derived and applied. Examples of some of the elements that constitute overhead are as follows:

Controllable overhead within the project
    Proposal preparation
    Supplies not directly required by the project
    Clerical assistance
    Staff support
    Equipment not directly required by the project
    Professional meetings and periodicals that cannot be charged to the
        project

Noncontrollable overhead outside the project
    Fringe benefits
    Depreciation reserves
    Maintenance
    Indirect labor
    Organizational memberships
        Dues
        Subscriptions
        Travel
        Seminars
    Training programs
    Corporate general and administrative expenses
    Nonproductive supplies
    Taxes
    Personnel recruitment
    Nonproductive chargeable telephone and postage expenses
    Utilities

The above list is only a partial but representative list. Some of the controllable overhead within the project is manageable. Sensitivity to costs and careful consideration of cost options by the project manager can often significantly reduce overhead costs generated within the project. Awareness of overhead cost external to the project and beyond the direct control of the project manager is also important. In some instances the project is a large contributor to the corporate overhead rate. Again, cost sensitivity can minimize such negative contributions. Where overhead costs are external and not controllable, the project manager should know how such rates currently affect the project, possible future changes in organizational overhead rates, and how such rates might affect the management of the project.

Another frequent problem associated with overhead rates is the application of such costs. How overhead is allocated within the organization is often a source of internal friction. The following are a few possible examples of how overhead might be applied:

According to the percentage of physical area used

Based on the percentage of profit contribution

Based on the percentage of organizational resources used

Based on the percentage of total sales

Based on the number of people assigned to the project as a percentage of the total work force

Estimating Labor Costs

If the amount and cost of labor on projects, particularly those projects where there is research and/or development, could be accurately anticipated, estimating would be vastly simplified and stabilized. On many projects the single, most important cost component is labor costs. For instance, labor costs have been calculated as accounting for 65–85% of total project costs where there are R&D activities.[18] If 75% were taken as representative, estimating the number of people to be assigned to a project would provide a basis for control. The difficulty lies in predicting which people, at what cost, and what length of time they will need to accomplish the objectives of the project.

Despite these variables, estimating project labor costs can be improved with sound methods of allocating personnel. One method is to figure the human resources required in each of the sequential phases of the project and to convert these requirements into estimated hours to complete the program. The calculation begins with the direct cost of the hours; adds overhead expenses, and general and administrative costs; provides a contingency or emergency factor for possible increases in labor costs and for unforeseen problems that might be encountered on the project; and makes an allowance for profit[19]:

Direct labor hour cost	$20.00
Overhead at 150%	$30.00
	$50.00
General and administrative cost at 10%	$ 5.00
	$55.00
Contingency factor at 10%	$ 5.50
	$60.50
Profit at 10%	$ 6.05
Total estimated labor cost per hour	$66.55

On the basis of this example, the project labor costs can be estimated by multiplying the total hours required by $60.50 for nonprofit or in-house work, and by $66.55 if the hours represent a service sold for profit to another organization. This method or some variation of it has often been used in determining labor costs for projects.

There are, however, several limitations to this approach. The direct labor outlay is usually computed on the basis of current cost or immediately foreseeable labor costs. And yet, because a project may cover months or years, adhering to present costs as an estimating base for projection into the future can be seriously misleading, if not naïve. As the project progresses, the situation depicted in Figure 9-1 develops all too often.

In Figure 9-1a the hours expended are following the program plan. Converting these hours into dollars (Figure 9-1b) indicates the real cost of labor.[20] The total of dollars actually expended is greater than the expenditure forecast to that point, although the hour inputs were accurately predicted.

The simple explanation is that the cost of the hours has been greater than originally estimated. In the method of computation being illustrated, inadequate allowance was made for increasing labor costs. This example represents an average yearly increase of almost 7%. In the model a contingency factor of approximately 28% instead of 10% would have been necessary merely to cover the increased labor costs, without any allowance for the additional hours or longer period of time that would accrue if the program encountered unforeseen technical obstacles. As has been amply demonstrated, it is highly optimistic to assume that an original estimate of the hours and the work involved in complicated and time-extended projects will be right on target. What are the alternatives when cost information shows a situation like that illustrated in Figure 9-1b?

The most obvious and direct solution, assuming that the discrepancy from the estimate is discovered early enough to take corrective action, is to cut the cost of the hours being spent. If the control system is not sufficiently sensitive to detect the variance until considerably more expenditure has taken place than was planned for, the cost of future hours

Figure 9-1. Forecast and actual project expenditures proceeding from an estimate based on present costs. From Daniel D. Roman, *Research and Development Management: The Economics and Administration of Technology,* Englewood Cliffs, NJ: Prentice-Hall, 1968, p. 307.

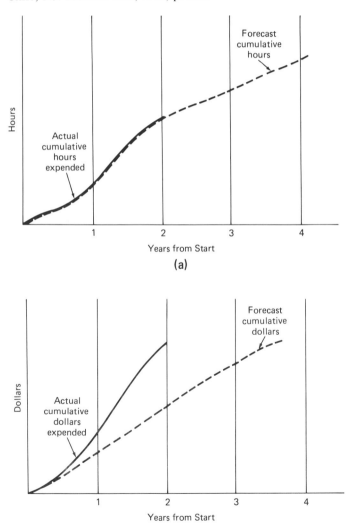

will have to be cut below the original estimate to compensate for the expensive hours already used and charged. Though the trend of increasing labor costs appears to be too strong for these methods to be workable, there are several alternatives along these lines that management can consider to bring the cost back into alignment.

One possible solution is to assign less expensive personnel to complete the program. This at first appears to be a logical step; however, realistically, the people who have been on the project from its early stages and are familiar with it are generally more efficient, even though the direct out-of-pocket cost might be higher for them than for more junior people. The need for continuity and for specific talents on some projects often precludes the advisability of transferring personnel freely from project to project.

A second possible avenue for adjustment would be to review the entire project to assess the accomplishment to date and the work remaining. It may be possible to contract, eliminate, or consolidate one or more work phases or to modify the project's technical approach. Changing the scope of the work might allow the project to be completed satisfactorily with the expenditure of fewer but more expensive hours than originally estimated.

A third possibility would be to reduce the overhead rate. In the example it was assumed that the average cost of a direct labor hour was $20.00 and the overhead rate was 150%. If the cost of the $20.00 hour were to follow the projected annual increase of 7%, it would mean that a corresponding cut in excess of 20% a year in the overhead rate would be necessary to maintain the same approximate cost level. To illustrate:

Project year 1		Project year 2	
Direct labor hour	$20.00	7% increase	$22.10
Overhead at 150%	$30.00	Overhead at 130%	$28.73
	$50.00		$50.83

Cutting overhead 20% a year would be very difficult. Overhead primarily consists of indirect labor and fixed costs like taxes, depreciation, and utilities. It might be possible to lower overhead by putting certain indirect work classifications on a direct charge basis. On the face of it, this would increase the direct hours over the figure originally budgeted. An audit of the functions, performance, and number of indirect people might allow management to reduce the indirect work force, yet indiscriminate layoffs could transfer some of these functions to highly skilled project professionals who are already on a direct charge. This approach can be self-defeating in that it may lead to distractions from the immediate project objective in sufficient degree to where overhead savings are offset by decreasing the amount of effort and contribution made by the direct people. However, organizations do tend to allow functions, individuals, and activities to exist and even grow that are noncontributive and not cost effective. There are times when operational crises force a review of the organization that can in turn lead to elimination or reduction of some cost elements without impairing the efficiency or morale of the organization.

There are many less obvious ways to reduce overhead. Some exploration can lead to cost savings that would not interfere, as mentioned in the preceding paragraph, with the efficient execution of functions and the attainment of operational objectives. Often the alternatives suggested only partially succeed in offsetting miscalculated costs. In this event management will need to review the project from other standpoints to determine the most feasible course of action, considering existing objectives and obligations.

If there is a contractual commitment at a fixed price, management must minimize remaining costs but complete the project, though it means less profit or even a loss. If the contract is a government cost plus fixed fee arrangement, the firm can request permission to continue on overrun funds. At this point the government contracting officer can review the project or program and decide whether to authorize additional funds or terminate the program. If the project is in-house, management will have to judge whether the potential is sufficient to justify additional cost, or whether some useful information can be salvaged from what has been accomplished with the funds already expended. Management might then look for other resources within the company to continue the work or decide to abandon the project.

Estimating to Complete

Control and responsive action are often difficult in project management because assessments of progress are frequently inaccurate. The intangible nature of the work makes the appraisal of accomplishment in relation to dollar and time expenditures subjective. If calculating the actual progress is hard for people directly assigned to the project because of their inherent optimism, their vested interest, and their usual unwillingness to acknowledge the extent of the technical problems they are experiencing, it is even more difficult for managers, who are one or more steps removed from the project. The result is that management must generally rely on the appraisal of the people more familiar with the work.

A method to aid in a realistic evaluation of a project's progress is to estimate to complete the project. It pinpoints what has been done to date and what is left to be done in terms of the time and dollars authorized and budgeted for the project.

The estimate to complete is a valuable tool not only for top management, but also for the project manager, because it helps him or her to assemble the various increments of the program. A form like that shown in Figure 9-2 can be drawn up to reflect the operational and financial status of the project.

In Figure 9-2 the estimate to complete identifies the project, shows an item and work phase breakdown as it relates to the authorized budget, and indicates the specific resources in direct labor hours and other direct costs allocated to the performing functions. The second column shows the forecast or estimated expenditures at the completion of the project. The third column shows the expenditures as of the issue date of the report, and the fourth column indicates the balance between the estimated cost at completion and the actual cost incurred to date. The fifth column indicates the total amount authorized converted into dollars, the sixth column the estimated completion costs, and the seventh column the difference between the authorized and estimated amounts.

A detailed analysis of this type will indicate where funds have been over- or underexpended and focus on trouble areas. It also forces the individual groups supporting the main project to look at the available resources, what has already been spent or committed, and what remains to be done. Any good planning and control must go into such detail in order to determine what is happening. This approach provides tangible evidence of what is happening on the project. To a large degree, it forces project people to provide a more realistic status on a project and, as mentioned, targets in on problem areas. On many projects the failure to accomplish the objectives of a single work phase can have drastic implications for the entire program, such as cost overruns and schedule delays.

Project Cost Control Problems

Total costs within a project organization can be determined, but procedural disparities and differing cost classification methods may make the allocation of costs to specific accounts less than accurate. Often cost identification breaks down at the project level.

Most organizations engaged in project activities have several projects in process simultaneously. These often can be grouped according to technical compatibility or similar resource requirements. The related projects may be placed under a single manager, even though each project represents a separate commitment and calls for independent technical planning and resource allocation. Grouping projects may be more effective organizationally, but this practice makes project cost accumulation and control more difficult.

The composite activity under the jurisdiction of a project manager can be forecast with reasonable accuracy. The dollars spent for outside services and equipment and the time charges of people reporting to the manager can be priced and recorded. With two or more projects under the

XYZ Corporation

Estimate To Complete

Date: 6 1 19XX

Project and Item	[1] Authorized Budget				[2] Estimated Costs at Project Completion				[3] Expenditures as of 6 1 19XX				[4] Balance Between Estimated and Actual Costs				[5] Authorized Project Cost^a	[6] Estimated Completion Project Cost^a	[7] Balance
	Engr. DLH^a	Mfg. DLH^a	Engr. DC\$^{b}	Mfg. DC\$^{b}	Engr. DLH	Mfg. DLH	Engr. DC\$	Mfg. DC\$	Engr. DLH	Mfg. DLH	Engr. DC\$	Mfg. DC\$	Engr. DLH	Mfg. DLH	Engr. DC\$	Mfg. DC\$			
Project X-12																			
Item 1	2,000	1,000	$5,000	$10,000	2,500	1,000	$5,000	$12,000	1,700	700	$4,000	$8,000	800	300	$1,000	$4,000	$104,860	$123,500	($18,640)
Phase 1	500	300	—	1,000	500	275	—	500	500	100	—	500	—	175	—	—	24,630	23,547	1,082
Phase 2	500	300	1,000	1,000	600	325	1,000	2,000	300	200	500	1,500	300	125	500	500	25,630	30,540	(4,910)
Phase 3	1,000	400	4,000	8,000	1,400	400	4,000	9,500	900	400	3,500	6,000	500	—	500	3,500	54,600	69,412	(14,812)

^{a} Engineering direct labor hours are priced out at $33.28 per hour; manufacturing direct labor hours are priced out at $23.30 per hour.

^{b} Direct charge dollars are the sum of such cost items as materials, trips, outside production, long-distance telephone calls, etc.

^{c} The procedure for computing this figure (and other figures in columns 5 and 6) is as follows:

2,000 engineering DLH @ $33.28/hour	$ 66,560
1,000 manufacturing DLH @ $23.30/hour	23,300
Engineering DC$	5,000
Manufacturing DC$	10,000
	$104,860

Figure 9-2. Estimate to complete project X-12. From Daniel D. Roman, *Research and Development Management: The Economics and Administration of Technology*, Englewood Cliffs, NJ: Prentice-Hall, 1968, p. 310.

domain of one project manager and where resources can be interchangeable between projects, the project manager is in a position to compensate
for poor estimates and inadequate performance. The project manager can
switch people among projects and have them record their time against the
project that is in the best financial position to absorb the charge. Similar
procedures can be used with equipment and other project costs.

Using a simple model to illustrate this situation, let us assume that the
project manager has two projects reporting to him or her. The project
manager makes the projection for the projects shown in Figure 9-3. As a

Figure 9-3. Estimated times and costs of two projects reporting to a single man-
ager. From Daniel D. Roman, *Research and Development Management: The
Economics and Administration of Technology,* Englewood Cliffs, NJ: Prentice-
Hall, 1968, p. 318.

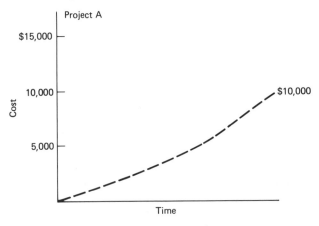

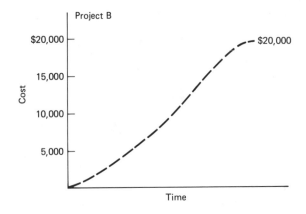

result of unforeseen technical problems or mistakes in planning and estimating, the actual costs might approximate those in Figure 9-4, which
shows an overrun or loss of $2,000 on project A and an underrun or profit
of $6,000 on project B.

Indubitably, management will ask the project manager why he or she
was 20% over on one project and 30% under on the other project. The
project manager's technical and administrative ability may be questioned

Figure 9-4. Estimated and actual times and costs of two projects reporting to a
single manager. From Daniel D. Roman, *Research and Development Management: The Economics and Administration of Technology,* Englewood Cliffs, NJ:
Prentice-Hall, 1968, p. 319.

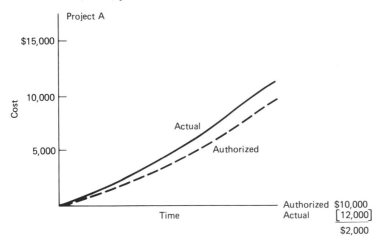

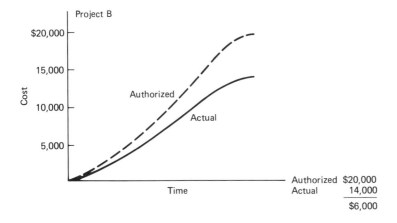

as a result of the cost experience; certainly his or her estimating capability would be closely scrutinized. Aware of the possible implications of the information shown in Figure 9-4, the project manager would probably maneuver costs to reflect the position illustrated in Figure 9-5.

Figure 9-5 indicates that the combined cost of the two projects remains the same, $26,000, but by distributing the costs more evenly, the project manager has given project A an underrun or profit of $1,000 (10%) and

Figure 9-5. Estimated and redistributed actual costs of two projects reporting to a single manager. From Daniel D. Roman, *Research and Development Management: The Economics and Administration of Technology,* Englewood Cliffs, NJ: Prentice-Hall, 1968, p. 320.

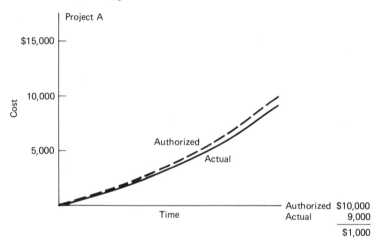

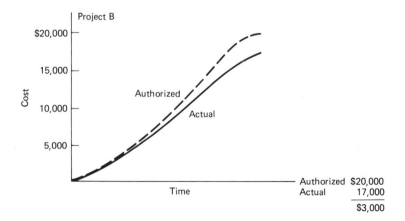

project B an underrun of $3,000 (15%). Displaying this cost experience, the project manager would probably be acclaimed for good performance instead of pressed for explanation and justification.

There are perils associated with mischarging that are not always readily apparent. If the misrecorded costs are used as the foundation for proposing additional project B work, the follow-on will not be authorized if an astute evaluator sees that the work is overpriced. Along the same lines, if more project A work were accepted as a result of the recorded costs shown in Figure 9-5, a loss would probably result unless the project manager has other projects to use in playing the same game the next time around.

Despite budget mechanisms, time cards, job time summaries, and other accounting devices, in the final analysis the project manager who is responsible for more than one project has control. Many a manager who considers himself or herself professionally honest ignores the ethical implications of mischarging. Mischarging may be defensive, but this all too common practice damages the accuracy of cost accumulation at the project level and encourages slipshod estimating.

Project cost control needs reappraisal. Technical people must be impressed with the fact that improper charging is unprofessional. Management must be more tolerant and understanding of cost variances, especially when there is reasonable justification. Finally, much of this practice goes beyond internal management; it can often be attributed to the government system of contracting if there is federal support for the project. If projects A and B are government contracts, the underrun funds on project B in Figure 9-4 would probably have to be returned to the contracting agency with an explanation, and there would be a delay before the required justification and authorization could be gotten for the additional funds needed on project A. Very often two separate government agencies are involved. The inclination, morally questionable as it may be, is to avoid the system and accommodate commitments with the total resources available.

Some Suggestions to Improve Cost Estimating

It is difficult to see how estimating technologically complex efforts can ever become a precise and mechanical procedure, but the accuracy of forecasting costs can be considerably improved if the problem is approached intelligently.

A first step to better estimating is educating the estimators.[21] Project estimates frequently represent a compilation of inputs from various individuals and functions that support the project, too often with insufficient thought and effort given to careful calculation and analysis of estimated activity. Another problem is the coordination of activity and costs in an extensive project. Estimates can be well considered and indeed correct as far as they go, but communication failures can lead to erroneous assumptions and planning. Poor estimating can also be attributed to the lack of uniform methodology; procedures may be so varied that they give rise to different interpretations of the same problem. Also, in the first phase of a multiphase contract, estimating may be intentionally optimistic in order to buy in and win a contract over the competition. There are times when estimates are made honestly and realistically, but management slashes the estimates in the hope that the revised bid will be more competitive and lead to a contract. Management rationale in such situations is "let's get the contract and then we'll find ways to do it within established cost constraints." The author has, unfortunately, been privy to such decision processes; when the contracts were subsequently authorized and the work and costs proceeded along the original estimates, the results were contract overruns and management unhappiness.

Contracts for research and development work for the government and especially the military branch frequently far exceed the original cost estimates. Too often the government contractors have not really thought out the nature of the problem(s) involved and the potential scope of the project. A more definitive work scope and explicit project objectives would enable better estimating as to what the project will ultimately cost. Because of the vagueness, many times, of specifically what the government wants and the frequent practice of changing the direction of the project, estimators are forced to calculate potential costs on the assumption that expected program changes will be the norm rather than the exception.

More emphasis must be placed on accurate estimating, beginning with a reasonable appraisal of the problem itself. Internally, management can and should stress the need for full and correct information on cost components. It must also adopt a more realistic approach to both the costs and the technical scope of the project. Enlightening decision makers and educating project people will produce more accurate approximations of cost. If necessary, management can impose sanctions when foreseeable problems are not recognized in calculations of project costs.

Cost estimating might be improved by greater detail analysis, including the identification of major blocks or items of work and phases of activity within these items, in short, a comprehensive work breakdown analysis as indicated in Chapter 5. Detailed analysis could give management better project perspective and be especially useful in helping to evaluate the prospective work phases before the authorization and to quickly segregate problem areas once the project is in force.

Another suggestion might be to break the program into progressive segments. The total project can be a composite of different modules. The modules would represent sequential phases that would permit evaluation as to accomplishment, value of the project, actual cost experience versus estimated cost, and, finally, the decision as to whether to proceed to the next module or discontinue the program. A modular approach might be more feasible with key decision points indicated rather than total commitment where the program has technical uncertainties.

The accuracy of cost forecasting can be increased by the use of trend analysis, which involves a study of the organization, industry, and economy over a time period. For example, if long-range commitments are being undertaken, wage rates can be analyzed and projected into the future. An emergency or contingency factor that initially appears more than adequate can prove to be entirely inadequate over a long term, owing to inflationary trends. It is therefore useful to establish the types of skill(s) needed in a project, the time phase during which they will be needed, and the anticipated wage rate when each skill will be used. Then, not only must the actual direct cost of the labor be computed, but future overhead rates must be forecast fairly accurately. Overhead, as indicated in the example shown earlier in this chapter, has a significant effect on the total cost of labor.

In line with the preceding discussion and by way of summarization, the following suggestions are offered to improve cost estimating:

Break down work segments into manageable modules.

    Identify work segment resource requirements:

        Human resources

        Facilities and equipment

        External support

        Costs

Realistically allow for inflation.

Provide a hedge for unexpected problems or changes in the project concept. Some possible factors that might affect the project are the following:

    Inaccurate work breakdown

    Omissions of work segments in original estimate

    Improper estimating techniques

    Failure to provide for risk and/or additional effort required to accomplish technical objectives

Get firm price/cost and schedule commitments:

    Internally

    Externally

Be alert to changes in overhead and how overhead changes might affect the project.

Explore possibilities of using knowledge or equipment from other projects.

If a physical end product results from the project, consider the quality control implications:

Inspection costs
Rejections
Rework
Scrap
Spares
Work in process
Warranty reserves
Product liability

Check past experience on technically related projects for guidance in cost estimating.

Maintain good communication with all internal and external project support activities.

Educate estimators on the following:
Judgment
Accuracy
Objectivity
Magnitude of effort
Time

Provide for change control procedures.

Budgeting

Authorization

The budget is the authorization of resources. It can be expressed in things, people, or—more commonly—dollars. Work authorization, by means of a budget against which charges for effort are made, can be to a function, division, project, or the total organization. The budget should be correlated with planning for the accomplishment of objectives. It should represent a decision on the utilization of resources after alternative courses of action are evaluated. The budget is a price tag.

The budget gives management a quantitative base for measurement and evaluation. It represents the delegation and delineation of responsibility and helps provide organizational stability and continuity. The budget is a management tool for communication and coordination.[22]

Budget Process

Budgeting is usually but not always done on a yearly basis. A 1-year budget allocation reflects management's decisions on short-range planning. Some projects extending beyond 1 year may require a long-term commitment and a budget period that is geared to the life of the project rather than a fiscal allocation.

Management must evaluate many factors in determining the budget. It must consider the amount of money needed to keep the organization at the level of operation consistent with commitments and a desired profit or return on investment. In doing so it is necessary to consider the skills available within the organization, the skill mix essential to achieve technical obligations, the amount of funds available, the mix of productive elements that promise optimum results, the amount of project activity to be performed internally and the amount of project work contracted outside the organization, the commitment to a long-range project or program which might transcend the immediate allocation of available resources, and the level of control that will enable management to correlate input–output relationships.[23]

The planning, budgeting, and control of each project in the organization are best carried out by people with technical proficiency who understand the problems and objectives of the project. However, many technically oriented people are unable to effectively cope with managerial planning and budgeting. As an example, Moranian,[24] in his observations on research and development operations, concluded that generally line engineers were either ignorant or disdainful of budgeting and did not understand the concept behind it. Technical professionals frequently tend to look at the budget as an artificial limitation on activity and are more concerned with the immediate accomplishment of the technical aspects of the project than with its costing. Yet, obviously, if every project were allowed to proceed beyond the authorizations granted by the budget, the resource distribution could be like a boarding house dinner—everybody indiscriminately grabbing off everything in sight. Some projects would stop short of achieving objectives because resources were unavailable; others might attain technical objectives at a cost disproportionate to their value. Over- and underexpenditures on different projects or by different functions upset internal planning. They can force management to make unrealistic trade-offs not compatible with the best technical and organizational objectives.

Normally the budget process starts with a forecast of total organizational activity. The forecast can include firm contractual or current obligations that are in process, anticipated follow-on work which extends beyond the present budgetary period, and prospective work that may be started within the next period. The budget under consideration serves as a framework for reviewing authorized projects in process and examining immediately contemplated projects. If funding sources are external to the performing organization, the budget review provides insight into the resources to be requested from the sponsors. If the project work is being subsidized internally, it provides guidance to the level and emphasis of effort that should be elected on the basis of available resources.

The budget process, properly performed, is also a medium of communication. To operate effectively, management must inform the various functional activities of organizational objectives, commitments, and resource expectations. At this time it asks for estimates of resources required to meet established obligations and also solicits suggestions for additional effort compatible with organizational goals and available resources. The operational segments translate their support requirements into budget requests, which are then assembled, compiled, coordinated, evaluated, and authorized. The flow of the process is shown in Figure 9-6.

The budget submitted by each organizational division is usually a compilation of requirements of the separate functions within it. In some organizations budgets are drawn up by activity or project rather than by operational division.

Frequently, when budgets are coordinated and compiled, some modifications are needed. Individual budget segments may appear reasonable in the light of committed and planned work, but when the individual segments are superimposed to make a composite picture, the total budget is found to be out of keeping with expectations or with available resources. Since it is extremely difficult for upper-echelon management to be technically and organizationally adroit enough to evaluate the accuracy and validity of individual budget segments, it frequently imposes an across-the-board budget cut to reconcile expenditures and expectations. Cutting a straight percentage from all budgets is poor management. This fails to take into account miscalculations or excessive requests by some activities that are not in line with actual performance requirements.

Figure 9-6. The budget process. From Daniel D. Roman, *Research and Development Management: The Economics and Administration of Technology,* Englewood Cliffs, NJ: Prentice-Hall, 1968, p. 324.

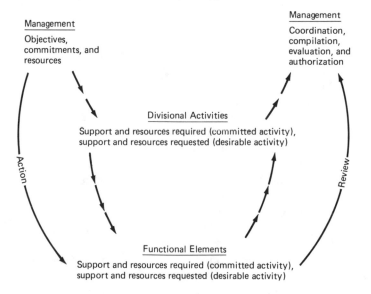

There usually is an inclination to pad the budget. The budget director, who is generally financially rather than technically oriented, is rarely equipped to evaluate the validity of a request founded on anticipated technical accomplishment. Adding to the difficulties is the fact that usually there is no useful precedent to serve as a guide for budget projections. Past authorizations can be misleading, since the project, even though it parallels similar projects that are active or have been completed, may be different enough to where past or existing activity is only partially applicable as a basis for determining resource requirements. If there is a straight across-the-board cut, it imposes a penalty on honest managers who have not padded their budgets and have submitted what they consider to be logical and representative requests. Indiscriminate budget cuts induce padding as a defensive measure to provide reasonable assurance that adequate resources will be available to get the job done.

Budgets must also provide some maneuverable resource surpluses in order to provide for unforeseen contingencies, which are typical rather than atypical in projects that are establishing knowledge frontiers. Such things as loosely defined specifications, changes in the state of the art, the availability and price of professional human resources, unanticipated technical problems, and shifts in costs can seriously affect the estimates that have been translated into budget requirements.

Another budget problem arises when expenditures have been less than anticipated and surplus funds are available. The natural inclination of the manager is to accelerate spending in order to use up these funds. The spending may not make any significant contribution to organizational objectives, but it does take the manager off the spot he or she would be on for tying up resources that they had represented as operationally necessary. It also enables them to maintain or expand their operation. Project managers are acutely aware of the fact that they are selling a technical capability, people and their skills, and on occasion overestimate their requirements as a means of supporting the organization assigned to them. Also, using up the current budget appropriation gives the manager a strong starting point in negotiating for new funds in the next budgeting period; if last year's budget has not been spent, it often is difficult to bargain for the same amount or more funds for the next budget period.

Management is a prime contributor to these dilemmas that arise during the budget process. Effective two-way communication would mitigate many of the misunderstandings and frictions consequent on budget decisions, which often appear arbitrary to technical people because they are unaware of the factors putting constraints on their requests. Management must bring them into more active and willing participation in the development of budgets. The technical manager usually delegates this activity to administrative assistants with only casual interest. Not until work is slowed down or stopped for lack of resources are technical managers more than mildly concerned. It is very important that the technical professional become cognizant of the broader organizational implication of budget actions that can directly or indirectly affect their sphere of operations. The budget must be flexible; it must provide for a shift of resources when changes or unanticipated problems do develop. The professional becomes frustrated when ideas are allowed to lie dormant because they cannot be implemented when resources are unavailable. This is a relatively common problem in many organizations where the major operational thrust is high technology. One possible suggestion is that a contingency reserve be established to provide support for technical explorations after requests and reviews have been made on the potential benefits of such new projects. Drawing the reserve from unexpended budget funds would provide an inducement for cost consciousness.

Budget as a Control

The budget, as mentioned, is a tool that helps managers manage. It can and more often than not does deviate from the original calculations. There is nothing sacrosanct about a budget; a fetishistic adherence to it can cause organizational havoc; on the other hand, ignoring the budget can also lead to chaos.

To repeat what has already been said, the budget is a synthesis of estimates that are only indicative of the anticipated scope of the program. A mechanism must be provided for reviewing actual expenditures in relation to estimated expenditures, time, and accomplishment. Are objectives being met? Is the plan still valid in scope, sequence, and duration? Have personnel requirements been accurately forecast? Was the amount of effort anticipated correctly? If the implementation of the program has deviated from the plan, where, how, and why?

A systematic analysis of budgets must start with detailed work elements, identified by item and phase. If the work elements can be isolated, it is easier to establish control and detect deviations in cost, time, and performance. A departure from plans in any work phase can have effects throughout the entire project. Bringing the variance(s) to light at the work phase level provides insight into the future applicability of the existing plan.

A cost comparison with the budget often provides the initial clue to program deviation. What is the basis of the deflection? Poor estimating, more work than anticipated, questionable performance, technical trade-offs? Have resources been available when and where they were needed? Has the program been delayed or accelerated? Any variation from the original budget must be immediately brought to management's attention for explanation and any necessary action. If it is anticipated that expenditures will exceed the original authorization, management's review and approval should be mandatory. Where many projects are in process at the same time, a change in resource requirements by one project may affect the others.

The budget revision request form in Figure 9-7 can be used to give management information for analysis and decision where there are budget deviation requests. The information provided includes the authorized budget, the amount of requested revision, the revised estimated costs, the cost of resources required, and the reason for the revision request.

Risk Management

Defining Risk

Risk can be defined as the probability of failure to accomplish an objective. *The Project Manager's Guide*[25] states the following:

> If success is the unqualified achievement of the goal, the probability of success is one minus the risk, since all probabilities are measured on a scale from zero (no chance of occurrence) to one (certainty of occurrence).

> Success and failure hinge on the definition of the goal; the well defined goal consists of the following characteristics:

>> A complete description of that to be attained including tolerance on each descriptive parameter

>> The resources to be spent in attainment

>> The time in which the goal is to be reached

>> Any constraints which may exist on the actions that may be taken to achieve the goal

Partial success can be achieved, and such partial success can be considered as being satisfactory or unsatisfactory. Partial success implies two underlying risk principles[26]:

1. There are a number of elements which, taken together, describe the goal; there is risk associated with each element.
2. There are consequences attached to the failure to attain each element which may vary from insignificant to catastrophic.

Risk Categories

If there is no risk, the probability for success would be unity: This is related to the goal of risk management, which is directed to minimize risk and improve the probability for success. A project operational environment completely devoid of any risk is an improbability. Where success is not a certainty, the implications and degree or prospects of failure must be considered. Such consideration is another aspect of risk management and involves taking an approach to maximize the probability of an acceptable outcome. It is necessary to define what is considered to be an acceptable

248

Budget Revision Request Analysis

Project No. _____ Name _____ Type _____

	Direct hrs	Direct DC$	Indirect hrs	Indirect DC$	Total Cost
Authorized budget					$
Requested revision					
New estimated total cost and requested budget					
Actual costs through ____ hrs. ($ ____ DC$ ____)					
Unexpanded balance--present budget					
Requested percent increase over budget					
Percent actual costs of present budget					
Estimated project cost					
New Estimated total cost					
New unbudgeted reserve					
Percent new unbudgeted reserve of remaining costs					

Notes

1. Conversion rates:
   Direct labor hrs. $ ____
   Indirect labor hrs. $ ____
   G & A ____ %

2. Initiating activity _____

3. Revised project cost _____

4. Reason for revision request _____

Prepared by _____ Date _____

Figure 9-7. Budget revision request form. Modified from Daniel D. Roman, *Research and Development Management: The Economics and Administration of Technology*, Englewood Cliffs, NJ: Prentice-Hall, 1968, p. 326.

outcome vis-à-vis an unacceptable outcome. Classification of unacceptable and acceptable failures has been suggested[27]:

Critical	A failure which is of itself unacceptable, i.e. catastrophic
Potentially Critical	A failure which is acceptable but which is unacceptable in combination with other failures
Probably Noncritical	A failure which is acceptable and must occur in combination with several other failures to lead to an unacceptable result
Noncritical	A totally inconsequential failure

In addition, a risk that might be classified as acceptable or unacceptable could be (1) an independent occurrence which is not affected by other risk elements, (2) a dependent risk that is totally determined by the outcome of other elements, or (3) interdependent where the risk is operationally or functionally related to other project elements and as a consequence each affects the others.[28]

The degree of risk independence, dependence, or interdependence and the potential consequences should provide a course of action to cope with such prospects. Risk criticality associated with project management can vary, as indicated, from minimal to crucial. Accordingly, contingencies should be factored into the project plan to permit operational latitude to blunt the possible negative effects resulting from highly probable or important risk situations.

Categories or Techniques for Risk Assessment

It may be advisable as a part of planning in the formative phase of the project life cycle to develop a procedural model for risk identification and analysis. On some projects a comprehensive procedural model might be indicated, whereas on other projects a more simplistic approach might be applicable. A universal model may not be practical, but it might be possible to indicate a general framework as a guide to manage risks. As indicated in *The Project Manager's Guide*,[29] eight general categories of technique might be applicable:

Defining the goal
Identifying risks
Assessing consequences
Assessing degree of risk
Manipulating consequences
Manipulating degree of risk
Assessing results
Developing a best plan of attack to achieve a goal

Handling Risk and Risk Strategies

Recognizing and handling risk[30] is one decisional avenue to allocating project resources. The amount and type of resources used in concert with propitious timing can be effectively used to minimize or eliminate potential risk if such risk has been identified. Those risks that appear most critical to the success of the project should be given priorities. Risks might be assessed in descending order of criticality to the project and treated accordingly. Risk evaluation should help the manager to determine which risks are acceptable and manageable. When risks are unacceptable and/or unmanageable, the project should not be authorized, or if the project is already in process, the most prudent action might be to abort the project.

In many cases risk can be acceptable and manageable. Risk assessment can help suggest some strategies for handling such risks. Several risk strategies can be considered.

Hedging. Hedging strategies are possible in some situations by providing alternative courses of action and useful results, even though there is only partial achievement of the ideal goal. Hedging is possible by using a parallel-path method whereby two or more approaches are taken concurrently that differ as to risk. One path should be a low-risk approach. A backup method can also be taken where more than one approach is taken and each approach has a different risk area.

Transfer or Exchange Strategies. In this approach an unknown risk is exchanged for a known risk that is considered acceptable. It is also possible in this strategy to exchange a known critical risk for a risk that is also known but considered less critical. The employment of a transfer or exchange strategy for risk management can be manifested by the use of warranties and/or guarantees, by insurance to limit potential future negative experiences, and by means of contractually shifting the risk to the vendor.

Reduction Strategies. Reduction strategies relate to resources allocation. Under this strategy it is assumed that the better the human and material resources directed to the project, the better the probability will be that risks can be properly handled and neutralized. This approach requires extensive management planning and coordination. A danger in this approach is that by directing prime resources to "a" project, other projects may be vulnerable.

Avoidance Strategies. This strategy is predicated on avoiding exposure to risk. Alternative paths are explored and taken where there are technologically oriented risks. Past related experience or current assessment of the magnitude of the technical problem(s) involved may be determinate in taking one technical approach rather than an approach involving a greater technical risk.

Evasion Strategies. Evasion strategies are based on comprehensive planning where risks are determined and possible consequences evaluated in the event there is a failure. Often this strategy is based on political considerations. Evasion tactics might ultimately be decided on after an evaluation of the influential people who support the project. If the influential and power support base is high, risk of subsequent failure may be low. On the other hand, if support is tepid and the power base of support is low, even a minimal failure might entail a high-risk position.

Risk Assumption. This strategy recognizes inherent risks associated with the project and builds in contingencies by padding estimates of resources and time required to complete the project objectives. In this strategy discretion must be used to provide an adequate pad for unforeseen contingencies while at the same time avoiding excessive cost estimates that might jeopardize the initial authorization of the project. Under this strategy it is possible that since the risk has been assumed, an ultraconservative technical approach will be taken, with questionable end benefits resulting. It is also possible that if a sufficient pad has been buried in the project cost estimate, a high technical risk position will be assumed and again cost/benefit may not be commensurate.

A Tool

Risks associated with project activity can vary from trivial to cataclysmic. The project manager should be sensitive to potential risks that might impact on the project. Risks are invariably entwined with the financial health of the project. Risks can result from technical problems, human activities, a change in the thrust of the project, competition, the availability or lack of internal or external support, politics, and a shift in the state of the art. On some technologically complex projects with a potential for an extended life expectancy, all or many of the risk factors indicated can come into play at some phase of the project's life cycle.

Risk management can be used as a tool by the project manager. Possible project problem areas can be localized and probability analysis used to give a general order of risk magnitude. However, a high degree of accuracy in determining where, when, how, why, and the extent of the risk is normally beyond existing analytical capabilities. Still there is precedent where risk management has been used with signal success. This concept has been used in the insurance industry, where it has been developed into a rigorous science. Comparable application in project management is not possible at this writing. Candidly, while this can be a useful tool and can help call attention to potential risk areas, its application is often heavily biased by intuition. Nevertheless, even though the decisions involved in the management of a technologically complex project will not be directly applicable to the statistical analysis of an actuary, some of the techniques can be adapted.[31]

Risk and Managerial Philosophy

Exposure to risk can well reflect management's philosophy and operational strategy. Risk can be centered on offensive or defensive operational strategies. Taking a risk position can depend on the organization's reputation or position within an industry or a technology, the state of the technological development, the perceived extent of risk considering the technology and potential rewards, the estimated time to reach technical objectives, and perhaps the organization's present and committed project portfolio. Can an incurred risk be spread over a mix of existing projects, taking into account the risks associated with such projects?[32] Are the potential rewards great enough to offset taking a risk position? Is there a large enough project base within the organization to where a few successful projects can neutralize many failures?[33] Might it "be advisable to reject a high-risk project, in spite of a high expected payoff from it, if the portfolio is small or if the portfolio already contains a number of other high-risk projects?[34] What percentage of the organization's resources will be required by the project? Do project selection and risk/benefit analysis entail essentially an all-or-nothing approach, a single roll of the dice philosophy?

Risk analysis generally includes some accommodation for cost/benefit evaluation. The ultimate decision to embark on a project may hinge on need and financial factors, including available resources, expected benefits, and the prospects for accomplishing technical objectives. Risk analysis is useful, but it may not be the final controlling force in the decision process. Need may circumvent risk. There can be situations where risk may be minimal and potential benefits promising, but resources may not be available. The risk analysis and evaluation may be based on questionable data, and, finally, the risk analysis evaluator(s) may be prejudiced or incompetent.

Endnotes Chapter Nine

1. B. Twiss, *Managing Technological Innovation,* London, Longman, 1974, p. 37.

2. C. J. Hitch and R. N. McKean, *The Economics of Defense in the Nuclear Age,* Cambridge, MA, Harvard University Press, 1963, p. 233.

3. *Ibid.*

4. *Ibid.,* p. 159.

5. *Ibid.,* p. 169.

6. This suggestion is only a short-run solution where economic conditions are temporarily depressed. In the long run, commercial organizations cannot survive unless fixed and variable costs (total costs) are covered, as well as a necessary profit residual to provide incentive for continuing operations.

7. This is not an unusual provision. In some areas of government contracting a set percentage of the contract is established for subsequent subcontracting to small businesses or minority entrepreneurs.

8. Security considerations make it impossible to identify the contractors or the federal agency involved.

9. *Accounting for Research and Development Costs,* N.A.A. Research Report No. 29, New York, National Association of Accountants, 1955, p. 48.

10. *Project Manager's Guide,* Technical Document 108, Naval Ocean Systems Center, San Diego, 1 June 1977, p. 1x-1.

11. *Ibid.,* pp. 1x-1 and 1x-2.

12. See also *ibid.,* p. 1x-2.

13. M. H. Spencer and L. Siegelman, *Managerial Economics,* rev. ed., Homewood, IL, Richard D. Irwin, 1964, p. 318.

14. B. N. Baker, *Improving Cost Estimating and Analysis in DoD and NASA,* unpublished doctoral dissertation, George Washington University, Washington, DC, January 1972, p. 72.

15. Spencer and Siegelman, *op. cit.,* p. 302.

16. *Ibid.,* pp. 302–309.

17. A good discussion on project overhead rates is contained in H. Kerzner, *Project Management. A Systems Approach to Planning, Scheduling, and Controlling,* New York, Van Nostrand Reinhold, 1979, pp. 379–385.

18. R. Villers, *Research and Development: Planning and Control,* New York, Financial Executives Institute, 1964, p. 20; J. B. Quinn, *Yardsticks for Industrial Research,* New York, Ronald Press, 1958, pp. 77–78.

19. In the illustration $66.55 is assumed to be the average cost for all direct labor hours expended. In practice, greater sophistication and accuracy can be achieved if the hours are time coordinated and priced by skill and work phase rather than averaged.

20. The model has been simplified by the exclusion of other than labor costs.

21. See Twiss, *op. cit.,* pp. 155–160.

22. J. B. Quinn, "Budgeting for Research," in *Handbook of Industrial Research Management,* C. Heyel (ed.), New York, Reinhold, 1960, pp. 281–313.

23. Villers, *op. cit.,* pp. 20–34.

24. T. Moranian, *The R&D Engineer as Manager,* New York, Holt, Rinehart and Winston, 1963, pp. 62–63.

25. *Project Manager's Guide, op. cit.,* p. XX1-1.
26. *Ibid.*
27. *Ibid.,* p. XX1-2.
28. *Ibid.*
29. *Ibid.,* p. XX1-3.
30. Comprehensive treatment of handling risk and risk strategies is treated in *ibid.,* pp. XX1-7 and XX1-8.
31. *Ibid.,* p. XX1-1.
32. Twiss, *op. cit.,* p. 51.
33. *Ibid.,* p. 149.
34. *Ibid.*

CHAPTER TEN

Project Controls

Control Objectives

Control Process

There are psychological problems associated with control insofar as most people, especially highly educated and specialized professionals, balk at being "controlled". Most professionals feel being "controlled" has a denigrating connotation and are unhappy about the prospect of operating in an environment where they feel their activities are closely monitored. On the other hand, few of these same professionals would be willing to accept operational (i.e., project) responsibility without having some procedural process that would give them reasonable assurance that the activity they were responsible for was proceeding in accord with planned objectives and inferred or formal legal commitment.

There can be a dramatic shift in attitude relative to control and accountability resulting from a change in the level of organizational responsibility. By way of illustration, there was the situation where a very senior project engineer constantly complained about the obligation for frequent reports to the project manager on technical accomplishment, schedules, and cost expenditures. As a professional, he interpreted such activity as being demeaning and felt that management should have enough confidence in him to give him complete operational latitude, without the restraints and harassment he felt were unduly imposed. This same individual was subsequently elevated to the position of project manager. After a few months in his new assignment he was questioned in regard to the transition and adjustment required by his new position. His response was that he enjoyed the challenge of being a project manager, but his major concern was the coordination and *control* of subordinates' activities. In effect, he said that leaving people to wander off in all directions, often of their own choosing, based on their interpretation of what had to be done, was to court disaster.

Control has to be brought into perspective. As indicated, perhaps the use of the word *control* is unfortunate. What actually happens is an active management process to see that objectives are accomplished with a minimal expenditure of resources. To be more explicit, control involves the correlation of functional activities in an integrated reporting system that is accurate, objective, fast, and action directed. To be effective, control must give the project manager early warning of variances from plans. If these are detected quickly enough, corrective action can be taken before resources have been overexpended to the point of impairing program objectives. Essentially, control includes the assessment and interrelation of three critical factors, examined in total perspective: (1) actual performance, compared with planned, (2) the schedule of accomplishment, and (3) expenditures of resources in relation to accomplishment.[1]

Establishing Standards

Control is immeasurably simplified when some bench mark of performance can be established. A standard can be set, maintained, or improved upon, with reasonable objectivity, where there is a predictable production cycle, resulting in products or services that are essentially similar in appearance and/or performance and which can be evaluated against comparable products or services.

Establishing a standard in project management is infinitely more difficult than in situations involving cycled activity. Projects, as previously mentioned, are ad hoc activities. There are few, if any, precedents on which to establish productivity norms. Each project, by the nature of its inception, is unique to some degree. It is possible that a project has evolved from previous activities where some operational experience has developed; however, different people may be assigned to the new project, mitigating any possible advantages of a learning curve. Also, even though there initially may appear to be considerable commonality between some projects, especially those projects involving product improvement, there ultimately may be significant differences.

An example of such a situation in product improvement would be where planning, including anticipated performance, product cost, and schedule for completion, is based on a commitment of a preliminary 90% release of engineering drawings that have previously been used. The 90% commitment is on the assumption that these drawings and parts will be used in the new product. Too often this is an overly optimistic appraisal of what finally has to be done. The remaining 10% needed to accomplish the product development may subsequently entail considerable modification and redesign of parts contained in the original 90% estimate of common parts. The result is a serious miscalculation of the actual magnitude of effort required on the new project. Additionally, in a dynamic technological field it is possible that there may be technological developments that obviate previous work.

A machine is reasonably predictable. The machine can normally turn out uniform parts or products. In projects people are generally the productive force. People performance is nowhere nearly as predictable as machine performance. People performance will generally vary in physical and mental activity between different individuals given the same or similar assignments. Even the performance of one individual is not always predictable, owing to physical and emotional changes that periodically take place. Setting people standards in project management is often very subjective. What may be a reasonable level of performance expectation for one person may be an impossible level of attainment for another person.

The project manager can hardly, under the environment in which he or she operates, establish categorical standards. First, in complex projects there are many unprecedented activities, and, second, it must be recognized that all people are not equal in ability in performing the same activity. There may be a tendency to overkill, that is, assign overqualified people to accomplish the necessary tasks and set standards compatible with the capabilities of the best people. This approach suggests many problems, such as incurring costs that are too high by underutilizing people, highly qualified people tending to become bored and disgruntled, and junior people being denied the opportunity for professional development, growth, and challenge.

As implied in this section, a standard of performance in project management often relates to the people assigned to the project and an evaluation of each assigned person's current and potential ability. This, as indicated, involves considerable subjective evaluation by the project manager, who must decide whether the individual's performance is satisfactory or not satisfactory. If performance is not satisfactory, the control process can be instigated by simplifying the person's assignment, providing closer supervision and more instruction, or reassignment. If performance is deemed to be satisfactory, but objectives are not being accomplished, the planning parameters must be reexamined and changes implemented as necessary.

Control: An Innovation Process

There is usually the tendency to look for simplistic answers in nonsimplistic situations. Control is a critical part of the project management process. To establish control the project manager must have a firm understanding of what technical objectives are to be accomplished and how these objectives must be achieved within time and cost constraints. Invariably, performance, time, and cost are tied into informational requirements, which must be current, accurate, and relevant in order to assess actual progress versus planned activity. To develop an informational system, which gives the project manager a high confidence level that the project is proceeding per plan, is not only extremely important, but also requires constant attention, revision as necessary, and considerable innovation.

Control, or a control system, is not static. Project operational objectives are susceptible to change. The project may be well conceived but could also be vulnerable to external influences outside the jurisdiction of the project manager. Establishing relevant controls requires intelligence and innovation. A relevant control system would focus on strategic factors to control. Too much or too little control is wasteful and defeats the concept of necessary awareness by the project manager to intelligently direct the project.

In organizations where operations are a composite of many projects, operational continuity often is erratic. Management in such situations may have difficulty in formulating control objectives, much less implementing them. Project people have a tendency to be optimistic and to minimize problems; indeed, they are often unaware of imminent technical difficulties. It is easier to assure management that potential achievement is consistent with objectives than to explain the problems that may exist.

To suggest that a categorical approach or a specific technique can be formulated to determine a project's actual status is unrealistic. Each project has distinct characteristics. The project manager must be able to determine the critical elements of a project in order to have control. In some instances key milestones can be identified. Despite assurances to the contrary, if these milestones of accomplishment are not achieved, the project manager is alerted to the existence of a problem area.

Another aspect of this situation is to determine the potential scope of a technical objective. Most project people, as mentioned, tend to be optimistic in their ability to solve technical problems. How much optimism should be factored into or out of a prognostication of ultimate achievement? The evaluation of the extent of optimism as a factor affecting the actual project cannot be taught. The shrewd project manager, based on past experience, will determine and plan on a person-to-person situation.

The aforementioned can be illustrated by what became a relatively common practice in one engineering organization. When the project managers were asked for an evaluation of resource requirements on projects that frequently pushed the state of the art, they generally minimized the magnitude of the problem by one-half. An estimate of 6 months to complete, a performance specification of 2, and a budget of $500,000 could more realistically be interpreted and translated into a 12-month schedule that would result in a performance specification of 1 and a potential expenditure of $1,000,000. And, of course, there was the project manager whose estimate, based on his past commitments and actual performance, invariably had to be factored by 4 rather than 2.

Managers in a volatile project environment will probably have few valid standards to use with confidence in order to verify the representation it receives. Piecemeal results may be misleading or difficult to determine, and it is frequently impossible to make an accurate assessment of cost in relation to time and progress. As a result, management is placed in a compromising position.

Rather than improvise and innovate to cope with the operational idiosyncracies of individual projects, management often succumbs to the inclination to develop blanket controls. An all-encompassing system will frequently lack individual project operational sensitivity and will rarely cover the different problems encountered in diffused projects. A management that attempts to control everything with one system may wind up not controlling anything. Procrustean controls cause confusion and provoke resentment or indifference; the costs to control can be out of proportion to benefit, paperwork can be monumental, and the control concept can be strangled by its own inflexibility.

Many useful control techniques have been developed and can be used effectively on projects. Many of these techniques or control areas are covered in subsequent sections of this chapter and in other chapters of the book. Techniques or control methods useful on some projects may not be applicable for other projects. At times recognized control techniques can be adapted and successfully employed on projects that are quite different. Finally, common or oft-used control techniques may not be applicable to a specific project. It is like trying to fit a size 13 foot into a size 7 shoe. In each project situation the project manager should be aware of the project scope, what is needed to effectively manage, what tools are available and applicable, what tools can be modified for applicability, and where innovative approaches may prove to be more feasible based on the distinct characteristics of the project. The extent of effective project management may be correlated with the extent of effective managerial innovation to provide the necessary ingredients for control.

Need for Project Control

Control must be objective directed. The exercise of control is a matter of getting people to do what must be done to achieve an objective.[2] When controls are properly established and thoroughly comprehended, they constitute one of management's most effective tools and one of an organization's best methods for creating a uniform understanding of policy. Controls are methods developed to assist management and must not be taken for management substitutes.

The project manager, in developing a control system, should be cognizant that controls must be shaped to correspond with the operational objectives of the project. The controls employed should accommodate the need to delegate authority and assign responsibility; a control system should have built-in stabilizers, which are also adjustable and usable at the various levels of project activity. Control should encourage creativity and anticipation and should be preventive and directive; project controls should not be after the fact or imply punitive action. A good project control system should be directed to minimize loss and protect the organization from the consequences of poor performance, unwise decisions, or errors made by those to whom responsibility has been delegated.

In addition, the objective of control should be to maximize effort and minimize the expenditure of the organization's resources. It should assure the fair and equitable treatment of personnel as uniformly as possible. Control should be designed to enhance organizational and customer relations and prevent internal disequilibrium and promote communication among functional groups. When control information flows among all levels of the organization, working goals are better defined, misunderstanding and confusion are minimized, and efficiency and morale are promoted.[3]

Project Control

Interface

Many of us have had the experience of learning to drive an automobile with a manual transmission. Unless blessed with an inordinate amount of natural dexterity, the preliminary learning stages were often an intimidating situation. The number of activities almost simultaneously required (i.e., shifting gears, using the clutch, proper acceleration, steering) called for a tremendous degree of coordination and concentration. With practice, these skills finally became almost like reflex actions and were performed with mechanical precision. To the uninitiated or novice project manager, the coordination, understanding, and exercising of control at the different internal and external operational levels can be a frustrating experience. More experienced project managers, like the driving illustration, learn to cope with the problem and, in many instances, probably react to given situations almost with a conditioned response. However, a cavalier approach should be avoided and careful analysis of the project and its operational environment made a prelude to the instigation of a system of project controls.

Project control can be exerted at various operational levels—on individual projects assignments, on functions or sections, on the composite project, or on the total organization. The controls used may be internal, external, or both. The kinds of control employed on a project differ according to whether the origin of the control is internal or external, the

technical complexity of the project, the resource requirements, the degree
of dependence on other projects, the ability and reputation of the project
leader, and management's policy and philosophy.

Control and the Project Life Cycle

The tendency is to think of project controls primarily in the operational
phase of the project life cycle. Actually, project controls can be effectively used in the conceptual, formative, and terminal phases of the project, as well as in the operational phase.

Figure 10-1, a project control schematic, indicates a range of possible
control areas. The project control schematic only identifies some of the
possible activities where controls can be employed. Some projects may
entail much more in the way of strategic activities where controls are
necessary. Other projects may be relatively simple and only need periodic
reviews of a few essential checkpoints. The schematic does, however,
indicate some of the possibilities. Of particular significance to the project
manager are the extensive factors that must be controlled and the variety
of control techniques and informational requirements which would be
needed to manage a complex project.

Control at the Project Conceptual Phase

Projects may be solicited, unsolicited, internal, external, simple, complex, and of short or long duration. Normally we do not think of project
control(s) at the conceptual phase, but in fact there are operational foun-
dations that subsequently affect the conduct of the project. In the conceptual phase feasibility studies may be conducted to determine the technical
and economic desirability of embarking on the project. The feasibility
study is a control to provide evaluation, based on relevant information, as
to whether to formally proceed or abort the project before resources are
committed. Preliminary feasibility studies may result in the decision to
develop or not develop a proposal.

Developing a proposal may entail the activities of several different
organizational functions. The proposed activity may involve considerable
technical complexity. Time or scheduling may be an important factor.
Competition could affect costs and price considerations. Legal issues
could also be a factor. To cope with the aforementioned, a project proposal team is often organized. It is possible that the composition of such a
team could include organizational representation from such functions as
contracts administration (legal), pricing experts (finance), proposals (coordination and assembly of the project components), logistics, and technical. The pivotal function is technical.

The technical representative on the project proposal team is usually the
authority in coordinating with the potential customer the scope of the
work to be performed on the project. At times the organization's technical

262

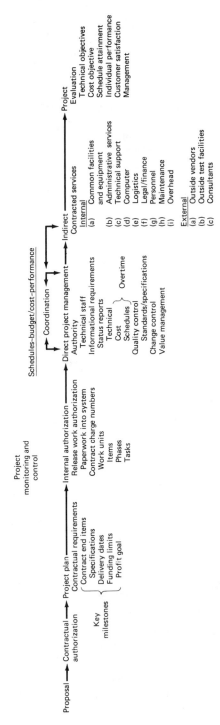

Figure 10-1. A project control schematic.

representative becomes so enthusiastic or obsessed with the project's technical potentials that other critical aspects are subverted. This is why it is common practice in the situation described to have a proposal team. The control factors are checks and balances to see that no undue commitments are made that are not compatible with the organization's technical, cost, profit, time, and legal objectives.

Often the technical representative in the conceptual phase becomes the project manager, if the project is authorized. This is a good project management control insofar as the technical representative has to be realistic in terms of anticipated technical accomplishment and resource requirements that would affect schedules and cost and profit goals. It would normally be unwise to have one person establish legally obligated work parameters and subsequently assign another person the responsibility for performance.

Control at the Project Formative Phase

It is not uncommon for the representatives of negotiating organizations to feel that legal authorization of the project is imminent and, in their enthusiasm and optimism, commence preliminary activity without formal commitment. The author has been involved on numerous occasions, especially with the federal government, in situations where there has been encouragement to proceed on a project in anticipation of subsequent authorization. Too often subsequent authorization was never received.

In mass production, where there is a standard product, inventory can be built up to meet expectant demands. In such a situation production is frequently before an actual sale. The market for the product is extensive and there generally are many buyers. Projects involve specialized and customized activity. The demand is specific and there is "a" customer. If there is preliminary work and the customer decides not to proceed with the project, in all probability little or none of the effort can be salvaged.

It should be a cardinal rule and a fundamental control that project work should not be initiated and costs should not be incurred until there is a firm legal commitment. The exception, of course, is where there may be preliminary work associated with proposal preparation in the event there is a decision to bid on a project.

Often the early negotiations involve people who overestimate the authorizing prospects for the project. Too often these people are at a level where they are not in a position to make a firm contractual commitment. It should also be pointed out that the vendor's technical representative must be extremely careful in making any commitment to a prospective buyer, because in some instances the law of agency could be invoked, obligating the vendor to an unwelcome contractual commitment.

Assuming that authorization has been granted, there are many areas requiring attention in the formative stage. The project plan should closely parallel the project proposal. In effect, the proposal should become the project plan. Realistically, this may not happen. Proposals are frequently developed under extreme time pressures; if and when the project is ultimately authorized, and there has been time to reflect on how to go about accomplishing the work, there may be subsequent changes in the approach outlined in the proposal and a reformulated project plan. On many occasions projects have been authorized and a new master project plan is subsequently required in order to meet the contractual obligations. The original proposal was bought and there was a formal commitment for deliverable end items, specifications, completion dates, and funding limits. These were firm commitments, but how to get from here to there changed dramatically between the time the proposal was submitted and when it was authorized.

The project manager has important coordination responsibilities in the formative project phase. Detail planning is required to support the project. Planning and control are closely related. Project controls must mesh with project plans. Planning inputs are required from the technical organization directly responsible to the project manager, as well as internal and external supporting activities. It is not unusual to find that once the project is authorized, the direct and indirect support functions reappraise their potential project contribution and request resources that are not compatible with resources which have been originally requested and subsequently authorized. It follows that if the project manager is to have a successful project, some reconciliation is needed between the commitments made leading to the proposal submission and the current assessment of resources required to support the project. This situation, unfortunately, is not uncommon, is frustrating, and calls for refined interpersonal skills on the part of the project manager to resolve the technical and managerial differences that have evolved. Time can also be a factor creating this change situation; work loads, costs, and available human resources can change from the time the proposal is generated until there is actual contract authorization and project go-ahead.

If the project manager releases work authorization before agreement has been reached on work scope, schedules, and costs, he or she has practically abdicated control. Agreement and commitment are essential before releasing the paper work into the system that authorizes the various activities or functions to start in support of the project.[4] As part of this process, it is recommended that there be some system of contract charge numbers, corresponding to a breakdown of work units, which include items, phases, and tasks to be accomplished. This approach will enable progress monitoring and some measure of cost control once the project moves into the operational phase.

Control at the Project Operational Phase

The most extensive use and diversity of control techniques are required in the operational phase of the project cycle. It is impossible to address every area where project controls can be used because of the limitless variety of projects that can and do exist. However, some representative examples can be cited. The project manager must be concerned with the use of resources, internal activities, external activities, and activities that affect the project but which are not directly controllable. The latter will be discussed in the next section.

Use of Resources. One of the very first activities in project management is identification of resource requirements. The project manager should know the type, quality, quantity, and time frame for resources needed to execute the project. The project manager should also know which of the resources would be directly allocated to the project, which required resources would have to be shared internally with other projects, and which resources might be unique or internally unavailable and would have to be procured external to the organization.

The planning, subsequent control, and effective use of resources are essential for project success. Resource identification and allocation involve human activities (i.e., skill mix, the number of people directly and indirectly assigned to the project, and the level of professional competence needed to achieve project objectives). Resources can also include different types of equipment, ranging from sophisticated production or test instrumentation to office equipment to computer support to logistic vehicles. Resources, in addition, can be a variety of facilities from office space to test ranges. And resource requirements external to the organization can reflect a variety of services, such as technical consultants, specialized subcontractors, and test facilities operations.

It is suggested that the project manager carefully evaluate the project work scope and develop a projected inventory of resource requirements. Too often there is only a vague or general feel for the total amount of resources required. The way a project is managed can materially be affected by the amount, type, availability, and cost of resources needed to support the project. Establishing resource requirements at the outset of the project operational phase, rather than improvising as the project moves through its operational phases, can provide important perspective and instigate calculated decisions.

Decisions, unfortunately, are frequently made under crisis conditions. Many times panic situations can be avoided if there is intelligent anticipation. Intelligent anticipation is part of the project control process and would certainly affect resource allocation. For instance, identification and allocation of resources would enable project managers to make considered trade-offs where costs may be a serious factor affecting the conduct of the project. Decisions could cover optional uses of resources, buy or lease strategies, and the use of outside contractors or services where there are distinct specialization requirements that are not economically feasible to develop in-house. Decisions on the use of resources may also involve situations where there is only sporadic need for the resources but, because of unavailability, there may be costly down time, where schedule conflicts might develop, and where resources are common to several projects. Resource need identification is critical for project management and control and should be a prelude to the actual commencement of project operations.

Internal Activities. If activity is organized along pure project lines vis-à-vis functional or matrix organization, the technical people required to directly support the project will report to the project manager. In this situation the project manager has a high degree of control of human resources. This includes level of staffing, skill mix, determination of competence needed, and specific work assignments. The project manager has administrative as well as technical control of human resources. This approach provides the project manager with some sanctions insofar as he or she can hire, reassign, or perhaps even terminate people. In addition, the project manager exerts another important human resource control, in that they are directly responsible for the periodic review, performance rating, and promotional prospects of their subordinates.

The degree of the project manager's control of human resources is lessened in matrix organization. In matrix organization the project manager's position can vary from having a considerable impact as to the determination of who is assigned to the project, to a passive position, where technical support people are unilaterally assigned by functional managers.

Work cannot be accomplished without people. It is assumed from the preceding paragraphs that the people organization is compatible with the work to be performed. Once the people organization is set, the project manager's most urgent responsibilities are to see that technical activity, schedules, and costs are accomplished within the authorizing perimeters of the project. To have control the project manager must be able to meaningfully correlate performance, time, and cost. Control to only one project phase is to not have total or realistic control. The following will illustrate this point.

As part of the project planning process, projections are made on schedules for performance attainment and cost accrual. Figures 10-2 to 10-5 represent a very simple example of such planning.

The project manager can develop planning and control methods and

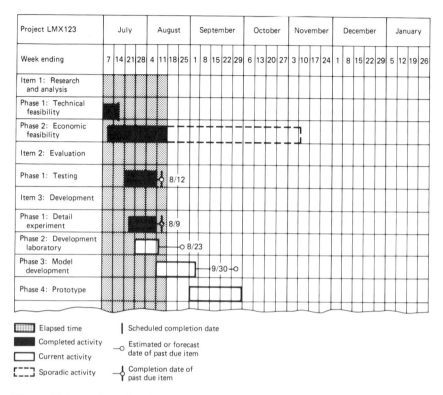

Figure 10-2. Project planning (Gantt method). From Daniel D. Roman, *Research and Development Management: The Economics and Administration of Technology,* Englewood Cliffs, NJ: Prentice-Hall, 1968, p. 350.

techniques, but these can be misleading or, worse yet, useless unless they represent relevant and accurate information. In Figure 10-2 some items and phases have been completed, some are on time, and some are behind schedule. If the information is correct, problem areas are indicated. The project manager can anticipate these problems and initiate activity to minimize or eliminate potential difficulties. What is critical is the validity of the information received. Also, it is very important to identify critical milestones. These are signal areas that indicate whether the project is moving or not properly moving toward its objectives. It is also essential that the project manager have the technical competence to recognize the validity of the information received as to the actual technical status of the project. Perhaps a vignette, based on experience, can be illustrative.

The author was in charge of a master planning and control operation in an aerospace company. Part of the functional activities included responsibility for project master plans and the scheduling of project operations.

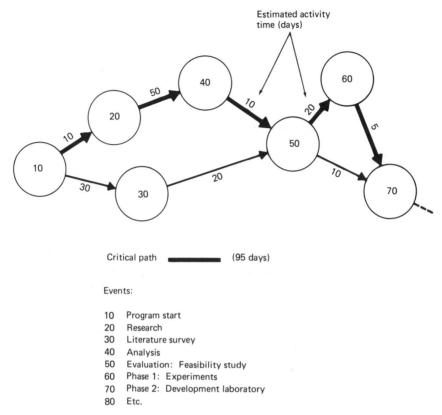

Figure 10-3. Project planning (PERT method). From Daniel D. Roman, *Research and Development Management: The Economics and Administration of Technology,* Englewood Cliffs, NJ: Prentice-Hall, 1968, p. 349.

On a large project, involving expensive and exotic hardware, there were major difficulties in maintaining accurate schedule information and, subsequently, meeting contractually scheduled delivery dates. When requesting progress information from functionally responsible project people, there were assurances that there were no undue difficulties and schedules would be met. Frequently, based on such assurances, project overtime, as requested, was authorized on the assumption that minor difficulties could be mitigated and the hardware would be available on time.

Assurances of on-time progress would be made almost to the actual deadline date. When the scheduled delivery date arrived, there were invariably excuses of unforeseen technical difficulties; often the result was a schedule slippage of several weeks. Generally the nature of the problems could have been foreseen and corrective action taken had there been

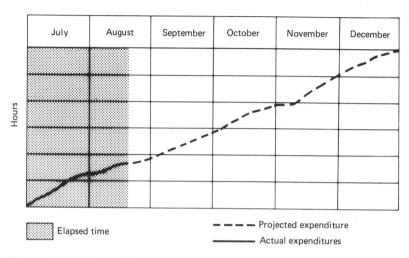

Figure 10-4. Planned direct labor hours.

relevant and accurate information that could be used to set up proper control procedures.

In order to try and maintain some semblance of performance and schedule control, about 20 people were assigned to watch the project's status; literally hundreds of parts were monitored. After a frustrating period during which there was no resolution or solution to the problem, it was decided to explore new avenues that might provide answers. The ultimate solution was found in the quality control reports. The technical problems

Figure 10-5. Planned dollar expenditures.

July	August	September	October	November	December

Elapsed time   Projected expenditures
                      Actual expenditures

were well disguised by the project people, who were optimistic relative to a solution and who were reluctant to have closer managerial supervision. The quality control reports indicated that 97% of all rejections occurred on work effort involving three subassemblies. There was only a 3% random rejection rate on what amounted to hundreds of other parts and subassemblies. The actual problems were correctable once they were localized. Problem localization enabled concentration on finding a solution. In addition, control was immeasurably simplified by adding the three subassemblies to the master schedule and carefully watching the progress on each of the subassemblies. There was approximately a 4-week lead time from the completion of the subassemblies to final completion and assembly of the hardware.

Locating the strategic factors provided control where control previously did not exist. It also enabled reassignment of people to where one person working part-time on this project schedule had infinitely better control than in the previous situation where almost 20 people were assigned.

Figures 10-4 and 10-5 illustrate another aspect of project control. As a generalization, organizational controls are frequently financially dominated. Such controls should be established, used, and analyzed in proper perspective.

In Figure 10-4 a projection has been made on the expenditure of direct labor hours. A little less than one-sixth of the planned project operational time has elapsed. According to the actual experience of direct hours expended, the project appears to be on schedule, but this might be misleading in that hours are being expended as planned but real accomplishment has not been achieved as scheduled. Or the costs for direct labor hours could be miscalculated. Miscalculation of costs can result from unanticipated salary inflation, increased overhead burden applied to direct labor hours, or inadvertently assigning high-priced people to the project.

In Figure 10-5 there is an indication that the actual dollar expenditures on the project are exceeding the projected dollar expenditures. An explanation and understanding of the deviation of actual from planned expenditures are supercritical. It is extremely important to have information that promptly flags any deviation of actual expenditures from planned expenditures. The control process breaks down if the information comes too late, is not accurate, is not properly analyzed, or if there is failure to take corrective action in the event that something must be done. A strict financial orientation, devoid of intelligent analysis and explanation, would tend to create a panic situation based on the information in Figure 10-5. The immediate prospects would indicate a project cost overrun.

There are several possible explanations for the cost situation depicted in Figure 10-5. On the positive side no problem may actually exist, since the project could be ahead of schedule, which explains the faster-than-planned rate of expenditures. It is also possible that long lead time procurement items are required to support the project and funds have been allocated earlier than originally anticipated for such acquisition and show up in current cost accruals.

On the negative side, several possibilities exist, such as the project running behind schedule and there being greater inputs than expected in order to put the project back on schedule. Costs may be realistic in view of the scope of the work being attempted. Expensive people have been assigned to the project. The extent of necessary support areas were miscalculated in the original project cost estimates. Facilities charges and the purchase of equipment may cost more than originally anticipated.

Once the cost deviation is known, the project manager can start looking for corrective solutions. If the project is behind schedule because of technical difficulties, expert assistance from outside the project can be sought. One or a few knowledgeable people may be able to solve project problems more quickly and better than several people with less experience or technical talent. Another possibility for higher than anticipated costs may be due to the enthusiasm of the project people who want to explore new or related areas and extend activities—and costs—beyond the scope of work that is contractually required. It may also be necessary to reexamine the proposed project methodology and work scope and see if the project objectives can be telescoped or accomplished by taking a different (i.e., more cost efficient) approach. Still higher costs than originally anticipated can develop because of the employment of high-cost people on the project. Can less senior people be used? Would it be cheaper to go to outside sources to do some of the work?

Cost escalation often occurs when support facilities and equipment are required to complete the project. The project manager should consider the cost, availability, and alternatives where there are facility requirements. At times extensive cost savings can be realized and costs brought back in line by a reevaluation of equipment needs. Rather than purchasing expensive equipment, it may be possible to rent or share such equipment, send the work out to an organization that has such equipment, buy used equipment, or realistically reappraise equipment requirements. There often is a tendency to purchase Cadillac-type equipment when much simpler and cheaper equipment could also be used.

Early detection of cost variance is important. It gives the project manager time for analysis and provides the opportunity to take corrective action if necessary. If the project manager fails to establish an effective cost control system, by the time it is recognized that costs relative to accomplishment are excessive, too many resources have been expended. The remaining dollars may be inadequate to complete the project within original cost commitments.

Some costs are obvious and the experienced project manager carefully watches such costs to prevent overruns. There are, however, many insidious areas where cost leaks that can impair the financial success of the project can occur. Some cost areas, such as human resources, facilities, and equipment, have been discussed. Cost can also be controlled in many other operational areas, such as materials, general supplies, utilities (especially telephone charges), travel, maintenance, inventory, production charges, buying practices, and scrap. Some specific clues as to excessive costs are a high rate of work rejection, including reworks, loss of inventory or equipment, unreasonable quality specifications, obsolete inventory, and duplication of facilities and equipment; theft by employees; poor buying as to price, quality, and quantity; planning failures, such as not anticipating operational problems; idle time; equipment breakdowns; excessive labor turnover; employee accidents; too much unnecessary paperwork; improper space utilization; too much overtime; and poor layout that might affect performance efficiency.

The ideas suggested in the preceding paragraph certainly are not all inclusive, but the possibilities for project cost control and cost management should be apparent. To illustrate how cost control can contribute to a project's profit, let us assume the following:

Project cost authorization	$1,000,000
5% profit	$50,000
Project costs	$950,000

If one penny could be saved out of every dollar spent to accomplish the project's objectives, there would be a saving of $9,500, and this would increase net profit from $50,000 to $59,500. At a 5% profit rate, it would take $190,000 of additional project cost authorization to generate $9,500 more profit, or, to be more explicit, a 1% cost reduction could contribute as much to profit as a 19% increase in project cost authorization.

Intelligent and systematic cost control and reduction are the exception rather than the rule. Cost reduction can take place without impairing operational efficiency, destroying or compromising the quality of effort expended to complete the project, or adversely affecting organizational morale. The project manager should recognize that cost control is a major activity and an ongoing process. Some guidance for cost control is suggested, in a cost control checklist, in Appendix A of this chapter.

Another project control area relates to quality, performance, and obligation. Quality should not be sacrificed. There are times when time and cost pressures lead to sloppy work, which may or may not satisfy project work requirements. Poor performance can negatively affect the probability of follow-on authorization. Poor performance (e.g., engineering, where a product is developed) can also lead to a tarnished reputation and, perhaps, litigation resulting from consumer liability.

The other side of the coin is where there is overkill. At times in product development there is a tendency to overengineer. This can result in production difficulties and cost escalation, which can affect marketability. There are also situations where no physical product is involved. The project end product may be a feasibility study. The author has experienced situations where a contract was negotiated based on an agreed-upon work statement. Once the contract was in force and the project operable, the contractor requested additional information involving extra cost-generating effort. The inclination in such cases is to respond favorably to the contractor's request. By doing so, obligated work can be jeopardized, costs can accelerate, and profits diminish. This is a relatively common occurrence. It is suggested that when such requests are made, the contractee be amenable to work change or inclusion, but that there should be negotiation with the purchaser to incorporate the added costs into the basic contract agreement. The original project work statement would also have to be amended.

The illustration cited is an example of a change request originating external to the organization. Change requests can originate internally or externally, especially on projects where there is hardware development. Common reasons for changes to the original work plan can result from poor developmental test results, new knowledge or new technology, which would enable a better end product, a desired change in end product specifications, the availability or unavailability of materials, or poor planning initially defining the project work statement.

An internal work change request may or may not result in incremental project funding. Externally, at times, the customer can be convinced that the change will ultimately be in the customer's best interests if added funding is available and it can be justified. This situation often arises on projects for the development of military weapons systems. Such programs are often cited as examples of high project cost overruns. This can be deceptive inasmuch as the system originally contracted for and the system eventually delivered could be significantly different in performance and technical sophistication. By analog, this is like starting out to buy a pair of roller skates and winding up with a Mercedes.

Frequently requests for changes in the project work scope are internally generated. These changes, for reasons cited, may or may not be eligible for incremental funding. In almost any event the changes requested will entail added project costs. The added costs might be insignificant or considerable. The impact of the change, if authorized, can affect the project minimally or considerably. In view of the potential impact of a change to the project work scope, it is very important that there be a procedure and control to handle requests for project changes.

Many organizations have control procedures to handle project change requests. Usually the final decision as to whether to implement or reject the change is not left to an individual. Generally, a representative change control board is established to evaluate the request and subsequently determine the favorable or unfavorable disposition of the request. The change control board may include representatives from such functional areas as engineering, production, quality control, procurement, finance, legal, and management. The functional composition of the change control board would probably reflect the nature of the project.

An example of some of the factors the change control board might investigate before a decision is made is as follows:

Impact
  Minimal
  Major

Need
  Absolute or critical functional considerations (performance)
  Desirable marketing considerations

Attendant factors
  Extend product project life cycle
    Phase in (lead time)
    Retro fit
  Risk
  Impact: this and other projects
    Support activities
    Legal implications
    Complexity, coordination
    Cost/benefit analysis
    Education and training
    Priorities, schedules
    Internal/external security considerations
    Patents/trade secrets

In this section some suggestions have been advanced relative to the control of internal activities in which the project manager could have an impact. The project manager should adapt an entrepreneurial posture. The project must be managed with perspective from both the technical and profit aspects. Neither aspect should be neglected.

The project manager should approach control as an attempt to control value. Value control can be looked upon as a method that aims to find ways to get equal or superior performance from a product, process, function, or activity, at lower cost, while retaining quality, performance, and reliability. The broad objective of value control is to eliminate cost factors, without jeopardizing the performance, salability, or usability of a product or the effectiveness of a function or activity associated with the project.

Indirect Control Areas Internal to the Organization. The project manager may have a project that requires extensive support from functions and/or organizations beyond his or her immediate jurisdiction. Support and impact may be from activities external to the project but internal to the total organization. Some examples of such required support are the use of facilities and equipment that are available to other projects in the organization, administrative services, technical support, the computer, logistics, legal/finance, personnel, and maintenance.

Control problems can be difficult for the project manager where support is required and no direct sanction exists. The normal procedure is to request inputs in the formative phase of the project as to the nature and extent of support services, schedules, and cost estimates. After the proposal becomes an operable contract, the project manager has to release work authorizations into the system to instigate the necessary support. The control problem is that the support areas usually request their full share of the budget when the project is approved. The rationale is that budget authorization is needed in order to plan support activities and channel resources. Once the total budget is released, the project manager actually loses control. This may not actually be a problem.

Support services may be simple and predictable. Also, good working relations may have been established on past projects between the project manager and the support area; there is a high confidence level that the support effort will be forthcoming as represented.

There are, however, situations where working relations are not as good as they might be. Cases can be cited in which proposals have been generated to accomplish highly technical and unpredictable effort, the scope of which could change drastically once the project was operable. An example could be in hardware development, where production support estimates in the proposal were based on relatively vague specification and design concepts. As the project evolves, and the specification and design concepts come into sharper focus, many support areas, including production, feel the actual approach is so significantly different from the planned approach that they cannot be held to the original premises. Support commitments as to performance, time, and cost are altered, even though the project manager is still obligated to the original estimate. This situation can be exacerbated when support activity is in process and a change in the project work scope negates work already performed. The examples cited are not uncommon dilemmas; categorical solutions are impossible. Such situations should be anticipated and avoided, but if they do occur, the project manager must use ingenuity to solve the problem and minimize negative impacts on the project.

Planning and subsequent control are often tenuous when the project manager is obligated to use organizational facilities and equipment that are common to other projects. When buying support services external to the project, the project manager is, in effect, acting as a contractor. In buying such services there are three potential problems: (1) Will the facilities and equipment be available when needed and scheduled? (2) Will the performance of such facilities and equipment be compatible with the project's technical requirements? (3) Are costs reasonable and compatible with budget allocations?

Often the cost of owning needed project support facilities and equipment cannot be justified or authorized for the project. In many instances the only solution is to have such equipment and facilities available for sharing and chargeable to several projects. Where there are many active projects operating in technologically related areas, it is very possible that the demand for such support is erratic. At times demand may far exceed support capacity and at other times there may be a lull and down time. The natural inclination is for the project manager to plan the projects on a logical work sequence, assuming support will be available as needed. Often the project manager is dismayed to find that other projects are already using the facilities or equipment, or, worse yet, he or she gets to the required support areas only to be bumped by projects that have been given a higher operational priority.

If the project manager finds the project held up by the unavailability of support resources, problems are likely to develop that could affect the ultimate success of the project. Usually such delays result in unanticipated project costs. Project people may have been working to a schedule on the assumption that continued effort will proceed as planned. The required facilities and/or equipment support may be essential to the next work phase of the project. Not having access to such support as planned can disrupt the entire project work schedule. Delays can cause unproductive labor charges for idle time. Larger than anticipated overhead allocations can lead to budgetary difficulties. There could be difficulty in keeping the project team intact, especially if there are serious morale problems where people have worked conscientiously and then are frustrated by being forced into a project stretch-out over which they have no control.

Many of the situations cited can be avoided if there is organizational provision for central coordination and control on requirements and schedules for the use of common resources. The project manager should build some flexibility into the project work plan to enable contingency activities in the event there are unforeseen holdups. The project manager should also know what other projects may be in competition for the use of common resources. In many instances coordination between the project managers can prove mutually beneficial. If the project manager is aware of probable scheduling problems, it may be possible to contract for the required support work outside the organization. Good control would enable the project manager to anticipate these types of problems, get authorization, if needed, for outside procurement, and have sufficient lead time to locate alternate sources.

There are also situations where existing organizational facilities and equipment are not compatible with the project's support requirements. The project manager might investigate the feasibility of the organization buying equipment that could also be shared with, and charged to, other projects. Another possibility is to modify the project's technical support requirements so that existing facilities and equipment can be adapted. A third possibility is to contract with outside vendors where ownership is not feasible.

The third potential problem, relative to buying facilities and equipment support for the project, revolves around costs. If the organization has made capital expenditures to provide facilities and equipment support for projects, there is understandable pressure for in-house utilization. Theoretically, in-house utilization can be convenient, provide more direct control, and save the organization money by avoiding outside procurement. In practice, in-house utilization, as mentioned, can involve scheduling difficulties. Additionally, the extent of control can be illusory if the internal sources are high-cost operations and there is questionable performance. The project manager may be very unhappy but have few actual sanctions to impose. On the other hand, if the performance of an outside vendor is unsatisfactory, the sanction of contract cancellation is a definite possibility.

Frictions often develop between project managers and internal support functions. Most organizations, as a policy, maintain that project people are free to use outside support sources if internal services are inadequate and costs are not competitive. In actual practice, unless there are very strong justifications, project managers tend to be captive in purchasing internal services, if they exist.

So far in this section the discussion has centered on the use of facilities and equipment that are necessary for project support. There are other required project support areas that are internal to the organization but beyond the direct control of the project manager. If all the resources to accomplish the project resided within the project, this would result in a product rather than a project organization.

It is unusual for a project manager to have all the functional support required under direct control. At times some functions are so important to the project that specialized people are assigned to and integrated into the project team. At other times the functional support needed by the project is peripheral or functional support requirements may be sporadic. Examples of the aforementioned are administrative services, which often include communications and the use of the computer center; very selective technical support; logistics, including any necessary procurement activities; legal and contracts administration; finance; personnel; maintenance; and production.

Many of the functions indicated are needed in projects. These functions generally are common resources available to many projects. A functional representative may service several projects, or a single project may be so large and complex that several people from a functional activity are assigned to it. This is another facet of project management.

The project manager must recognize a division of labor, specialization, jurisdiction, and the need for functional support. At times project managers get impatient and try to encompass all the project-related activities within their direct control. This usually is not a wise operational approach. Expensive labor may be used in performing tasks that could be delegated to less expensive or more specialized help. Jurisdictional disputes and attendant frictions can develop. And, because of past experience of poor working relationships when functional support is required, the functional people may not be as helpful or as cooperative as possible. It behooves the project manager to develop and maintain good working relationships with all the functional support managers.

The project manager may also find his or her position compromised by an inability to control the allocation of overhead costs to the project. The overhead charges allocated to the project and the actual applied overhead rate can be determining in the decision to bid or not bid on a project. Overhead charges can significantly affect the competitive position of a potential project. Some representative indirect or overhead costs are maintenance; clerical help; general and administrative salaries; fringe benefits, including sick leaves, vacations, health insurance, educational programs, and tuitional reimbursement; utilities; taxes; interest; rent; nonproductive supplies; and depreciation.[5]

Indirect Control Areas External to the Organization. There are times when outside sources and support represent a significant part of the project work scope. Outside support can range from trivial to essential. There are situations where the project manager is primarily a contractor who disperses different segments of the project to subcontractors and coordinates their activities. On other projects most of the effort can be accomplished in-house and relatively little effort is farmed out.

The more common external areas where the project manager cannot exert direct control are situations where outside vendors are used to provide project technical support, where specialized outside test facilities or equipment is required, or where consultants are retained on an ad hoc basis. Even though the aforementioned activities may be contracted out, the project manager does not necessarily have to abdicate control prerogatives.

Controls by the project manager can be exerted prior to actual commitment and during the performance phases. Control, a prelude to actual authorization, can result from vendor evaluation and certification. Evaluation and certification would entail review of past experience by and with the vendor on such factors as related technical experience, quality, cost, adherence to schedule commitments, reliability, excellence and reputation for performance, capacity, and demonstrated managerial competence. There are situations where project support might not involve a standard product or service for comparative purposes. In such situations the project manager can issue a request for proposals to determine relative methodologies, promises of performance, and estimated costs by competing vendors.

Once the contract for actual project support is authorized, control becomes tenuous; however, the project manager still has a variety of controls at his or her disposal that can be used to reasonably ensure performance. Some techniques that can be employed for control purposes are establish key milestones which signal major accomplishment points; arrange for on-site inspection, especially where there are unusual hardware requirements, important schedule considerations, and critical specifications and quality standards; stipulate a requirement for periodic comprehensive progress reports; set up coordination meetings to discuss technical progress and problems; and arrange a schedule of progress payments based on the accomplishment of specified technical goals or the delivery of hardware.

The insertion of a contractual provision for progress payments for work performed is an important project control when dealing with supply sources external to the organization. This is a relatively common but not universal practice. To illustrate, the author was brought in as a consultant for a nonprofit organization that funded research. The consulting assignment arose from the organization's poor experience with completion of the research projects. The existing procedure was to have peer review of research proposals and, if there was favorable reaction, to release the funding to the applicant. A large percentage of projects that had been funded had never been completed. It was suggested, and subsequently implemented, that if peer review deemed the project worthy of support, funding should be released on an incremental basis. The specific recommendation was that 25% of the funding be released at the time of the initial project authorization, based on milestone accomplishment identification; an additional 25% of the funding was to be authorized and released when the project was one-third completed; 25% more funding would be forthcoming at the two-thirds completion point; and the final 25% of the funding would be granted when the project was completed and a final report submitted. The improvement was dramatic. Before incremental funding, less than 20% of the projects were completed. After incremental funding was practiced, over 80% of the projects authorized were satisfactorily completed.

Control at the Project Termination Phase

Many projects may operate on incremental funding, which is periodically subject to review and which can have a bearing as to whether the project is continued or terminated. There are situations where projects are undertaken on a "best effort" basis. A few representative examples of such projects might be to solve operational problems and research to seek a cure for a disease, develop a new pharmaceutical, or conduct a feasibility study. Projects where there are no specific time limits often involve knowledge generation and can be open-ended; as mentioned earlier, a restraint is funding.

In situations where the project life is related to a definite operable and time objective, the project termination is, in effect, predetermined. There are, of course, exceptions where the life of the project may be extended owing to changing requirements, added information, new technology, and so on. A question frequently encountered and posed by top management is When do you terminate a project? When does the law of diminishing returns become operable?

When there are no established milestones leading to the completion of a project, the decision to continue or abort project effort may be very difficult. Where problems are significant and the solutions sought evasive, project people are often highly motivated and feel confident of an eventual breakthrough. After they have extended considerable effort, they are loath to give up. They want the project to continue and generally maintain that the solution is imminent. Is the answer really close by? Has the approach been correct? Would the result, even if successful, justify the expenditure of resources? Would it be a case of spending good money after money poorly spent? Are there possible side benefits to be derived by continuing the project? These are questions and control points that must be satisfactorily answered if the project is to be continued.

Another control problem is terminating projects that have essentially accomplished their objectives. In large organizations, where there are many interesting and technologically diverse projects, intraorganizational mobility is usually good. In fact, control by the project manager, in the described situation, may be to retain essential project people until the project is technically completed. Where there are promising alternatives, project people may be anxious to leave a dying project before all the work is completed. They may be eager to jump aboard a new project that has a much longer life expectancy.

It is hard to retain interest and enthusiasm for a project that is nearing completion. The project manager must recognize such emotional and motivated factors and also be aware of his or her obligation to complete the project. One suggestion that might at times mitigate the transition problem is a temporary dual assignment. Project people can spend part of their time on the terminating project and, at the same time, phase into activity on a new project. Control here is essential if this route is taken. The project manager must be confident that the effort he or she is buying and being charged for is the effort that is actually being expended to complete the project. Where people are dividing their effort between projects, time and cost controls are very important.

A reverse situation can develop where organizational project activity has been curtailed and there are limited or no opportunities for reassignment to new projects. In this type of situation the tendency is to find excuses for extra effort on the project, even though the authorizing objectives have been accomplished. Continuation of project activity, which may be questionable as to relevance and contribution, can escalate costs, erode profits, and lead to morale problems, since this is a form of featherbedding.

People are involved in project management. Where rapport has developed between members of the project team, it could be traumatic for the project manager to exercise control and terminate the project, on the basis that contractual objectives have been accomplished, and break up the project team.

Project control in the termination phase of the project life cycle entails review. Before the project is actually shut down and authorized charge accounts closed, the project manager may, based on the type of project, have to coordinate internally and externally to see if technical and schedule objectives have been met and cost goals have been achieved. In addition, even though actual work has been completed, there may remain the disposition of equipment, parts, spares, and partially completed work. Often a final report to the customer is required, and, before walking away from the project, the project manager should coordinate with the customer to ascertain that the customer was satisfied. The project manager should verify with the organization's legal department that contractual requirements have been accomplished; the project manager should arrange for a briefing session with top management to review the history of the project and, hopefully, be able to demonstrate successful project results and contribution to the total organization's welfare.

Avoiding Problems and Improving Control

Synthesis

Much of this last section reviews either information covered earlier in the chapter, problems or possible solutions not directly discussed but alluded to, problems that can be avoided, or solutions which can be used in a common sense approach. The tragedy is the number of problems that develop owing to the inadequacy of controls and because managers fail to use elementary common sense.

Control Problems

There are many problems in establishing and maintaining a good informational system. Relevant, accurate, and timely information provide the project managers with a high degree of confidence so that they know what is happening on the project, how it is happening, or what should be done if what is happening is not compatible with the project's objectives. This is the essence of control.

First, there is a tendency to overload the informational system. In some organizations information seems to be the major product rather than a facilitating by-product. Being inundated with too much information can be as bad or worse than not having enough information. In such cases the relevant information may be buried along with nonessential trivia and extracting the information is difficult or impossible and is certainly time-consuming.

Second, the information should be accurate and reliable. Too often the accuracy or reliability of information received can be questioned. People report on their activities. How objective can people be in appraising their own performance? If there are failures, it is easier to place the blame on other people, other functional areas, or on circumstances beyond their control. Or they may be optimistic and contend that, even though objectives have not been met to date, a solution is imminent. Is such a solution really on the horizon? Another related problem is that information is often fragmented or partial. At times this reporting is deliberate to obscure the real problem; at times fragmented or partial information is the product of a poorly designed information system. At times a half or partial truth is insidious and makes a true appraisal of the actual situation very difficult.

Third, the information should be timely. Late, after-the-fact information limits the project manager's options. If a problem has already occurred, the only alternatives may be consideration of which corrective actions have the best prospects for putting the project on-line again. Timely information should provide insight into developments that can negatively affect the project. Before-the-fact information infinitely expands the options available to the project manager.

Related to information, and an attendant problem, is the frequent failure to properly coordinate project activities. One support group may be proceeding along work lines originally agreed upon, but the work scope, or work effort, or schedule of other groups may have changed. Such changes could very conceivably affect the effort of other groups. It is very important to have periodic coordination meetings. Such meetings should communicate progress, problems, and possible changes in the work scope so that all project support factions are alerted to what is happening and they understand the potential impact of such happenings on their effort.

Another control problem relates to the control of strategic factors. There may be a managerial inclination to either over- or undercontrol. Or management control may be sporadic and the boom lowered after there are frequent or serious problems. Control is an ongoing process. It can be time-consuming, ineffectual, and at times organizationally demoralizing. It is not how much or how little control is exercised; what is important is that control be related to accomplishment factors vital to project objectives. Identification of strategic factors and a continuous monitoring process of these factors are essential for good project control.

Improving Control

Earlier in this chapter it was mentioned that "control" often conjured up negative reactions. Unless properly understood, implemented, and managed, the control process can organizationally lead to psychological barriers. What really is possible is a better or improved system of control in most project organizations if managers reflect on and consider the operational climate.

Project organizations usually have a high density of professional employees. For the most part these people, by their career choice and educational attainment, want the dignity of accomplishment and the recognition of their efforts. They are professionals and expect treatment accordingly. Unilateral decisions and control processes should be avoided whenever possible.

Project control can generally be improved by a participative or consultative approach. The people responsible for performance should be involved in evaluating the magnitude of effort, setting performance standards where possible, and being made responsible and accountable for results. Most professionals prefer to work in a permissive and participative environment and welcome responsibility and accountability.

A great deal of control involves communication and explanation. People will usually favorably respond to action situations if they understand what is happening. Too often orders are arbitrarily passed down in the organization without explanation, rationalization, or education. What often becomes a sticky situation could, if properly handled, be a team-building and project morale-building experience.

Control can be improved by constant attention and review of the factors to be controlled and the techniques used to control the strategic factors. Control should be flexible, adaptive, and innovative. What worked once in one situation may be inapplicable under current conditions.

Control should be predicated on helping people do their jobs better. They should feel comfortable that they have the necessary tools and information to do what has to be done. They should be educated to the fact that a sharp organization achieving its objectives is normally a healthy organization. Being a member of a healthy organization promotes individual pride and generally affords career development opportunities.

Finally, control can be improved by encouraging people to be operationally honest in recognizing and communicating potential problems. Anticipation is critical in a good control system. This approach can be fostered by an enlightened management approach, where the identification of potential problems signals the need for and subsequent deliverance of help. Too often people associate punitive actions or managerial hysterics when potential or actual problems are communicated. A positive, rather than negative, operational control environment can be more productive and beneficial.

Endnotes Chapter Ten

1. D. Roman, *Science, Technology and Innovation: A Systems Approach,* Columbus, OH, Grid Publishing, 1980, p. 370.
2. C. C. Higgins, "Management Controls for Small Business," in *Top Management Handbook,* H. B. Maynard (ed.), New York, McGraw-Hill, 1960, p. 442.
3. Stanley de J. Osborne, "Management Controls for Large Business," in *Top Management Handbook,* H. B. Maynard (ed.), New York, McGraw-Hill, 1960, pp. 427–428.
4. Work authorization and control are discussed in R. D. Archibald, *Managing High Technology Programs and Projects,* New York, Wiley, 1976, pp. 180–191.
5. See S. E. Stephanou, *Management: Technology, Innovation and Engineering,* Malibu, CA, Daniel Spencer, 1981, pp. 149–151.

Appendix A. Cost Control Checklist

This list is by no means intended to be all inclusive; it is only a suggested starting point. Each manager can add or eliminate relevant or nonrelevant factors.

A. Records
   Do you have adequate information?
   Too much nonusable information?
   Unused forms?
   Unimportant or unused reports; paperwork tied up for dust-gathering records?
B. Travel
   Is this trip necessary? Would a letter or phone call be quicker or cheaper and just as effective?
   How are you traveling? Consider method and cost and do not omit time, which is a valuable asset.

C. Human resources

Do you have too many or too few people to do the job?

Are the people paid commensurate with their contribution?

How valuable are they to the organization? What would happen if you did not have them? Would things continue with a little belt tightening or reorganization? Would there be confusion? Lost opportunities? Would you have to replace them and perhaps pay as much or more to get somebody who may be no better or even worse?

Remember, labor turnover is expensive; there are many costs besides out-of-pocket salaries.

Do you have expensive people doing jobs that could be done by cheaper help?

Would it be cheaper to use temporary help? Purchase services outside the organization?

D. When you purchase

Do you have unreasonable quality specifications?

Have you shopped around for the best price and quality?

Have you considered possible substitutes that could do the job better or cheaper?

Do you have a lot of capital tied up in inventory?

Are you put in a compromising position by not having goods or material to service a customer?

Have you figured all the costs of maintaining an inventory, such as obsolescence, spoilage, tax, and cost of space used?

E. Scrap

Do you have excessive scrap?

How do you minimize scrap?

How do you dispose of scrap?

F. Are you using your facilities properly?

Do you have an effective layout?

Do you know where things are?

Is it convenient to reach goods and materials, and do they flow in relation to their need?

Do you have unused space? What does it cost? Can it be profitably used?

Are you anticipating space requirements so you will not be in trouble in the near future if you have to expand or contract operations?

G. Utilities

Telephone: unnecessary calls

Gas

Electricity: lights not on when not necessary

H. Maintenance costs

Do you have frequent breakdowns that disrupt operations, lead to idle time, and prevent meeting commitments to customers?

Do you schedule maintenance to coincide with possible slow periods?

I. Product changes

How much standardization?

Can better and cheaper products be developed to do the same job?
What is the product supposed to do; what else and how else can it be done?

J. Use of capital
   Are you using your funds wisely?
   Do you have a cash flow problem?
   If you are financing your customers, have you considered this as an operating
     cost? The money costs you and should be incorporated into the price you
     charge your customers.

K. Some general areas that you might want to explore:
   Preventive or positive maintenance
      Outside or inside maintenance capability
   Paying creditors; discounts, net 60 days, etc.
   Consignment of inventory
   Alternate uses of facilities and equipment
   Off-season diversification
   Cost of employee benefits
   Waste reclamation
   Standardization of equipment and services
   Use of a computer for information
   Security measures that might help reduce losses through destruction, loss, or
     theft
   Energy conservation
   Volume buying for discount and reselling surplus
   Excessive overtime costs
   Too much handling and rehandling of materials

CHAPTER ELEVEN

Some Legal Aspects of Project Management*

Legal Implications of Project Management

Introduction

It is not the objective of a project to become involved with the law, yet, from the inception of the project to its termination, the law pervades its activities. Project decisions and their implementation can often cause an organization to commit acts that infringe on the rights of others or which are injurious to society as a whole, and such acts can be considered a crime by a government. It is also incumbent on a project engaged in the development of new technology and innovation to protect the interests of the organization to the fullest extent afforded by the law. The problems of the law are best left to the legal profession, and particularly to the legal specialists, where warranted. It is prudent for project personnel to become familiar with the various aspects of the law in order to appropriately guide their activities and know when to effectively seek counsel from the legal profession. The fees of attorneys engender a high expense and often the extent and success of an attorney's efforts depend on the appropriate decision and conduct of the client. The purpose of this chapter is to impress upon project personnel not to be oblivious to the law and essentially understand the legal implications of their activities to avoid stumbling into legal entanglements and make prudent use of legal support.

Sources of Law

Since the United States is a union of 50 states, there are in effect 51 legal systems: 1 federal legal system and 50 state legal systems.

* The author is indebted to Professor Max Weiner, who submitted this chapter.

Federal Law

1. The United States Constitution is the fundamental source of law and its authority is absolute on all points covered by it.

2. Statutes. These are laws enacted by Congress and signed by the President, unless there is a veto, in which case Congress can still enact the statute by a 2 to 3 vote. These statutes are embodied in the U.S. Code. No statute can be contrary to the provisions of the Constitution.

3. Administrative Regulations. These are rules adopted by federal agencies—under the authority of a statute—that have the full force and effect of law. They are authorized to permit government agencies to carry out the tasks of government and generally they are issued pursuant to the Administrative Procedures Act, which formulates a method of adoption. They are embodied in a Code of Federal Regulations. They cannot be contrary to a statute or the provisions of the Constitution.

4. Judicial Law. This consists of decisions whereby judges apply a principle of law to a set of facts developed in a case. In subsequent cases that are similar the principle is applied on the basis of precedence. If there are conflicts, the precedent of a higher court prevails. Thus decisions of the U.S. Supreme Court guide the decisions of all federal judges. The decisions of the Circuit Court of Appeals are binding on federal judges in their respective circuits. Decisions of other circuits and other judges have an influence in formulating a decision. Judges review challenges against regulations and statutes and decide if they violate a law or provision of the Constitution to the extent of nullity.

The federal legal system has jurisdiction over matters that involve the provisions of the U.S. Constitution, a federal statute, a treaty with a foreign nation, a decision by an administrative quasi-judicial agency, or in civil cases where there is a diversity of citizenships among parties from different states. Civil cases must present a claim of $10,000 or more.

State Laws

1. All states have a Constitution that distributes the powers of government to three branches, as the federal government, and provides for the distribution of power to political subdivisions, such as counties, cities, townships, school districts, and fire districts.

2. Statutes. These laws are enacted by the respective legislatures and signed by the Governor. Some states have constitutional provisions permitting the citizens to nullify a law by referendum or generate a law by initiative.

3. Ordinances. These are laws enacted by local governing bodies of counties, cities, and townships that are authorized by the state constitution or statutes. In some jurisdictions the laws are enacted by the people at periodic town meetings, and in some they are enacted or nullified by initiative or referendum.

4. Administrative Regulations. A number of states permit their agencies to adopt rules under the authority of a statute that have the full effect of law. This applies to local jurisdictions under their charters.

5. Judicial Law. State courts render decisions in cases litigated before them, or reviewed upon appeal, that establish applicable principles of law. The decisions of the highest state court guides the decision of all state judges. Some states have intermediate courts of appeal, whose decisions are binding on all judges in their respective districts.

The states have jurisdiction over all legal matters not delegated to the federal government by the U.S. Constitution or prohibited by it to the states.[1]

Legal Environment*

Projects are established by organizations that are usually established under the law and operate under the rules of law. They are members of the nation, the states in which they operate, and the communities that house and protect them. It is expected that they abide by the law and pay penalties for any infringement or violation of law. They have a relationship with others and rights. They also have a duty to act or refrain from acting when the act or omission would violate the rights of others. Any conduct that violates this relationship is subject to legal action, which may be in the form of a civil suit or criminal prosecution. When the relationship is a private matter among individuals or organizations, any violation is considered a breach, which may result in a civil action, compensating an aggrieved party for damages suffered. When the relationship involves a breach against the public or the government, it is a criminal matter, subject to prosecution by a State Attorney or a U.S. Attorney.

From the inception of a project, when the selection process is considered, if the project is considered for seeking new knowledge, product development, improvement, or improving a process, the rights of others should be borne in mind. Someone else may have acquired a patent on this contemplated innovation, which gives an exclusive right to its fabrication, use, or sale.[2] Use of that patent without consent is an infringement, subject to injunctive action restraining its further use and a suit for damages. It is necessary to first make a search for a patent, contact the inventor or holder of the patent, and negotiate for a license, which usually entails the payment of a royalty, unless the organization holds patents that the other party may desire and be amenable to a cross-licensing agreement. This would require an evaluation as to whether it is economically advantageous to generate the project. The support of a legal special-

---

* Much of the material in the following sections addresses legal issues as they might apply to government contracting for projects. In most instances the law might similarly be applied on project contracts between two parties in the private sector.

ist, such as a patent attorney, would be the appropriate route to seek under such circumstances.

Often projects are tentatively established when an organization submits a proposal for a contract. If the contract is awarded to the organization, it will be the responsibility of the project to fulfill its provisions. At this point it is incumbent on the project manager to become familiar with the provisions of the proposed contract to consider the possibility of performance and required resources in order not to subject the organization to a breach of contract and assure profitability. If it is a construction project, there are problems involved with zoning and local ordinances pertaining to licenses, permits, and rights of obstruction. There are numerous subcontractors and purchase orders for materials and equipment and rental of equipment. There may be access rights and labor problems with unions and the Department of Labor. If it is a government job, there are the Davis-Bacon Act, minority subcontracting, and security requirements. There are also insurance and bonding requirements. Projects involved with nuclear plants have to cope with environmental and nuclear regulatory laws and regulations.

If it is a project for research and development, the laws pertaining to patent rights, copyright, and trade secrets have a significant impact. The project should consider the unpatented proprietary information the organization possesses that would enhance its proposal, and the extent and method of divulging it as a selling factor and protecting its status. It would be wise at this point to evaluate the intended use of technology to ascertain the use of processes that have been patented by others requiring a license for use and initiate suitable negotiations for such use. The identity of potential subcontracts should be viewed with capable sources and the extent of royalties that may have to be paid. This would entail identifying organizations that may possess a competitive advantage as a result of possessing rights or access to pertinent technological innovations. No doubt the properly managed organization will have legal and contracting talent available in the preparation of a proposal, but its efforts are only effective if the project can supply data that would then permit it to submit a meaningful proposal containing a competitive advantage and protect the proprietary interests of the organization.

If the proposal is made to a government agency, there should be knowledge of the extent of progress the government has made in the field. The government requires contractors to send copies of scientific and technical reports to either the Defense Technical Information Center at Cameron Station, Alexandria, Virginia, or the National Technical Information Service, Department of Commerce, Springfield, Virginia.[3] These activities provide a central service for the interchange of scientific and technical information, which may be used in developing the approach presented in a proposal. Items that are classified under security requirements are not released to those who do not have an appropriate security clearance and a need to know. When work is contemplated on classified materials, the project's organization would have to be cleared for security requirements and be a party to a security agreement.[4]

On the other hand, a project may be established to fulfill a program for an organization that would require the use of other organizations as an extension of its resources. This would normally be accomplished through the contracting instrument, which is a legal document whereby a party assumes an obligation to perform on a prescribed task in return for some consideration, which is usually payment of a prescribed amount or an amount established by a prescribed procedure. Although the organization may use contract negotiations and an acquisition system in its procedure in the selection of sources and awards of contracts, the crux of any resulting contract is the description of the requirements for performance. This would be the responsibility of the project. Its input would determine, to a great extent, the success in the proper selection of a contractor, the effective negotiation of a contract, and the sound administration to assure satisfactory performance and completion. In this relationship the project encounters the rules of contract law and the law of agency. In the process it is also exposed to laws affecting labor, safety, patents, copyrights, trade secrets, and property rights.

Projects that are established to develop, improve, and market products may find themselves running into a legal maze on product liability and warranties, which could prove costly to the organization, and they must guard against false or misleading advertising. Where imports and exports are concerned, there are customs laws and restrictions on imports and the necessity of permits for export of technology. There are a multitude of legal barriers and problems facing a project, but primarily projects are generated and operate under an aura of contractual commitments and obligations and perform in furtherance of an organizational objective. These conditions dictate a basic knowledge of the laws of contracts and agency.

Basic Concepts of the Law of Contracts

Basically, a contract is an agreement between two or more parties whereby one makes an offer, another accepts an offer, and there is the presence of consideration. The important word is *agreement,* a meeting of the minds, and the offer must be valid and available for acceptance by the one to whom the offer is made.

If A offers to sell a black vehicle to B for a price, and B accepts the offer to buy A's white vehicle for that price, there is no meeting of the minds. If A requires an acceptance by a specific date and B accepts it subsequent to that date, there is no valid offer available for acceptance. If A makes the offer to B, C cannot come along and accept that offer, since it did not apply to C. Consideration is where one obligates oneself to do something that one had a legal right not to do, or forbears from doing something one had a legal right to do. Mutual promises in exchange for each other are consideration: a promise for a promise.

Under judicial law an offer could be withdrawn at any time before acceptance. Once there is an acceptance, it is a contract. A party may be bound to keep an offer open for acceptance for a specific period under an option that, in effect, is a contract to permit the offer to be available for acceptance for that period. Usually an offeree gives some consideration for that right. However, with one exception, all states have adopted the Uniform Commercial Code, which has changed the judicial law in many respects pertaining to the sale of goods. Therefore, under Section 2-205, an offer must last out its term. If an offer is specified as open for 10 days, it may not be revoked before 10 days. If no time is specified, it has to be open for a reasonable amount of time, but in no event for more than 3 months. When the mails are used, judicial law makes the U.S. Postal Service the agent of the offeror. Therefore when an acceptance is deposited into a mailbox, it establishes a contract. Today, if it concerns the sale of goods, Section 2-206 of the Uniform Commercial Code permits acceptance of an offer, in any manner and by any medium, reasonable under the circumstances. If A sends an offer to B, which the latter has not received, and B sends A an offer with identical terms, it is not considered an acceptance of the offer. It is, in effect, another offer, and cross-offers do not constitute a contract.

Parties to a contract must make their offers and acceptances freely, and not under duress, coercion, or undue influence. This is fairly clear when a person is deprived of liberty or property through physical force or even the threat of physical force. Courts have also held that economic threats or business compulsion may constitute duress. Undue influence results from an inducement by a dominant party taking advantage of one under mental or emotional strain. Parties must be capable of seriously making a choice for an offer or acceptance. They must be mentally competent and not impeded by the use of alcoholic beverages or drugs. An offer or acceptance made in jest is not serious. A minor or mentally abnormal party is not competent.

A contract must be for a legal purpose and not cause a violation of the law. Most jurisdictions forbid gambling, so a contract to pay a gambling wager is unenforceable. Limitations are set on interest rates, and no contract is enforceable that requires excessive interest rate payments. Contracts entered into by parties in a capacity requiring a regulatory license by a state are not considered legal without that license. Therefore one who is instrumental in effecting the sale of real estate may not sue for a commission without a broker's license. Contracts whose performance would violate a zoning law, an antitrust law, or a patent or copyright law, or interfere with the public's general welfare, health, safety, or morals will not be entertained by the courts. Section 2-302 of the Uniform Commercial Code permits courts to refuse to enforce an unconscionable contract or clause.

A contract may be unilateral or bilateral. A bilateral contract is the exchange of a promise for a promise. If A promises to fight B at a boxing event, for 15 rounds, on a specific day at a specified place, and C promises to pay a certain amount for that performance, this is a bilateral contract. If C promises to pay an extra amount if A knocks out B before the 10th round, this is an offer that is a promise for an act of performance: A has not promised to knock out B in the 10th round; there is just a unilateral offer by C that can be accepted when the performance occurs. The problem unilateral contracts present goes back to the legal principle that an offer may be revoked before acceptance. Judicial law has had conflicting views over the subject, from requiring such an offer to stand until the other party has a chance to perform to the stringent rule that it can be revoked at any time before the act. In the sale of goods under Section 2-206 of the Uniform Commercial Code, an offer to buy, for prompt or current shipment, is construed as inviting acceptance by either a prompt promise to ship or current shipment of conforming or nonconforming goods. Section 206(2) recognizes the beginning of a requested performance as a reasonable mode of acceptance; however, an offeror should be notified of acceptance in a reasonable time.

Does a contract have to be in writing? Not necessarily, unless it is required to be in writing by a statute. The first statute requiring certain contracts to be in writing was passed by the English Parliament in 1677 to prevent frauds and perjuries and is commonly known as the Statute of Frauds. A written instrument is required in six situations:

1. A promise by an executor of an estate to pay the debt of a deceased out of his own funds
2. A promise to pay the creditor of another person the debt of that person
3. An agreement in consideration of marriage
4. A contract for the sale of real estate
5. An agreement not to be performed within 1 year
6. A sale of goods for $50.00 or more

Although the English Parliament repealed the Statute of Frauds, except for contracts involving the sale of real estate and the promise to pay the debt of another, our Uniform Commercial Code requires writing sufficient to indicate a contract for sale of goods for $500.00 or more, signed by the party against whom enforcement is sought,[5] or $5,000.00 for other personal property.[6]

Our states have not followed the action of the English Parliament, except that agreements in consideration of marriage have been limited generally to property settlements. The common conception of a contract by laymen usually visualizes a formal legal instrument, signed by both parties, with all provisions contained therein. This is a perfect situation, but not really necessary. If enough written pieces of paper can be gathered to spell out the terms of an agreement, and there is a signature by the party against whom enforcement is sought, the statute is satisfied. The statute is also satisfied if the agreed terms are omitted or incorrectly stated in the writing but the quantity of goods is established. Then it may be enforced for fulfillment of the quantity of goods. The Uniform Commercial Code permits enforcement of an unwritten order for goods of a special nature not suitable for sale to others in a standard market if the seller substantially performed fabrication before receiving notice of repudiation.[7]

When there is a written contract no parol evidence, which means oral or written items, not incorporated in the contents of or by reference in the document can be used to vary the terms of the contract. However, this does not prevent the use of parol evidence to clarify or resolve differences in the interpretation of the terms of the contract. The Uniform Commercial Code permits a course of dealing, or usage of the trade, as a basis of explaining or supplementing the terms of the contract.[8] Unfortunately, contracts at times contain inconsistencies, and, in considering which provision prevails, generally a handwritten word prevails. A typewritten word prevails over the printed word. A written specification prevails over a drawing. A provision in the body of a contract prevails over a specification appended to a contract and made part thereof.

Generally, contracts embody the identity of the parties and their obligations. One party is required to perform and the other is required to provide the consideration. Both the performance and the consideration should be described in clear and unequivocal terms; otherwise problems present themselves from ambiguities and inconsistencies. Courts do not correct ill-prepared contracts. They will merely attempt to ascertain the true intent of the parties from their conduct, correspondence, past relationships between the parties, and the customs of the trade. This is affirmed by the Uniform Commercial Code.[9]

In this context the role of a project is of crucial importance. Although the responsibility of negotiating and consummating a contract usually rests with an acquisition, procurement, or other contracting function, it is the project that is responsible for establishing the performance requirements. It is the duty of the project to describe to the contracting function, in clear and unequivocal terms, what it desires from a contractor as to quality, quantity, time of delivery, and place of delivery. This is the basis of solicitation by the contracting function, its negotiation and preparation of the contractual document. A description that is ambiguous, inconsistent, and vague will be deficient in attracting good reliable sources, will be negotiated on erroneous premises, and will result in a contract that will be difficult to enforce. When it gets to a court, the drafter of the instrument is at a disadvantage. Courts consider that one who solicits should know what is required and not put the other party in a position of uncertainty. In a difference of interpretation, a court will hold with the other party if its interpretation appears reasonable under the circumstances. On the other hand, if the project is established to perform on the contract, it owes a duty to examine the performance requirements of the contract and warn the organization of the deficiencies that will present problems and the gravity of consequences which may be encountered. This should present a basis for the organization to decide whether it should include contingencies in the negotiation, attempt to correct the situation at negotiations, negotiate on the customer's terms, and perform as it sees fit with a view of future modifications, or not enter into the transaction. Knowledgeable conduct by a project at this stage will tend to result in a legal document that will fulfill an objective rather than invite a lawsuit.

At times parties may not have entered into any negotiations for a contract and yet, in spite of an intent not to enter into a contract, the law will imply a contract. This situation may exist when one under either an erroneous impression or force of circumstances performs for the benefit of another who may not have asked for it. The situation may be further aggravated if the other party permits the performance to be completed when there is a duty to speak out and object. The law refers to such situations as a quasi-contract. It occurs when a party receives or retains a benefit, thereby becoming what the law considers unjustly enriched, and there is no other legal recourse for the victim. The victim is entitled to recover the reasonable value of the benefit. A says to B, "I am sending you a terrific gadget for only $200.00 and please send the check as soon as you receive it"; B did not order the gadget and may even express a desire not to have it sent. However, if B receives it, keeps it, and uses it, then there is an implied contract. The law considers that B is unjustly enriched. This poses a problem for projects to exercise caution in dialogue with personnel of solicitors seeking to gain a foothold in furnishing the organization goods and services. The conduct in a sincere intention to evaluate may create an impression of an acquisition and subject the organization to a claim.

Government Contracts

Government contracts are covered by statutes, such as the Armed Services Procurement Act, the Federal Property and Administrative Services Act, and acts establishing the agencies with their authority. Although the government is a sovereign body, it subjects itself to contract law in its relationship with the industrial and business community in the acquisition process. However, it is restricted in its approach and methods by the statutes, and in the course of historical events, judicial law has extended an aura of protection to safeguard the interests of the taxpayers. Furthermore, the government has issued the Federal Acquisition Regulation, which implements the various laws, and this is further implemented by agency regulations, which supplement the Federal Acquisition Regulation. Although the principles of contract law apply to government contracts, there are some differences. All government contracts are written and, even if the instrument omits provisions required by law or regulation, the law implies that such provisions are included in the contract. The contents of the law and regulations are published and available to the public, and the law considers that the public should be aware of the mandatory provisions in a government contract. A government contract is structured to contain general provisions and a schedule. The general provisions are mandated by law and regulation. The schedule describes the required performance and payment. It may contain or incorporate by reference specifications that agencies are required to use unless they obtain waivers. In case of inconsistencies, the general provisions are usually paramount. The schedule prevails over specifications that, in turn, prevail over drawings.

In the acquisition process government agencies must adhere to the procedures outlined in the law and regulations. They indicate a preference for open competitive bidding, where the lowest prices of a responsible and responsive bidder prevail; however, under certain conditions, agencies have a latitude to negotiate contracts preferably with sources in a competitive range. In the latter case factors other than price receive serious consideration. If an agency abuses the restrictions imposed by law or regulation, aggrieved bidders or offerors can protest the action to the Comptroller General, who can nullify the agency's action. They may also resort to court action to restrain the agency from proceeding with an award of the contract, pending a determination of the regularity of the agency's action. Government agencies are also bound by socioeconomic laws, requiring preferential treatment of small businesses, disadvantaged business firms, and firms in labor surplus areas. Projects that become involved with government contracts may find themselves bound to deal with firms in a program with which their organization is obligated to comply.

Types of Contracts

Fixed Price

In the normal commercial atmosphere there are contracts for real estate transactions, contracts for the sale of goods and services, and construction contracts. All are generally on a fixed price basis. Passing of title, delivery of goods, or completion of services requires a payment of an agreed price. The payment is usually in a lump sum. If payments are deferred or set up in installments, we may have, in the sale of personal property, a conditional sales contract, where the seller retains title in the item or has a security interest. In real estate transactions there is usually another instrument in the picture, a mortgage or trust. In construction contracts there is usually a lien. Construction contracts may have provisions for partial or progress payments as performance progresses. Partial payments may also be provided for interim deliveries of goods.

Escalation Provisions. Construction contracts for long lead time projects may have escalation provisions, changing the price if certain direct costs go beyond an established index, such as applicable labor rates or materials peculiar to a trade. With the advent of inflation, sellers of goods were reluctant to enter into term contracts of long duration without an escalative clause. When the petroleum crisis occurred in the 1970s, many state and local governments and large business firms like the utilities could not obtain petroleum delivery contracts for more than 1 month without an escalation clause. Rarely in the commercial community are other types of contracts used. On the other hand, in the government there is an array of some 15 types, in addition to indefinite delivery types of contracts. They run a spectrum from the firm fixed price contract through the loose letter contract.

Fixed Price with Price Redetermination

In addition to the firm fixed price and fixed price with an escalation provision, the government has a fixed price type with prospective price redetermination. The price is fixed for an initial period and then, according to the provisions of the contract, as experience is gained for a calendar period or unit of production, the costs are determined for the period and a redetermined price is negotiated prospectively. Usually a ceiling price is established for the whole contract or the redetermined portion, and there may be more than one redeterminable period. It is appropriate for long-term quantity production for which a fixed price can be agreed upon for only part of the contract period for lack of adequate cost data at the outset. There is also a retroactive redetermination after completion, limited to research and development, up to $100,000.[10] It provides for a fixed price at the outset, with an established ceiling price. Upon completion costs are evaluated and a final price is redetermined that cannot exceed the ceiling price. It is used in instances where a fair and reasonable price cannot be established initially for a firm fixed price, the amount of money is considered small, and time is too short to render the use of another type contract practical.

Firm Fixed Price Level of Effort Contract

There is a firm fixed price level of effort term contract. This usually describes the scope of the work in general terms, calling for an investigation or study. The end product normally is a report to show the results achieved through the application of the required effort, and payment is based on the effort expended, and not the results achieved. It is used in the research and development contracts, when the work cannot be clearly defined, or the technical results are very difficult to predict, and the level of effort can be identified and agreed upon in advance. It may also result in a design or a breadboard. There is no assurance of successful results when this type of contract is used.

Fixed Price Incentive

When there are some technical and cost uncertainties, but they can be identified at a range with some confidence, a profit motivation is attempted to attain more economy and efficiency by offering higher profit for outstanding, effective and economical performance. This is the purpose of the fixed price incentive type of contract. It offers some flexibility to restructure a price from an original agreed-upon total of target costs and target profit to a revised price upon completion, which increases the profit for lower costs or decreases the profit for higher costs, up to a range of a ceiling price, which cannot be exceeded. This is accomplished by the application of a formula, which is included in the provisions of the contract.

Cost Reimbursement Contracts

The government also makes extensive use of cost-reimbursable types of contracts. They are used when the requirements are uncertain and it is impractical to expect the ordinary, reasonable, and prudent person to assume the risk of successful performance without providing for extensive contingencies. It provides for the payment of applicable and allowable costs, within the constraints of prescribed principles, not in excess of a negotiated estimated cost ceiling. The buyer assumes all of the risks, in contrast to a fixed price contract, where the seller is obligated to complete the requirements at the agreed price. If there is no completion after the estimated costs are expended, the seller can stop performance and the buyer has the alternative of increasing the estimated cost or discontinuing. There are a variety of cost-reimbursable contracts that add features for different purposes. The most common form is the cost plus fixed fee. The fixed fee is a negotiated percentage of the estimated costs paid, in addition to the costs, as a reward for managing the performance of the contract. This fee cannot exceed 15% in any cost type of contract the government awards.[11] If it is not a research and development contract, the limit is 10%, and for architectural and engineering service it is 6%. The payment of the fee, unlike the costs, is contingent on satisfactory and successful performance. If the estimated costs are increased when the original amount is expended, in order to permit performance to continue, the fee remains static, unless additional requirements are added to increase the scope of work.

Cost Sharing Contracts

The government also uses a cost sharing type of contract, where only an agreed-upon percentage of the allocable and allowable costs is reimbursed. The government restricts its use to situations where there is a high probability that the contractor will have substantial commercial benefits from the experience acquired under the contract. The straight cost reimbursement type of contract, without fee, is prevalent among contracts with educational, nonprofit institutions. On occasions, organizations for profit will enter into such contracts, for an experience factor, or to create productive effort in a facility operating below capacity.

Cost Plus Incentive Fee Contracts

The government provides a cost plus incentive fee type of contract, where a fairly firm target cost is not reasonable as a result of the magnitude of technical uncertainty. It provides for a target cost, as in the fixed price incentive contract, but a target fee instead of a profit. A maximum fee is established that may not exceed the ceiling imposed by law.[12] The minimum fee may go down as far as the parties agree, even to a negative phase, which, in effect, becomes a cost-sharing arrangement. An adjustment formula is included in the provisions and, upon completion, is applied to increase the target fee when the resulting costs are below the target costs, and decrease this fee for cost overruns. Incentive fee increases may be included for exceeding performance and delivery requirements.

Cost Plus Award Fee Contracts

There is also a cost plus award fee type of contract, which combines characteristics of the cost plus incentive fee and cost plus fixed fee. There an estimated cost is established and a base fee is tantamount to a fixed fee. Although there are no specific restrictions on this portion of the fee, agencies usually keep it within the range of 3%, leaving room for the award portion to become meaningful as an incentive to perform. The total fee cannot exceed statutory limitations.[13] The award fee is periodically determined by a subjective, unilateral evaluation of performance under a criterium contained in the contract. It is a very useful incentive type of contract when quantitative objectives cannot be adequately defined.

Time and Materials Contracts

The government has a type of contract which is used to a great extent in the private sector by service people. The time and materials type of contract provides for payment of direct labor hours, at fixed hourly rates, which includes direct labor costs, indirect costs, and profit. Materials that are used are reimbursed at cost. A ceiling price is established that may not be exceeded. In the private sector car repairs, plumbing, and other similar services are usually charged on that basis and quoted as a fixed price.

Letter Contracts

Reluctantly, the government uses letter contracts. It is preliminary to a negotiated contract, authorizing commencement of work pending negotiation of a definitive contract. It sets forth the maximum liability of the government, the type of contract anticipated, and as many provisions as possible at the time that are contemplated in the definitive contract. It is used when time is of the essence and it is not possible to negotiate a definitive contract to meet the requirements. It should be replaced by a definitive contract within 6 months or before 40% of the work has been completed and the amount spent is not more than 50% of the total estimated cost.[14]

Indefinite Delivery Contracts

Indefinite delivery types of contracts vary. One is for a definite overall quantity for which funds are obligated. Deliveries for specific quantities, to designated locations, within specific periods, are made upon issuance of orders. It is used generally for quantity buys of common items, of recurring need, where quantities are known in advance and items are readily available or require short lead times. The requirements type of contract of indefinite delivery is used when precise quantities, by designated activities during a period, are not known. It provides for the purchase of actual requirements of specific items by designated activities during a specific period. It establishes an estimated total quantity and a limit of the contractor's obligation to deliver an order. It may establish maximum and minimum quantities for each order. Funds are obligated by each order. There is a contract that provides for the delivery of prescribed, limited quantities on order, from designated activities, which obligates funds in the contract. These contracts are awarded usually by the General Services Administration or the Defense Logistics Agency as central keepers of prescribed items required by other agencies or activities. It prevents the stocking of unduly large inventories. Large business organizations, with dispersed facilities, use these types of contracts when they have a centralized purchasing system.

Performance

Contract Administration

After the parties have entered into a contract, the phase of performance is associated with contract administration. In that phase the project is charged with a duty, in the case of the seller, to assure that the organization complies with the provisions of the contract, and, in the case of the buyer, to enforce the provisions of the contract. It is emphasized that one does not have to perform beyond the scope of the contractual provisions. It is the duty of the project to closely monitor the functional activities to meet the requirements. Less than this subjects the organization to a suit for breach of contract. Going beyond the requirements will affect the economic welfare of the organization. On the other hand, the project of a buyer should maintain surveillance during performance to assure that the objectives of the contract are fulfilled within the prescribed time. To await results on a due date, without liaison during performance, may prove to be a disaster if the project schedules the item to channel into other activities of the overall project. This is why it is important for the project to require its contracting activity to insert provisions to give it access to the seller's facility to observe progress and obtain progress reports. It is also important for the project to provide the contracting activity with structured reporting requirements and formats. It may be necessary for the project to retain the services of experts if the organization lacks internal capability in certain areas. Then a provision in the contract should contain a condition for access by that third party, or even approval, if necessary.

Performance Variations

In a perfect atmosphere contract law requires parties to perform exactly as provided in the contract, and the law is inclined to enforce this. However, parties do not operate in a perfect atmosphere. One party may not perform properly, to the satisfaction of the other, as a result of misinterpretation, which may be due to an imperfect description of requirements generated by the project. Circumstances may prevent a party from performing properly as a result of unforeseen weather conditions, shortages of vital materials curtailed by foreign upheavals, or prolonged strikes in an industry, or even attempting to go beyond the state of the art. In the latter case a project should make its contracting activity aware it is pushing the state of the art beyond the barriers of existing knowledge. Impossibility of performance is a good defense against a breach of contract suit, and a contracting activity should be forewarned of the problem in order to negotiate a suitable contract or give the organization the prerogative of not pursuing such contractual relationship. Under certain circumstances there may be a defense of substantial performance against a breach of contract. This can happen in a construction project, where the court may find no willful or intentional departure from the provisions of the contract and an honest effort to comply, yet there was no literal fulfillment of every detail of the contractual obligation. This may bring some deviation from the contract price, but there is still an obligation to accept less than expected, and a requirement to pay, as long as the essential purpose of the contract is fulfilled.

Acceptance

Every buyer normally has a right to inspect the performance before accepting and paying for it. This inspection must be done at a reasonable place, at a reasonable time, and in a reasonable manner. In the sale of goods this is specifically stated in the Uniform Commercial Code.[15] This principle applies to other items. Inherent in the right of inspection is the right to reject nonconformance with any specifications or other performance requirements. If there is nonconformance, rejection must be manifested within a reasonable time after delivery or tender[16] and must state the basis for the rejection. Failure to do so constitutes a waiver of the defect.[17] Failure to inspect in a reasonable time signifies acceptance, in spite of a condition of nonconformance.[18] This is definitely the case if the end item is used, even partially.[19] These rules should impress a project that it has a duty to inspect an item promptly or make sure that the organization has arranged to inspect it and take timely action to properly reject it, if warranted. Laxity in performing such functions may result in the loss of rights established under the contract. Another feature to this problem is the right of a seller to correct or replace a nonconforming item. The law permits a seller the opportunity to make good, if this can be done before a due date.[20] It also permits a seller to notify a buyer reasonably for further reasonable time to substitute a conforming tender.[21] This corrective action has to be accomplished at the expense of the seller, including the additional transportation charges that are involved with returns and reshipment. The organization is also entitled to charge the seller for the undue inspection costs. If projects make cozy deals with the personnel of the seller that, in effect, nullify the rights afforded by law, they lose this economic advantage for their organizations.

Time for Performance

Contracts normally establish a time for performance. Courts have often found and held that adherence to the exact date specified in the contract is not always vital. Often it is a date of convenience. It depends on circumstances. In a contract for the sale of winter coats it is vital that delivery be accomplished in the early part of fall. Where the circumstances are not this obvious, it is sound to include in the contract an indication that "time is of the essence.'' The law also permits a party not to wait to the bitter end to spell out a breach for failure to make a timely delivery. If it can be reasonably established that the progress of performance cannot possibly meet the required date, the contract may be considered breached before the due date. This is known as the anticipatory breach or repudiation. If the situation is not obvious, it may meet with severe resistance, which may be successful; however, if an item requires 30 days of testing before delivery on November 30, and it is not ready for testing on November 1, there is definitely an anticipatory breach and a party does not have to wait until November 30 to repudiate the contract. If the performing party tells the other party there is no intention of meeting the delivery date, this is solid grounds for considering an anticipatory breach. This principle is codified in the sale of goods.[22] Projects that fail to monitor a contractor's performance closely will lose, for their organization, this right established by contract law.

The foregoing rules generally apply in government contracts. The government requires its agencies to include inspection and quality requirements in its contracts.[23] It also requires agencies to insert clauses in contracts to require the contractor to provide and maintain an acceptable inspection system, give the government a right to make inspections and test while work is in process, and require that records of inspection be kept complete and available to government personnel.[24] As the requirements become more complex, a higher level of quality control is mandated.[25] The government has a farflung system of field contract administration, with a number of offices established throughout the United States, including resident offices at major government contractor facilities. The agencies delegate various contract administration functions to these offices, including quality control and scheduling surveillances. The government reserves the right to reject nonconforming items and permits correction and replacement, if these can be accomplished within the delivery schedule, at the expense of the contractor.[26] It provides that its personnel give the reasons for rejection. Government contracts contain a clause permitting the government to terminate, for default, because of the contractor's actual or anticipated failure to perform its contractual obligation.[27] When there is a failure to deliver on time, or perform any other provisions of the contract, the government may exercise a termination notice unilaterally. It is discretionary with the contracting officer to issue a letter advising the contractor of the deficiency and require the contractor to show cause why there should not be a termination for default. The contractor has an opportunity to explain the reason for the failure to perform and cite an excusable situation. If the government anticipates a breach, it may issue a notice of the situation and give the contractor 10 days to cure it or face default action.[28] This is used if it can be reasonably anticipated that there can be a cure in 10 days. In cost-reimbursable types of contracts a 10-day show cause notice is required before a termination notice can be issued.[29]

Fines

A contract is completed when the parties have fulfilled their obligation. Complete performance as required within the prescribed time discharges a party from further obligations. Parties may mutually agree to rescind a contract, discharge each other from further obligations, and restore themselves to the positions they occupied before they entered into a contract. A party may be discharged from performance by the occurrence of a condition that prevents performance. For example, a contract to construct a plant cannot be done if the land is declared a historical site by the authorities. Parties to a contract may be discharged from performance by the substitution of a mutually agreed upon new contract whose terms are inconsistent with the replaced contract. This is not to be confused with changes or modifications to a contract. After parties have entered into a contract, it may occur that one desires some modification of its provisions. Parties may enter into a supplemental agreement to modify the existing contract, but generally there should be consideration to validate this new agreement. However, in the sale of goods the Uniform Commercial Code eliminates the need for consideration.[30] Thus, say there is a contract to sell fuel at $1.00 per gallon and, as a result of market conditions, the seller cannot get it for less than $1.25 per gallon and balks at delivering under the contract price; if the buyer agrees to pay $1.30 per gallon, in spite of the existence of the contract, this is a valid, enforceable modification. In government contracts no agency can give up any rights obtained under a contract without receiving consideration. An agency cannot increase the scope of a contract, since this is considered new procurement and must be awarded through a procedure that resulted in the original contract. Under certain conditions the agency may justify the award to the existing contractor on a sole source basis and add the additional work in a supplemental agreement to the existing contract. The government has a unique class in its contracts, entitled ''changes,'' to provide flexibility in its operations. Under this clause, contracting officers have the unilateral right to direct the contractor to perform under changes in the specifications, place of delivery, and packaging. The contractor is obligated to comply forthwith and claim an equitable adjustment in the contract price. Changes in specifications may not increase the scope of work, since that is to be treated as a new procurement; nor may the work reduce in scope, since that is to be treated as a termination for the convenience of the government under the termination clause. However, there have been occasions when changes contained such conditions in the specifications that were substituted. In complex technical projects this is often difficult to discern. Insofar as projects for contractors are concerned, format is immaterial, as long as the equitable adjustment covers the cost of the modification. Changes can also occur by implication from the action of personnel responsible for the contract. These are considered constructive changes. Changes also result from lack of assertion, which may be construed by the law as waiver of rights. This leads into the matter of conduct by project personnel and the subject of the law of agency.

Law of Agency

Right to Obligate

Individuals in business can buy and sell as contracting parties and partnerships can enter into contracts. One partner can bind another partner, even though the other partner had no knowledge of the contract, provided that the contract was on behalf of the partnership enterprise. In this day and age the preponderance of people work in a business community comprised of impersonal legal entities called corporations, or they may be nonprofit, unincorporated associations. When Frankenstein, Inc., enters into a business transaction, who has authority to obligate the organization? The authority really exists in the owners of the corporation, the stockholders. In an unincorporated association the authority is vested in the membership. It would be ludicrous to expect consensus from the thousands of stockholders or members of a large organization to meet and decide on each of the thousands of transactions entered into by the organization each year.

The law provides for a practical solution: the concept of agency. Under the articles of incorporation, the stockholders elect a board of directors to manage the business. In an unincorporated association the body may be called trustees. These bodies, as representatives of the stockholders or members, establish organization policy and appoint a management team of officers, such as presidents and vice-presidents, to implement that policy. So the authority flows down through a board of directors or trustees to a chief executive officer or director. As a practical matter, it is impossible for such executives of a large organization to become personally involved with each transaction. So the authority flows down further under organizational procedures to focal points, such as a purchasing manager to buy, a sales manager to sell, a controller to borrow and dispense funds, and a personnel manager to hire and discharge employees. Usually organizations limit authority to obligate to those officials to maintain management control. They are authorized agents of the organization in transactions with the external business community.

Special Agents

An agent may also be retained for a specific purpose, such as a real estate broker to sell property. The organization or individuals who retain agents to represent them are known as principals. A principal may be disclosed or undisclosed. An agent binds a principal when acting within the scope of his or her authority as if the principal acted directly.

Authority

The law recognizes three types of authority: express, implied, and apparent. Anything an agent does, pursuant to a direction or within general guidelines established by the principal, is express authority. It is not always possible to express every detail of an agent's authority. To provide flexibility in fulfilling a function, an agent is allowed additional implied authority to perform activities that one might reasonably infer are incidental or necessary to carry out the principal's instructions. Factors such as usage in a trade or an emergency situation, where it is impractical to contact the principal, may spell out implied authority when the action is in the principal's best interests. If the principal's conduct causes others to reasonably believe that the agent is authorized to act on behalf of the principal, there is a situation of apparent authority. If a storekeeper leaves someone to mind the store while the storekeeper is temporarily absent, any customer walking into that store might reasonably believe that person has authority to sell, and any sale made to that customer is valid. From all appearances, the person had authority to transact business with anyone who entered in good faith to buy. Unless a third party is made aware of the scope of an agent's authority, through specific knowledge, constructive notice, or practices of the trade, a principal is bound by the acts of the agent, under any type of authority, unless the acts of the agent are contrary to the law. Everyone is presumed to know the law, and a third party may not take advantage of the agent's ignorance or willful misconduct. Constructive notice is an impersonal notice to the public in a publication or posting in a conspicuous place. It is a proper notice to everybody except those with whom there has been a prior relationship; they require a specific notice.

Ethics: Conflict of Interests

The law of agency covers what is commonly considered as ethics. An agent operates in a fiduciary capacity, a position of utmost trust. An agent cannot deal with any entity in which the agent has an interest, or act in the agent's own interest, or the interests of another, to the detriment of the principal. An agent cannot engage in conduct that conflicts with the interests of the principal. The principal is owed an obligation of full disclosure of the agent's dealings on behalf of the principal. An agent should not compete with the principal or act on behalf of the principal's competition. Agents may not buy from or sell to themselves. They should not make use of any information obtained in the course of their relationship for their own benefit, contrary to the interests of the principal. They are not permitted to make a profit out of items acquired for the principal. Such profits are considered kickbacks, which belong to the principal. An agent must act with reasonable care and exercise all special skills on behalf of the principal. An agent's acts should not bring disrepute upon the principal. An agent must obey the principal, unless required to do an illegal act. Ignorance of the law is no excuse and cannot be used as a shield on the premise that the agent complied with the instructions. In many jurisdictions there are statutes that impose criminal liability on the corporation, unless management used due diligence to prevent the commission of a crime. In some jurisdictions officers of corporations are criminally responsible for violations of law, even when they do not personally participate in the unlawful activity.

Legal Liability of the Agent

If an agent acts outside the scope of authority, then there is personal liability for the consequences. The law implies a warranty of authority to act on behalf of the principal. If the agent harms a third party while conducting the principal's business, that agent is liable for damages, as well as the principal. Individuals are considered responsible for torts committed by them. The fact that they commit the tort while pursuing a principal's objectives makes the principal also liable.

Legal Liability of the Principal

The law imposes a duty on the principal not to harm the agent's reputation and not to unreasonably interfere with the agent's work to make it impossible to perform the required duties with self-respect. A principal is obligated to reimburse the agent for any authorized expenses or losses suffered by the agent while acting for the principal. If the agent suffered damages while acting for the principal's benefit or was exposed to liability to a third party, there should be indemnity by the principal. In the latter type of situation the agent should notify the principal of the legal proceeding to permit the principal the opportunity to defend the agent.

Termination of Agency

An agent's duties terminate, generally, when the principal suffers death or incompetence. They also terminate upon the occurrence of an event that renders the agent's ability to act for the principal futile, such as bankruptcy of the principal or destruction of the subject matter. Of course, a principal may discharge an agent and an agent may renounce the position at any time, since it is unconstitutional to force people to work against their will, which constitutes slavery. However, this does not bar legal liability for breach of contract if a valid agency contract exists for a specified time. In cases where the parties enter into an indefinite distributor relationship or franchises, the law requires a manufacturer to have cause for termination and give due notice.[31] In any event, an agent must be notified of the termination. Third parties who have been dealing with the agent in that capacity should also be notified.

Agency and Government Contracts

The government, as any private corporation, is an inanimate entity. Its authority lies in the people. Under the Constitution the people act through their duly elected representatives, the congress of the United States, or a state legislature. This, in effect, is the board of directors. Congress enacts the laws that are the policies of our government. The Constitution establishes the executive branch to execute those laws that, in effect, implement the policies. When congress establishes programs and appropriates funds for them, it authorizes the executive branch to administer the government operations. It also conveys on agencies formed by law the authority and responsibility to fulfill the objectives of the programs. Included in these acts is the authority to contract and obligate the government in fulfillment of the objectives. There we have the authority flowing down to the president and heads of agencies. It is not reasonable to expect the president or head of an agency to become personally involved in each of the transactions entered into each year by the agencies. Therefore regulations enter the scene, providing for a focal point where the authority is delegated to individuals. In the area of contracting for the United States, and obligating the government, regulations focus that authority on an individual, designated as the contracting officer. This individual is the spokesperson for the government in contractual relations. This appears to be similar to the commercial organization. However, the law offers the government a degree of protection not afforded to private principals.

The Constitution provides that no money shall be drawn from the Treasury but in consequence of appropriations made by law.[32] Therefore, if no money is appropriated for any programs, it is unlawful for any government representative to obligate the government in furtherance of such programs. Statutes exist to confirm this by establishing penalties for such violations. Since government budgets and appropriation laws are matters of public record, a party cannot take advantage of such a violation. The government gives that agent no authority to obligate it, and the government is not bound by that agent's wrongful action. This concept is extended further to cover acts by government agents that are contrary to a statute or a regulation.[33]

The government's operation is, on the whole, an open book. Its laws are contained in the U.S. Code, annotated where the purposes, authority, and responsibilities of the agencies are found. The regulations are found in the Code of Federal Regulations. Ignorance of the law and regulations, which have the full force and effect of law, cannot be used as an excuse. The public is charged with knowing the law and regulations. Those who deal with the government are deemed to know the full extent of the authority of the government personnel with whom they relate in the transactions. Even if the government agent who is authorized to act on behalf of the government willfully or through ignorance acts outside the scope of authority, the government is not bound by such action, and the third party is subject to the requirements imposed by either the law or regulations as if the agent had acted pursuant to the scope of authority.[34] The government in its regulations sets forth who is authorized to act on its behalf[35] and in the general provisions of the contracts defines the authority of the contracting officer and establishes the exclusive authority in that individual. The regulations permit that individual to delegate authority to perform required functions in administering a contract. These functionaries become the representatives of the contracting officer for the purposes set forth in the delegation. Under this type of operation there can be no apparent authority as in the private sector, and implied authority is very limited.

Projects, Agency and Authority

Projects are generally not the expressed authorized agents of the organization in its contractual relations entered into in the course of business. However, there may be many instances of implied authority resulting from the conduct of the project that the organization permits in the course of operations. There may also be a situation of apparent authority established by passively permitting project personnel to assume authority not originally expressly authorized. Usually project personnel are also delegated functional authority as the technical representatives of the contracting official of the organization. In performing functional assignments, overenthusiastic project personnel may pursue the work to an extent that exceeds their authority, and they should be mindful that, if their principals are able to legally squirm out of an obligation claimed by a third party, as a result of their unauthorized action, the party may turn to them for recourse. The safest course of conduct for a project is to become familiar with the organization's policies and procedures and comply with them meticulously; thereby action would be within the scope of authority. This does not relieve project personnel from liability for any torts committed or protect them from criminal action for any public offense committed in performing required duties. If personnel injure a third party in an accident while driving on organization business, they are jointly liable with the organization. If they drive under the influence of intoxicating beverages, they stand alone, since the principal did not authorize them to drink. If they make unauthorized use of a patented item, contrary to organizational policy, and the organization rejects such use, then they cannot impose the liability on the principal. This is beyond the scope of authority. However, if the principal takes advantage of the infringement, the authority is implied. If they order goods or services directly, without use of the procedures, the organization can renege on such orders as an unauthorized action and a seller can have recourse to the project personnel. If, in spite of written procedures, the organization permits the action to go on, lulling a third party into a sense of security in dealing directly with a project, there is a case of apparent authority.

In the 1950s victims of an electrical equipment price-fixing conspiracy were able to recover hundreds of millions of dollars from corporate giants such as General Electric and Westinghouse. These civil suits were successfully pursued under the Clayton and Sherman Acts. These acts, in substance, prohibit monopolies and combinations and conspiracies in restraint of trade, including price-fixing, price discrimination, group boycotts, division of markets, tying arrangements, and exclusive dealings. Violation of the Sherman Act is also a felony, which may result in the imposition of fines up to $100,000 per count for individuals and $1,000,000 per count for corporations. It may result also in imprisonment for up to 3 years. The electrical equipment cases shook the business community by reaching individuals in the corporations who were involved in those arrangements, and many corporate management-type personnel found themselves sentenced to prison terms. The inanimate corporation cannot go to prison, but its agents can. In civil suits for violation of antitrust laws, the damages are treble. The Robinson-Patman Act prohibits price discriminations when selling to buyers of a like class, thereby giving a buyer a competitive edge. Included in that act is a provision holding both the buyer and the seller liable for a violation. However, there is an exception, if the product is made to a buyer's specification; thus it is not a like product. Projects will generally not be directly involved in all aspects of violation of antitrust laws, but it is conceivable that a project may be the instrument of designing products to facilitate tying arrangements or cosmetically applying specifications to standard items to circumvent the full effect of the Robinson-Patman Act.

Product Liability

Shift in Legality Regarding Product Liability

There was a time when the doctrine of caveat emptor prevailed. When a buyer purchased an item, the law considered that buyer was responsible to practice caution and prudence in the selection of the item in the exercise of free choice. If the item was of poor quality, was unsafe, or did not measure up to standards as offered by a seller, the buyer paid the penalty of exercising poor judgment or ignorance. Over the past few decades there has been a trend toward consumer protection. Courts began to recognize liability on the part of sellers, especially of used goods, for negligence in inspecting an item before sale when a buyer suffered damages as a result of using the item. This was even extended to anyone who might reasonably come in contact with the item.[36] At first liability was limited to the seller on the premise that the buyer had no privity or contractual relationship with anybody but the seller. Therefore a producer was liable only to a wholesaler or a distributor. A landmark decision in 1916 by the New York Court of Appeals departed from this requirement of privity and held the manufacturer liable for injuries resulting from the use of its product because there was evidence of negligence in the manufacture or assembly of the product.[37] In 1960 the neighboring state of New Jersey's Supreme Court went a step further and imposed an implied warranty of fitness for use on the manufacturer, Chrysler Corporation, holding Chrysler and the dealer liable for injuries sustained in the use of the car, in spite of a disclaimer of such warranty by Chrysler in the sales contract.[38] A manufacturer who fails to exercise reasonable care in the fabrication and assembly of an item that harms a user who uses it in a manner and for a purpose for which it is intended is subject to liability for the consequential harm.[39] Furthermore, a manufacturer must also exercise care in the design of a product. If the design makes it dangerous for the use for which the item is intended and a user is injured, the manufacturer is thereby liable for failure to exercise reasonable care in the design.[40] When General Motors Corporation claimed, as a defense, that the automobile was not made to collide with other cars, a court held that a defect in design by a manufacturer that enhances injuries upon impact, a frequent and inevitable contingency of normal automobile use, subjects a manufacturer to liability.[41] Manufacturers must reasonably test and inspect a product for visible or latent defects before putting it on the market. A manufacturer also has a duty to warn the public of the potential danger of a product and is responsible not only to a buyer of the product but anyone who is expected to use it with the consent of such buyer.[42] A manufacturer should be able to foresee that the product may be dangerous if used improperly.

Subcontractor's Liability

So far it appears there is an imposition of liability on the prime manufacturer. Under today's techniques and methods of production, a manufacturer is virtually an assembler. More than 50% of the fabrication is accomplished by secondary sources that make parts and components which are purchased by the manufacturer. What about these fabricators of parts and components? Do they escape or can an end user pierce through a seller, distributor, and manufacturer to hold them liable? The Restatement of Torts Second follows the position that the manufacturer of parts to be incorporated in a product is liable if the parts are so negligently made as to render the product in which they are incorporated unreasonably dangerous for use. Thus both the assembler and the parts maker are liable, one for failing to discover the defects and the other for producing the defects. This liability is even extended to a bystander who is injured as a result of the product's use.

Basis for Liability

The basis for liability entails three concepts: negligence, breach of warranty, and the doctrine of strict liability. It should be of no concern to a project which approach a user's attorney will pursue. Regardless of the premises of the legal principles, the project that is engaged in the design and development of a product or the improvement of a product should consider in the design of the product the potential dangers involved in the use and the consequences of the liability for harm to others. Often there are conflicts in design, whether or not to sacrifice a feature for economic or marketable considerations. The project is the focal point to evaluate the possibilities and probabilities of the consequences and take a position for management to consider. It is the prerogative of management to take the calculated risk, but it is the duty of the project to direct management's attention to the potential problem. Under the doctrine of vicarious liability, an employer is liable for the negligence committed by an employee within the scope of employment. It imputes negligence, regardless of the employer's fault or blame. Therefore a project's withholding of information of the existence of such a problem places the organization in jeopardy. If it involves professional misconduct, the project personnel would share the liability. Willfully hiding a design defect, resulting in unsafe items, or allowing usage through gross incompetence involves project personnel as joint tort feasors.

At the Ford Motor Company management made the wrong decision on the Pinto model gas tank. The project's design engineers opted for a position and the safety engineers highlighted its danger in case of collision. The memorandum of the safety engineers was introduced into evidence in a later lawsuit for negligence when a passenger was burned in a Pinto that was hit in the rear and where the gas tank exploded. Management gave undue emphasis to cost cutting. A project's memoranda should be carefully considered in view of its potential use in a product liability case. This holds true for warranties.

Warranty

Breach of Warranty

When a seller represents to a buyer that an item has certain features and conforms to certain standards, it expressly warrants the existence of these features and standards. If the item does not contain them, there is a breach of warranty. Not every warranty need be expressed. There are warranties implied by law. When one sells an item that is supposed to perform a certain function, an implied warranty is established that it will do so—the warranty of merchantability. If the item fails to function properly, there is a breach of warranty. If a buyer informs a seller of the need of an item to meet certain specific requirements and the seller sells the item forewarned of those requirements, there is a breach of implied warranty of fitness of use for the particular purpose if the item does not function as required. Here a buyer relies on the seller's skill and judgment to select a suitable item for the specific purpose. There is a third implied warranty—title. Everyone who sells anything automatically warrants rightful, free, and clear ownership with a right to sell.

Under the Uniform Commercial Code for the sale of goods, a seller does not have to specifically state an expressed warranty. As long as there is an affirmation of fact, or a promise relating to the goods that is the basis of the sale, an express warranty is created that the goods conform to the affirmation or promise. A description of the goods in the sale creates an express warranty that the goods conform to the description. If there is a sample or model that is part of the basis of the sale, then there is an express warranty that all the goods conform to the sample or model.[43] Not all statements or promises create warranties. Some statements made by sellers are considered by courts to be mere puffery, such as "this is the best product made," "this is the best quality," or "this is in perfect condition." These are considered expressions of opinion or judgment.

Implied and Expressed Warranties

The Uniform Commercial Code defines the implied warranty of merchantability in part as fit for the ordinary purposes for which such goods are used and conforming to the promises or affirmations of fact made on the container or label, if any.[44] It is to be noted that this type of warranty is implied only if the seller is a merchant dealing in the line of those goods.[45] In the implied warranty for fitness for a particular use, the Uniform Commercial Code requires the seller to have reason to know any particular purpose for which the goods are required and reliance by the buyer on the seller's skill or judgment to select the suitable goods.[46] So a buyer who gives a seller data on the dimensions of a structure when buying an air-conditioning unit and is sold a 2-ton unit when a 3-ton unit is required has grounds to claim breach of warranty. If the buyer furnishes specifications to the seller, there is no breach, even if the seller knows the purpose for which the product is to be used, since there is no reliance on the seller's skill and judgment. In the above example, if the buyer orders a 2-ton unit that is inadequate, there is no breach of warranty. Parties may agree to exclude or modify implied warranties; however, the Uniform Commercial Code requires such exclusions or modifications to be in writing, clearly excluding merchantability, and state there are no warranties beyond the description.[47] General language as a condition of sale, such as *as is* or *with all faults,* will exclude implied warranties. An express warranty may disclaim an implied warranty, but the language has to be in conspicuous type. If warranties are in conflict with each other, courts will attempt to give effect to the intention of the parties. However, the Uniform Commercial Code sets forth rules to determine the intention. Exact or technical specifications displace an inconsistent sample or model or the general language of the description. A sample displaces inconsistent general language of description. Express warranties displace inconsistent implied warranties other than that of fitness for a particular purpose.[48] If a seller offers a buyer an opportunity to examine the goods and requires such examination, the implied warranty is thereby excluded, except for latent defects.

In 1975 the Magnuson-Moss Warranty Federal Trade Commission Act went into effect. It expanded the power of the Federal Trade Commission, specified minimum disclosure standards for written product warranties, and set minimum standards for these warranties. It is primarily an act for the benefit of consumers to know at purchase the nature of the warranty and permit effective enforcement in case of breach. It applies to consumer products of more than $15.00 containing a written warranty. It does not cover goods purchased for commercial or industrial purposes or for resale in the ordinary course of business. It does not permit the disclaimer limitation or modification of any implied warranty, unless it is a limited warranty that may limit the duration, if reasonable.

The warranty must clearly give the name and address of the warrantor, the product or parts covered, a statement as to what the warrantor will do at whose expense and for what period, and a detailed procedure to follow for enforcement. If the warranty is limited, it must be so clearly indicated. Under a full warranty there must be correction of defects, without charge, for a reasonable time and a replacement after a reasonable number of attempts to remedy the defect has failed. A warrantor is liable for consequential damages, unless it is limited or excluded by a conspicuous note on the face of the warranty.

Project Warranty

Projects concerned with purchase of goods should be guided accordingly in preparation of requirements. If they prepare detailed specifications, they assume a responsibility if the product does not fulfill the purpose for which it is intended. Under such circumstances there will be no implied warranty of fitness for a particular purpose. Performance specifications would be more appropriate on the acquisition of the seller's product upon assurance it will fulfill the purpose. If a seller allows a bench test or a laboratory test of a sample and it does not work when installed in the project's product, then there is no likelihood of recourse to an implied warranty. Testing and approving a first article and inspecting the remaining units is not a situation where one can take advantage of implied warranties, unless there is a latent defect.

Warranties cost money. If a project considers it to the best interests of the organization to pursue such methods, it can be a basis for negotiating cost factors of warranties out of the price. On the other hand, in the development of a product for sale, a project should be mindful of the implied warranties facing the organization and analyze the probable expectations of defects and malfunctions that will furnish data for the marketing unit in structuring the price to cover potential liability for warranties. It can also prepare specifications for its product that will inform buyers or consumers of the limitations for the performance or use of the product.

Warranties and Government Contracts

The government does not mandate that agencies require warranties. It establishes a criterium for contracting officers to consider. Factors to be considered include complexity and function, degree of development, state of the art, end use, difficulty in detecting defects before acceptance, potential harm to the government from defective items, cost included in the price, cost of administration and enforcement of the warranty, location and proposed use of the item, storage time for the item after receipt, distance of the using activity from the source of the item, difficulty establishing the existence of defects, and difficulty in tracing responsibility for defects.[49]

If the trade of the product customarily warrants an item, then the government will take advantage of the warranty since its cost is already included in the price. Ordinarily warranties are not included in cost-reimbursable types of contracts. If a warranty clause is included in a contract, it is of course an express warranty, and it does preclude the provisions of the inspection clause relating to a contractor's continued liability for latent defects, fraud, or gross mistakes that amount to fraud.[50] The govern-

ment will take partial warranties on such items as installation, components, accessories, subassemblies, and packaging. If it specifies the
design of the end item, then the warranty is limited to defects in materials,
workmanship, or failure to conform to specifications. Its warranty clauses
negate the implied warranties of merchantability and fitness for a particular use.

The duration of the warranty must be clearly specified in the contract,
and—in establishing the duration—contracting officers must consider the
estimated useful life of the item, the storage or shelf life expected, and the
lead time for furnishing notice regarding the discovery of a defect, considering the possible time necessary to discover the defect and the time
required to take the administrative steps for such notice.

Although the Federal Acquisition Regulations involve the contracting
officer as the responsible individual, this does not exclude the project's
responsibility with respect to determinations on warranties. The regulations of many agencies require the technical officers to cooperate and
advise the contracting officer on the appropriate decisions. In some agencies the contracting officer is a member of the project team.

The government has standard warranty clauses to fit different situations, depending on the type of item, specifications, and type of contract.
There is a clause for a fixed price supply contract, an alternative for a
government-specified design or a contractor's design, an alternative for a
fixed price incentive type of contract, an alternative for items of a complex nature, one for systems and equipment acquired under performance
specification or design criteria, another for services, and one for construction. The last alternative specifies a duration of 1 year from the date of
final acceptance or from the date the government takes possession. The
warranty clauses indicate the preferences of having the contractor repair
or replace the defective item. Usually any transportation charges are at
the contractor's expense, but not in excess of the original delivery costs.

In construction contracts contractors are obligated to obtain warranties
from subcontractors and enforce them. If it is not practical to direct the
contractor to make the repair or replacement, or such repair or replacement does not afford the government an appropriate remedy, then the
warranty could provide other remedies, such as retaining the defective
item and reducing the price, or the government can repair or replace the
item by its own or other resources and charge the contractor for the costs
thereof.

Government weapons systems projects are often plagued with the problem of warranties, which have a severe impact on their budgets. In 1983
Congress passed a law requiring the U.S. Defense Department to obtain a
warranty on every large weapons system. It found that the warranty for
40 engines from Pratt-Whitney, for F-15 aircraft, would cost $53,000,000,
one-third of the costs of the engines. This caused Congress to consider an

exemption.[51] There is another type of warranty in government that is not usually considered in the commercial community: Often the government requires the submission of data in contracts covering research and development. Agencies can develop and use clauses requiring warranties of data.[52]

Patents

Intellectual and Proprietary Property

Generally no one is inclined to spend a great deal of time and money developing an idea only to have others appropriate the idea free to their own advantage. Usually, when the commandment "Thou shalt not steal" is considered, it is associated with tangible property, something that one can feel, hold, and see. An idea cannot be felt, held, or seen. It is considered, in law, as intangible property and further classified as intellectual property. Knowledge is intellectual property, which is freely disseminated by our educational systems. What they impart is common knowledge, available to the public for the public good. There is, however, certain knowledge that society considers in the public interest and which should be protected from free use by the general public to provide those gifted to create and develop the incentive for innovation. This was recognized by the framers of our Constitution when they established the power of Congress to enact certain forms of protection "to promote the Progress of Science and useful Arts, by securing for limited times to Authors and Inventors the exclusive Right to their respective Writings and Discoveries."[53] Congress exercised the power by enacting patent laws and copyright laws.

Patent Protection

A patent is a protective grant, issued by the U.S. Patent Office, of a right, for 17 years, to exclude others from making, using, or selling the invention.[54] It includes a right to license others to make, use, or sell it. In effect, it grants a monopoly. Therefore, when one applies for a patent, it must be established that the composition, device, or process is novel[55] and the principles involved are not obvious common knowledge. The term *obvious common knowledge* does not necessarily mean that every person on the street knows about it. If a Ph.D. in a certain field would know it, it is considered obvious common knowledge. Therefore no abstract idea or principle is patentable, but a device or process that uses such principle may be patentable if it does not preempt the field of science or mathematics, which is obvious common knowledge to those who engage in the field.[56]

In the repair of a road, a machine was used to spread the asphalt, another was used to bind it to the old asphalt, and a third to roll it and compact it with the remainder of the road. A machine designed to perform all three functions, at one time, using the process of the three machines, was not considered patentable since it involved the use of processes that were not novel and which were obvious to those in the field.

Another element is utility. Nothing is patentable if it has not been reduced to practice.[57] A patentable item must be established as useful. If a bench model has been perfected and tested in a laboratory, it cannot be patented until the prototype is finished and proves its usefulness. It also must not have been used and written up more than 1 year before the date of application, since it is then considered to have been divulged to the public and cannot be protected for the applicant's exclusive use.[58] This is true even if this took place in another country. When one registers or applies for a patent, the U.S. Patent Office makes a search for existing patents and applications to ascertain that a patent has not already been granted on the same subject matter.[59] This still offers no assurance. If the application is filed under the wrong classification and someone else filed it under a proper classification, either before or after the application, the applicant may not have a valid patent. A classification may be a machine or process. Therefore, if it is filed as a novel machine, when one already exists, but this filing should have been for a novel process, there is no patent on either.

Assignment

Patents can be assigned to others. In many cases the assignment is made before the origination of the idea. Most companies engaged in technology have their employees assign their rights to patents as a condition of employment. Even where one originates the item on one's own time at home in the basement workshop, if the basis is knowledge gained at the place of employment, the company may claim the rights to the patent. This also is true of government employees and especially military personnel considered to be continuously on duty.

Generally, a project's organization will have a procedure for maintaining laboratory notes and records, the reporting of novel processes and hardware, and the processing of patent applications. Companies maintain extensive portfolios of patents, and organizations such as IBM, RCA, and AT&T, to name a few, cherish these portfolios as valuable assets and watch products on the market that may infringe the use of the patent— without a license—for which a royalty is exacted.

Companies have cross-licensing agreements where they share the use of each other's patents. This rigid control may relieve a project to an extent from safeguarding its organization's rights, but the heavy burden a project may face in this area may arise when contracts are awarded to other organizations in furtherance of the project's activities. Two problems arise: One consists of safeguarding the rights of the project's own organization to obtain patents for innovations developed by the contractor or supplier, which are financed by the project's organization; the other consists of safeguarding the organization if the contractor or supplier infringes on the patents of others in producing for the organization. Usually the contracting activity will include clauses establishing the rights to patents resulting from a contractor's development and a provision for indemnity in the event a suit arises from some party claiming a wrongful use of that party's patent.

The project is the unit with the technical knowledge to administer these clauses. It should be aware, if the work entails advancements in the state of the art, to warrant vigilance in monitoring possible patentable developments and coordinate with the organization's counsel or patent counsel, if there is one, to assure that patent applications are made and they are assigned to the organization. A project's technical knowledge should permit it to be alert to the use of technology that is known to be the product of another in the trade. If royalties are paid, it may not be necessary as a result of cross-licensing agreements the organization may have. The project may also be able to show a contractor that substitution of another approach, which the organization is free to use, would be more advantageous.

Patents and Government Projects

Projects involved with government contracts have a special problem area of complying with government requirements. Government agencies are required to maintain an inventory of patents.[60] The patent policy of the government varies with agencies and the type of contract. The statute that establishes some agencies requires that they obtain title to patents derived from contractors; otherwise, agencies have to obtain a nonexclusive, nontransferable, irrevocable, paid-up license to use any invention derived from a contract and even obtain the additional right to sublicense any foreign government pursuant to a treaty.[61] Any agency has the right to reserve title for the government when the contract is for the operation of a government-owned research or production facility, to protect security, or if it is in the best interests of promoting the objectives of the government.[62]

If the statute requires the government to obtain title, then the patent is public property; however, the agency has the right to give a contractor a greater right to the invention for a specified period, if it is determined that the public is better served thereby.[63] In making such determination, the agency has to consider the objectives of promoting utilization of inventions arising from federally supported research and development, promoting public availability of inventions by U.S. industry and labor, ensuring that inventions are used in a manner that promotes free competition and enterprise, and that the government obtains sufficient rights to meet its needs and protect the public against nonuse and unreasonable use of inventions.

If the government contract is with a small business concern or a nonprofit organization, it permits the contractor to retain title to a patent.[64] It may permit retention of title by any contractor if it is necessary to obtain a unique or highly qualified contractor or the contractor shared the costs of the work, but this does not necessarily apply to the U.S. Department of Defense, U.S. Department of Energy, or the National Aeronautics and Space Administration.[65] If a nonprofit institution retains a patent, it may not assign it without approval from the agency, or grant a license to anyone—other than a small business—for a period in excess of 5 years from use of the invention or 8 years from the date cleared for sale by a regulatory agency, whichever is earlier.

Government patent rights clauses in its contracts vary with the type of contractor to implement its policy with the objectives of promoting the utilization of inventions arising from federally supported research and development, encourage maximum participation of industry in federally supported research and development efforts, ensure that the inventions are used in a manner to promote free competition and enterprise, promote commercialization and public availability of inventions made in the United States by its industry and labor, ensure that the government obtains sufficient rights in federally supported inventions to meet the needs of the government and protect the public against nonuse or unreasonable use of inventions, and minimize the cost of administering the policies in this area. The clauses cover any invention of the contractor considered or first actually reduced to practice in performance of the work under the contract.

In any of the clauses the contractor is obligated to disclose an invention to the contracting officer, in writing, within 2 months after the inventor discloses it in writing to the contractor personnel responsible for patent matters. In a contract with a business organization, not classified as a small business, a contractor is obligated to disclose an invention in any event within 6 months after becoming aware of it and before any sale, public use, or publication of such invention is known to the contractor. Such contractors are required to establish and maintain procedures to assure identification and disclosure that include maintenance of laboratory notebooks and other records to document the conception and the first actual reduction to practice. The clauses also require contractors to furnish the contracting officer interim reports every 12 months, listing the inventions during the period and certifying that all inventions have been disclosed or that there are no such inventions. After work is completed, a final report is due, listing all inventions under the contract or certifying there were none, and all subcontractors at any tier must be listed if these subcontracts contained patent clauses; if there were none, it should be certified to that effect.

Contractors are required to insert patent rights clauses in their subcontracts with flow-down provisions requiring subcontracts to include such clauses. Contractors under the clauses agree to file patent applications or notify the government of a decision not to prosecute a patent application. When an application is filed, it must include language that the invention was made with government support, under a contract identified by the number and federal agency, and the government has rights to the invention. Even if the government retains title, the clauses give contractors nonexclusive royalty-free licenses. A contractor loses the right to any invention if there is a breach in making a timely disclosure to the government. The clauses authorize the government to examine the contractor's records to determine compliance with the clauses within 3 years after final payment on the contract. The government also withholds payment, amounting to 5% of the contract amount, or a maximum of $50,000, up to final payment to assure compliance with the clause.

If security is involved, patents are not disclosed. If the Commissioner of Patents considers disclosures detrimental, he may refer the application to the Secretary of Defense or the U.S. Department of Energy, who may freeze the disclosure on a year-to-year basis.[66] If it is disclosed in a foreign country, the penalty may be $10,000 fine, 2 years of imprisonment, or both.[67] From the foregoing, projects can discern the responsibility imposed in this area of research and development. It is usually the duty of project technical personnel to assure that procedures are followed to safeguard the interests of the organization and its obligation to comply with contractual provisions. It is important that adequate records be established and maintained to document the work accomplished. This provides the data to establish conception and reduction to practice. It may be necessary to curtail an enthusiastic professional from writing a paper to read in glory at a conference or seminar. This is a publication that tolls the time for filing a patent application.

Insofar as the use of the patents of others is concerned, the government generally will not refuse to award a contract on the basis that a contractor may infringe on a patent. To cover such situations the government inserts in contracts an Authorization and Consent clause, which permits the contractor to use any item or process patented in the United States when performing pursuant to specifications or work statements of the contract. It assumes liability for infringements, but the government, unlike private parties, cannot be sued in a U.S. District Court and is not subject to injunctions.[68] The contractor is protected from any suit by this clause, since the government assumes the responsibility for the infringement. The recourse for an aggrieved party lies in a claim against the government and an action in the U.S. Claims Court. When a party claims infringement by the contractor, or the contractor is otherwise aware of an infringement, under a clause, entitled "Notice and Assistance Regarding Patent and Copyright Infringement," the contractor must report to the contracting officer the details of such infringement or claim. At the contracting officer's request, the contractor is required to furnish the government all information and evidence pertaining to the matter. This also applies to subcontractors.

If the contract is for the acquisition of goods and services sold in the open commercial market or is awarded on an open, competitive, formally advertised basis, the government will include a Patent Indemnity clause. Under this clause the contractor agrees to indemnify the government against liability for infringement of a patent. However, if the government issues a change to the contract, which will entail the use of another's patent, it will waive the indemnity. In other than formally advertised contract awards, the government may require reports on royalty payments. This permits the government to evaluate whether it is necessary to use the patent of another. Often the government may already have a royalty-free license as a result of another contract from any agency. It will also determine whether it is reasonable, or it may already have a license with a lower royalty rate.

Copyrights

Areas of Protection

Another protection the federal government offers is a copyright. The law gives copyright protection to original works of authorship, fixed in any tangible medium of expression, now known or later developed, from which they can be perceived, reproduced, or otherwise communicated, either directly or with the aid of a machine or device.[69] Therefore written matter, recordings, video tapes, photographs, motion pictures, art, drawings, and musical compositions may be copyrighted. A ruling by counsel for the Copyright Office makes computer programs subject to copyright protection, even though they are not specifically mentioned in the statute. Protection is extended to any idea, procedure, process, system, method of operation, concept, principle, or discovery, regardless of the form in which it is described, explained, or illustrated.[70] Only the words, phrases, and exact contents are protected. Therefore one cannot copy or paraphrase, but the ideas presented by the words or phrases can be used. Under a "fair use" doctrine developed by the courts, an intermittent quotation from an authored work may be used as explanatory to impart an idea, as long as the user gave substantial input. Copyright protection since 1978 is for the life of the author plus 50 years. To gain protection the work must contain a notice of copyright, as follows.

©   Year   Name of author

It should be registered with the Copyright Office.

Projects and Copyrights

Generally, projects involved in research and development will encounter copyright exposure in the publication of results of the research, development, and demonstration activities. Projects of various studies undertaken for health or social welfare purposes may get involved with publications. Computer programs may be developed and technical manuals prepared for products to be marketed. Once the publication is disseminated without a notice of copyright, there is no protection.

The government often considers it necessary to acquire or gain access to data to ensure appropriate use of any research and development it financed. It also requires data to ensure future competitive procurement and logistics support. Agencies profusely engaged in research and development have Rights-to-Data clauses, which gives the government a royalty-free license to use copyright material. Such contracts require contractors to furnish scientific and technical reports, with copies, to either the Defense Technical Information Center or the National Technical Information Center of the Department of Commerce. This presents a problem, especially with universities, when the scientist or engineer requires publication to survive or gain stature in the field. No publisher would touch any publication with awareness that it will appear as a government publication. Thus some agencies will waive a license to a copyright if private publication will be accomplished in a reasonable time. This, of course, does not apply to classified materials.

Proprietary Data and Trade Secrets

Patent and copyright protection is afforded by the federal government, as prescribed by the U.S. Constitution. However, not everything is patentable, and copyright does not protect ideas or concepts. Additionally, filing for a patent makes the contents available to the public. What happens if the patent is denied? Something unique has been exposed and there is no protection. Anyone may use it. Therefore organizations have unique knowledge and processes that give them an advantage in the competitive market which they do not disclose to others. This is proprietary data and also known as trade secrets. Most states consider a trade secret a property right and have trade secret laws, with criminal penalties for this violation.

One may also sue in civil courts in tort as a conversion action, using the property of another without consent. Of course, as the nomenclature implies, to qualify as a trade secret the data must be a secret. Once it is divulged to anyone, it is no longer a secret. However, if that other person is bound not to reveal it to others, secrecy has been maintained. Thus employees are bound not to breach confidentiality, and they often sign agreements not to divulge or use data for their personal benefit. Subcontractors and suppliers obligate themselves not to divulge data furnished by the customer. A franchised dealer or service organization binds itself to maintain the secret. Even a customer who gets technical manuals for maintenance and operation that divulge some secret with markings that it is confidential and not to be used for purposes other than maintenance and operation is bound not to disseminate that data. Furthermore, if a competitor has independently obtained that secret and maintains it as a trade secret, it is still considered a secret.

The secret must be novel, it must represent a real economic interest or investment on the part of the owner, it must prove to be commercially valuable, and it must be reasonably protected by the owner. Once these factors are established, the unauthorized use of the data constitutes a violation of a trade secret. Some states have more stringent laws than others. California and New York lead the states in laws to protect trade secrets. It is no accident that an organization such as IBM, which is a New York corporation, inserts in all its contracts a provision that any legal action resulting from the contract will be decided under New York law. This company was successful in its violation of trade secrets action against Hitachi and some of its employees in California. Most thefts of a trade secret involve the state; however, when the secret is taken across a state line or transmitted through the U.S. Postal Service, it then becomes a federal crime.[71]

Anyone who embezzles, steals, purloins, or knowingly converts to one's own use or the use of another; or without authority sells, conveys, or disposes of anything of value of the United States, any department or agency thereof, or any property made or being made under a contract for the United States, or any department thereof; or whoever receives, conceals, or retains same with intent to convert to one's own use or gain, knowing it to have been embezzled or stolen, is subject to criminal penalties.[72]

There is often a pragmatic problem in protecting a trade secret from unauthorized use. It is not unlawful for one to independently discover and use the trade secret. It is often difficult to contest the defense of independent discovery, since it is necessary to prove wrongful acquisition by tracing its derivation from the source.

Many trade secrets are derived from the work of employees who are usually under contract, binding them to give their discoveries, made on company time and facilities, to the employer. Some contracts extend this requirement to discoveries made in the area of the subject at any time and place during the period of employment. What happens when that employee switches jobs? Can the employee's discoveries benefit the new employer? Generally such an employee is not free to disclose to another employer the unique development of the former employer. Courts have gone as far as to hold that a new discovery for a subsequent employer should not be done using the unique knowledge gained at a former employer. Nevertheless, as a practical matter, it has to be proved that the new discovery did not use just common knowledge, but the unique knowledge gained at the former place of employment. That is often very difficult. Normally people cannot forget all that has been learned. They are familiar with the techniques in the field and become familiar with more as experience is gained. Employers seek experienced employees to derive benefits of the knowledge gained during productive years. This is a pattern of business management. What has to be avoided is actively pirating an employee, with full awareness of the special knowledge gained from the employer, and exploiting that factor to the advantage of the new employer. This is considered an improper action to gain disclosure of the trade secret of another and will subject that employer to liability.

Impact of Proprietary Information on Government Projects

Projects involved with government contracts face very sensitive problems. In research and development projects the government has a practice of demanding data in the solicitation phase for the purposes of technical evaluation and for the delivery of data for the work performed under the contract. When the data are included in a proposal, they are in effect published. There goes any trade secret that is included, unless it is marked with a legend that it is confidential, proprietary data, and to be used only for evaluation purposes. Then it is even protected from exposure to the public, under the Freedom of Information Act, as an exception to access by the public, as well as the cost data. Government employees who divulge it to any competitor are guilty of misconduct and subject to criminal prosecution.

Once the contract is awarded, the government's project decides the extent of data to be required from a contractor. It is the policy of the government not to require any more than it needs to fulfill its objectives. The government is entitled to unrestricted use of technical data developed through direct application of government funding. If data are developed through support of an overhead pool, as part of an internal research and development program, the data are not considered government funded, even if the contractor is engaged 100% in government work. These have to be covered by direct costs. This does not mean that a contractor will get away with a scheme of intentionally charging the work of people engaged in the government contract to the overhead development pool when the discovery is made or is imminent.

If the government decides it needs data developed by the contractor, other than data produced directly under the contract, which is often the case when future production of the developed item is contemplated, then it negotiates for the additional data, which is included as a deliverable item under the contract. It would require a complete set of manufacturing drawings, with bills of materials keyed to drawings and specifications developed for materials, components, assemblies and subassemblies, plus manuals for installation, maintenance, operations, or training of personnel. On occasion the government may require not only data, but also assistance for another source to become capable to produce the developed item. If there is only one capable source in the field, it may pay for the government to develop another source.

The legal subjects included in this chapter were selected as having a bearing on a preponderance of project activities. It should impress project personnel with a sense of responsibility in the conduct of their functions. Legal problems are complicated to the extent that lawyers specialize in the various subjects. When in doubt, consult the appropriate counsel.

Endnotes Chapter Eleven

1. Amendment X, U.S. Constitution.
2. 35 U.S. Code, paragraph 154.
3. Federal Acquisition Regulation, paragraph 35.010(b).
4. *Department of Defense Security Manual for Safeguarding Classified Information* (DOD 5220.22M).
5. Uniform Commercial Code, paragraph 2-201(1).
6. Uniform Commercial Code, paragraph 1-206.
7. Uniform Commercial Code, paragraph 2.201(3)(a).
8. Uniform Commercial Code, paragraph 2-202(a).
9. Uniform Commercial Code, paragraphs 2-207(3) and 208(1)(2).
10. Federal Acquisition Regulation, paragraph 16-206-2.
11. 10 U.S. Code, paragraph 2306(d); 41 U.S. Code, paragraph 254(b).
12. *Ibid.*
13. Federal Acquisition Regulation, paragraph 16.404-2(c)(2).
14. *Ibid.*, paragraph 16.603-2.
15. Uniform Commercial Code, paragraph 2-513(1).
16. *Ibid.*, paragraph 2-602(1).
17. *Ibid.*, paragraph 2-605.
18. *Ibid.*, paragraph 2-606(1)(a).
19. *Ibid.*, paragraph 2-606(2).
20. *Ibid.*, paragraph 2-508(1).
21. *Ibid.*, paragraph 2-508(2).
22. *Ibid.*, paragraph 2-610 and 611.
23. Federal Acquisition Regulation, paragraph 46.102.

24. *Ibid.*, paragraph 46.202-2.
25. *Ibid.*, paragraph 46.202-3.
26. *Ibid.*, paragraph 46.407.
27. *Ibid.*, paragraph 49.401.
28. *Ibid.*, paragraph 49.607.
29. *Ibid.*, paragraph 49.403.
30. U.S. Code, paragraph 2-209(1).
31. *Ibid.*, paragraph 2-309.
32. U.S. Constitution, Article 1, Section 9.
33. Federal Crop Insurance Corporation vs. Merrill 332 U.S. 380.
34. G. H. Christain & Associates vs. U.S. 312F2d 418, 160 Ct Cl 1 rehearing denied 320F2d 345, 160 Ct Cl 58, cert denied 375 U.S. 954.
35. Federal Acquisition Regulation, paragraph 1.6.
36. Chamberlain vs. Bob Matick Chevrolet, Lic. 4 Conn Cir Ct 685.
37. MacPherson vs. Buick Motor Company, 111 N.E. 1050.
38. Henningsen vs. Bloomfield Motors, Inc., 161 A 2d 69.
39. Section 395, Restatement of Torts Second.
40. *Ibid.*, Section 398.
41. Larsen vs. General Motors Corporation, 391 F 2d 495.
42. Section 388, Restatement of Torts Second.
43. Uniform Commercial Code, paragraph 2-313.
44. *Ibid.*, paragraph 2-314.
45. Sieman vs. Alden, 341 N.E. 2d 713.
46. Uniform Commercial Code, paragraph 2-315.
47. *Ibid.*, paragraph 2-316.
48. *Ibid.*, paragraph 2-317.
49. Federal Acquisition Regulation, paragraph 46.703.
50. *Ibid.*, paragraph 46.705.
51. *Wall Street Journal,* May 10, p. 8, 1984.
52. Federal Acquisition Regulation, paragraph 46.708.
53. U.S. Constitution, Article 1, Section 8.
54. 35 U.S. Code, paragraph 154.
55. *Ibid.*, paragraph 101.
56. Gottschalk vs. Benson 409 U.S. at 71-72, 35 U.S. Code, paragraph 103.
57. 35 U.S. Code, paragraphs 101, 102(g).
58. *Ibid.*, paragraph 102(a)(b).
59. *Ibid.*, paragraph 102(e).
60. Federal Property Management Regulation 41C FR, chapter 101, part 4.
61. Federal Acquisition Regulation, paragraph 27.302(c).
62. *Ibid.*, paragraph 27.302(b).
63. *Ibid.*, paragraph 27.304-1(a).
64. *Ibid.*, paragraph 27.303(a)(i).
65. *Ibid.*, paragraphs 27.303(a)(i) and 27.304-1(f).

66. 35 U.S. Code, paragraph 181.
67. *Ibid.*, paragraph 186.
68. *Ibid.*, paragraph 146.
69. Copyright Law, Section 102(a).
70. *Ibid.*, Section 102(b).
71. 18 U.S. Code, paragraphs 659 and 2314.
72. *Ibid.*, paragraph 641.

CHAPTER TWELVE

Human Factors

Introduction

The People Factor

People are the driving productive force on projects. In physical production processes the machine frequently is the major determinant as to the quantity and quality of output. In projects machinery can be employed, but in most projects where mechanical equipment is used, it is subservient or incidental to the human element. In short, there is a shift in emphasis on the significant factor for production between mechanistic and organic operations. This chapter examines some of the people factors that might be influential in project management, and Chapter 13 takes an in-depth approach relative to productivity in project management.

There is no intention to minimize the importance or contribution of the human element in mechanistic organizations; it is recognized that even in tightly cycled and highly standardized operations the machine is ultimately dependent on human interaction. The point is that machines are normally reliable, predictable, and generally somewhat rigid or limited in the range of operations. People, on the other hand, are far less predictable. There are performance variations between people; there are even performance variations for the same person within a workday, day to day, or over an extended period of time. But people do not suffer from the rigidities of the machine. People normally are adaptive, flexible, and can be more responsive when there is frequent and unforeseen change.

In a functionally oriented mechanistic organization people with similar skills are departmentalized. Departmental functionalism requirements can range from extreme professionalism, versatility, and competence to relatively little skill and specialization. The operational situation usually dictates the assignment. If variations of ability are needed, there probably is a talent reservoir to draw upon. At times a combination of functional skill levels can be utilized. The emphasis is on functional involvement and identification.

In the project situation a required skill inventory is determined as a part of the planning and organization process. Ideally, specialists are assigned to the project consistent with the degree of functional ability needed to accomplish project objectives. The project team can be composed of many diverse specialties. A significant metamorphosis takes place in projectization in that functional identification and affiliation become relatively incidental to a shift in emphasis on the contribution to project objectives. Functionalism is processed into an interdisciplinary team effort.

Of course, the aforementioned assumes a reasonably complex project entailing the merging of many diverse skills. Projects can also be relatively simple, requiring only a few skills, or a project may essentially be initiated to solve a specific functional problem, and subsequently the project team may be composed of people with the same basic functional skills.

The Critical Human Resource

Many times the objective of projects involves knowledge generation. Knowledge generation may be a prelude to subsequent projects involving the application of the information. The generation of knowledge is dependent on professional skill, conceptual power, the ability to act, and personal energy; the aforementioned are subject to considerable variation. The usual dependence on unpredictable human skills and inputs compounds the difficulty in managing projects.

As indicated, the human resource is normally the critical production factor in projects. Generally each project requires a unique combination of knowledge, aptitudes, and skills. The project manager should, where possible, select individuals with the best qualifications for the work undertaken. It should be noted that the best qualifications for a project may not be the highest level of functional ability. A functional overkill can be costly and misuse scarce talent.

Projects are usually selected because of perceived need or anticipated benefits; often controlling in the final selection process is the faith in the demonstrated ability and reputation of the project director and the project team. Consequently, favorable managerial impressions of the present and prospective capabilities of the project team can be very influential in the decision to authorize a project. Conversely, a proposed project that appears to have potential for success may be discarded because there is the impression that the project would be assigned to people who have questionable technical and managerial qualifications. Management might not approve the project even though it is possible for much of the project effort to be contracted out. Dependence on outside sources might compromise the organization's position on proprietary information or might entail unacceptable loss of managerial control.

Professionalism

The project work environment generally includes a high percentage of professional employees. Most professional employees attain such status as a consequence of formal educational attainment. There are also employees who have professional classifications and who have attained such status through experience rather than by way of education. Most of these people started as technicians and were subsequently promoted on the basis of experience and competent performance.

We live and work in a very status-conscious society. Management must be sensitive to professional attitudes and aspirations. One area where frequent reconciliation is required is attitudinal. People with professional classifications desire to be treated as professionals. In a true sense they are not pure, economically independent professionals; they are, in fact, professional employees. Many times these people do have transferable skills that can be directed to independent professional activity. But as long as they operate under the aegis of a formal organization, they are not independent professionals.

There often is a push–pull situation. Professional employees desire special treatment and professional prerogatives. Management often feels that these people are basically employees and question the advisability and propriety of privileged treatment. The work environment for these people usually falls somewhere in between the relatively extreme freedom of an independent professional and the operational restraints imposed on less skilled, nonprofessional employees. The degree of operational latitude can also vary owing to economic conditions, the need and availability of certain professional talent, the type of project activities within the organization, past practices, and managerial attitudes.

The Manager

Organizational frictions often develop because of managerial inability to cope with professional employees. Managers of projects are usually selected on the basis of demonstrated technical competence. Even though they emerge from the professional work environment, they frequently have transitional difficulties in recognizing the significant change in their responsibilities and activities from technician to manager. In the transition from technician to manager, they may lose their perception of the needs of colleague employees. Some technical professionals turned man-

agers make the transition gracefully; for others the transition is a traumatic experience, but they eventually do become effective managers; and
for some the transition is an impossibility and the net result is the loss of a
first-rate technical professional and the incurred obligation of a poor
manager.

The transitional problem may reflect the nature of the organization's
operations. In organizations where the major thrust is on technical problems, professional effort may primarily be directed to introverted activities. Managers in dealing with professional employees must be extremely
responsive to these people. They must remember, but unfortunately frequently forget, those operational factors that motivated them when they
were working professionals and those factors which had negative motivational impacts. The intelligent manager, recognizing the operational restraints that invariably exist in all organizations, will try to perpetuate the
positive factors and minimize or eliminate the negative or distracting
elements.

Project managers not only must be aware of the motivational requirements of professional employees, but also should be sensitive to and
accommodate motivational factors affecting the nonprofessionally classified people assigned to the project. Treatment of all personnel assigned to
the project should be fair and equitable. The project team should represent a proper mix of professionals and technicians; the range of skill levels
should be consistent with the skill levels needed to support the project;
education and experience should relate to the desired technical inputs. As
part of the input process, the people assigned to the project should feel
such exposure affords them the opportunity for professional and technical
growth and contribution. The aforementioned are relevant considerations
and would in most instances be applicable in many project operational
environments whether the operational base would be in for profit, nonprofit, government, or military organizations.

Economic Realities of Maintaining a Viable
Project Organization

In this introductory section some of the basic people factors in project
management have been discussed. It has been iterated that professional
people are the critical productive resource and management must be responsive to the needs, motivations, and idiosyncracies of professional
project people. Concern for the welfare of these people transcends hu-
manistic considerations. The ultimate concern is the economic reality to
maintain a viable project operation if the organization is to grow and
prosper.

In mechanistic organizations hiring is usually based on relevant experience or training, and the hiree becomes productive within a relatively

short orientation period, if not immediately. This is not the case involving professionals in organic organizations. Professionals have to be located, recruited, and integrated into a project operation. It takes time before these highly trained and expensive people can become productive.[1]

The recruitment process for professionals is far more involved than the hiring of unskilled, semiskilled, or technician employees. Need has to be identified. If the professional skill is highly specialized, analysis is necessary to determine whether the required skill is for an ad hoc situation or if such skill can be effectively employed and transferred to either existing projects or future projects. This analysis is extremely important in that it takes time to locate potential employees and go through the various processing phases leading to integration into the organization. If the present need is so unique and the future prospects for using such a highly specialized talent are remote, a better course of action might be to temporarily bring in a consultant or contract the work out to individuals or organizations with the required specialized ability. In the situation indicated it probably would be unwise to make any long-term commitment to an individual unless such an individual's skills could ultimately be employed on anticipated projects or as a possible lead-in to enter new operational areas. The time and cost involved in the recruitment and termination of professionals are invariably substantial. The implication of termination of an employee should be thoroughly considered before undergoing a recruitment process. The benefits derived from a short tenure of employment might not justify the inconvenience and problems attendant to termination.

Jundal and Sandberg[2] identify seven stops in the hiring process that are also cost categories:

1. Conceptualization of the position by the hiring manager.
2. The search process.
3. Interviewing.
4. The offer.
5. Agency fee payment.
6. Relocation of the new employee.
7. In processing of the new employee.

Even after a careful recruiting routine there is no guarantee that the person hired will perform up to the level of perceived expectations, even though they may appear to have the proper qualifications, including relevant education and experience. The qualifications may be overstated in that they have not kept up with recent developments in their field, they may be slow and indecisive in actual performance, their stated experience may be more fictional than real or so long ago as to be obsolete, and there may be personality problems not apparent at the time of hiring that inhibit their becoming an effective and contributive member of the project team.

Besides recruiting and building a project organization, it is also important to selectively maintain project teams that have proven records of accomplishment. The turnover or attrition rate of employees, especially professionals, should be carefully monitored by management. Who is leaving? Where are they leaving from? What projects or functional skills are being affected? Where are these people going? The answers to the aforementioned questions can provide insight to management relative to the human organization.

Inasmuch as project work is usually in a dynamic technological environment, some employee movement in and out of the organization is desirable. Poor performers can be encouraged to leave. Sometimes people who have not performed up to expectations can be recycled and become productive as a consequence of changed assignments. At other times there is no place in the organization for these people; they might be better off with a fresh start in another organization. And, realistically, there are some people who will drift from organization to organization and never find an acceptable niche. The recruiter should be very skeptical about hiring a person who might appear to have glowing credentials and lots of experience but who never seemed to establish a career anchor with any organization.

There are situations where it is desirable to bring new people into the operation. Carefully chosen people can bring new skills and insights into the organization. Propitious turnover can help stimulate the organization and conversely prevent stagnation.

Turnover of project professionals cannot categorically be considered good or bad. Turnover is costly, time-consuming, and at times operationally disruptive. Turnover can also, as indicated, be beneficial, but beneficiality has to be qualified. The turnover of employees has to be analyzed and answers to the questions raised in a preceding paragraph could be helpful. In addition, what is considered an advisable turnover rate for people in your technological field and geographic area? Managerial action is indicated if the turnover rate is either excessive or negligible. If the rate is excessive for the entire organization relative to comparable organizations, management should localize and neutralize the negative factors that precipitate employee exodus. If the rate is excessive but only in a few operations, intelligent investigation can also lead to corrective action. It is also possible that the organization is developing exceptional people and is being used as a recruiting base by competitive organizations to build up their technological capabilities. For example, exodus of proven professionals has been quite common in the computer industry. If this is the case, the challenge to management becomes more intense in that management must consider inducements to retain key people. Inducements must be very carefully thought out so that such inducements encourage the desired people to stay with the organization and provide motivational incentives. Long-term commitments that could ultimately prove to be restrictive and nonmotivational can become counterproductive and organizationally embarrassing.

Perhaps negligible turnover is a more insidious problem. People can become complacent. Complacency leads to stagnation, and stagnation is disastrous in a volatile technological environment. It may be that the organization has developed a poor operational reputation. There may be few or no professionally stimulating projects. Economic conditions may be such that interorganizational mobility is restricted. Worse yet, the project professionals may not be desirable to other organizations and may consequently not have much interorganizational mobility even during active economic periods.

The turnover rate is an operational barometer. As mentioned, the loss of key people can have a significant bearing on operational performance. Management should also be alert to who is being hired, where they are being placed in the organization, and how they are being used. Too often, unless turnover becomes obviously critical, management is inclined to exercise only casual interest and control. On the assumption made earlier, that the human element is the dominant productive force on most projects, it behooves management to carefully control turnover and be aware of the economic realities of maintaining a viable project organization.

Some General Characteristics of Project Professionals

Change

One of the most important distinguishing characteristics of organizations where operations are primarily a composite of many ongoing projects is the force of change. Most people tend to fear the unknown and consequently actively or passively resist change. Modifying work patterns in the organization where there are cycled operations and a productive standard usually creates management problems. In the project environment change is a normal, accepted, and usually welcome part of the operation. Project people work in a constantly shifting environment. New situations are always developing, new problems are always arising, and routine is minimal in comparison with most occupations or operational environments. The average project professional thrives in this environment, and in all probability would be bored if he or she were doing more static or routine work.

However, the continual transformation of work is not an unmixed blessing. It both attracts and repels. It attracts because it offers intellectual stimulation and the opportunity for professional exposure and growth. It repels because of the uncertainty of future assignments. A new project, a project with unexplored facets and extensive resources, provides frequent and stimulating change. But an expiring project or an impending situation that promises limited prospects for professionally rewarding assignments represents an unwelcome change situation. If immediate or future prospects for assignment are professionally and emotionally disturbing, project people can become overtly or subtly disruptive. Resistance to change that is perceived to have negative connotations can take place during any phase of the project life cycle. The project manager has to be especially guarded against such situations that could be critical to the success of the project.

There are also other types of changes that can have negative impacts. Some changes, especially where sensitive and introverted professionals are involved, can emotionally be disruptive and in turn affect performance. Peripheral changes, as in the availability and assignment of physical facilities, administrative procedures, and even seemingly trivial changes like new parking arrangements, are likely to be more disconcerting to the project professional than to people who are engaged in more routine day-to-day activity.

Work Environment

There is no geographic region that has a monopoly on intellectual activity. However, there are geographic clusters of organizations engaged in activities that tend toward operations amenable to projectization. Representative areas include Boston, Washington, DC (including parts of Maryland and Northern Virginia), New York, Houston, and Northern and Southern California. People with marketable professional qualifications are usually concerned with the quality of life prospects offered in different geographic regions. Probably a primary consideration in accepting a position is the potential for professional and economic benefit. Nevertheless, a decision to accept or reject a job offer may hinge on the perceived advantages or disadvantages of the external and/or internal work environment.

Some of the external environmental factors that might be attractive to professional employees are adequate housing, service facilities, good transportation, efficient local government, geographically related technological activities, educational facilities for themselves and their families, cultural opportunities, a relatively crime-free area, and the ability to interface with other professionals outside their immediate organization.

There are internal working conditions that also can be influential as to accepting or rejecting a position. Such conditions can even prove to be persuasive in a decision to stay with or leave an organization. The size, location, and appointment of facilities for professional employees are much more significant to these people than they will overtly admit. The facilities provide a working atmosphere in which the greatest part of the day is spent, and these surroundings should be comfortable and conducive to productivity. A very pertinent corollary factor is that the assigned quarters represent a status symbol.

The professional employee usually wants a comparatively secluded work place, free from distractions. In recognition of this need, there has been a trend to provide these people with either individual or partially shared offices and related appointments. This is a distinct departure from the oft-employed practice after World War II of grouping professionals in a open or bull-pen type of arrangement. Besides the immediate surroundings provided for the professional employee, management must appreciate the necessity to provide adequate auxiliary facilities such as proper dining accommodations, parking space, library, conference rooms, and clerical and technical support. Finally, and it should go without saying, that if special equipment, instrumentation, or facilities are required to support professional activity, they should be available, when needed, properly maintained, and adequate to properly support the required work requirement.

Education

Not all project activity requires a high concentration of professionals with advanced college degrees. However, project activity entailing knowledge generation such as research and/or development or other creative work will probably involve people with a formal college education and intellectual capability. Intellectual attainment, as evidenced by graduate degrees, is not a guarantee of competence or performance. Nevertheless, realistically, in some professional disciplines a master's degree is almost a minimal requirement for peer acceptance or as a prerequisite to participate in some projects. In some organizations a doctorate may be essential for one aspiring to upper-echelon positions.

The possession of an acceptable university degree has become almost as relevant in some scientific organizations as it is in the universities for a faculty position. The degree is often equated as a standard of intellectual achievement and may be the ticket for initial entry into the organization. The degree is no guarantee of performance. Where the degree is an essential part of the system, there is apt to be discrimination against a person who either does not have a degree or has a degree in a discipline not considered germane to the main-line operations. Discrimination can be manifested in the nature of assignments, salary, and promotional opportunities. In addition, real or imagined intellectual compatibility often acts to facilitate or impede internal communication and organizational alliances.

Personality

Of course it is difficult to generalize and especially to categorically state that all professionals invariably have certain personality proclivities that should be recognized. There tends to be some commonality as to attitudes, professional aspirations, and personality traits. Still these people are highly individualistic and it would be a serious mistake to attempt to manage a project without taking into consideration personal differences and make accommodation for such differences.

Project work involves team effort. A good project team will have the requisite skills and individuals who can also work together effectively. It may appear to be a paradox, but most professional people want relative operational freedom; operational freedom and a team obligation may seem contradictory, but actually they are not. The professional wants freedom to make technical decisions and determine the direction of the work effort. Such decisions may be made after some give-and-take with the professional's colleagues. What is important is that the decision is compatible with colleague effort and the project objectives. Individual decisional latitude can be based on the desire to avoid close and potentially stifling supervision. Professionals normally want to feel a sense of pride, accomplishment, and obligation; they want the leeway to interpret what has to be done and be allowed to employ their ability, dedication, and self-discipline to accomplish goals. Again, a word of caution: This is a generality that might apply in most situations; there are always exceptions. Also, depending upon the individual, his or her level of experience, and the nature of the assignment, the amount of supervision required might vary from slight to extensive.

Professionals are inclined to be status conscious. They are impressed with other professionals who have demonstrated accomplishments. Educational levels and intellectual attainment are important as currencies for interface and operational negotiations. By way of illustration, the author at one time reported to G. W. Carr, who had been a vice-president at Lockheed, Boeing, executive vice-president of McDonald, and president of Menasco. The author was disturbed by the constant practice of having his division intercede between production, procurement, administration, quality control, and so on, on problems involving the scientific division of the company. Such concern was communicated to Carr, and he was informed that the scientists considered themselves a professional division and that there was a general feeling within that division that there was no intellectual compatibility with the aforementioned operations. Hence the practice was developed to use a neutral operational division as an intermediary. This is indicative of insiduous prejudice and may be an extreme example. However, in many organizations there are first- and second-class organizational citizens and a definite hierarchical order, even if it is not obvious on the organization chart.

Professional people seem to be more apt to be personally sensitive than nonprofessionals. They are acutely aware of their professional stature; anything that may be interpreted as professionally demeaning will in all probability be so interpreted. A sulking professional can be disruptive to a project.

Professionals also thrive on acclaim. Recognition by their peers, subordinates, and superiors often provides incentive for additional effort. Again, as a generalization, frequent encouragement, figurative applause, and overt recognition can be applied in liberal doses. Any appearance of patronization should, however, be carefully avoided.

Professionals usually feel more comfortable working with other professionals. The interface can be with colleagues within the same discipline or colleagues from another discipline. The significant fact is that there should be mutual professional respect. In line with the aforementioned, the extent of experience, accomplishment, or organizational level may not be the same and probably would not be critical factors relative to encouraging interface. In a professional environment these differences usually do not lead to operational domination or personal subordination. What usually exists is a colleague relationship between peers and a modified supersubordinate relationship.

Many professional disciplines involve introverted activities. Introversion for members of a project team should be discouraged. Professional project people are often involved with problem solving. Problem solving and the application of the solution usually transcend the operational sphere of a single person. Many times professionals are reluctant to communicate problems or the magnitude of perceived difficulty to come to a solution. Because of ingrained attitudes of professionalism and the desire for relative freedom from close supervision, professionals often fail to communicate difficulties they are experiencing. Failure to communicate problems can have serious downstream impacts on the successful completion of the project.

There are also situations where professionals have accomplished technical objectives but are weak in communicating the results to colleagues. This particular problem has been discussed with several executives in project organizations. One vice-president of a large aerospace corporation seemed to sum up the concensus of impressions. He felt that there are many situations where professionals have done exemplary work and have made a substantial contribution, but the accomplishment was minimized as a consequence of their inability to lucidly explain the effort, accomplishment, application, and derived benefit(s).

The Expanding Role of Women

Professional Women

A separate section dealing with women as professionals is considered important. Women as professionals is not a new concept; however, women as part of the professional work force were statistically insignificant prior to the 1970s. Since then there has been a very rapid acceleration of women into professional job classifications. The 1970s and 1980s represent a transitional period; this section will attempt to identify some of the transitional factors. As of the mid-1980s it would appear that the transition should essentially be over by the 1990s. In the meantime productive integration of women into the professional ranks is a necessity.

In the past women were generally limited to lower-level support-type or technician jobs. There were traditional areas, such as teaching and nursing, that offered some modicum of professionalism. Most professions were male bastions, and the brave women who attempted to infiltrate these professional bastions had an extremely difficult time in being accepted as a professional equal. Women were generally societally conditioned from an early age to expect little in the way of a professional career. The big tragedy was the loss of a vital source of competent human resources.

As implied, there was the impression that, if the opportunity for higher education were given, such education should be centered in the liberal arts. Women were discouraged from the professions. Perhaps the dramatic change in attitude and career direction can be attributed to such factors as women's liberation, the periodic shortages of educated professionals, the realities of economic pressures for financial independence, the increased commonality of two-career families, and a desire for more materialism and hopefully a better quality of life.

More and more women have come into the work force. It has been estimated that both the husband and wife work in half the U.S. families. "By 1995, more than 81% of married women aged 35 to 44 will be employed or seeking work, the Labor Department projects, up from 64% in 1982."[3] Women are no longer conditioned to accept menial assignments with little prospects for career development and self-fullfillment. Many of the women entering the job market are strongly career oriented and educationally qualified to hold responsible professional positions. Professional recognition and organizational advancement often place a heavy personal burden on the aspiring woman. She frequently has the added obligation of attempting to fulfill the role of homemaker, wife, and at times mother, as well as maintain a full-time demanding position.

From all indications, in spite of the transitional problems, women are succeeding in establishing professional career patterns. The past distinction between male and female career opportunities has certainly become blurred, and in some professional classifications all but obliterated. Since the 1970s capable women have had time to establish their careers. These women are progressing through organizational pipelines and are assuming managerial roles. There are increasing promotional opportunities that have resulted from performance. Competent and reliable performance has, in many instances, dispelled erroneously founded prejudicial attitudes. An attendant development has been the acceptance by peers and subordinates of women as professionals and managers. However, while there are positive signs of professional progress and the erosion of preju-

dice in the more enlightened organizations, there still are attitudinal problems that exist and which should not be ignored.

Prejudice

Despite encouraging career progress, women's professional capacity and
talent have in the past, and even currently, too often been underrated by
employers. Employers have been, on occasion, reluctant to hire professional women. Worse yet, if they hired women, employers may not have
provided them with challenging assignments and promotional opportunities. Much of the failure in some organizations to provide equal career
opportunities can be attributed to lingering employer attitudes and prejudices. According to Torpey,[4] these employers assert the following:

1. Women are less objective than men, specifically in science and technology. This is only an impression which has no statistical proof or substan-
   tiation.
2. Women are less reliable than men in job attendance. This may or may
   not be true depending on the stage of a woman's career and her family
   obligations, especially if there are young children at home.
3. In science and technology the tradition has been a male-dominated area.
   Women, if involved at all, were usually delegated support or clerical
   type positions. Experience has proved that women can perform as well
   as their male counterparts. Performance can be related to educational
   background. In the past women were discouraged from taking the
   "hard" subjects such as advanced mathematics and science.
4. Women do not have the intellectual capacity to perform effectively in
   highly technical disciplines.
5. Women as professional employees represent a questionable investment
   insofar as their tenure as long-term employees can be affected by marriage, children, and being subject to geographic displacement due to the
   transferability of their spouses. It is not uncommon to find highly specialized professional women making more money than their husbands. It is
   also a more common situation that where there are two career patterns in
   one family one of the mates, and not necessarily the female, does have to
   consider a transfer in the light of their spouse's career.

Besides the prejudices indicated by Torpey, it is often felt that women
are too emotional, indecisive, and reluctant to make critical decisions,
that they cannot take the pressures that usually accompany positions of
responsibility, and that when put in a difficult situation, retreat to fem-
inism, which many men resent because they feel they are maneuvered
into a compromising position.

Some of the Problems

Prejudices are slow to die. Some of the prejudices are eroding as the new
breed of women is making professional inroads and the old female stereo-
types are fading. Nevertheless, while there is strong evidence of career

progression, women still frequently operate in a job environment where there are problems. The problems encountered by professional women are not universal, are not found in all organizations, and may on occasion be localized and counter to organizational policy.

The male who has responsibility for people should examine his attitudes and question his objectivity to determine if he has prejudices and is subtly or obviously discriminating in dealing with female employees. Accordingly, the female who considers job opportunities should carefully try to determine the attitudes of her prospective superior and colleagues to decide whether the actual work environment will be conducive to a meaningful and potentially productive career opportunity. It is suggested that a serious career-oriented woman should conduct some pre-job interview research to see if the position has professional dimensions that are compatible with her career objectives. She should not be timid or intimidated during the job interview. She should ask relevant questions in order to ascertain if the job is as represented or is fictionalized for recruitment purposes. She should attempt to determine whether professional opportunity really exists and that the job offer is not merely a subterfuge in order to bring a token female professional aboard.

There are several career-related problems encountered by women. These problems have been publicized but still persist in many organizations. For instance, many men feel threatened by professional women. Even though traditional roles are changing, it is more than occasionally difficult for a man raised in a male-dominated cultural setting to accept a woman as an intellectual equal, let alone as a supervisor. Many men still view women as sexual objects and are unable to disassociate sexual overtones from the exigencies of professional operational requirements.

Salary structure is another problem often encountered by women. Salary differentials for comparable rank, responsibility, and performance have been rationalized on the basis that the man has more economic responsibility and that the woman is not the primary wage earner in the family. Salary discrimination can also reflect prejudice that the woman is not as capable as her male counterpart, even though the real facts do not substantiate such attitudes.

Another frequent problem revolves around the nature of the work assignment. There may be a tendency to underutilize female professionals. The assignment may not be professionally rewarding, may actually be boring, and may be used as leverage in salary discrimination. Conversely, the assignment may be purposely too difficult in order to prove that the female professional does not have adequate competence. In either event, the woman may find that future promotional opportunities are restricted.

There are times when women are treated in a patronizing manner. Differential treatment can be an insidious form of discrimination. The perceptive woman cannot help but be concerned if she thinks she is not treated as a person and a professional and differential treatment is sexually motivated.

Another problem encountered by professional women is less than total acceptance and integration into the work force or project team. She may be treated politely and her professional inputs may be respected, but she is de facto isolated from the mainstream of the male-dominated human organization. She may well feel a sense of organizational isolation by not being accepted as one of the "boys."

Another serious problem encountered by professional women that was alluded to earlier is the demands on her time. The professional woman, as mentioned, has to prove herself on the job. Frequently she has the added responsibilities of being a wife, a homemaker, and a mother. Many times motivation for undertaking a career is twofold, self-realization and economic necessity. Often a second family income is necessary to maintain a desired standard of living. The burden of a dual role can be extremely difficult, and, in some instances based on individual temperament, an impossible situation. The problem of maintaining a career and a marriage would vary in intensity owing to such factors as the energy and organizational ability of the woman, whether there are any children at home, the ages of the children, and spouse support in accepting and dividing household chores that are traditionally related to women.

Managers cannot be oblivious of the problems indicated. The problems cited are relatively common. Some or all of the problems indicated exist in many organizations. No doubt there are other problems encountered by women in different organizations that have not been mentioned. The enlightened manager will recognize the inevitability of change and adapt procedures and modify behavioral patterns to utilize women as a productive, contributive, and professional part of the organization.

A Few Suggestions

In line with the preceding section, integrational problems can be minimized or eliminated by intelligent management. The manager should treat all people equally and fairly. Patronization, which really is demeaning, should studiously be avoided. The manager should be aware of the aspirations and needs of professional women. Young women with professional qualifications probably will not have extensive job experience. They may initially require even more guidance than comparably experienced male professionals in the same job classification. Initial supervisory guidance may be required because the woman has to this point in her career led a relatively sheltered life and because in all probability she is a minority in the project organization.

Reasonable, and not discriminatory, supervision is important. The manager has to evaluate the individual in order to determine what constitutes reasonable supervision. A capable, self-assured manager will act as a mentor to less experienced people. The mentor concept is important, especially for young women embarking on professional careers. As mentioned, women often early in their careers need more supervision than their male counterparts; properly directed guidance, encouragement, and reinforcement can be the foundation for a productive career and attitudinal perceptions.

Men have frequently grown up in a more competitive environment than women. Much early male conditioning results from team activities and sports; competition has often been a part of the male growing-up process. Women are increasingly beginning to participate in games and competitive team activities. Nevertheless, many women, especially older women, entering the job market find the competitive environment alien to what was previously a comparatively sheltered life-style. These women can be vulnerable at the outset of their careers. Unhappy experiences can color their attitudes and subsequently affect their careers. A good manager will evaluate each individual and each situation and will help in the transitional period.

Obsolescence

Obsolescence Isn't Always Obvious

Much concern has been expressed about the outmoding of professional knowledge. What constitutes individual, group, or organizational obsolescence? What meaningful criteria can be established to serve as guides to minimize the obsolescence factor? How can it be recognized? How can it be prevented? The ability to make contributive professional inputs that enable the individual and organization to survive and grow in a technologically competitive environment might well be a meaningful indicator of obsolescence.

There are times when obsolescence is apparent. A few good examples are the U.S. steel industry, textiles, and probably to some extent the U.S. automobile industry. The marketplace in the aforementioned examples is the determinant. On the other hand, individual, group, or organizational obsolescence may not be immediately obvious. Where there is political protection, industries may survive and even flourish as a consequence of being sheltered from more advanced technology or more effective productive processes.

Individual obsolescence may be insidious. The problem with individual obsolescence is that the individual is rarely consciously aware that he or she is outdated. It is possible that the organization may also not appreciate individual limitations that are the consequence of obsolescence. In project organizations, where knowledge is a critical commodity, obsolescence is operationally cancerous. If the organization's management is alert, it can detect trends and effectively evaluate the human organization. People who do not appear to be developing professionally become vulnerable. However, too often management is not perceptive. People who have failed to intellectually respond and grow to meet the challenge of change persist in outmoded approaches—either out of ignorance or for self-preservation—and the result is organizational deterioration. At times organizational erosion can be so severe that recuperation becomes impossible.

Types of Obsolescence

According to Ferdinand,[5] there are three types of obsolescence: professional obsolescence, in which technical competence is not deep enough; areal obsolescence, based on the individual's lack of knowledge in his or her own technical speciality; and ex officio obsolescence, in which the individual's knowledge does not encompass the body of knowledge needed for the specific technical tasks the person is required to perform in the current position. Where there is professional obsolescence it may be possible to organizationally survive. Survival might be due to the fact that the organization is not engaged in technologically sophisticated work, or the individual may be assigned to relatively simple tasks that require minimal professional competence. Assignments that require greater technical competence may go to people who are perceived to be more professionally accomplished and current.

Individuals, as mentioned, may survive in spite of professional or even areal obsolescence within certain operational environments. Such people would probably have little intraorganizational mobility and would have little or perhaps even no interorganizational mobility.

The worst possible obsolescence is ex officio obsolescence, where the individual is unable to satisfactorily perform the assignments related to his or her current position. Inasmuch as we are concerned with professionals who are a vital productive factor and a high-cost productive element, it follows that ex officio obsolescence leads to extreme individual vulnerability. It can also be operationally disastrous if these individuals are not weeded out of the organization.

Criticality

Projects are often formed to solve nonroutine problems. Often the successful completion of a project is based on imaginative and creative solutions. The people assigned to a project are crucial in order for project objectives to be accomplished. People who are professionally obsolete may not be able to come to successful project resolution or the end product may be a poor compromise. Obsolescence is perhaps more critical in knowledge-generating project activities than any other sector of the economy.

In a highly competitive technological environment it is important for management to establish guidelines that can be used to monitor obsolescence. It is very easy to become complacent, especially if there appears to be no immediate threat to the organization's operational survival. Most managements fail to anticipate. Management response usually is crisis directed. Waiting for a crisis to initiate action may well be too late. Constant and relevantly directed effort is necessary to keep the organization and its individuals current and technologically productive. Avoiding operational obsolescence must be a high management priority. Unfortunately, obsolescence cannot be seen, handled, weighed, or measured. Obsolescence is also relative. An obsolete individual, organization, or even industry in one environment may be functionally adequate in another operational environment.

Each management must determine what factors contribute to obsolescence in their particular operational situation. Each management must also determine what can and should be done to minimize the threat of obsolescence. Procedures of explicit guidance might be found by examining the organization, its competitive technological position, its reputation, its progress, including the identification of new and useful innovations, evaluation of its potential, and a discerning analysis of its people. The strategic factor in a case of individual obsolescence might be a determination of the person's professional versatility by seeing what assignments have been made in the past, the current operational responsibility, and possible avenues to which the professional might be directed to in the future.

The Project Manager and Obsolescence

The project manager is generally forced to rely on inputs from diverse professional specialities. Each speciality and each input can be likened to a link in a chain. A weak link can lead to the disruption of project objectives. In viewing the role of the project manager, relative to obsolescence, two assumptions are made: First, the project manager is professionally competent and is not obsolete, and, second, the project manager can and will take an active role rather than a passive posture in minimizing the possibility that the project team or individual members thereof will be obsolete.

In some instances the project manager is a mentor and a teacher. On other occasions the project manager may not have the specialized indepth knowledge required to teach but can create an operational setting that encourages subordinates to be exposed to new ideas, new situations, and the opportunity to experiment with innovational approaches. Educational exposure can provide stimulation.

Education, per se, is no guarantee of performance or that obsolescence will be retarded or avoided. Can obsolescence be related to education or, more specifically, to recency of education? Does educational exposure in fact afford a means of averting individual professional ineptness? Some people are exposed but do not learn. Some people have no formal educational exposure but learn by observation, experience, and individual study. Encouraging professional development usually does assume added educational experience, but added educational experience should be approached on an individualistic basis. Age, work experience, current and projected job assignments, level of operational responsibility, and—perhaps most important—motivation should be carefully considered before any commitment to educational exposure.

In most high-technology project environments management has often sponsored education to combat intellectual erosion. Professionals have, in many instances, been given the opportunity to go back to school. In addition, in-house training programs have become common. People have been allowed to attend professional meetings and urged to publish scholarly papers. Such exposures are provided on the assumption that there will be professional update, including the addition of new skills, and that productive intellectual effort will be stimulated.

Even though educational exposure suggests several possible pluses to help avoid professional obsolescence, education is not an unequivocal panacea. Management in general and the project manager specifically must be supportive. In periods of declining economic activity management may view the cutting of educational expenditure a short-term expediency to cost reduction, or management may be reluctant or restrictive in supporting educational activities.

Generally, high-technology professional organizations do make provisions for educational benefits for their employees. Educational opportunities can be an attractive fringe benefit in attracting employees, especially younger professionals. The organization may subsidize the employee's education by remuneration for educational expenses and by providing release time from the job. An extremely serious and all too frequent situation occurs after the educational process is completed. Usually, after sponsoring additional educational attainment, the organization fails to respond to the individual's need for recognition or reassignment compatible with the newly acquired skills. The employee with added educational credentials will probably find his or her job horizons expanded—if not within the organization, probably outside the organization. A combination of failure to accommodate the professional's newly acquired skills/knowledge plus their enhanced marketability often results in the individual seeking career opportunities outside the organization. The sponsoring organization, by failing to recognize and accommodate accomplishment, suffers a double loss. It loses a good professional, who has, by virtue of expending time and effort, demonstrated a willingness for professional development. The organization also loses out-of-pocket expenses incurred to train and develop the professional. As is often ironically the case, the professional probably will leave the organization to join a competitor who derives the benefits that should have accrued to the sponsoring organization. If there is no internal system to provide for recognition and review when individual status has changed, the project manager should accept this obligation. Recognition of added attainment and job accommodation by way of increased responsibility, promotion, salary adjustment, and so on, is of the utmost importance. Positive action reinforces the objective of greater individual professional capability and is tangible evidence to provide incentive for personal development.

The project manager can be the pivotal factor in either a positive or negative managerial environment. The project manager can offer subtle or direct educational inducements to subordinates. The project manager can also adopt a negative posture that discourages subordinates from outside educational exposure. Often negativism is reflected by demanding work assignments, frequent travel and an unwillingness to adjust travel schedules to educational schedules, and a stated reluctance by the project manager to give professionals released time to engage in outside educational activities.

Another very essential condition can exist relative to resistence to educational exposure. Individuals, for a variety of reasons, may not want to participate in continuing educational activities. A few reasons are the following: a lack of desire to be updated; poor motivation to take a few courses if no graduate degree can be obtained; reluctance to be gone any extended period of time from the job; the inconvenience, time, and effort involved in continuing educational programs; reluctance of older professionals to compete educationally with younger and organizationally junior professionals; and the change in academic programs that requires considerable updating of older people in order to understand new educational approaches.[6]

While educational exposure is frequently considered as a general standard of professional attainment and currency, it is not the only avenue that can be used to minimize obsolescence. As indicated earlier in this section, people can professionally grow and avoid obsolescence in several ways. Different approaches may be more or less effective, depending on different individuals. The competent project manager should know his or her people. Sometimes the clues to a professional's ability are not obvious. How is the individual accepted by his or her colleagues? Are they a problem solver or a problem maker? Do they have operational perspective? What is their conceptual ability? Are they receptive to new ideas and approaches? It is possible that he or she has concentrated to the point of being too narrow, with subsequent loss of perspective? Is their degree of specialization compatible with present need and utilization? Future need and utilization?

The project manager is pivotal in providing incentive to people for professional growth and the avoidance of human obsolescence. In providing a positive and constructive operational environment, the project manager has to consider several possible ways to stimulate individual development and avoid obsolence. The following paragraphs offer a few suggestions that might be relevant.

It is a natural tendency to keep people in the same or similar assignments where they have a high level of expertise and past accomplishment. Restricted assignments can be the prelude to boredom, burn-out, and subsequent indifference and obsolescence. Periodic rotation of assignments, where possible and within the project, can be challenging and stimulating. Exposure to new situations can be instrumental in moving people into new career areas, give them broader operational perspective, and be a factor in encouraging communication by providing an interdisciplinary bridge.

The project manager has an inclination to want to maintain a technically successful project team, especially if the team has demonstrated emotional and operational compatibility. At times there may be a short-run sacrifice in promoting people and allowing them to leave the project team. There can, however, be a long-term benefit by integrating replacements into the project team who will infuse new ideas. People can become too "habitized" and get to the point where they are not receptive to new ideas. A danger and a prelude to obsolescence is that people and project teams can become inwardly directed and communicate only within the restricted boundaries of their immediate project. They become a small world unto themselves, with the inherent limitations that develop as a consequence of curtailed exposure, and often are unaware of the existence of prejudicial attitudes. Turnover on a selected basis can be extremely beneficial in avoiding individual, group, and organizational obsolescence. The key is that the project manager must appreciate the long-term implications and be willing to make adjustments for short-run inconveniences.

One other suggestion that can have merit in some operational situations is to establish career progression steps. Career progression and achievement goals should not be established unilaterally; this should be a participative exercise. Establishing career accomplishment points can be a variation of management by objectives. Definitive steps or goals compatible with professional growth and contribution should be recognized, agreed upon, and achievable with reasonable effort, proper motivation, and within an ascertainable time frame. An all-or-nothing approach in contrast to setting up a program with incremental accomplishment points can be intimidating and discourage effort. People generally like to see attainable milestones and some tangible return for effort as incentive to continue. Incremental goals can be building blocks for continued professional development and help avoid professional obsolescence. As Confucius is purported to have said, the longest journey starts with but a single step.

Creativity

Creativity: Overview

Creativity is usually essential in project work. Projects may involve some transference of past experience that is reasonably applicable or may involve almost totally new activity. In either situation there are elements that have not been previously encountered and which, depending on the nature of the project, can call for creative solutions if the project is to be successfully completed.

Volumes have been written on the creative process.[7] The understanding of creativity and creative applications, especially in projects, is a most important goal; yet obviously the understanding and an application of methodology cannot be taught with the precision of the exact sciences. This section is intended to point out some of the factors and problems associated with creativity. Creativity is often closely allied with productivity, which will be discussed in the next chapter. Hopefully, the following discussion will provide some added dimensions to an understanding and stimulation of creativity.

It has often proven to be a humbling experience, but the author, in a wide variety of operational situations, has found new and exciting approaches generated by people at all organizational levels. It is always possible to learn something from someone, if a person has an open mind. It is maintained that every person has some spark of creativity in him or her. However, creative impulses are normally used poorly because people are not exposed to situations in which a creative response is really encouraged or fostered. Young and relatively inexperienced people are frequently turned off early in their careers because of operational environmental constraints. When they are recruited for their job, they invariably are told, especially in professional positions, that what is wanted is an aggressive, imaginative, and *creative* approach to their job activities. Once ensconced, they are disillusioned to find little receptivity to new ideas, especially any innovations that are a radical departure from the established norm of the organization. The result is that the timid tend to give up trying to promote new ideas or creative inputs rather than fight the system.

Many people who seem dull, unimaginative, and mediocre in the performance of their work possess creative instincts that are manifested in hobbies or other personal activities outside the job. These activities are psychologically satisfying and reaffirm self-esteem and respect. It is necessary, especially on projects requiring complex solutions, to fan the spark of creativity in the individual so that it may be exploited for the individual's and organization's benefit. When creative impulses are suppressed in the work environment, the worker loses, the organization loses, and there is a societal loss; generally the result is dissatisfaction on the part of both management and the worker.

Creativity: Some Possible Explanations

Definitions and interpretations of creativity vary widely. For instance, creativity has been described as an intuitive process that reaches a solution for a problem without going through step-by-step reasoning; it employs the whole of an individual's knowledge, often subconsciously, and may follow a period of unstructured thinking.[8] Randsepp[9] feels that the creative process entails a selective structuring of vague ideas and is largely a product of intuitively discerning what is applicable and what is not. Taylor[10] distinguishes between creativity and productivity: Creativity is reflected in the originality and value of the product, and some productivity is required before the creative person is identified and recognized by society. There may be a moderately high correlation between productivity and creativity, according to Taylor, but there are instances of high productivity and low creativity and situations where production quantity is slight but creativity is significant.

Further elaboration is provided by Twiss,[11] who notes that creativity can encompass the following:

New combinations or patterns of existing knowledge and concepts springing from the imagination or resulting from techniques of systematic analysis.

Association of ideas, often from widely different spheres of learning, which enable new patterns to emerge.

Creative solutions arising from or resulting in a redefinition of the problem.

Mutual stimulation between persons of different intellectual backgrounds.

A freeing of the mind from the constraints of normal logical rational thought processes.

The role of fantasy in achieving a state of detachment.

What, then, is creativity? Is it a new breakthrough? Is it a solution to a problem? Is creativity a part of everyday activity in the operational environment? Is it the formulation of a new context for old ideas? Can an individual be considered creative if he or she just dreams and talks but fails to implement? Is an unexploited idea a worthless commodity?

Another Look at Creativity

There is a tendency to be too simplistic in looking at creativity. Creativity can take many forms. The child is positively creative. Without the inhibitions subsequently acquired in life, the child is inquisitive and constantly discovers new vistas. Childhood is a period of rapid learning. The childhood learning process involves a form of creativity that enhances the child's perspective even if the creativity adds nothing new to the store of knowledge and is, in fact, a variation of reinventing the wheel. There is productive creativity. This is the type of activity that results in a usable end product. In productive creativity there is a tangible result—a new product, process, procedure, idea, or theory. There is some socially desirable and useful innovation.

There is also negative creativity. Some people do not have the aptitude to develop productive creativity but are extremely creative in detecting flaws in plans or ideas advanced by others. For example, some organizations have so-called "red teams," which are composed of people selected from within the organization to evaluate, criticize, and detect flaws in proposals or prospective projects. These people are, in effect, the devil's advocate. The fact that they can see shortcomings in ideas suggested by others is still a creative input and an organizational benefit in that scarce resources are not dissipated.

Creativity can also be nonproductive. Many people engage in daydreaming and Walter Mitty-type mental sojourns. Most of us have known someone who had great ideas and forward vision but who never managed to execute the ideas—ideas that often were later developed and exploited through the effort of other people.

There is still another form of creativity, and this is destructive or socially undesirable creativity. A good example is criminal activity, which frequently, unfortunately, is ingenious. Often, if the mental effort and ingenuity were directed to socially beneficial projects, both the individual and society would benefit.

Some Methodologies

Various techniques or methodologies for stimulating creativity have been developed and used with varying success. A few of the more prominent methodologies that have been developed and used since World War II have been brainstorming,[12] the value engineering–value analysis approach,[13] and morphological synthesis.[14]

Brainstorming was widely publicized and used in the 1950s and early 1960s. It is still used, often in an altered or modified form. Brainstorming is a spontaneous group attack on a problem. To encourage freedom of expression, no criticism or editorializing is allowed on the comments volunteered by the participants, although they may hitchhike on ideas suggested. Ideas are recorded without comment during the session and are later screened for possible applicability, elaboration, and implementation.

In value engineering–value analysis, procedures are established to stimulate creative solutions. The methodology attempts to minimize detours of the creative impulse caused by normal mental roadblocks. The theory is that by setting up a pattern of suggestive questions, the usual reservations or mental obstacles can be avoided and a creative solution developed.

Morphological synthesis aims to convert a problem into a solution by relating or establishing empathy between elements and their environment. It involves the association of unrelated ideas and sets up phases of the problem to be solved, such as the general and subordinate objectives and the major obstacles in the way of a solution.

The aforementioned and other possible methodologies can be useful in some situations. However, no approach or methodology will be useful unless there is a permissive environment. A permissive environment is a prerequisite for creativity and is more important than method or technique. Sporadic encouragement of creativity in an otherwise hostile climate does not build an energetic innovative organizational attitude.

Method or technique can provide stimulation and added dimension, but the vital element is leadership. Leadership is of paramount importance in providing the proper atmosphere. The project manager should set the example by having the courage to tangibly innovate rather than profess empty platitudes on the desirability for creative solutions. The project manager must recognize the creative ability in individuals and encourage their effort. Many times creative solutions can be reached as a result of innovative procedures or methodologies. If ideas are solicited, and in the project environment they should be solicited, they must be utilized, or a plausible explanation must be given for why they are not feasible. As already stated, vocal tribute unsubstantiated by action fools few people.

Barriers to Creativity

Establishing a creative operational setting is not a simple or easy process. Invariably there are negative forces that are overtly or subtly present to minimize or discourage creativity. Awareness of negative pressures can be an important first step in eliminating or neutralizing these barriers to creative processes.

It must be recognized that creativity suffers in the face of social pressure to conform. Pressure for conformity is more obvious in mature organizations where there is cycled activity. There is a tendency in most organizations for cliques to form, representing a community of interest. These people usually have vested interests, and any change or significant innovation is often perceived as a threat to their established position. Consequently, these people who may be organizationally strategically situated are prime pressure points for conformity. In organizations where project operations represent a significant part of activities, it is important to objectively evaluate the power structure and determine whether there are indeed sacred cows, and what might be done to circumvent these obstacles in order to initiate necessary creative and innovative activity.

Another frequent barrier to creativity is associated with timing. The creative person's timing of their activity can be critical. A good idea at the wrong time will probably be doomed. Enthusiasm should not obscure rationality. Many times patience is necessary in order to introduce the creative input into a work environment that has been primed for receptivity. In line with the aforementioned, a creative suggestion or a significant innovation usually requires support from various individuals or activities. Failure to bring these people or activities into the scheme as active participants can be disastrous, because if their alliance and support are not forthcoming, there may be a formidable barrier when the time comes to implement the creative process.

Another deterrent to creativity has been the indiscriminate use of committees. There are times, of course, when a situation is so complex that it becomes virtually impossible for any one individual to untangle. Many technical problems are solved by a group approach in which interdisciplinary inputs and added insight are applied. This can be stimulating and creatively productive, but often enough committee action represents a compromise solution to a problem and a dilution of the issue. Committee and group solutions are not necessarily the same, but in practice the procedure often becomes so similar that the forms merge. Unless the creative person has tremendous stature and the ability to dominate the group, he or she is often overwhelmed by the force of numbers.

There are other recognizable barriers to the creative process, such as "We've always done it this way, so why change now." Ignorance, lack of ability, negative attitudes, indecision, overspecialization, extreme caution, fear of failure, and subsequent ridicule can also be obstacles to developing or implementing creative activities. Most people have some degree of susceptibility in these areas. Acute personal sensitivity can prevent the individual from attempting anything that is significantly different. An environment permeated by apprehension of criticism and concern over professional and social ostracism would discourage creativity.

Another serious and frequent reason why creative inputs are not employed can be the impatience of the instigator(s). The instigator wants too much too fast. People, even in a highly charged creative environment, can usually absorb and accept only so much change in a given time frame. Normally change has to be propitiously phased in. The exception is where change is mandated to avoid an operational catastrophe. The incremental introduction of creative change, reinforced with explanation, and solicited participation can generally succeed if the creative change process is addressed to need or contribution, has properly been planned, and is thoughtfully implemented. Creative changes should be directed to those areas where prospective contribution is obvious. There should also be a reasonable probability of accomplishment in introducing creative inputs into the organization. Success tends to breed success and a record of beneficial creative contributions should find increasing organizational receptivity on successive attempts.

Stimulating Creativity

It has strongly been intimated that creativity in an organization is often the product of a conducive environment. This thesis is predicated on the assumption that all people have some level or area of expertise where they have the potential to make creative inputs if the opportunity does exist.

How can the creative process be reconciled with conflicting organizational and group pressures? Establishing a creative climate is absolutely essential in project organizations; this is especially true where project objectives involve knowledge generation and/or innovation. Karger and Murdick[15] suggest that certain steps can be taken to promote creativity in scientific organizations; these steps can also apply to any organization where the work is professionally oriented and lends itself to projectization:

1. Where possible, give professionals a choice of problems.
2. Permit freedom for responsible professionals.
3. Give time for ideas to incubate.
4. Minimize distractions and trivia.
5. Be receptive to new ideas.
6. Allow for personal difference.
7. Provide proper tools to accomplish the job.
8. Encourage personal intellectual growth.
9. Establish a review and recognition system for technical achievement.
10. Set the pace and establish a pattern for creativity in the organization.

Much project activity involves research and development. Twiss[16] maintains that, relative to creativity, the R&D manager can and ought to take action to ensure the following:

1. The amount of creative ability in his organization at all levels is adequate.
2. The creative potential of his staff is identified.
3. The opportunity for the exercise of creativity in each job is analyzed.
4. Tasks and people are matched so far as possible.
5. The creation of a working environment in which:
   a. Unplanned creative ideas are received with an open mind and are not rejected out-of-hand because they do not accord with current plans or conventional practice.
   b. Creative solutions within on-going projects are encouraged, particularly in the early stages when exhaustive searches should be made to ensure that the subsequent investment of time and effort is well placed.

There are many effective stimulants to creativity that project managers can employ. As mentioned earlier, a shift of assignment or job rotation can activate the creative process. People can lose their edge and even become dull with constant exposure to routine or predictable work. The change inherent in project operations is a stimulating force, but even in this environment a long-term project can vitiate the excitement and challenge of the work.

Rotation to different types of assignments or projects that broaden the individual's perspective can strongly stimulate creativity. The exposure to new people, the change of the immediate work environment, and the crossbreeding of ideas can inspire added insight, leading to creative suggestions.

The project manager can also encourage assignments that may at first appear prosaic but which can stimulate curiosity and lead into fertile, new professional areas. Something that is provocative, something which brings the professional into a thinking situation can be vitally instrumental in nurturing individual creative activity.

Endnotes Chapter Twelve

1. Gopi R. Jundal and Carl H. Sandberg, "What it Cost to Hire a Professional," *International Journal of Research Management,* Vol. 21, No. 4, p. 28, 1978.

2. *Ibid.,* p. 26.

3. "More Spouses Receive Help in Job Searches When Executives Take Positions Overseas," *Wall Street Journal,* January 26, p. 35, 1984.

4. William G. Torpey, *Optimum Utilization of Scientific and Engineering Manpower,* Richmond, Whittet and Shepperson, 1970, p. 31.

5. T. N. Ferdinand, "On the Obsolescence of Scientists and Engineers," *American Scientist,* March 1966.

6. Torpey, *op. cit.,* pp. 133–134.

7. Some of the representative literature includes W. I. B. Beverage, *The Art of Scientific Investigation,* New York, Random House, Vintage Books, 1957; C. W. Taylor (ed.), *Creativity: Progress and Potential,* New York, McGraw-Hill, 1964; E. Randsepp, *Managing Creative Scientists and Engineers,* New York, Macmillan, 1963; R. Taton, *Reason and Chance in Scientific Discovery,* New York, Wiley, 1962; R. B. Braithwaite, *Scientific Exploration,* New York, Harper and Row, 1960; A. D. Ritchie, *Scientific Method,* Totowa, NJ, Littlefield, Adams, and Co., 1960; T. W. Costello and S. S. Zalkind, *Psychology in Administration,* Englewood Cliffs, NJ, Prentice-Hall, 1963; B. Twiss, *Managing Technological Innovation,* London, Longman, 1974.

8. D. W. Karger and R. G. Murdick, *Managing Engineering and Reseach,* New York, Industrial Press, 1963, p. 134.

9. Randsepp, *op. cit.,* pp. 4–5.

10. Taylor, *op. cit.,* pp. 156–157.

11. Twiss, *op. cit.,* pp. 98–99.

12. See A. F. Osborn, *Applied Imagination,* rev. ed., New York, Scribner's, 1963.

13. See L. D. Miles, *Techniques of Value Analysis and Engineering,* New York, McGraw-Hill, 1961.

14. See M. S. Allen, *Morphological Synthesis,* Long Beach, Institute of Applied Creativity, 1963.

15. Adapted from Karger and Murdick, *op. cit.,* pp. 143–145.

16. Twiss, *op. cit.,* p. 96.

CHAPTER THIRTEEN

Factors That Affect Project Productivity

Determining Productivity Levels in Projects

A Valid Index to Measure Productivity

Uncertainty leads to anxiety. If the elements that create uncertainty cannot be neutralized or eliminated, anxiety may evolve into some form of hostility. On many occasions during the course of consulting assignments or field research, the author has encountered senior level managers who expressed concern over their inability to determine, with some reassurance, the productive contribution of their project organization. An explicit example involved one vice-president in a large research and development organization. He said, in effect, that when one of the scientists has his feet up on the desk and his eyes half-closed, is he thinking systems development or is he contemplating the coming weekend at a ski lodge?

Positive productivity is vital to the health of any organization. Ideally, managers would want some standard or index to gauge productivity. A valid productivity index could provide the manager with a standard that could serve as a comparative norm, help establish meaningful operational ratios, and afford guidance to instigate productivity improvements. Productivity evaluation should entail both quantity and quality of the operational end product.

The simplest approach to developing a productivity index is to determine input–output relationships. For instance, if it takes 100 working hours to produce 100 widgets, the productivity index is 1. The productivity index 1 can be used as a base point upon which to measure increases or decreases in productivity. If subsequent productive experience shows that in a 100-hour work period 105 widgets have been produced, the productivity level would rise to 1.05 against the previously established base point. If only 95 widgets were produced, the productivity rate would fall to 0.95 against the base point. In either situation management should direct effort to ascertain what factors contributed to improved productivity or what factors had a negative impact.

The aforementioned example is an oversimplification; it is also only applicable in limited operational situations. Where the machine, not the human, is a controlling factor and paces the operation, a reasonably meaningful input–output relationship can be established. In the aforementioned situation each end product would essentially be a clone of its predecessor and quantitative and qualitative standards could be set for comparative purposes.

Setting a standard or productivity index for nonroutine or thinking activities is infinitely more difficult and in some instances a virtual impossibility.

Some Difficulties in Establishing a Productivity Index on Noncycled Activities

There have been attempts to improve performance and productivity in such areas as secretarial work (letters typed), filing, and purchase requisitions processed. In each situation where productivity indices have been attempted on jobs where activity varies by time spent in performing different job elements and the level of difficulty also is a factor, the results have been inconclusive. The time required for typing letters, filing material, or issuing purchasing requisitions can fluctuate considerably. To determine a reasonably valid productivity index, the work must be repetitive and relative or absolute in terms of effort required. If people are assigned corollary tasks, it becomes, as indicated, virtually impossible to set some productive norm when the amount of time devoted to the tasks varies from day to day.

Input–output relationships are possible in some cycled production operations. There often is a problem in establishing agreed-upon productivity standards. The problems that would be encountered in trying to standardize productivity norms where noncycled, thinking, and creative activities are involved are infinitely more complex. What constitutes good effort? Reasonable effort? What is the value of the end product? Can it be compared to a similar product or effort? What did it cost? How long did it take to achieve the objectives? Was the time involved reasonable? Were there failures and/or setbacks? Was anything learned from failures that could be used to avoid future difficulties?

A few relevant questions were raised in the preceding paragraph. Generally a response or analysis to these questions is based on a subjective evaluation. A true input–output relationship in project work may not be valid, because inputs may be carryovers from knowledge gleaned from previous projects. The output from completed projects may have a multiplier effect that benefits new or future effort.

There are other difficulties in reaching an acceptable agreement on a productivity standard relative to effort. People differ, and what is a major effort for one person might only be a minor excursion for another, or, where there are intangibles involved, one person may grasp a concept much sooner than another. Another possible standard is cost. On the assumption that cost can be accurately segregated, it is often difficult to decide whether the end product was worth the cost. In noncycled operations there frequently is no directly related product that has used the same inputs and which can be used for comparative purposes.

In creative activities new frontiers are often attacked. There often is failure to immediately accomplish objectives. In pushing knowledge into previously unchartered areas there well might be a trial and error process. Error normally connotes failure. Was the trial logical? Was the error reasonable in light of the problem? Was there an applicable learning process? Can the knowledge gained be applied to future project activities that could ultimately result in positive productivity? How can failure in such instances be reconciled with productivity, which is associated with incremental contribution? A negative result would in the short-run affect productivity, but in the long-run could have a beneficial impact on productivity if the lessons learned can be applied on the current or future projects.

Some engineering and scientific organizations have attempted to correlate productivity to the number of papers published or presented at professional meetings, citations of published work, and the number of patents that have been issued. Such indicators of productivity have obvious limitations. The impact and quality of publication are more important than the actual quantity. Peer review and the adaptation of concepts and subsequent acclaim are relevant, but can they be measured? Unfortunately papers presented at professional meetings are frequently dull and the information, because of organizational proprietary interests, may already be outdated.

There are also limitations in using the number of patents issued as a productivity indicator. There are many instances where engineers hold several patents. May of these patents may have had little application or impact in their professional sphere. There may also be situations where other engineers might hold only one or a few patents but these have extensive applications that result in impressive economic and sociological returns.

This introductory section has provided an overview of some of the issues or problems that affect the establishment of productive standards in noncycled activities, for example, in the management of projects. Subsequent sections of this chapter deal with other aspects of the operational environment that affect productivity, such as quantitative and qualitative productivity indicators, productivity motivators and demotivators, the dual career ladder, counterproductive operational conflicts, and some recommendations which might improve productivity.

Localizing the Factors That Affect Productivity

Some Variables

It would be desirable to ascertain and isolate the specific factors that affect productivity in thinking and creative effort. The difficulties in establishing productivity indicators stems from the fact that projects vary considerably as to objectives, organization, required resources, technical complexity, and so forth. Developing productivity indicators on some projects could be extremely difficult, if not impossible. In other instances, in some organizations, and for some projects it may be possible to design a reasonably valid and acceptable system to ascertain project productivity.

There are possible project situations, where quantification of factors that affect the project goals is possible. Quantification of important project accomplishment points may be possible to serve as productivity guides; such guidelines should, if possible, be developed in conjuncture with the project professionals who feel comfortable with and committed to such standards. On the other hand, these same people who may operationally embrace quantitative methodologies as relevant to the solution of project problems are often unwilling and may even be belligerent when an attempt is made to employ quantitative methodology to evaluate their personal effort.

More often managers and peers have definite impressions of individual productivity based on subjective impressions rather than quantitative evaluation methods. On several occasions the author has posed the following questions to managers: How do you evaluate a person? What tangible indications do you use to determine a professional's productivity? The responses almost certainly follow a similar pattern to the effect, "They get things done. They are reliable. When I want a problem solved I give it to _____." This same general pattern of responses has been encountered in a variety of project operational settings where the primary effort was intangible mental activity. Despite the fact that hard and fast quantitative reinforcement is not available and evaluation attitudes reflect subjective impressions, there generally are very strong feelings on the part of peers and managers relative to individual performance.

One possible approach, based on the aforementioned, would be to attempt to identify the productive individuals and to as objectively as possible try to isolate the critical incidents that nurtured the impression of productivity. Personality traits and performance experience should be segregated. At times the two become entwined, and this can color an objective evaluation. It could be fruitful to take an additional step in attempting to segregate technical skills, educational attainment, experience, and in some instances job assignment, as well as personality characteristics, to see if the "productive" people can fit into any discernable profile. If so, positive performance and personality factors can be used for guidance in directing the improvement of less-gifted members of the project team.

It is important to bear in mind that no system or approach has universal application. Even a system that may have some acceptance within a project organization has to be constantly reviewed, modified, or reinforced over a period of time because of changing conditions. Also, factors that may be productively desirable in one organization may be counterproductive in another organization owing to the types or range of project activities or the organizational mores.

An excellent and highly recommended study on productivity was conducted under the auspices of the Hughes Aircraft Company. The following was stated in the aforementioned reference[1]:

> To be effective, any system of productivity evaluation must be readily understood, simple to implement, easy to administer, and clearly cost-effective. It should require minimal paperwork, be timely, and especially important—it must be endorsed and conscientiously implemented by its users.

Measurable Productivity Indicators

Quantitative productivity indicators may not be conclusive, but they can give a picture of trends and point out areas where operational improvements are possible. Also, since projects are subject to considerable operational variations, not all quantitative, or for that matter qualitative, indicators would be applicable for all projects. The participants in the Hughes Productivity Study Report cautioned that an evaluation of productivity factors should analyze the work performed, being careful to distinguish between valuable work and unnecessary work; recognize the difference between activity and work; understand the difference between efficiency and effectiveness; and realize that it is possible to confuse working "hard" with working "smart."[2]

The Hughes study presents examples of organizational quantitative productivity indicators and individual activities that could be quantified. The following are some of the quantitative organizational indicators that were identified by the study participants and which have been adapted with some additional suggestions by the author[3]:

Sales per employee

Sales per direct employees

Sales related to payroll

Profit relative to employees

Profit as a percent of payroll

Production dollars generated by employees

Correlation of R&D expenditures to sales and profits

Percent of proposals won

Dollar value of proposals won compared to expenditures on marketing effort

Overhead in relation to direct charges

Comparison of planned work completions and costs versus actual completion and cost experience

Mechanical activities such as design and drafting work, schedules, errors, processing time, engineering changes

Ratios of direct to indirect employees

Hours per test

Recruiting performance, labor turnover, job offers accepted/rejected, recruitment costs, processing time for new employees

Absenteeism

The above list is not all inclusive. As mentioned, unique factors not suggested might be applicable in some project environments. It is also possible that some quantitative factors will be highly significant in some organizations as productivity indicators, whereas other quantitative factors will have relatively little impact on productivity or may be beyond the control of management.

Individual quantitative productivity indicators have to be selectively determined to meaningfully relate to project activities. Any attempt at numbers correlation with individual productivity determination has to be reconciled with the difficulty of the assignment. Determining the difficulty of the assignment is inherently based on subjective evaluation. Another factor to consider is the degree of complexity and ultimate level of achievement that can reflect personal differences in ability and exposure. Just to give one simple example, the quantification of individual effort based on the number of designs produced or drawings completed fails to take into account the technical difficulties involved or the details that have to be accommodated.

A poorly conceived system for determining individual productivity indicators can, as mentioned, wind up being counterproductive. Such an attempt will probably affect the morale of professionals; it is also possible that such an approach would encourage volume activity with a sacrifice of qualitative effort. In projectization quality effort is generally a paramount concern. Often project work involves thinking activity. Creative thought processes are qualitative. How can thinking activity be quantified?

No explicit quantitative method has had general acceptance in measuring individual productive performance. As already mentioned, there generally are impressions of individuals as to the quantity and quality of their work by their peers and their supervisors. Individual reputations are developed over a period of time. Attitudes and impressions may be slow to change—either positively or negatively—even after current performance warrants a performance reevaluation. It is also possible, especially for newer employees, that attitudes will be based on the most recent interface and experience.

Despite the difficulties involved in setting up individual quantitative productivity indicators, there can be projects where some quantitative productivity indicators are relevant. Identification and agreement, in concert with those involved, of critical production elements is perhaps a first step. In order to determine the prospects for establishing some quantitative productivity guidelines, a few possibilities are suggested:

Discuss the project assignment with the individual. Together agree on technical objectives, schedule commitments, and cost goals. This is an application of management by objectives.

Recognize that mental work cannot be scheduled and measured on an hour-by-hour basis. Establish a reasonable time frame, for example, a quarterly review period to determine the level of accomplishment relative to the work assigned during that period. Review would encompass technical accomplishments, schedule achievement, and cost experience.

Establish a simple weekly backlog report. Such a report would indicate work in progress, work completed, and work initiated with relevant comments.

Subjective Productivity Elements

The study participants in the Hughes report identified organizational and individual indicators of productivity that are relevant but difficult or impossible to quantify. Many of the qualitative factors reflect internal and external impressions. Favorable or unfavorable impressions can materially affect the success and future of the organization. Some of the organizational indicators suggested and adapted from the Hughes report[4] are as follow:

The success rate in winning competitive proposals

The experience of the organization in meeting its commitments

The internal operational experiences in achieving technical goals, cost objectives, and schedule milestones

Customer satisfaction

Transformation of R&D activity into productive activities

The performance of the product resulting from the project

The external organizational reputation

The internal organizational reputation–motivation–morale–employee attitudes

The organization's professional approach

The quality and recency of ideas generated with the organization

The technological currency of the organization—a leader in its areas of activity

The organization's reputation for quality of work

The organization's responsiveness to meet change and operational challenges

The ability to resolve difficult problems

The foul-ups such as delinquencies, deficiencies, and errors

Internal and external coordination problems

Excessive red-tape or paper work

Internal functional disputes

The aforementioned are subjective or qualitative organizational factors that could have a bearing on productivity. There are also subjective individual indicators that can affect productivity. Many of the individual indicators relate to personality traits. To be sure, a difficult person can be operationally disruptive, but some people who have personality problems can be contributive if they are properly used and organizationally placed. Some of the individual indicators identified in the Hughes report[5] are the following:

Quality of performance relative to assignment

Comparative evaluation to others with similar background doing the same type of work

Ultimate value of contribution

Reliability—work habits

Compatibility of individual professional career objectives with goals of the organization

Employment of innovative methodologies

Relationship between relevant and current technology and job assignment(s)

Completion of work as scheduled

Errors and/or problems resulting from work

Adaptability—moving forward quickly and smoothly into new assignments

Personal relations with superior, peers, and subordinates

Professional acceptance by peers—solicitation of professional advice

Ability to develop rapport with customers

Willingness to take on new assignments—aggressive versus passive approach to work

Productivity Motivators and Demotivators

Value Systems

Individual performance and productivity are generally related to motivational or demotivational factors. What may motivate, or for that matter demotivate, individuals depends on such things as age, personal aspirations, and value systems. Different people will react differently to the same stimuli; a person's reaction to the same stimuli may even vary over a period of time. Values change and since, as Stephanou[6] indicated, professionals are often guided by their values or goals, it is worthwhile to examine factors that affect value systems. It is also important to recognize that there are organizational as well as individual value systems. Conflict can arise when individual and organizational value systems are not compatible.

Many people are ostensively outwardly motivated by materialism. They may gravitate to organizations where they feel their material desires can be satisfied. Too often they fail to objectively consider their own values to determine if the material goals can be achieved without a major alteration or compromise of their personal values. It is possible that joining an organization that has values which may be in conflict with individual values can develop into a traumatic experience. In order to cope with such a situation the individual (1) discovers there is no basis for reconciliation and leaves the organization, (2) modifies or compromises his or her values in order to survive as part of a process of reprioritizing values, or (3) tries to exist in an environment where there are conflicts in organizational and individual values. In the last situation individual emotional problems can develop and the organization is saddled with a person who may not be responsive or who may even be disruptive to the achievement of organizational goals.

Organizational value systems may involve accommodation for statism, degrees or levels of integrity, expected employee loyalty, company loyalty to employees, demands for individual dedication and contribution, latitude for creative inputs, extent of operational permissiveness, participation in decisional processes, individual and organizational security, intraorganizational policies, and attitudes in dealing with external constituencies. These are just a few representative organizational values. In addition, the nature of the operations and projects might be controlling in determining individual or organizational value compatibility. For example, a person with a strong ecological sensitivity might emotionally be repelled by the prospect of working on a project that might ultimately result in environmental pollution.

A person's value system might reflect cultural or religious influences, conservative or liberal inclinations, a level of personal integrity and willingness or unwillingness to raise or lower such standards, an extent of commitment to a career, a desire to personally and professionally grow, ambition, a desire to interface with peers, subordinates, superiors, and potential customers, a sensitivity to operational pressures, and the extent of responsiveness to react to a volatile operational environment.

Again, the above is only a partial indication of what values individuals may find influential. Individual values do change. People do intellectually and emotionally grow or even retrogress. An appreciation of an organization's mission and its value system that is more often implied rather than explicitly stated can provide a foundation for establishing motivators which enhance project productivity. Personal and organizational value compatibility is normally crucial for harmonious working relationships. In the personnel selection process organizations normally search and screen to seek out individuals who have the requisite professional talent. Another very important consideration that usually is an intangible in the final determination to employ or not employ a person is whether that particular person will fit in the organization. "Fitting in" transcribes into "does he or she not only have the professional qualifications but also will accept and will be accepted by other members of the organization?" In other words, do they come within the bounds of some general people profile that exists in the organization? If organizational and individual values do not reasonably mesh, the prospects for productive working relationships are dim even though the person may have the professional qualifications.

Productivity Motivators

Where individuals and organizations subscribe to the same general system of values, it is easier to develop a blanket of motivators that will cover most people. However, it would be a serious managerial error to assume that the same factors would motivate all people at a comparable rate and in the same direction. In project organizations it must be constantly remembered that the project team is composed of professionals who have strong individualistic characteristics. While each of these people may respond in degree to some motivators, the intensity of response will tend to vary to reflect timing and personal need differences. In some situations a motivator may have an immediate and positive impact; in other situations the response may not be commensurate with the cost and effort involved to provide productive motivation. It is also possible that what may be a motivator for one person will be a demotivator for another, or productivity motivators may be neutralized by demotivational factors that exist in the organization. Demotivational factors will be discussed in the following section.

Perhaps productivity motivators can be segregated into three distinct areas. First, there are motivators directly related to the work assignments. Second, there are motivators that are, in effect, rewards and recognition for exemplary performance. Third, there are motivators that are attendant to the job, such as perks and the actual working environment.

Motivators Directly Related to the Work Assignment.   The motivators directly related to the work assignment have an immediate impact on productivity. Most professionals, especially scientists and engineers, according to Stephanou,[7] want to have a choice in technical assignments. Wherever possible, people should be placed where their interests and talents can best be utilized. This contention is reenforced by Frohman,[8] who emphasized the importance of matching skills and interests. Where there is no match, performance is apt to suffer as a consequence.

In mechanistic, functionally oriented organizations matching skills and interests is relatively easy. In organic, project-oriented organizations matching skills and interests presents a constant challenge to management. In a project-oriented organization it is possible that, because of the existing mix of active projects, individual inputs may be required from professionals who are less than enthralled with the assignment. However, most professionals working in a multiproject environment are willing to accept periodic assignments that are not personally exciting if they feel management is aware of their professional interests and will accommodate them when there are projects falling within that sphere of professional interest.

Most professionals take pride in their work. They strive for excellence. To attain excellence usually takes time. Unfortunately, in most project situations there are extreme time pressures. Time pressures are especially controlling in proposal preparation. Constant time pressures can have a debilitating effect. Managers should avoid the temptation to make commitments that are unrealistic relative to the work to be performed. The professional should feel that management is aware of the magnitude of effort and has allocated a reasonable time frame in which to allow for commensurate activity. Given a reasonable time frame, consistent with the perceived amount of effort involved, a person will usually be motivated to do a professional job.

Another productivity motivator is providing a sense of assignment security. Assignment security can be related to having the opportunity to stay with a project or projects until they are essentially completed. Disruptions are distracting. Project people normally feel a sense of involvement on the assigned work and want to experience the satisfaction of seeing the project successfully completed.

Often in the process of completing the technical phases of a project new and technologically related vistas appear. There has to be some balance and control between excursionary explorations and the immediate project contractual obligations. Where possible, some slack should be built into the schedule, especially if the project is pushing knowledge frontiers. There should also be some available funding to enable the pursuit of technical opportunities that were not apparent when the project was initiated.

Communication failures can occur between the project manager and members of the project team. What is perfectly obvious to one person may be a complete mystery to another. If there are communication gaps, people can go off on tangents that have little, no, or casual relationship to the assignment. Productivity can be improved, the possibility of errors minimized, morale heightened, rapport developed, and motivation stimulated if there is a firm understanding between the project manager and members of the project team on the explicit nature of the assignment. Feeling confident that there is a firm understanding of the work assignment can be a productivity motivator.

The project manager should be aware of the aspirations of the individual members of the project team. Different people grow at different rates. Even fiercely ambitious people need an occasional hiatus to professionally coast, rest, or assimilate the knowledge or absorb the experience they have been exposed to.

Response to operational or personal pressures can result in positive or negative productivity. Some people respond favorably to pressure; other people have a negative reaction. The project manager should recognize how different people might respond in different situations and under different conditions. People can, in some instances, be reasonably predictable. On other occasions the individual's response to operational pressures may reflect, among other possibilities, existent personal problems at the time an assignment is made, their current career pattern, the level of individual energy, and their experience and confidence in their own ability relative to their present assignment. There are times when the project manager may have to make adjustments in work assignments for people in order to accommodate a period of emotional stress that could cause performance to suffer. In periods of personal stress people may negatively rather than positively respond to added exposure to job-related pressures. There are times, and there are some people, when a pressure situation encourages high performance and productivity. Some people thrive under pressure, which for them is motivational and encourages productivity, stimulates personal growth, and contributes to job enrichment.

Most professionals are productively motivated when they are given increased responsibility. This is usually interpreted as reflecting managerial confidence in their ability. Attendant to the granting of more operational responsibility is the level of supervision. Supervision should be reasonable and conditioned by the person to be supervised and the operational situation. What is reasonable supervision for a neophyte professional would be professionally repugnant to a more experienced person. The amount of supervision and control can be either an emphatic motivational factor or lead to resentment and become demotivational.

Closely allied to increasing responsibility and providing relevant supervision is extending the professional's decision-making latitude. Project professionals usually want to be participants and consultants in decision making. Intelligent participation is predicated on communication and an awareness of what is happening on the project. If the professional is made a participant in the decision process, he or she might be able to offer possible insights to better achieve project objectives. Participation would entail commitment and would encourage a feeling of moral and professional obligation to make their proposed solution work. If management imposes rules or decisions autocratically, the results can be counterproductive. The subordinate may respond reluctantly rather than by overt insubordination, or there may be passive resistance. If there is direct or indirect reluctance to perform or if the performance is less than enthusiastic, it follows that the end product might be suspect and the productivity questionable.

Motivators That Involve Recognition. Recognition, in the context of this discussion, is to provide incentive for productivity. Recognition has been defined as formal acknowledgement, as a fact or a claim, or an entitlement to attention.[9] Recognition can take many forms. The forms of recognition can also vary in effective response owing to individual differences. Despite possible variations relative to effectiveness, there does seem to be general agreement that recognition properly implemented is a positive motivator.

Recognition, as intimated, is a complex and necessary process. It is a very natural desire to seek acclaim when it is felt that there has been commendable performance. Managers too often are prompt and vocal in pointing out performance that is considered poor or unacceptable. Recognition for outstanding performance, too often, is either relatively slow in coming or, worse yet, not forthcoming at all. Some managers have a philosophy that high performance levels are to be expected of professionals. Even though some of the productivity motivators indicated in the preceding section do exist, recognition is still important for reinforcement. Recognition for good and bad performance is part of the system.

Recognition is often ignored, but is also very important, for people who do a professionally conscientious and reliable job day in and day out. There may be no spectacular performance breakthroughs or monumental foul-ups by such people. They are, nevertheless, an important part of the project team. A periodic, nonpatronizing, figurative slap on the back indicating that they are needed, contributive, and appreciated is an intelligent and motivating approach.

One positive form of recognition is remuneration as a merit reward for job performance. According to Kopelman,[10] "Individuals rewarded on the basis of job performance tend to be more motivated and more productive than individuals rewarded on various non merit bases." Merit awards are associated with expectancy theory. Expectancy theory assumes that there is a positive motive to work based on a subsequent relationship between effort and work-related rewards. Therefore, if rewards are associated with performance levels, individuals can aspire to higher rewards resulting from increased effort; the result is greater motivation.[11]

Monetary rewards are undisputably important; however, monetary awards may lack consistency as a motivational factor. For instance, money may have diminishing marginal utility. A $2,000 a year increase would probably have more immediate economic impact for a person making $20,000 a year than a $4,000 a year increase would have for a person making $40,000 a year. At the higher income range other forms of recognition might take some direct or indirect precedence over monetary rewards. Herzberg and co-workers classify salary as a hygiene factor (dissatisfier). They feel there would be job dissatisfaction if there was not a perceived adequate salary level.

Herzberg and colleagues are of the opinion that motivators (satisfiers) are inducements to get people to work harder. The motivators indicated by Herzberg and co-workers involve responsibility, achievement, prospects for advancement, the nature of the work assignment, recognition, and potential for personal growth.[12] Some of these motivators are directly related to the work assignment and some relate to recognition.

So far in this section we have discussed recognition as acknowledgment of performance. Performance recognition can be praise to the individual, group, or project team. It can be private or public and oral or written. Recognition can also be in some material form, the most obvious, of course, as mentioned, being financial reward. Other forms of recognition could be promotion and subsequent increased organizational status. We live in a very status-conscious society. Impressive titles embellished with attendant appointments such as privileged communication, access to the executive dining room, a fancy office with a wooden desk, a private secretary, reserved parking place, adequate library facilities, and accessible conference room facilities are status related and motivational factors that reflect organizational recognition.

Recognition can, in addition, take other forms such as representation of the organization or the project outside the internal operational environment. Being placed in the position of spokesperson for the organization can carry a great deal of prestige and positively affect relationships within the inner organizational structure. It may also be possible, if no proprietary organizational information is involved, to publicize the person and his or her work outside the organization. A few such examples involved Kelly Johnson and the "Skunk Works" at Lockheed, Lowell Steele and Larry Miles at General Electric, and Jack Morton at the Bell Laboratories.

Favorable peer acceptance and recognition are also productivity motivators. Peers may recognize individual technical competence, but peer acceptance of the person may be missing. The ability to productively interface with one's peers is essential in order to have a harmonious and properly coordinated technical project team effort. Lack of peer acceptance can lead to negative synergism; lack of acceptance can result from personality clashes, failure to reconcile technical difference, or absence of respect for a person's technical competence.

Recognition, internally and externally, may be reflected in meaningful professional activity outside the direct operational sphere of the project. Papers can be presented at professional meetings and articles can be published, especially in refereed journals. Professional involvement and peer recognition can result from national or regional offices held in professional associations. In addition, the organization may encourage internal or external consulting assignments.

Attendant Motivators. Attendant motivators are usually in some form of "perk." Perks are subsidiary benefits and can be substantial motivators. The availability of perks may relate to reaching higher organizational levels where different perks become available. Perks can materially add to the total compensation package. Perks also represent a tangible form of recognition.

Attendant motivators may be packaged according to the job classifications and automatically bestowed on attaining such job classification, or they may be individually negotiated between the organization and the person and become part of the employment compensation package.

As a generalization, perks would probably become more important after there was some career progression. The type or nature of the perk could also reflect the stage of one's career, the level of professional attainment, the perceived importance of the person to the organization, income bracket, and age. For instance, younger and organizationally more junior professionals might only logically expect and opt for payment of memberships in professional and work-related organizations, subscriptions to technical journals, and the subsidization and opportunity for educational advancement. The chances are that older and organizationally more senior people would not actively pursue advanced formal educational degree programs. They might want instead to periodically participate in short, specifically work-oriented informal courses.

Attendant motivators could be supplementary compensation packages. These are frequently negotiated by people in upper organizational echelons. Supplementary compensation packages represent a wide range of alternatives and are beyond the scope of this book. Suffice it to say that most supplementary compensation packages are tied into the operational success of the organization. Just a few examples of the many supplementary compensation options would be stock purchase plans, profit sharing, productivity incentive plans, retirement benefits, the use of a company car, membership in the country club, and extended vacation periods. Increased productivity and subsequent profitability in the private sector would add to the compensation package and could provide motivation.

A few other relevant attendant motivators would be a life insurance policy paid by the organization. The nature and amount of the insurance would in all probability reflect the salary compensation and the person's place in the organizational hierarchy. The amount of travel budget, including the wheres and whens of travel, is a recognition factor. Another attendant motivator, as mentioned, could be the allowable yearly vacation period. In many organizations the yearly vacation period may be extended from the normal 2 weeks to as much as 6 weeks, depending on organizational position and length of service. In practice, people at the top of organizations are often reluctant to take extended holidays because of job pressures and responsibilities.

Many organizations provide an automobile as an attendant motivator. Such a motivator, as previously indicated, could be negotiated or an established perk related to job responsibility. The make and model of the car can provide a strong motivation for organizational recognition. The annual cost of owning an automobile is another factor to be considered. Even though having a company car provided represents a definite means of recognition in the United States, the car provision recognition factor is not as significant in the United States as it is in many foreign countries. The author was very impressed with the importance of the automobile as an attendant motivator in England. In England personal income taxes are extremely high and take-home salary somewhat limited. It was surprising that in discussing promotional opportunities and improved economic affluence with English scientists and engineers that such opportunities were often associated with the availability of a more prestigious automobile.

Considerations in Initiating Productivity Motivators

In this section we have discussed a few attendant productivity motivators. The motivators discussed are perhaps the more commonly used attendant motivators. Most of these motivators are primarily used in the private sector. It is also possible to tailor attendant motivators to fit unique operational conditions and accommodate key people. Nonprofit organizations, particularly the government, are limited in the application of compensatory motivators. Nevertheless, some nondirect compensatory motivators should be considered and innovated in these economic sectors, even though it is acknowledged that supplementary compensation packages are more difficult to initiate.

Establishing a motivational system that will positively affect productivity is not a simple undertaking. As has been mentioned several times, people are different and individuality can be a controlling consideration in attempting to inaugurate any motivational program. Not all motivators turn all people on, let alone at some comparable or predictable rate. Motivation aimed at improving productivity is situational. Management must not embark on motivational programs without thought and investigation as to potential ramifications. Once a commitment is made, it becomes virtually impossible to withdraw. If the intended motivational commitment fails to achieve its objective, management has probably added another cost without a corresponding operational benefit.

The manager, that is, the project manager, is the pacesetter. The project manager can implement or retard motivational concepts sponsored throughout the entire organization by upper-echelon management. Incentives for productivity can also be instigated within the project by the project manager consistent with the project manager's operational latitude. The awareness and employment of productivity motivators are preliminary steps. Proper employment of people can be the ultimate factor as to whether the motivator is successful in improving productivity.

Demotivators

It is very possible that even though a productivity motivational system is operational, counterproductive factors exist in the organization. There is no natural balance between productive and counterproductive motivational factors. One intensely negative demotivator can neutralize many positive motivational factors that were instituted on the assumption that productivity would be improved.

Most productivity demotivators are controllable and can usually be traced to poor management. Management may be indecisive, or the response to a situation may be inadequately thought out with a predictable poor result. Worse yet, there can be a complete avoidance in addressing the issue(s). In the latter instance failure to come to grips with the problem can be the result of purposely avoiding a potentially unpleasant event. It is also possible that management may be oblivious to what is happening and what has to be done.

Managerial inaction, when the situation requires an active decision process, is organizationally demoralizing. There are too many instances when time, rather than responsible management, makes policy. By not taking directive action, management might feel that the problem will ultimately be resolved or an unpleasant decision can be avoided by letting a subordinate take the decision-making action.

Management practices can be contradictory and counterproductive relative to productivity. According to Hall and Wolff, dissatisfiers often reflect perceptions. Professionals tend to become unhappy with the organization if they are of the opinion that people are not being properly managed, that business opportunities are being lost that affect individual prospects within the organization, and that people are not being treated fairly.[13]

In the Hughes report on R&D productivity the study participants identified 25 factors that were felt to create a counterproductive operational environment in R&D organizations; these counterproductive factors would generally be applicable in all project organizations[14]:

1. Poor planning, direction, and control
2. Improper organization
3. Excessive staffing
4. Inadequate attention of management to productivity and the elimination of counterproductive elements
5. Internal communication problems
6. Failures to exploit technology exchange possibilities
7. Lack of sufficient investment in R&D
8. Work environment problems
9. Insensitivity to people
10. Improper use of employees
11. Poor structuring of work assignments
12. An inadequate personal performance evaluation system
13. Ignoring impact of low producers
14. Technological obsolescence
15. Questionable reward system which does not properly correlate compensation with productivity
16. Failure to provide equal opportunities for advancement in managerial or technical career paths
17. Operational inequities
18. Ineffective interface with customers

19. Ineffective functional interface within the organization
20. Ineffective interface and control with vendors
21. Internal red tape—operational complexity
22. Too much internal political machinations
23. Internal provincialism
24. Inadequate management development
25. Failure to properly invest in and maintain capital facilities

By way of elaborating upon and in some instances reinforcing the Hughes study, some other productivity demotivators are often present in organizations.

There are situations where employees are kept in the same general work area even though the employee wants and is receptive to a change in his or her work assignment. Slotting a person can lead to individual and professional stagnation. There is little or no professional growth; the employee becomes frustrated and unhappy and may even become productively disruptive. If the work does not present a technical challenge and the opportunity for professional development, a person may well feel that their career is compromised relative to promotional prospects and an improved salary position.

There are negative or demotivational factors associated with the work environment that include, among other things, inconvenient access to the work facility, extensive travel time to and from work, inadequate parking arrangements, poor public transportation, lack of availability or access to necessary library material, poor eating accommodations, uncomfortable office arrangements, and insufficient technical and clerical support.

Productivity may also be affected by the obligation of reporting to two superiors who have operational and philosophical differences. This type of situation places the person reporting to them in a difficult position of trying to satisfy two diversely different people. Placed in such a position, a person can easily be reluctant to take any initiative and may take a wait-and-see attitude. Vacillation is usually counterproductive. The situation described is very possible where there is a matrix organization, where a person reports to one administrative person and another person in a technical capacity.

It is also possible to become indecisive, confused, and reluctant to go beyond minimal activity because one's superior is erratic, moody, or overly critical. The superior may not properly delineate the assignment, or, to the other extreme, be so definitive as to eliminate all possibility for creative and interpretive contribution. Work frustration can result as a consequence of reporting to a poorly organized superior who has questionable technical and managerial ability. Often such managers fail to properly think out work obligations before making assignments. The impact of such inadequate planning is the frequent need to change work in process or be forced to redo work that has already been completed.

Much project activity involves some plowing of new ground. Moving into new areas means incurring various degrees of risk. A risk-avoiding managerial philosophy can discourage professional initiative, which, in some projects, can be very counterproductive.[15]

Many professional people are underutilized. Underutilization can result from the direct work assignment that inefficiently uses professional skills, or it can reflect the individual's lack of comprehension of their work obligation. Highly skilled professionals are often criticized for spending too much of their time and energy on casually related work activities that could, in many instances, be delegated to other people. If professional people spend 50% of their time in work not directly related to their speciality or work assignment, shifting 25% of these efforts to their professionally specialized activity would be tantamount to increasing the professional labor force by a fourth. Too often professionals do relatively menial work and compete with subordinates in areas where less than highly skilled professional work can be delegated. The example cited may be oversimplified, but the principle is valid. Productivity and morale can be improved by proper organization and direction of professional effort.

There are times, however, when project professionals are purposely, at least in the short-run, underutilized. The demand for project professionals can be erratic owing to the operational environment. In periods of relatively low project activity project professionals might, in effect, be stockpiled. Stockpiling may be in anticipation of future projects even though the current work load will not properly support the present professional organization. This practice distorts supply–demand relationships. In addition, specialists who are simply figuratively standing by in reserve may develop less than desirable work habits. Thinly spread available work or a make-work project is not professionally fulfilling. Financial inducements can temporarily offset personal dissatisfaction; however, prolonged inactivity leads to professional deterioration and reduced productivity. Ultimately, the quality of the people and the organization are affected. The good people with professional mobility will tend to leave the organization if no promising projects are on the horizon. If operational activity is only at a temporary lull, managers could initiate in-house projects, provided that funding is available, which have genuine potential benefit for professional growth and promise for future organizational operational opportunities.

The practice of unproductive stockpiling has contributed to a widely held management attitude that project professionals, especially scientists and engineers, are less than ideally productive.[16] Yet this image can frequently be traced back to management that perpetrates the situation and then criticizes the result. Part of the problem is the time it takes to build a project organization. In the interim between the planning stage—characteristically high in expectations—and the actual authorization of projects, people are hired or retained. All too often the expectations regarding both plans and personnel are not achieved. To minimize the costs and problems associated with stockpiling, it might be wise to consider, in the short-run, the advisability of maintaining the essence of a capable technical corps and subcontract work out where future or follow-on activity is highly uncertain.

Discrimination is another demotivator. Discriminatory practices are at times insidious and in other instances are only too apparent. Discrimination usually is associated with bias related to age, sex, race, or religion. Discrimination can also reflect bias resulting from personality differences, functional affiliation, professional specialization, educational attainment, educational institutions attended (the old boy network), or previous employment.

The implications of discrimination, relative to productivity, are considerable. By not assigning people on the basis of ability, it is possible to lose the potential for the best probable performance on a specific project activity. The people directly affected invariably are aware of and sensitive to discriminatory practices. Their more enlightened colleagues will also be cognizant of discrimination and probably harbor resentment that capable people are precluded from being properly utilized on the project team. Preclusion of capable people from maximizing their potential contribution affects the quality of work on the project and can throw an undue burden for performance on other professionals assigned to the project. Resentment might also fester, because if there are discriminatory practices, the possibility exists that such practices could expand. People currently not directly affected may feel that in such a work environment they too can become vulnerable. Having a vested interest in the organization or fear of losing their job may significantly color their activities and put them in a patronizing position.

This section has dealt with productivity demotivators. Many common productivity demotivators have been identified and discussed. Perhaps many more not so obvious demotivators exist. Most of the demotivators indicated can be attributed to management. In some instances management may be unaware that problems exist. To use a cliché, management cannot see the trees for the forest. It is also possible that management is insensitive to the human element. There are still people in authoritative positions who operate under a philosophy that assumes that people are being paid to do a job and management has the right to expect professional performance without the obligation to coddle individuals within the organization.

How a Dual Career Progression Ladder Can Affect Productivity

Career Progression

The projects within an organization would image the organization's special operational abilities. For instance, if the organization concentrates on doing economic analysis and studies, entry into main-line operations would probably be based on having degrees or demonstrated competence in such professional specializations as economics, operations research, statistics, computer science, and perhaps sociology. If the organization is scientifically directed, entry into project operations would be dependent on having the requisite scientific skills. What might be a main-line professional activity in one organization could be a staff or support activity in another operation. An example would be where a financially trained professional could be involved in main-line projects in a financial institution or be a staff specialist in a scientific operation.

The usual way to the top of an organization is through main-line activities. There are exceptions where a person with a strong marketing background or with finance and/or legal expertise is promoted to the top of an organization. This is not an uncommon practice in mechanistic organizations. In organic project organizations there tends to be a strong inclination to move people up in the organization based on technical ability and contribution consistent with the organization's basic operational objectives. There is normally a very strong professional bias in such organizations in that there is reluctance, if not overt discrimination, in accepting anyone in a leadership position who does not have organizationally acceptable technical credentials. This operational philosophy acts as a preclusion to non-mainline professionals or staff people as far as aspiring to the top position(s) in the organization. Because of limited promotional opportunities, these people, particularly staff professionals, usually spend their entire organizational life within their functional specialty. What promotional opportunities do exist are generally restricted to promotion within the functional specialization.

Professionals within the organization are often confronted with the prospects and possible choices of different career paths. They can advance up the technical ladder, concentrating their effort in their field of technical specialization; they can move into other professional functional areas, which may or may not be main-line activities; or they may decide that the best career opportunities are in management. If they opt for the management career path, there is a divergence in required activities and skills. This section will discuss some of the implications where a technical professional is faced with possible options of remaining in their area of technical specialization or moving into management.

Some people embark on formal educational programs in technical disciplines because of an intense interest in the field. They enter into such an educational contract with the explicit purpose of making a career and to establish expertise in that technical area. There are people who are less dedicated to the discipline; they embark on formal technical training and the attendant degree(s) as a means of job entry. They have no intention of making a life-long career in the immediate technical field; their career planning is to expand into peripheral activities. There are also situations where people initiate technical training with the intention of pursuing a career in such an area but subsequently decide to move out of the technical sphere.

In each of the three possible career progressions mentioned in the preceding paragraph management is dealing with a valuable professional resource. It is not always obvious to managers, or even at times to the individuals directly involved, as to what ultimate path careers will follow. There are instances where the professional does have a pretty definite idea of what type of career they want. If the professional is indecisive, different career opportunities can be explored. Subsequent career experience could indicate that their career pattern is not compatible with promotional and recognitional opportunities within the organization. They may not be maximizing their productive potential and may decide to deviate from a previously planned career approach.

Career development is affected by individual choice, often chance opportunity that was not anticipated, and the organizational operational environment. Periodic assessment of personal interests and capabilities might be suggested relative to maintaining an existing career path or altering such path. There are times when unanticipated vistas appear that were previously unknown or not considered but which, upon reflection, offer promising career prospects. There are also situations where the organization can be a directive force by encouraging new career directions or positively emphasizing the contribution of the current technical specialization.

Dual Ladder for Career Progression

Organizations where the major activities are technical and professional are generally dominated by people who are qualified to participate in these activities. Technically dominated organizations usually have either an explicit or implied hierarchical structure. It is relatively rare, as already mentioned, to find a nontechnically trained professional holding an upper-echelon line position in a technical organization.

As technical people move up the organizational ladder, their decisional latitude normally is expanded. Decisions entail more technical choices. They additionally are apt to get more involved in managerial decisions. Most technically trained people are used to dealing with "things." Many technical specializations involve introverted activities. People with this type of background feel confident and comfortable in determining avenues for technical effort. In management there is a different decision process. Management is an extroverted activity and "people" rather than "things" become the decisional focal point.

The career direction problem normally does not become acute until technical people have promotionally advanced several steps within their specialization. There may be a gradual transition as a consequence of increased responsibilities. In all probability, professionals will find more and more of their time taken up with making decisions that involve both the technical and people. The transition may be relatively easy, but it is possible that professionals will resent the effort and time directed to decisions that have little or no direct impact on their immediate technical obligations. Very often professionals are forced to evaluate their career status in the light of their current position. They have to ask themselves such questions as the following: Career-wise, where am I? Am I happy doing what I'm doing? Am I productive? What are the future prospects or opportunities based on my present situation? What are the negative and positive aspects of my job? My career?

A change in the direction of a career is not simple after a person has invested a significant part of his or her productive life in achieving a status level associated with technical accomplishment. The professional has to consider whether he or she has the talent and inclination to be productive and contributive in the professional sphere. These professionals have to consider whether the organization will provide opportunities for professional growth and advancement within their technical field. They also have to consider whether more or better opportunities exist on the managerial ladder. In short, what are their options? Are there parallel ladders for professional advancement? Equal opportunity would involve comparable salary and organizational status by either moving into management or deciding to continue to concentrate on technical effort. If there is honest parallelism, there is a strong inference that individuals are encouraged to stay in their professional fields.[17]

Managers have titles usually denoting with some extent of accuracy their level of accomplishment and status within the pecking order of the organization. Professionals should also have titles that signify accomplishment and place in the organizational structure. Managers are generally visible and recognition is reasonably established. Technical professionals, by the nature of their work, may not have extensive organizational exposure. It is important that these people are also recognized. Recognition should be related to professional progression up the technical ladder. Accomplishment should be publicized. Peer acclaim is an important motivator for productivity for most professionals.

The discussion to this point has indicated some of the factors involved relative to possible career choices of technically educated professionals. The opportunity should be present for some individual self-determination as to what career path to follow. Usually, even if a dual ladder is present, the prospects for career advancement based on technical activity are more illusory than real. First, many technical professionals feel that the real promotional opportunities are on the management side of the operation. Second, many feel technically defensive as to their future ability to be competitively contributive and productive in their professional specialization. This feeling is exacerbated in technologically volatile fields, where young professionals often bring into the organization new concepts and techniques that may be alien to older professionals. As a consequence, many professionals move into management because they are insecure in their professional areas and they neither want to nor feel able to keep up with professional developments.

Many older and experienced professionals gravitate to the management side of the organization. The movement is related to the various factors discussed, such as promotional opportunities, recognition, salary, status, and professional insecurity. Many of these people, unfortunately, are unable to make a graceful transition from technical professional to manager. They frequently lack interpersonal skills, which are very important in dealing with technical professionals. They also tend to minimize the complexity of skill levels involved in management. They may, in addition, find it difficult to understand and apply the decisional processes that are different between managerial and technical activities.

The influential factors in the technical versus the managerial arenas that have been previously indicated can range from slight to significant, depending on the project. If there are transitional problems in converting from technician to manager, there can be negative operational impacts. A project manager unable to make an effective transition from technician to manager places a project in jeopardy from its outset.

Some Pros and Cons of the Dual Ladder

A dual ladder system can be effective, depending on the situation and the people involved. The installation of a dual ladder system for organizational progression should be deterred until the pros and cons of such a system are evaluated.

Some possible pros and cons relative to the dual ladder are the following[18]:

Pros

- It provides opportunity for advancement and recognition for technical professionals who prefer to remain in their field.
- It does not force technicians who have limited managerial potential into managerial positions in order to advance in the organizational hierarchy.

- People can remain in the work area where they feel most comfortable, competent, and, hopefully, most productive.
- Better organizational morale where there is individual choice on direction of career progression.
- Management recognition of the technical organization. Recognition would include awareness of individual effort, sensitivity to the professional needs of the technical people, and added emphasis on the necessity to maintain a high level of professional competence in technical operations; this would include the proper selection of projects and a continual educational program to update and reinforce technical professionalism.

Cons

- There is a sharp divergence of skills and knowledge requirements in performing technical and managerial work. Cross-over to parallel rungs on the opposite ladder may be very difficult. It would be particularly difficult to go back to the technical ladder and pick up after being away from a hands-on approach for an extended period.
- Despite promotional opportunities on the technical side there are still limitations. The management ladder is the route to the head of the organization.
- A pure technical environment may really be illusory. As professionals progress up the technical ladder more and more decisions have to be made. Some administrative decisions are inescapable.
- Management may appear to support a dual ladder but the support may not correspond to actual promotional opportunities. If technical professionals perceive greater opportunity in management they will, perhaps reluctantly, channel their careers in that direction. If such a situation exists it follows that management has made a commitment with a questionable corresponding benefit.

Conflict

Sources of Conflict in Project Management

Conflict[19] represents incompatibility, an adversary position, a clash, or a divergence of opinions. Conflicts can arise as a result from many operational situations. Conflict can be between individuals because of personality problems, professional orientation, or organizational affiliation. There can be conflicts between functions, product divisions, and projects. Some organizational conflict, due to operational decisions, is predictable. Some organizational conflicts are spontaneous and arise out of unpredictable events that cause anxieties. Some organizational conflicts smolder and periodically flare up, reflecting jealousies, politics, and internal competition.

On a positive note, conflict reflects concern and an active position. There probably would be a minimum of conflict in an apathetic organization. On a negative note, conflict is disruptive and can leave organizational scars that mar future working relationships and seriously impact on productivity.

Even in reasonably stable operational environments there is bound to be some conflict. In the project environment change is an ongoing process wherein new and often unanticipated situations develop, with a resultant change in the work scope and perhaps subsequent priorities. Such changes often become operational irritants and lead to conflict. In highly complex, technologically involved projects the project manager has the obligation to motivate his or her people to adapt to a fluid work environment.[20]

There are many operable conditions in project organizations that can fester into conflict situations. Some of the more common sources of conflict in project management are the following:

Technically trained people tend to be weak in interpersonal relationships.

Differences in the evaluation and interpretation of the technical results.

Personality clashes.

Jurisdictional disputes can develop as to who is responsible for project inputs.

Control: Functional support areas invariably lobby for authorization and release of resources in order to plan for and commence project support activities. If the project manager releases the resources and does not have functional authority, he or she, in effect, loses control over that part of project activities.

Project managers are vying for the best people to be assigned to their project. Assignment of personnel to projects can create conflict, especially in matrix organizations.

It is possible to misassign a person to a project. The wrong person and the wrong time can lead to difficulties.

Often conflict arises out of poorly communicated assignments. There may be a different level of expectations between the project manager and the professional who is assigned a project task or phase. If the work has to be repeated because of performance discrepancies or if it has to be repeated because there was inadequate communication as to what was expected in the way of the end product, there are bound to be frictions.

Trial and error are often a part of the process before coming to a successful resolution of a project. Undue criticism where there are failures can ferment resentment.

Conflict can develop as a consequence of competition for resources.

The establishment of priorities can lead to conflict.

Differences in opinion and commitment as to schedule obligations.

Failure to recognize or involve some individuals, activities, or functions in the project planning process. Subsequent participation or commitment may be reluctant owing to hurt feelings resulting from the perceived slight.

Cost of various project activities can create conflict.

There can be conflicts generated by functional incompatibilities.

At times project work involves pushing into new areas. Unforeseen problems and/or the unveiling of new technological vistas may dictate the necessity to make changes in the project work scope. Changes where work is in process, where work has been completed, or commitments have been made can be a major source of conflict.

Conflict can also arise as a result of playing politics. Internal gamesmanship can affect administrative decisions and certainly can be considered as being disruptive to the best interests of the organization.

Related to the preceding, conflict, internal to the project, can develop if the project people are of the opinion that the project manager is a poor leader and is being outmaneuvered in acquiring resources, recognition, and so on, by more managerially adept project leaders.

If the project manager has insufficient clout to control his or her subordinates or is incapable of successfully dealing with related support activities.

Conflict can result owing to a difference of opinion as to the proper approach to achieve the project objectives.

The aforementioned sources of conflict have been presented randomly without any attempt to prioritize intensity or frequency of conflict. In a study conducted by Thamhaim and Wilemon the frequency of conflict in descending order of intensity was schedules, priorities, human resources, technical issues, administrative practices, personality conflicts, and cost.[21]

Dealing with Conflict

Conflict is situational. Some sources of conflict can be reasonably anticipated; some conflict sources develop as a consequence of the often unpredictable nature of project work.

A competent project manager should know his or her constituency. The degree of involvement and the decisional range for the various project participants has to be assessed. Where there is a long project life cycle and considerable technical challenge, there is a very high probability that some project planning will go awry. Contingencies should be established and communicated to cope with the unanticipated. In effect, the unexpected is to be expected.

Where possible, the project manager should foster a spirit of involvement and commitment. People who have a strong sense of participation can often anticipate problems in their area that are not readily apparent to a project manager. Also, if they have a sense of commitment they will usually respond positively and productively to situations that were unanticipated and unplanned for. Without a strong sense of participation and commitment, they may be indifferent and passive rather than active in coping with unforeseen situations.

The project manager, in dealing with his or her technical organization and the external factions involved, must evaluate the extent to which these forces will bear on the project decisional apparatus. If the project manager is too authoritarian, people can be turned off and conflict and resentment can result. If the project manager consistently tries to mollify all project participants, such behavior may well be interpreted as being indecisive and weak. Trying to satisfy everybody is generally impossible. Action, consistent with the best interests of the project, is a normal and desired course and is usually justified even though all parties may not be totally happy.

There are times, again depending on the situation and the people involved, when the project manager has to defer authority and decisional response. There are other times when conflict can be resolved by reasonable compromise. There are other situations where the project manager is thrust into a decisional position. Vacillation or, worse yet, avoiding a necessary decision can have an operationally eroding effect and maybe lead to later organizational conflict that could have negative productive implications.

Establishing an Organizational Climate to Promote Productivity

Some Suggested Managerial Guidelines

This chapter has dealt with some of the factors that can impact on productivity. Some of the factors discussed would be applicable in most organizations. Some of the factors mentioned are more unique to organizations composed of highly trained professionals who are primarily engaged in projectized activities. In some organizations managers have more directional leeway in initiating programs that could affect productivity. A thought out, well-planned, and at times innovative management approach can be instrumental in creating a productive operational climate.

If the operational climate is unduly rigid, the chances are that professionals will avoid such a work situation. More often than not, managers, particularly in professionally oriented organizations, do have some discretional lattitude in lauching programs or policies that might have a favorable incentive to stimulate productivity. In order to develop a productive atmosphere, thought and effort are required. Every organization, group, project, function, and individual has some unique characteristics. A rigid or stereotyped approach can promise only moderate results at best. Relevant considerations in setting up a system to stimulate productivity would be the nature and scope of operations, the type of people, the prevailing value system governing the organization, the technological umbrella covering operations, and the composition, that is, age, sex, and professional mix, of the work force. No two situations are identical. Each manager has to assess his or her particular operational setting. However, there are, perhaps, a few ideas that might be considered and which could be applicable.

Eliminate poor performers. They tend to be demoralizing to the productive people. This is more pronounced if the system is sticky in allowing for salary differentials based on performance variations. At times poor performers can be stimulated by reassignment. At other times they should be encouraged to leave the organization. In the worst possible situation where reassignment or dismissal is not possible, some way should be found to neutralize such people.

Beware of the cheap employee. Too often there is a tendency to hire inexpensive or lower-level people who may not really be effective. Hiring practices are frequently dictated by short-run considerations. In such situations there may be an inclination to hire a person who can immediately make some contribution but who has definite limitations for long-term growth and contribution. The end result is that the operation is stuck with a person who is a questionable asset. The cheap employee with questionable qualifications may have only moderate productive possibilities and may even detract from more productive people who are assigned to monitor his or her activities.

There are situations where people are exploited by being hired at less than their competitive worth. The qualified person who is hired-in "cheap" invariably discovers the exploitation and becomes disgruntled. A disgruntled employee is rarely a productive employee. Added to the aforementioned is the probability that such an employee will actively pursue other employment and, in ultimately leaving the organization, will disrupt operations and possibly affect productivity.

Watch the human inventory. Are people intellectually growing? Are there professional growth opportunities afforded by the internal projects? The nature and scope of the projects can stimulate professional intellectual growth and productivity. What other educational opportunities are available to the project people other than their work assignment? Outside exposures from the project and the internal organization can be beneficial in leading to technological transfers and possible improved productivity. And, in line with an assessment of the human inventory, an objective evaluation should be made relative to the type and caliber of people who are attracted to the organization.

Encourage people to recognize the value of time. Hard work does not automatically ensure high productivity. Educate people to be time effective. The productive person works "smart" as well as "hard."

Provide people with the necessary tools and support to get the job done. It is a tragic waste of talent to force expensive people to dissipate much of their time and energy on menial tasks that can be delegated.

Encourage new ideas and procedures. Too often there is only lip service for innovation. People who try to be innovative in a nonreceptive work atmosphere are frustrated and ultimately become turned off by the restraints in the system. The project manager must set an example. The project manager is the pace setter. Reward and recognition for productive effort are reinforcing.

Monitor labor turnover. Losing good and productive project people during critical phases of the project life cycle is not only disruptive, but can also materially affect the successful outcome of the project. Personnel assignments should be selectively made. Motivational inducements should be provided to avert or minimize counterproductive transfers out of the project.

People should feel that the work assignment and the project afford individual and organizational professional growth potential. Career prospects within the organization should be optimistic. The professional generally wants to feel that there is upward mobility, the avoidance of individual obsolescence, promotion by merit, and easy infiltration of new ideas.

Organizationally, management should studiously avoid the inclination to develop proprietary interests (sacred cows). Concern should focus on total organizational welfare and attendant human considerations.

Communication should be simple and direct. Proprietary treatment of communication for internal competitive advantage should be discouraged.

There should be fast reaction to problems.

The organization should encourage esprit de corps. Foster an image that promotes personal pride in being associated with the organization. This should be translated into demonstrated quality work, cost consciousness, meeting schedule commitments, exemplary treatment of employees, an influential market position, a good physical working envirionment, profitability (where applicable), technological leadership, and a favorable organizational image reflecting social awareness and community involvement.

Endnotes Chapter Thirteen

1. *R&D Productivity—Study Report,* 2nd ed., Hughes Aircraft Company, Culver City, CA, 1978, p. 40.
2. *Ibid.,* p. 42.
3. *Ibid.,* pp. 44–45.
4. *Ibid.,* pp. 46–47.
5. *Ibid.,* p. 47.
6. S. E. Stephanou, *Management, Technology, Innovation and Engineering,* Malibu, CA, Daniel Spencer, 1981, p. 162.
7. *Ibid.,* pp. 162–164.
8. A. L. Frohman, "Mismatch Problems in Managing Professionals," *International Journal of Research Management,* Vol. 21, No. 5, pp. 20–25, 1978.
9. *Webster's New Collegiate Dictionary,* Springfield, MA, G&C Merriam, 1961, p. 707.
10. R. E. Kopelman, "Merit Rewards, Motivation and Job Performance," *International Journal of Research Management,* Vol. 20, No. 3, p. 35, 1977.
11. *Ibid.*
12. F. Herzberg, B. Mausner, and B. Snyderman, *The Motivation to Work,* New York, Wiley, 1959.
13. An interview with C. Dennis Hall and M. F. Wolff, "Companies and Careers," *International Journal of Research and Management,* Vol. 23, No. 4, p. 8, 1980.
14. *R&D Productivity—Study Report, op. cit.,* pp. 4–5.
15. L. W. Steele, *Innovation in Big Business,* New York, Elsevier, 1975, p. 23.
16. An informal poll of presidents and vice-presidents of organizations engaged in research and development, conducted by the author, indicated that these executives estimated the productivity of engineers and scientists to be between 5 and 30% of possible efficiency.
17. See W. G. Torpey, *Optimum Utilization of Scientific and Engineering Manpower,* Richmond, Whitlet and Shepperson, 1970, p. 60.
18. See Stephanou, *op. cit.,* p. 174.
19. Good discussions on project conflict are covered in H. Kerzner, *Project Management, A Systems Approach to Planning, Scheduling and Controlling,* New York, Van Nostrand Reinhold, 1979, pp. 250–258; R. D. Archibald, *Managing High Technology Programs and Projects,* New York, Wiley, 1976, pp. 46–54; University of Wisconsin, Extension Department of Engineering and Applied Science Course on Professional Development, "Managing the Development and Introduction of New Products," June 22–25, 1982.
20. Kerzner, *op. cit.,* p. 251.
21. Hans J. Thamhaim and David L. Wilemon, "Conflict Management in Projects Lifecycles," *Sloan Management Review,* Summer 1975, pp. 31–50.

The Project Termination Phase

CHAPTER FOURTEEN

Project Termination and Evaluation

Project Termination

A Complicated Process

There has been relatively little effort and literature devoted to project termination. The interest and major concern has been on the conceptual, formative, and operational phases of the project life cycle; the termination phase, usually neglected, often is critical and, when put in proper perspective, can be influential in determining whether a project was a success or a failure.

Termination signals the end. If the organization has other technologically and economically promising projects on the horizon, the inclination is to wrap the present project up as quickly as possible and move on to new and more promising areas. Project termination, however, is not always a simple or straightforward process. The project termination process can be based on an internal management decision; project termination can be initiated by forces or sources external to the organization; termination can also result de facto because project objectives were met. At times, as indicated, the decision is practically predetermined or outside the realm of internal jurisdiction. At other times the decision to terminate a project is internally generated.

An internal decision to stop an ongoing project can be approached like a new project selection.[1] A periodic review process can internally be established to look at all existing and prospective projects. Current operational projects can be viewed relative to actual versus planned objectives, evaluation of continued technical and economic feasibility, and, in the light of prospective projects from a competitive angle, where new projects may be more promising than existing projects. In such situations, existing projects would have to be examined as to the stage of completion, the possibility of reducing resource allocations and stretching the project out, after diverting some of the resources to new projects, or possible salvageable elements from the project in the event the decision is made to terminate.

The termination decision process indicated in the preceding paragraph could also be applicable in situations where the decision to stop a project is made external to the organization. In addition, the internal or external decision to terminate a project could reflect a composite risk evaluation analysis, which was discussed in the chapter on project financial management.

Reasons Why Projects Are Terminated

Projects can be concluded because the project objectives were met, the project can be terminated for convenience, or the project may be terminated for default or failure.

Completion.   In some projects achieving technical and/or contractual objectives signals the end of the project. Termination may simply involve the submittal of a final report. On other projects much remains to be done after the technical work has been completed in order to legally conclude the project. Charges to the contract may continue well past the ostensible completion because attention must be paid to one or more of the following: work in process, the disposition of special project equipment and purchased raw materials, procurement commitment to long lead time items, miscellaneous reports, outstanding bills and claims, unconcluded contractual commitments, returning the project (area) back to its original condition, disposal of finished inventory, disposition of scrap, interorganizational transfers, royalty or patent licensing costs, final settlement negotiations, terminal project audit, storage costs, warranty reserves, field service requirements, and instruction manuals.

Project completion represents a phasing-out process. It involves the scaling down and dismantling of the project organization. The completion phase also involves the reassignment of project personnel and, where possible, the transfer of resources to other projects. Completion should be anticipated and planned for to enable an orderly and effective transition.[2] Scheduling is extremely important. Resources should not be transferred too early so that existing project obligations are impaired. Also, if resources are held too long by a terminating project, unnecessary costs are charged to the project or other projects that can use the resources may adversely be affected.

In a multiproject organization, even a successfully terminated project can require considerable time and effort and involve many problems. Termination procedures require specialized people. Cleaning up project residuals is often tedious and unglamorous. Project termination, as indicated, frequently is not given sufficient attention in organizations where the paramount interest is in professionally directed technical effort. The orderly phasing out and phasing in of resources should not be neglected and termination procedures definitely should be reviewed and evaluated.

Termination for Convenience. There are also many reasons why projects may not come to successful fruition. It is possible that a project is aborted for convenience before it has achieved its franchised objectives. Termination for convenience can result because organizational resources are constrained and other projects are perceived as having higher priority for available resources. It is also possible that the project may have a high organizational priority but is stopped because of insufficient resources. Other reasons why projects may be terminated for convenience are new technology may make the present project not feasible; the initial project cost expectations have been exceeded; the potential market has changed and sales prospects, in line with costs, do not appear encouraging; there are legal implications; competitive forces are such as to discourage project continuation; other investment opportunities promise better returns for the allocated resources; the potential contribution to organizational objectives does not warrant the project investment; there is questionable probability of technical success; and the internal or external political environment may shift, with a subsequent diminishment of interest and support for the project.[3]

Termination for convenience often is a difficult decision; there is a connotation of failure to plan and/or properly assess technical and economic risks. As a consequence, unless the decisional elements are clearly evident, there is a reluctance to abort an operational project. Another factor for consideration in termination for convenience is the present stage of the project. How much time and resources have been spent? Can some of the project effort be productively transferred to other projects? Does a little more effort promise a commensurately greater return? Or is the assessment such that it is perceived to be a situation where good money would be expended without relative returns? If this is the case, the resources can obviously be more productively channeled elsewhere.

Termination for Default. The worst situation for project termination is where the project activity is stopped because of default. Default most often is related to unsatisfactory technical performance. Termination for default can also result because of cost overruns, delivery delinquencies, quality discrepancies, legal violations, unsatisfactory material or other substitutions, inadequate project planning, customer (internal or external) dissatisfaction, poor project management, insufficient internal or external management support, or lack of quality resources allocated to the project.[4]

Termination for default obviously would impact on the organization's reputation. A publicized termination for default could compromise the organization's survival. As a generalization, operations that lend themselves to projectization are comparatively rarely canceled out because of default. More often projects that are terminated before completion are terminated for convenience, as indicated in the preceding section. Where termination is for convenience on a project authorized external to the organization, there usually are contractual provisions covering such terminations. Where termination is for default, coming to a mutually agreeable termination process can be sticky.

In some instances the nature of the project can be relevantly explicit as to specific objectives. Failure to achieve such objectives would clearly put the project in jeopardy and make it vulnerable to default proceedings. In other instances project objectives may be somewhat indeterminate and subject to interpretation. Default procedures instigated by the sponsor could result in legal actions if the parties involved with the project differ in their appraisal of what was to be accomplished and what has been accomplished.

Some Suggestions for Project Termination

In the project termination, termination for convenience may indicate poor planning and termination by default would be presumptive of poor performance. Both situations should, of course, be avoided. In project termination, whether termination is due to successful completion, convenience, or default, management should determine the following: What did we learn from the project? What can be salvaged? How can we transfer what we learned on the project to other projects? Can we improve termination procedures with subsequent reduction in termination time and costs? Are there any unique termination problems associated with this project that might provide guidance for the selection and implementation of future projects?

Actually, several possibilities exist in looking at project termination that might be constructively employed on future projects. First, and most important, is the recognition of potential benefits that can be derived from an analytical evaluation of a terminated project. The tendency, as has been mentioned, is to pull out of the project as quickly as possible once the technical objectives have been accomplished. The technical people rapidly lose interest in the terminating project, unless they see possibilities for technology transfer from the terminating project to a forming project. Too often there is a failure to appreciate the potential of a managerial knowledge transfer from a terminating to a forming project. In the following paragraphs some suggestions are offered as guidance for the transfer of managerial knowledge, gleaned from a terminated project to a new project.

One possible approach would be to ask what technical and managerial lessons were learned from the terminated project. What new areas were encountered? What problems developed? How were these problems handled? Were the outcomes satisfactory or unsatisfactory? What improvements might be adapted to similar situations in the future? What recurring technical and managerial situations were there on this project that related to previously completed or presently active projects? Did we improve? Did we make the same mistakes? Did we instigate any new technical or managerial innovations that can be adapted to future projects? Can specific technical and managerial modules be identified? Can the knowledge derived from this project be communicated as an educational process to other project people? Can a procedural manual be developed to incorporate knowledge generated on a completed/terminated project? How might the lessons learned be phased into organizational policies affecting future projects?[5]

Another suggestion for a more orderly approach to project termination is made by Archibald.[6] He feels that projects may stay alive long after their usefulness and contribution can be justified. Undue extension, because of continuing changes to the project, can turn a financially successful project into a financial failure. One way to facilitate termination, according to Archibald, is to assign a project termination specialist who will be responsible for winding down the project. Related to the aforementioned is the advocacy for a project close-out plan and schedule, including applicable checklists of remaining obligations to be accomplished, delegating project close-out responsibilities, and provisions for postcompletion evaluation.

Balachandra and Raehn indicate that there are discriminant quantitative and qualitative factors that can be applied in the decision to stop R&D projects. Quantitative factors include evaluation of probability of economic success, potential growth prospects, capital expenditures, risk, return on investment, anticipated technical accomplishment, and schedule considerations. Some of the qualitative factors to be considered would be consumer attitudes, government regulation, competitive forces, perceived innovation, management support, technology transfer implications, and the role and ability of the project manager and people assigned to the project.[7]

Another approach could be procedural. A procedural approach could be the development of a comprehensive checklist of actions required, forms to be completed, and the sequence and scheduling of activities required to terminate a project. Since projects differ, an all-encompassing checklist may not be feasible, but some representative factors to be included on a checklist would be contractual end items completed, reports, disposition of materials, work in process, equipment, facilities closed down and charges, disposition of applicable patents, provision for licensing or royalty payments, audit, if required, and final determination of project allowable and nonallowable costs, any open items and possible renegotiations, final payment, and provision for reserves in the event of warranties.

As has been emphasized in this section, project termination is an important phase in the project life cycle. It is perhaps, under normal project operations, the most neglected phase in the life cycle. Terminating a project, especially a complex project, entails specialized skills and considerable effort.

In this section the concentration has primarily been on the mechanical aspects of project termination. The following sections will deal with evaluation procedures associated with project management. Evaluation will be examined from an individual perspective, as a project postmortem audit, and as an operational evaluation, looking at the total organization and its prospects for survival and growth in a competitive project environment.

Evaluating Individual Performance

Levels of Performance Evaluation

This and the next two sections concentrate on levels of performance evaluation. In this section evaluation is on individual performance and contribution. The project manager, owing to working proximity with people assigned to the project, is in the best position to make a performance evaluation. The next section is concerned with project evaluation. Evaluating a project has many facets that must be examined. The project manager usually has a strong vested interest in the completed project and understandably might lack objectivity or fail to evaluate the project holistically from an organizational position. The third section examines the total organization. A conducive operational environment, consistent with operational objectives and efficient management, is essential for survival, growth, and prosperity in a dynamic technological setting.

The Project Manager's Responsibility

Performance evaluation of professionals assigned to projects is very important. It is a natural inclination to want favorable professional recognition. Favorable recognition usually is a positive motivational force. The concept of individual performance evaluation is sound in that it establishes communication patterns and does, hopefully, provide acknowledgment of contribution where such contribution has been forthcoming. Unfortunately, the implementation of performance evaluation procedures frequently creates problems rather than serves as a motivator or morale booster.

The problem in dealing with and evaluating people on some projects is that there is little or no precedence to serve as a yardstick for a standard that can be used for performance evaluation. As a consequence, it can be very tenuous in some project situations to determine performance competence and contribution. Individual performance evaluation by the project manager is often based on subjectivity. As often happens, there are sharp differences of opinion regarding performance between the evaluator and the evaluatee.

In many operational situations poor performance becomes readily apparent. Where performance is deemed inadequate, managers usually are quite prompt in calling such shortcomings to the attention of the perpetrator. Exceptionally good performance is generally but not always recognized. It is the reliable day-to-day performer who does his job who tends to be overlooked, unless there is a periodic accounting period to review accomplishment.

A project represents a socially oriented and professionally dependent unit. Members of the project naturally seek organizational recognition. Informal recognition can be manifested by peer acceptance. Formal recognition can normally only result from review and evaluation; some responsible superior, for example, the project manager, must determine contribution and have the authority to reward effort. What appears to be an obvious and simple situation is not because, as indicated, there is the lack of adequate criteria for establishing performance standards. Professionals who manage professionals are frequently loath to review their work. Instead of rectifying a situation, which pained many of them when they were subordinates, they perpetuate the problem after they achieve management status.

A Work Management System

The crux of the problem is to establish a means of evaluating individual project performance that encourages productivity and creativity, avoids burdening professionals with myopic administrative detail, and concretely assesses activity without hour-by-hour or day-to-day harassment and distraction.

A work management system can provide such a means. The system envisioned will be considerably simplified if the project has been planned. When the project components have been identified, the next sequential step is to establish a work management system. This process, in broad terms, consists in relating individual assignments to project objectives and commitments.

Work management encourages better execution of the project plans by breaking them down into more detailed units and clarifying the obligations of each implementing person and group. It enables management to delegate authority more intelligently and to trace accountability, and it serves as a channel for information feedback and as a method for control down to the individual level.

A work management system helps personnel to operate efficiently. For instance, a schedule of project operations is based on estimates of the effort that will be required and an anticipation of the problems that will be encountered. Planning and estimating usually stop at supervisory levels. Because detailed inputs from subordinates are generally excluded, resource requirements are necessarily based on rough subjective calculations, and safety or contingency factors are used as a hedge. Each subsequent planning review level may add hedge factors, until the program appears technically and economically unfeasible. Realizing that the hedge process exists, management may scale down estimates, but specific work elements often defy evaluation; maintaining work control under such circumstances is practically impossible.

This suggestion might help simplify the problem: that management concentrate on planning, controlling, and developing individual work segments as coherent units. Analysis of these components will generally establish planning factors and will thus make it possible to set optimum schedules and subsequently improve operational efficiency.[8] In addition, work management should interrelate functional activities, show the total work load for the project, and provide a sequential plan of action to indicate progress correlated with performance, time, and cost.

To illustrate how the proposed work management system can be instrumental in partially solving the evaluation and measurement problem, a charting of functional responsibility on support assignments, like that in Figure 14-1, helps managers plan and assign the work in keeping with program objectives and available human resources and capability. The assigned work blocks give participants perspective on the program, signify responsibility by defining areas of contribution, signal deviation from goals or technical difficulties, and afford a context for the recognition of accomplishment. Delineating the support assignments also gives management a sensitive control over operations. Problem areas can be located quickly and allocations of resources modified or redirected.

From the simple system suggested in Figure 14.1, it is possible to derive a model of an individual work log (Figure 14-2) that represents a further refinement of work management. In Figure 14-1 the model shows item 1, phase 1A, assigned to Sam Brown. In the individual work log, Figure 14-2, that segment of work is enlarged to indicate the responsibility assigned to Sam Brown.

Sam Brown may have many project assignments during an audit period; assignments can vary considerably in scope and duration. As illustrated in

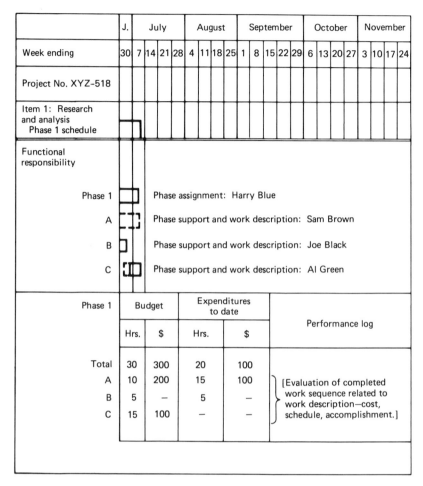

Figure 14-1. Project support assignment. From Daniel D. Roman, *Research and Development Management: The Economics and Administration of Technology,* Englewood Cliffs, NJ: Prentice-Hall, 1968, p. 399.

Figure 14-2, Sam Brown may be involved intermittently on assignment 4, concurrently on assignments 1 and 2 or 3 and 4, or sequentially on assignments 2 and 3.

The work log is a simple form to be maintained by each project professional; it is not designed for an hour-by-hour or day-by-day accounting of his or her time. A report of the professional's occupation during small increments of time is meaningless, since productivity in most project environments cannot by cycled with the regularity of more mechanical operations. On the other hand, some tangible evidence of accomplishment should be apparent over a reasonable period, say 3–6 months.

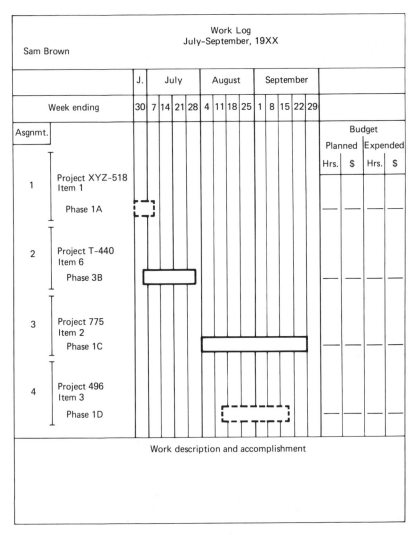

Figure 14-2. Work log for Sam Brown. From Daniel D. Roman, *Research and Development Management: The Economics and Administration of Technology,* Englewood Cliffs, NJ: Prentice-Hall, 1968, p. 400.

Within such an interval management has sufficient evidence of activity to make an appraisal of accomplishment and performance.

A work management system will encourage better superior–subordinate relations. The superior has specifics to use in evaluating subordinates' performances in relation to assignments, accomplishments, professional growth, and cost of effort. The work log enables the project professional and management to determine quantitative as well as qualitative productivity. It also helps to eliminate generalized impressions or images of employees by focusing attention on the assignment proper and its ultimate contribution to broad objectives. The subordinates receive credit and recognition for work performed and appreciate what is required of them, and management has a basis for comparing each of them with other employees. The system further provides the executive with a sturdy foundation for decision making and control, because it documents his or her organization's capacity, efficiency, economy, and relative accomplishment.

The author believes that the proposed work management system represents an improvement over most methods now generally being used to evaluate project professional performance. The procedure may represent a radical innovation for organizations that have no system whatsoever.

As is the case with most systems, this one also has limitations. For example, it is possible to define the individual's volume of accomplishment during a given time period, and this is a significant factor, but deciding on the degree of accomplishment and the value of the effort remains a subjective process.

Cost can be measured, but value is quite difficult to determine because, generally, no basis exists for a direct comparison of performances. There is no certainty that the effort, although performed within cost, time, and technical constraints, might not have been done better, equally well, or possibly worse by another individual. In other words, could the performance have been better, even though the results were good? Or was the performance good in view of the type of solution attempted, even though the results were not? There may be good performances but poor results, in that a particular approach is found to be impracticable. Reaching such a conclusion early in the program allows management to avoid expending additional resources, an important benefit. But would someone else have discovered this fact earlier or later, or not even have attempted the approach in the first place? Moreover, it will probably be impossible to ascertain the subsequent value of knowledge derived from such abortive efforts.

Weekly Backlog

Another and even simpler instrument for determining the individual's level of activity is a weekly backlog report, as shown in Figure 14-3. Here there is responsibility for reporting only on (1) current work in process, (2) new work initiated, and (3) work completed.

In reporting work in process, the performer indicates how long the assignments have been in process and the percentage of time or effort devoted to each. Comparing existing obligations with new responsibilities, shown in the section on new work initiated, the supervisor can

Weekly backlog report
(time in weeks)

Name: Sam Brown   Period: 6 1-6 7 19XX

	Project	In process	Estimated to complete	Scheduled to complete	Portion of work time allocated
I. Work in process					
Description:					
1. ∿∿∿∿∿∿	R-23	2	1	2	50%
2. ∿∿∿∿∿∿	59	7	10	12	20
3. ∿∿∿∿∿∿	R-26	3	2	6	20
II. New work initiated					
Description:					
1. ∿∿∿∿∿∿	L-14		10	10	5
2. ∿∿∿∿∿∿	L-17		1	1	3
3. ∿∿∿∿∿∿	M-2		1	1	2
III. Work completed					
Description:					
1. ∿∿∿∿∿∿	P-8	10		10	100
2. ∿∿∿∿∿∿	R-13	3		1	40

Comments:

_____

_____

_____

Figure 14-3. Weekly backlog report for Sam Brown. From Daniel D. Roman, *Research and Development Management: The Economics and Administration of Technology,* Englewood Cliffs, NJ: Prentice-Hall, 1968, p. 402.

quickly get a picture of the individual's commitment, the nature of his or her work, and an approximation of his or her time distribution. The supervisor can also use this information to see whether assignments are on schedule, whether the individual is overloaded, and whether the effort is being properly directed.

The inclusion of a section on work completed gives the supervisor a summary of the time period covered, hours charged, work accomplished, and schedule attainment on completed assignments.

The weekly backlog method is crude in many respects. It gives only a general estimate of effort and allows the reporter considerable latitude to maneuver his or her time on the assignments for which he or she is responsible. On the positive side, the report is simple and does provide information on the individual's responsibilities, time schedule, and progress.

Organizational Benefits from Work Management and Performance Evaluation

Uncertainty often breeds resentment. Uncertainty of performance and contribution frequently exists in project management, especially where there are research and development activities. Consequently, while many organizational activities can be evaluated with some degree of success, many project assessments prove difficult to make and provide an insecure base for performance determination and decision making.

Establishing a system for ordering and measuring project performance at the level of the individual benefits the whole organization. It makes it easier to target in on substandard areas of performance and raise them. It gives management a clearer picture of human resource utilization and reduces the possibility of its being hoarded or misused. Work management can help uncover inadequate professional skill, departures from standard procedure, and improper scheduling of work. By showing assigned areas and subsequent accomplishment, the system places the organization in a position to improve its planning and apply it more effectively. Slacks and bottlenecks are communicated promptly, so that effort can be redirected where necessary. Finally, the system makes management aware of requirements for additional work units to reflect changes in technology and work loads.

Only a few methods for appraising individual effort have been suggested in this section. Many innovations are possible and certainly warrant additional research. Work management and performance audits focus attention on the type of activity, procedures, and contribution of a professional over a reasonable period of time. Of course, such a system may meet with some opposition, because it isolates individual performances and exposes the incompetent, but it will be welcomed by the dedicated and productive professional, for it establishes criteria for recognizing merit and accomplishment.

Project Evaluation

Progress Evaluation

Evaluation of progress and problems on active projects is an integral part of the project management process. The literature is replete with examples of evaluation for ongoing projects.[9] Evaluation methods are also employed as part of the project selection process. Some of these methods were discussed in Chapters 2 and 3. What has generally been ignored is postmortem project analysis.

Postmortem Analysis

Project postmortem analysis, if conducted at all, is generally cursory. There may be organizational pressure to wrap the project up and move on to new areas. Such pressure, plus a vague notion that a project has been successful where there have been no significant customer/client complaints, no major organizational disruptions, and reasonable profitability, mitigate against incentive for constructive outcome evaluation.

An intelligent and comprehensive examination of completed projects can be instrumental in improving the conceptual, formative, and operational project phases for existing and future projects. Was the project terminated because its objectives were accomplished or was it terminated for convenience or, worse yet, for failure?

Was the project compatible with organizational objectives? For instance, does the organization have an operational strategy? Did the project complement such strategy? Was it consistent with short-, intermediate-, and long-range goals?

A project audit or outcome evaluation can be an extremely constructive and valuable tool for both the technical and managerial organization. It can help focus on objectives, establish commonality between management and technicians, and lead to reconciliation of relevant factors involved with evaluating the project.

Postmortem Evaluation Procedure

Projects differ considerably, reflecting environmental and operational variances and managerial philosophies. It is possible that different procedural models might be applicable in evaluating a completed or terminated project within the same organization. Procedural models should be devised to provide management a reasonable and accurate picture of what problems were encountered on the project, how they were handled, what was accomplished on the project, and its organizational contribution.

As indicated, the postmortem evaluation model will probably represent an innovative managerial approach. A procedural model can vary from simple to highly complex, reflecting the nature of the project and the operational climate. A relatively simple approach might be based on a scoring model with a range of 1–10 or 1–5, with 10 or 5 being best and 1 being least desirable. Such factors can be scored as meeting technical objectives, perceived customer satisfaction, follow-on business prospects, profits, new technical opportunities developed, education of technical staff, efficient use of human and material resources, schedules, market expansion or penetration, and organizational image.

Another approach might be based on evaluation of activity during each phase of the project life cycle. For example, in the conceptual phase were the underlying technical and economic premises of the project valid? Did they stand up during subsequent phases of the life cycle? Was the project selection methodology or approach satisfactory? Was the proposal representative of actual project work? In the formative phase, evaluation could center upon effective organization to carry on project objectives, a review of the adequacy of planning, and the use and integration of relevant tools or techniques to facilitate project accomplishment. The operational phase experience can be examined as to the level of actual to planned accomplishment. Also included would be attention to financial and control aspects involved in managing the project, as well as evaluation of productivity and cost/benefit analysis. The terminal phase could concentrate on the various aspects of completing the project and evaluation of procedures and processes in phasing out the project, including disposition of project resources.

Still another possible procedure would be an evaluation in selected operational areas. This will be elaborated upon in succeeding sections.

Suggested Areas for Postmortem Project Evaluation

To effectively conduct an outcome evaluation, it is suggested that a comprehensive analysis be conducted in five areas: technical objectives, cost and budget, human resources, project termination, and the technical and managerial project implications. The element in each of the five evaluation areas are subject to variation in their degrees of importance, depending on the nature of the project. What is important is to identify the relevant and strategic project components in order to provide perspective for project evaluation and future project management. Too often one overwhelming factor in one of the five evaluation areas can lead to a positive or negative perception of project success or failure. In all probability, most projects of any magnitude have had both good and bad experiences. Evaluation, in proper perspective, can provide guidance to perpetuate the good aspects and, hopefully, avoid or minimize the bad experiences in future projects.

Technical Objectives. Postmortem evaluation of how well the project's technical objectives were accomplished can be divided into three distinct phases: the technical conceptual phase, the technical operational experience, and the ultimate technical product achieved.

In the conceptual phase the project's technical objectives can be over- or underestimated. There can be a failure to appreciate the magnitude of the technical problems encountered. At times underestimating the degree of technical difficulty is done purposely in order to solicit project approval. Postmortem evaluation of the project's conceptual phase should look at such factors as the project requirements, including primary and secondary technical objectives, the proposed technical approach, and the supporting technical services required. Additional concerns include performance specifications, the reasonableness of quality standards, the identification of facilities and equipment needs, and the achievement of schedule commitments.

Once the project is operational, some of the objectives set in the conceptual phase may change. Final project evaluation geared to the conceptual objectives may be unrealistic from the technical product originally envisioned. Changes from original technological objectives to the final technical product can occur for several reasons. The state of the art may shift after the project inception. New and better technological approaches may be dictated in order to avoid obsolescence and/or to turn out a better end product than was originally planned.

Some other factors that could modify the original technical objectives are the tendency to overengineer the product (this is especially applicable to military and other government products), the inclination of technical people to seek perfection (this is related to the tendency to overengineer), the discovery late in the project's life that there were significant flaws in the original technical approach, and pressure from management for quick and cheap results (this can be related to competitive, cost, and time factors), and it is possible that, in the initial project start-up enthusiasm, the scope of technical problems was underestimated and, as a result, overoptimism on the solution of the technical phases of the project influenced the original commitment.

The third phase involving the ultimate technical product achieved would entail evaluation of the following: meeting contractual technical objectives, extra or unforeseen technical accomplishments that were not anticipated in the conceptual phase, technical objectives not achieved, the success or failure in meeting technical milestone schedules, with an explanation thereof, and customer relations and satisfaction.

Cost and Budget. Evaluation of cost and budget achievements in relation to project objectives can, to some extent, be analyzed quantitatively. However, cost and budget evaluation should not be oversimplified inasmuch as several factors can affect original cost and budget estimates. Some cost and budget elements can be reasonably controlled, some can be anticipated, and some, such as major changes in the thrust of the project once underway, may be difficult to predict.

Assuming there has been no drastic change in the technical aspects of the project, it would be meaningful to compare actual expenditures of resources again planned expenditures. Resource expenditures reviewed could include comparison of staff requirement projections against actual persons employed, overhead allocations, facilities and equipment use, supporting services required, and external resources contracted for.

Provisions can be made in the postmortem evaluation for some types of cost and budget expenditures that can be anticipated, if not directly controlled, such as contingencies for inflation, unforeseen technical difficulties, uncontrollable customer-dictated program stretch-outs, and added costs resulting from the unavailability of material, equipment, or facilities when needed.

Some cost and budget factors that could be difficult to forecast are significant changes in the technical scope of the project resulting from internal technical miscalculations, customer-requested changes, and/or a shift in the state of the art, which would affect the final product if not accommodated. Comparative cost and budget evaluation, based on original estimates, can be inconclusive, if the final project product is quite different from the project product originally planned.

Despite the range of difficulties indicated in evaluating cost and budget performance on a completed project, such evaluation is critical. The other four evaluation areas may score positively, but if costs and budgets are exceeded without some strong reconciliation or mitigating factors, the ability of the organization to survive and continue operations could be jeopardized. Further justification for review in this area would be to look for patterns. Are there some project expenditures that are repeatedly miscalculated? Identifying such areas could be very meaningful in providing better project managerial control. It could help identify project phases or functional activities where there are tendencies to consistently pad, areas of perennial overoptimism, technical incompetence, or out-and-out estimating ineptitudes.

Another consideration for cost and budget evaluation would be to review how budgets are derived and costs are experienced. Project budget changes, overhead allocation methods, and actual cost expenditures can be instrumental factors in the ultimate profitability or cost effectiveness of a project. By carefully comparing actual against planned expenditures, it might be possible to segregate areas where cost reduction would be possible without impairing the project objectives or the morale of the people assigned to the project. This could lead to added profitability and organizational flexibility.

Human Resources. In the final analysis, it is people who make or break organizations. Project objectives frequently are related to knowledge generation and employment. The project product may be nonstandard, somewhat intangible, and it is often difficult to comparatively evaluate. In almost all professions hard and fast quantifiable standards of excellence for evaluative purposes are virtually impossible to synthesize.

Despite subjectivity in evaluation within the profession, peers generally know who is a good doctor, scientist, engineer, lawyer, or professor. Conceding subjectivity in evaluating human factors in project management does not diminish the need or the importance of such evaluation.

Several avenues pertaining to human factors can be explored. What were the internal project working relationships? Did the project people interface well with other functional support areas? Were there too few or too many people assigned to the project? What type of people were assigned? What qualitative and quantitative people support was required external to the immediate project? Were there learning and professional growth? Were the project people professionally flexible? Transferable? Promotable? What was the actual ultimate disposition of the people assigned to the project? Were there any significant accomplishments as a result of the project? Was there a participative/consultative environment? What about communication? Motivation? Delegation? Did the people assigned to the project use their time effectively? Can some productivity index on the project be established? If so, were the project people productive? To what extent?

Project Termination. Project termination was discussed at some length earlier in this chapter. By way of a quick review, the project termination can be evaluated from three different perspectives: The project was concluded because its objectives were met; the project was terminated for convenience; or the project was terminated for default.

Regardless of the cause for termination, as cited in the preceding paragraph, termination procedures should carefully be examined. A quick and orderly transition should be effected whenever possible. Loose ends and delays create problems, divert resources that might be more productively used elsewhere, and add to operational costs. As stated earlier in this chapter, this is a neglected phase in the project life cycle. Winding up a project can be unglamorous and tedious. It can also materially affect the final profit picture and the organization's prospects for follow-on business.

Unfortunately, unless there are obvious foul-ups that become significant problems, little managerial attention is directed to this phase. Termination problems can often be anticipated and transition from operations to project wrap-up can be expedited by establishing termination procedures and assigning qualified and responsible people to see that this phase in the project's life cycle is accomplished.

Managerial Implications. Evaluating a terminated project from a managerial perspective to some extent reviews the effort from the four previous sections, as well as provides additional insight. Managerial evaluation, while entailing some overlapping, can be justified because project performance, as perceived by technicians, might not be perceived in the same light by management.

A postmortem project evaluation, from management's position, would probably focus on such factors as the following: What was the customer/client reaction? Degree of satisfaction? On some type of scale from 1 to 10, with 1 being worst and 10 being best, how would the project rate and why? What organizational benefits can be attributed to this project? Organizational benefits would be actual or potential follow-on projects, compatibility with organizational goals, planning, and strategies, transferable learning or educational knowledge derived by professional and managerial components of the organization, effective use of available resources, and developing new or expanding existing physical and human resources.

Some additional managerial considerations that might be relevant are as follows: To what extent did this project contribute to the maintenance and development of the professional organization? Was it completed as planned, or did its project life extend beyond a defensible period? What specific technical expertise resulted from the project? Were there any managerial or technical innovations? Were these innovations marketable? What did the project teach us in order to provide guidance for better future performance? Was there any sociological significance attached to the project? Did the project expose potential legal or ethical consequences? What did the project contribute to the organization's present and potential profitability?

As indicated earlier, projects are apt to vary considerably in technical complexity. All the evaluation factors indicated in this section would not apply to all projects. Some projects might require managerial evaluation in areas not suggested in this section.

An Outcome Evaluation Audit Model

Two-Phased Model

In the preceding five audit areas, several evaluation possibilities were indicated. The outcome evaluation audit model is a two-phased model. Phase one is procedural or descriptive to provide guidance for identification of relevant evaluation factors. Phase two is prescriptive in that, once the pertinent evaluation factors are identified, problem areas can be isolated and corrective action, where applicable, can be initiated.

Also, appropriate planning can be facilitated to avoid similar problems on future projects. The following two phases are only suggestive. Each project environment would probably require innovative modifications. As indicated, phase one factors will vary. Phase two can also be modified or adapted to specific situations.

Phase 1

1. Technical objectives
   a. Primary objectives
   b. Secondary objectives
   c. The proposed/actual technical methodology
   d. Other objectives

2. Cost and budget
   a. Actual versus planned expenditures
   b. Adequacy of contingency allowances
   c. Profitability
   d. Other objectives

3. Human resources
   a. Internal working relationships
   b. Interface with other projects
   c. Professional development
   d. Other objectives

4. Project termination
   a. Completion, convenience, or default
   b. Termination procedures and problems
   c. Legal implications
   d. Other objectives

5. Managerial implications
   a. Customer/client reaction
   b. Contribution to organizational objectives
   c. Expansion of physical and human resources
   d. Other objectives

Phase 2. A Prescriptive Model

Factor	No problem	Periodic problem	Constant problem	Degree of importance	Explanation of the problem
Technical objective Methodology		X		Very important	Tendency to miscalculate magnitude of technical effort and difficulty
Cost and budget Expenditures			X	Very important	Cost overrun
Human resources Low productivity			X	Very important	Inadequate planning: unavoidable support resources

Phase 2. A Prescriptive Model (continued)

Factor	No problem	Periodic problem	Constant problem	Degree of importance	Explanation of the problem
Project termination			X	Important	Failure to expedite contractually required termination procedures
Managerial implications Contribution to organizational objective		X		Very important	Project not compatible with growth objectives or available physical and human resources

Some Concluding Observations

In an organization where there are many and at times diverse projects, the tendency is to complete the project and move into something new and, hopefully, professionally stimulating. By the time the project has evolved into its final phase, people assigned to the project may be bored and anxious to move to another project, since the professionally challenging work has already been accomplished. The possibility of an enlightening and more than casual postmortem evaluation promises little professional stimulation. Worse yet, a postmortem audit can disintegrate into a finger-waving accusing exercise. The purpose of a postmortem review is not accusation, but professional and organizational performance improvement.

Project evaluation should be holistic. This section has stressed five significant audit areas. It has also been mentioned that one overwhelming factor can subvert many other pertinent and important factors. It is urged that any postmortem project evaluation procedure involve representatives from the different organizational elements that have contributed to the project. This is very important in order to minimize distortion based on narrow functional orientation. For example, in evaluation, technical project people can be pleased with accomplishments to the exclusion of other factors that are essential elements to project success. Even though technical objectives have been achieved, management can be dissatisfied for a variety of reasons, such as an excessive cost, low or no profitability, little potential for follow-on, questionable contribution to organizational objectives, and poor utilization of scarce resources. Conversely, management might be satisfied, but the project professionals might feel the results are not technically as good as possible. There is always the conflict between the managerial pressure for fast results and minimal expenditures and the professional's aim for technical perfection.

Lessons learned from a comprehensive evaluation audit can lead to improved organizational profitability, efficiency, and competitiveness. It can be instrumental in improving organizational productivity and this, in turn, can lead to greater operational flexibility and provide an expanded operational base. With proper communications and people education, it should become apparent that if the organization prospers and thrives, the people within the organization will also benefit professionally and economically.

The Operation Audit

Periodic Review and Evaluation

The operation audit is a technique to inventory and evaluate the total organization and its management. Organizations can stagnate or grow, be losers or be profitable. The operation audit can vary from a very complex technical procedure for a large organization to a simple but relevant operational review for the smaller organization. Regardless of organization size and complexity, a periodic audit can be useful in providing perspective, affirming objectives, pointing out areas that suggest inefficiencies, and perhaps lead to new or modified operating procedures.

Designing the Audit

There is no set methodology. Each manager should identify the critical organizational elements and systematically proceed on an evaluation. The following ideas represent only one possible approach.

Some General Questions

1. What do you think will be your operational environment in the next 5 years? In the next 10 years?
2. Is your operational environment expanding or contracting?
3. Can new competitors easily enter the field? How would this affect your organization?
4. What markets might expand or contract?
5. What functional changes can be anticipated within your field of operations? By functional changes, how will present activities be affected? To what extent do you feel technology might affect your industry, company, or organization?
6. As an owner or manager, how do you feel you will be affected? What new knowledge can you identify that would help you in any technological transition (e.g., the computer, new energy sources, new materials, new production processes)?
7. How are you affected by industry or legal standards that dictate or limit your operating prerogatives?

Management Philosophy

1. Does the organization have specific goals or objectives?
   a. Is there a periodic review of these goals or objectives?
2. What are your operational policies?
3. Does the organization concentrate in a single activity, technological phase, or product, or tend toward diversification?

Organization and Management

1. What is the skill mix?
2. What is the age mix within the organization?
   a. What is being done to provide continuity, nondependence on indispensible person?
3. To what extent do people within the organization need training to improve their job skills?
4. How is responsibility handled? Is there delegation of authority and is there proper accountability?
5. Is there a periodic review of the human organization as it relates to the business and to the people in the organization as individuals?
6. Are the leadership philosophy and style compatible with your type of organization and its employees?

Competitive Appraisal

1. Are financial ratios used for competitive comparison and analysis?
2. How does the organization stack up with competitors on physical plant and equipment?
   a. Have capital and labor-intensive activities been looked at as to their impact on being competitive?
3. Can your organization be evaluated and compared in the light of a competitive operation position?
   a. What competitive advantages do we have?
   b. Is our competitive position improving or deteriorating?
4. What competitive advantages and disadvantages do we have for the following?
   Management
   Technical
   Marketing
   Production
   Procurement
   Personnel
   Accounting and finance

Industry Characteristics

1. What is happening in the industry?
   a. What is our relative position in the industry? Are we typical or atypical? Why? Are we a leader (innovator) or a follower?
2. Is the industry growing or declining?
3. To what extent is diversification possible? As an operational hedge? To minimize seasonal fluctuations? New project possibilities?
4. To what extent are we subject to government regulation—local, state, or federal?

People Evaluation

1. How are we organized? Who does what and why?
2. How much personnel turnover do we have? Is the turnover rate reasonable? In terms of cost and operational disruptions?
3. Are we losing good people? Why? Where are they going?
4. Do some functions appear to be performing better than others? Why? What are our major functional strengths?
5. How are decisions made? Is there some kind of an orderly analytical process, or are decisions made spontaneously off the cuff?

Marketing

1. Do we attempt to forecast sales? Customers' requirements? Evolving technology?
2. Do we have any marketing strategies that might give us a competitive advantage?
3. Do we use marketing controls? So we know what the goods or services really cost us? What we really receive from the customer? Do we have inventory controls? Are we paid in a reasonable time and are payment schedules factored into marketing costs? Have we made a distribution analysis? Some business for the sake of business may not be profitable now or have future potential profitability.
4. Are our selling goals being realized? How effective is our selling?

Accounting and Finance

1. Do we have planned growth? Are we achieving an orderly growth process without putting ourselves in a highly vulnerable financial position?
2. What is our return on investment? Is this as good or better or worse than other similar organizations?
3. Do we plan and budget our resources?

4. What is our credit rating? Are we compromised and perhaps embarrassed by a poor credit rating?

5. Have we analyzed our debt/equity ratio?

6. Have our resources grown? How?

7. What are our capital expenditure policies?

8. Do we have inventory balance and control related to financial goals?

9. Are depreciation practices reasonable? Are we providing reserves and resources for necessary modernization?

10. Do we have a system of checks and balances to account for resources and prevent loss from deterioration, unaccountability, and theft?

11. Do we know our true operating costs? What each operational component costs and contributes?

12. Do we analyze financial trends?

13. What tests are used to ascertain the following?
Liquidity
Solvency
Cash flow
Profitability
Investment balance

Some Miscellaneous Audit Factors

1. Material control goals
Make, buy, or lease
Subcontracting procedures
Vendor selection

2. Production
Economic production runs
Product life and reliability
Are we turning out a good product at the cheapest possible cost?
Do we meet our production schedule commitments?

3. Facilities and equipment
Are our facilities adequate to do the job?
Are they modern or obsolete?
Do we have the capacity to meet our requirements?
Do we have unutilized facilities and equipment?

4. Quality control

5. Materials
Buying
Handling
Storage

The questions raised in the preceding sections primarily applied to project organizations where an end material product could be anticipated. In project organizations where the end product would be the knowledge gained from research, study, or report, many of the questions posed would not be applicable. The main theme, however, is not necessarily the specific questions asked or operational areas audited, but the emphasis on the need for periodic review and evaluation of operations. Frequent review, reaffirmation, or reassessment is essential for organizations operating in a volatile technological environment.

Endnotes Chapter Fourteen

1. R. Balachandra and J. A. Raehn, "How to Decide When to Abandon a Project," *Research Management*, Vol. 23, No. 4, p. 25, 1980.

2. L. T. Goodman, J. N. Hawkins, and T. Hiyabara, *Food and Agricultural Waste Projects, Planning and Management*, New York, Pergamon, 1982, p. 15.

3. D. Roman, "A Proposed Project Termination Audit Model," *IEEE Transactions on Engineering Management*, Vol. EM-30, No. 3, p. 125, 1983.

4. Also see I. Avots, "Why Does Project Management Fail?" (condensed from *California Management Review*), *AMA Management Review*, January, pp. 36–41, 1970.

5. Some of the ideas expressed in this section have been suggested in *Project Manager's Guide*, Technical Document 108, Naval Ocean Systems Center, San Diego, 1 June 1977, p. viii–4.

6. R. D. Archibald, *Managing High Technology Programs and Projects*, New York, Wiley, 1976, p. 234.

7. Balachandra and Raehn, *op. cit.*, pp. 27 and 28.

8. Norman J. Ream, "Planning and Control in Engineering Management," an address at the Management Conference of the American Society of Mechanical Engineers, Los Angeles, CA, September 17–18, 1957; Paper No. 59-NGT-7, New York, American Society of Mechanical Engineers, October 1959, pp. 45–46.

9. A few representative samples: W. E. Souder, "A System for Using R&D Project Evaluation Methods," *Research Management*, Vol. 16, No. 5, September, pp. 29–37, 1978; R. D. Archibald, *op. cit.*, Chapter 9.

CHAPTER FIFTEEN

The Project Manager and Project Management

The Project Manager

Technical and Managerial Competence

Project management starts with the project manager. The activities and skills required for efficient and effective project management are considerable. More often than not, as has been stated several times, the project manager is selected because of demonstrated technical competence. There are occasional exceptions, however, to the aforementioned, in that there may be projects and situations where the project manager is selected because of managerial ability or broad qualifications, such as in the military.

Project management normally involves both technical and managerial competence. As a generalization, it could be said that in research projects there would be greater emphasis on technical skills, whereas in large developmental projects the major emphasis would shift to managerial ability.

Shifting Job Emphasis

Frequently an individual goes into business or is promoted in an organization on the basis of demonstrated technical ability. The new position almost invariably requires more management of technical activity than technical management. The roles are not completely disassociated, but there is a major shift in emphasis in the requirements for professional performance. Technical awareness is important to understand the problem, but if the manager persists in maintaining technical competence and activity, he or she will give short shrift to the elements vital to the job of being manager.

To manage technical activity, the manager must be familiar with the various functional aspects of the organization, functional tools and techniques, and the contributions of the different functions in achieving organizational objectives. The manager must understand finance, accounting, production, marketing, personnel, and other operations. The manager of technical activity must be able to use and integrate these functions to support technical activity.

The project manager has to be aware of distinctive operational characteristics in technical management and the management of technical activities. There are also significant differences between managing a project and managing a functional activity; many project managers achieve this position subsequent to serving as functional managers. According to Archibald, "functional management may be said to be 'dividing' or perhaps 'divisive' management since the organization is divided along functional lines, while project management, like general management, is 'integrative' in nature."[1]

Technical managers are generally absorbed in the technical aspects of the job and have a far narrower purview. They thus have a quite different set of decision factors. They determine the feasibility of the project, how to approach the problem, what materials or methods might best be used, which skills are available to them, and which they need to accomplish the technical objectives. In short, the technical manager defines the technical problem, decides on a possible method or methods of solution, and identifies the resources required to accomplish program objectives. The manager of technical activity acquires, uses, and coordinates resources. The technical manager is concerned with the specific resources called for by the project; the manager of technical activities is concerned with the general as well as specific resource requirements.

Selecting the Project Manager

In view of the diversity of activities that might be anticipated in project management, and the well-above-normal managerial ability required to cope with such activities, selecting a project manager includes careful consideration of the skills and aptitudes relevant to the position. Upper-level management must be cognizant of the type of project, its duration, knowledge requirements, and technical objectives. A prospective project manager may do well under one set of project operational conditions and be a failure when assuming project management responsibilities under different operation circumstances.[2] Accordingly, management must factor into the selection decision process not only the competence, experience, and professional growth potential of the prospective project manager, but also personal characteristics that ultimately might be influential on the project's success or failure.

The theme throughout this book has been that project management normally is an extremely complex activity. The management capability requirements can range from challenging on short and relatively simple projects, to extensive on technologically complex projects covering a considerable time period. This chapter is, to some extent, a recapitulation of material discussed in previous chapters. It is also an attempt to synthesize the concept of project management by focusing in on the various aspects of the project manager's job. The following sections in this chapter will look at the job elements of project management (i.e., what the project manager does); the different operational environments where there is projectization and how the operational environment might impact on project management; some of the more persistent problems associated with project management; an attempt to develop a profile of a good project manager; some suggestions on what might be done to improve the project manager's performance; and, finally, a graphic overview of the project management process, showing the range of activities in the different phases of the project life cycle.

What Does the Project Manager Do?

Scope of Activities

The scope of the project manager's activities can range from very general managerial actions to managerial obligations that are quite explicit. Furthermore, the scope of operational latitude can be expanded or restricted by the operational environment, the type of project, the phase of the project life cycle, and degree of management support for the project, as well as managerial operational philosophy.

Project managers may have some very specific job obligations that can be incorporated into a formal job description. Again, bearing in mind some of the restrictions indicated in the preceding paragraph, the specific job components can situationally vary. There are also some very general skills or job-related activities that are difficult to state specifically and incorporate into a job description. However, many of these general activities are often crucial to project success or failure. These general activities are usually intangibles; how well they are performed and to what extent they are influential are usually based on subjective evaluation.

Some Explicit Job Requirements

As a starting point, project management job requirements follow the fundamentals applicable to any general area of managerial responsibility. "The project manager ideally will plan, organize, monitor, and direct the project to its goals as effectively as possible."[3] Of course, executing the management fundamentals in some situations is relatively straightforward, whereas planning, organizing, monitoring, and directing a project to its goals can entail very sophisticated effort.

It is safe to assume that the fundamentals indicated in the previous paragraph will have general applicability. Other job elements can be specifically applicable in some situations and not relevant under different project operational conditions. For instance, the job description could indicate a requirement for interface with the various constituencies with which the project is involved. The project manager may have liaison responsibilities with the immediate project team, internal functional support activities, outside contractors, consultants, the customer, and upper-echelon management. Another specific could relate to technical qualifications, educational attainment, and related experience requirements as a prelude to qualification as a project manager. Other job-related activities that could be subject to explicit responsibilities could include the obligation to issue periodic reports on project progress, cost management, personnel selection and placement, scheduling, and project resource management and allocation.

Archibald[4] concurs with the fundamental job requirements mentioned and indicates peripheral responsibilities, including the following: accomplishing project cost, technical, and schedule objectives consistent with available resources; meeting profit objectives when the project is contracted outside the organization; progress liaison with management; obligation for decisional processes germane to the project's success; an obligation to review and determine the feasibility to continue or terminate the project; to be the contact point for the various internal and external forces dealing with the project; and to determine and agree upon the support requirements from activities outside the immediate project domain.

Kerzner essentially agrees with Archibald and identifies another specific responsibility to resolve all conflicts resulting from project operations.[5] He sets up implicit responsibilities under three major classifications, including interface management (product and project interfaces), resource management, and planning and control management.[6]

Some General Job Requirements

There are many critical skill requirements associated with project management that cannot be quantified or even explicitly spelled out as part of the project management job description. Many of these general job requirements are conceptually related; some entail considerable interpersonal skills; and some are no more complex than exercising good old-fashioned common sense.

Leadership is an essential ingredient of good project management. Leadership can be based on position and absolute authority or on respect and accepted authority. People want to look up to leaders. Subordinates often see in the leader a means for achieving their own aspirations. They want an aggressive and progressive manager who creates a favorable internal and external organizational impression. People will follow, respect, and support a strong individual who is fair, even if he or she is aloof, more readily than they will the good-fellow type who is a nonprogressive wheelspinner. The effective leader is liked and admired; if the choice had to be made, it would be more important for the project manager to be admired and respected than to be personally popular.

In a volatile technological environment the leader's position is precarious. There is constant pressure to maintain a stimulating and professionally rewarding atmosphere. Subordinates often have received their education more recently than the project manager; they are usually impatient for the opportunity to test new ideas and methods. If the project manager is overly conservative and technically out of date, his or her people will probably be frustrated. Frustration would be a by-product of an operational situation where the project manager is not competent and, as a consequence, indecisive. In such situations there would be a reasonable probability that the more capable people will leave the group. Considering the aforementioned, as part of the leadership obligation, the project manager must constantly keep alert to technological developments that could impinge on the project. The project manager must also be flexible and be willing to innovate, adopt, and implement new ideas.

An all too common societal development is the fact that people want identification but are often reluctant to put forth commensurate effort or commitment. Managers are frequently reluctant to acknowledge the price of leadership. The manager paces the organization; if he or she stagnates or takes defensive action primarily to maintain their position, the entire project organization can easily deteriorate in short order. By example, the project manager must set a pattern for continued development and improvement.

A good clue to the caliber of the leadership is the overall reputation of the project organization and the individual prestige enjoyed by its members. Normally an organization seeks its own level; people tend to gravitate to their own type. A capable leader recognizes that organizational strength reflects composite abilities; such a leader will surround himself or herself with good people. It is unusual to find good people and a poor leader, or a good leader and poor subordinates. The incompetent person who has managed to achieve a leadership position is invariably afraid to subject himself or herself to comparative appraisal by employing competent lieutenants.

The leader must be emotionally stable. Reasonably predictable performance on his or her part is a soothing organizational influence. The project manager should avoid indulging in temper fits or allowing personal considerations to affect their dealings with subordinates. It is difficult for the leader to run away and hide from people on "off-days." Subordinates who have a much narrower operational range are in a much better position to avoid personal involvement on bad days.

Certain leadership prerogatives and status symbols are generally recognized and accepted. But leaders cannot indulge in such luxuries as sloppy work habits or unreasonable privileges without finding that the organization apes them in these respects. It is much more difficult to get people to follow the good example than the bad. Good work habits must be drilled into people; sloppy practices are more readily emulated.

Time is a critical resource to the project manager. Often time is not recognized as a resource and is not properly utilized. The project manager should avoid burying himself or herself in administrative trivia or pursuing technical activity that could be better delegated to subordinates. The inability to disassociate himself or herself from details and technical competition with subordinates is a common failing in project management.

Decision making is another vital aspect of leadership and project management. Despite the importance of anticipating and resolving problems in advance, project managers may not recognize problems or, on occasion, are loath to make decisions. The project manager must not avoid the decision-making part of the position. If the project manager vacillates, this becomes painfully apparent to everyone in the project organization. At times a questionable decision is better than none at all. Often managers do not know how to identify problems, how to explore for possible solutions, or how to sound out the organization for the implications of a potential course of action if a decision were forthcoming. Inaction could result from indecisiveness. Where decision making or policy is not under the guidance of a firm hand, time rather than the project manager becomes the influential factor in resolving decisional issues. This is not conducive to external respect for the organization or internal admiration for its leadership.

Problem solving is a prime justification for the project manager's existence. The project manager must bear in mind the operational facts of life, that, if people were self-starting, naturally highly motivated, properly oriented, inherently talented, basically cooperative, capable of resolving problems independently, and willing to continue indefinitely in the same environment, in the same position, and at the same reward level, there would be no need for managers. Managers often complain about not having ideal resources allocated to the project and tend also to ignore the paramount fact that people, conditions, and things are less than perfect. An important part of the project manager's job is to solve problems and achieve objectives without optimum resources.

Another important aspect of leadership relates to the project manager's ability to understand the people organization and to motivate subordinates. A good part of the success of a project organization can be attributed to the responsiveness and ingenuity of its people. The technically educated and oriented manager must rechannel the inclination to be thing centered to a people-centered approach.

Motivating technical people can be a by-product of good organization. Technical project people desire a professional image, a reputation for excellence that is fostered by technical competence, and corresponding assignments and activity. An improper utilization of the professional in his or her sphere of competence can deteriorate a project organization into a quasi-clerical or semiprofessional group.

Conversely, as they look outside their own activities, the project professionals are prone to minimize the contribution to the project of other than technical functions and to infringe on these functional areas. Project managers must educate their people to the concept of the division of labor and to the importance of support functions. If they do not do this, their people may spend a disproportionate part of their time on activities outside their professional responsibility, and technical effort will suffer. The project manager must encourage coordination, communication, and understanding among the various functions within the orbit of the project.

Project managers must recognize that the drives and desires of the people who report to them include nonmaterial as well as material needs. As people seek satisfaction for these needs, organizational pressures develop. A reward and punishment system is effective as a means of inspiring motivation, but there are other methods that, when supplemented by reward and punishment techniques, can bring out the prime performance in an organization.

Project professionals are perhaps supersensitive and must have recognition for their professional contribution. Individual development should be encouraged and performance and accomplishment acknowledged with publicity and appreciation; people will often accept sincere direct acclaim in lieu of monetary or other tangible rewards if they realize that the manager is unable to grant such rewards. Consequently, project managers should try to develop some system for measuring individual as well as group attainment. They should help people who have done good work to move ahead rather than hoard them under their control. Finally, because they are dealing in a area charged with technological innovation, project managers must encourage a creative environment where creative people can make a recognizable contribution.

The preceding paragraphs have dealt with intangible aspects of the project manager's job of leadership and motivating subordinates. There are several other general job requirements that are essential elements of project management but which do not lend themselves to inclusion in a project management job description. These general requirements can be inferred and, while subjective, represent intangibles that would have a significant bearing on the ultimate success or failure of a project.

Steele is of the opinion that the manager acts in the following capacities[7]:

a critic—to evaluate

an agent—contact point with prospective clients

a producer—the acquisition and utilization of resources

a stagehand—to take care of the details associated with the project; relieve subordinates of such responsibilities

Besides the aforementioned, Steele feels that there are institutionally imposed managerial roles. Some of these institutionally imposed rules are contingent on the manager's place in the organization and could be applicable in project management. These roles, identified by Steele, are achiever, the advocate/salesman, the resource allocator, and the goal setter.[8]

The author would include some other factors that are not explicit but which are considered an essential part of the project manager's job. The project manager should operate from a frame of reference; the suggested frame of reference is that of an entrepreneur. The project should be envisioned as an entrepreneurial activity, including sensitivity to profit goals, cost controls, effective use of resources, and prospects for new or follow-on project activity. In line with the entrepreneurial orientation, the project manager should be a change agent to facilitate the initiation of activity in technologically promising fields and should act as a risk manager, performance evaluator, communicator, and mentor.

Activities and Skill Requirements Can Differ During the Project Life Cycle Phases

The explicit and general requirements discussed are reasonably comprehensive, but certainly not all inclusive. Either category can be expanded or contracted, depending on the project. In some instances, what have been indicated as general job requirements could become explicit obligations and subsequently be incorporated into a job description.

Another way to look at the project manager's job is to examine the various activities and actions required in each phase of the project life cycle. The project manager in many operational environments would assume a participative role from the conceptual phase. It is possible that the proposed project manager, by participating in the project activity from its inception, would benefit from continuity and be in a good position to facilitate necessary integrative efforts. It is also possible that the project manager's sphere of authority would vary according to the required activity in the phase of the project lifecycle. By way of illustration, in the conceptual phase the project manager might have to defer authority in such areas as initial customer liaison, proposal coordination and preparation, and project selection. In the formative phase the project manager's role could be determined by the amount and type of resources under his or her direct jurisdiction, the level and nature of effort performed external to the organization, interrelations with other internal or external projects, and the organization's managerial operational philosophy. In the operational phase the realm of the project manager might be determined by available resources, priorities, schedule constraints, and the extent of active customer involvement with the project. In the termination or completion phase, the project manager might find the project aborted for such reasons as resource availability, competition for available resources, a change in mission, and a shift in the technology.

A breakdown of required actions during the different phases of the project life cycle could provide valuable clues as to the skill level and characteristics requirements for a person to manage that particular project. If the project involves major technological effort, an anticipated long time frame, and the allocation of extensive resources, it could well be beyond the capabilities of an individual. By examining the project activities during the various phases of its life cycle, it might provide insight for the human as well as the material resource requirements that should be assigned to the project manager. It would encourage the formation of a representative project team to augment the project manager's talents and provide necessary support in areas where the project manager has limited experience or operational deficiencies.

One other advantage in looking at the project life cycle phases for organizational purposes is when there might be situations where the project manager does not administer the project from its concept to completion. The project manager can be changed during some phase of the project life cycle for several reasons, including rotation and reassignment (common in the military), transfer to another project, dismissal, or resignation, illness, or death. If provision has not organizationally been made for project continuity, the loss of the project manager can be a severe blow to the morale of the people assigned to the project and negatively affect the prospects for the project achieving its objectives.

Authority and Responsibility

It is essential to effective project management that there be a clear delineation of authority and responsibility.[9] The project manager makes many decisions concerning people, material, costs, and technical performance. These and other activities are management functions that require that they be given the authority and responsibility of a manager.[10]

Authority and responsibility are not really coextensive in the project management scheme. Project leaders are given the responsibility for but have little or no authority over the functional areas that do not report directly to them. If each manager had his or her own functional support in each area required by the project, the organization would, in effect, be a product-type rather than a project-type organization. It is obvious that the cost of such a practice would be prohibitive. Intraorganizational dependence is what makes coordination a large part of the project manager's job.

The project manager rarely has direct authority over general service functions within the company, such as administrative, personnel, finance, purchasing, plant engineering, and production. Control and evaluation of the intangible technical aspects of the program are difficult enough where there is direct authority; the difficulties are compounded by the project manager's lack of authority and frequent inability to assess the contribution or progress of the various support operations. An organizational paradox exists in the title "project manager," since decision making and control latitude are restricted.

By way of summary, the project manager normally does have the authority to plan the project, control project resources under his or her direct jurisdiction, select personnel, represent the project in various liaison capacities, delegate authority to subordinates, and head up the project management office. Some of the areas where the project manager usually does not have authority are functional support activities that are not directly assigned to the project, individuals who may be temporarily assigned but who have the option of transferring to other projects or functions, equipment and/or facilities which are common resources to other projects, the establishing of operational priorities outside the project manager's immediate sphere of influence, and control of resources once allocated to internal or external support activities.

Project Management: Operational Environments

Operational Environments

There are many fundamentals in project management that are applicable whatever the organizational affiliations, the operational objectives, or the type of project; however, there can be some significant distinctions in conditions and practices among government, nonprofit, military, and commercial organizations. The following sections will highlight some of the operational differences. Also, since there is much in common between the government project operational environment and project management in the nonprofit sector, a separate discussion on the latter has been omitted.

Government Project Management

Government project management has certain characteristics that differ from the leadership function in military and commercial projects. For example, while some government laboratories undertaking research and development paralleling commercial firms operationally, workers have Civil Service coverage and enjoy greater job security than is found in commercial projects. The government project manager normally does not have his or her commercial counterpart's concern about organizational continuity. In government laboratories project continuity may be subject to technological and political considerations, and economic factors are often secondary. Connected with this is the fact that in government project management there is no profit expectation to use as a criterion for measuring and evaluating performance. Actual in-house work rarely extends through various technical phases to hardware development; the bulk of project effort is related to testing and evaluating.

Because much project work performed under federal sponsorship is farmed out, the emphasis in government project management often shifts from technical to administrative responsibility. Government project managers must have technical competence to select potential sources and evaluate the progress of a program, but essentially they have no direct technical control. They are primarily a contract administrator and coordinator, and they may perform these functions on several projects. To a large extent, their work is concerned with checking on the contractor's progress through either reports or personal observation.

In the commercial environment, unless there are unusual circumstances, the project manager stays with a project from its inception to its completion. In government the project manager may readily be reassigned during the project life cycle. This creates serious problems of operational continuity.

The government project manager often is responsible for an entire system and sublets segments of the system to various contractors. Each contractor may have a project that is really only a component of a system. The government project manager in such situations acts as a supercoordinator.

Military Project Management

The project manager in the military is frequently a general officer who may or may not have adequate technical and administrative ability. He is often assigned to a project already in process so that he is confronted with the problem not only of familiarizing himself with its pecularities but also of developing the dual competence needed to do an intelligent job of managing. The military officer's tour of duty is usually limited, and it rarely coincides with the complete life cycle of a project. As a result, project management is often interrupted.

The military must train, transfer, or promote people to manage its projects, as it cannot usually go out and hire officer personnel. A partial solution has been the use of qualified civilians to provide technical support and continuity. This practice has frequently created internal conflict. Civilian employees usually assigned to technical projects are specialists, not generalists; they are not subject to duty rotation as military personnel are, and thus have the advantage of program continuity. While they are usually subordinate in military organizations, they often receive higher compensation than their service superiors. Because of the inherent characteristics of the military organization, the military project manager often operates at a psychological as well as technical disadvantage.

Armed forces projects primarily have the purpose of testing hardware that has been developed by contractors. The military project manager must make sure that test range facilities are available and must procure equipment that can be modified to carry out the test of the weapon or weapons systems.

More and more project management in the military is related to the weapons system approach. The manager cannot treat the project as an isolated mission, but must relate it to the total system into which it will go. Systems concepts change, and this leads to problems in military project management. The operational life cycle of a weapons system is generally limited to a relatively few years. If the military project manager works intensively with a weapons system over an extended period of time, he may find that his career potential has been curtailed by exposure to only one type of system with a relatively short life expectancy.

In military as in government project management, profit is not an objective and therefore is not available as a means of evaluating performance. Finally, the project manager in the military operates within the organizational philosophy of the military, which is crisis oriented and which relates authority to rank. In the normal scientific organization there is more colleague authority; technical give and take is the practice rather than the exception.

Commercial Project Management

Project managers in industrial organizations are generally more technically involved than are their military, government, and nonprofit counterparts. They are required to have administrative ability, but their administrative operational sphere is much more restricted unless the bulk of the project activity is performed outside their immediate control.

In the commercial operational environment the manager usually takes the project through the entire cycle of phases to the ultimate development of hardware or solution of the technical problem. He or she coordinates various functional elements in the company and is primarily engaged in operations and the development of a concept.

Motivation and evaluation criteria in commercial project management are strongly profit centered. In commercially directed R&D projects, it is difficult to ascertain the contribution of R&D to the total organizational profit, but in government-sponsored or government-directed programs, contractual arrangements control both expenditures and income, and the profit from a completed project consists in the residue after all contractual commitments have been satisfied.

Project management in commercial operations requires a broader liaison base than it does in military or government projects. The project manager is responsible for liaison with the customer to assure him that the project is progressing according to plan. Project managers must keep top management informed of progress on contractual commitments and profit objectives. They also maintain contacts with vendors if outside contractors are used, and with internal functions in their own organization as well as their project team.

Commercial project managers are usually technical specialists and the project organization is often built around their technical competence. They work to specifications established either by top management or by the customer, but they are responsible for establishing test specifications to make sure that the product will perform according to the customer's requirements.

Project managers also face the unhappy situation that if they and their people do a good job, they ultimately work themselves out of a job. People at lower echelons have a great deal more elasticity in moving to different positions within the organization. The project manager who has achieved a certain organizational status has to find another project to head. If there are no other projects requiring senior-level talent, the organization must decide what to do with managers, for they represent a substantial nonproductive cost. Military and government operations are so extensive that the displaced project director is far more likely to find another comparable assignment.

Because of the ever-present threat of project cancellation or completion, the industrial manager may be constantly involved in proposal preparation. This is a time-consuming and distracting process, but it is a necessary part of the project manager's objective of maintaining his or her position and project organization. New projects may evolve from existing work or from the technology being developed on other projects. Project managers must evaluate the technical effort in their project area and decide whether there are commercially feasible possibilities of extending the project concept or exploring additional areas which the technical information derived from the project has opened up.

Problems in Project Management

Decision Making

A considerable problem area for the technically oriented project manager is the decisional process. Decisional processes that are professionally acceptable in the technical environment may be inapplicable in the managerial environment. The technical professional often wants operational freedom to explore areas that may or may not be directly related to the project objectives. The tendency is to take a long-range view relative to decisions affecting technical inputs. Problem-solving methods relative to technical matters generally emphasize thoroughness. Thoroughness implies waiting for all the facts and then conducting a comprehensive analysis, often after extensive testing and evaluation, before reaching a decision.

The managerial decision process is generally quite different from the decisional methodology used in technical determinations. The project manager usually does not have the time or the resources and subsequent luxury to indulge in any activities or explorations but those directly related to accomplishing project objectives. The project manager normally cannot look beyond the immediate project requirements and thus is forced to take a short-range view on decisions affecting the project. The managerial problem-solving approach also differs from that employed in the technical area. The project manager operates in a volatile environment where facts affecting the project are constantly changing. As a consequence, the project management decisional process often is forced into quick action with limited knowledge in order to keep project operations moving and get results.

The differences in decisional methodology in technical versus management spheres can easily lead to conflict situations. The problem can become more pronounced if the technically oriented project manager persists in continuing to make managerial decisions using the technical decisional approach. Managerial decisions, as indicated, are often forced to deal with less than total information. There frequently is pressure for rapid action-directed decisions. The manager usually cannot wait until all relevant information is available and often, once additional information is gathered, the status on activities received earlier is apt to change. Waiting is akin to vacillation and managerial vacillation can be equated with indecisiveness.

Communication

Communication problems are frequently inherent in project management. Communication difficulties can develop where there are extensive project operations covering diverse activities or functions and involving physical separation of the various project operational components. There can be communication failures because of inadequate coordination and dissemination of relevant information or because pertinent information was not communicated on a timely basis.

Communication failures can also result from the different orientations of the people assigned to the project.[11] Orientational differences can create barriers in understanding or interpreting project objectives. Where such possibilities exist, the project manager should take extra precautionary measures to make sure that there is a meeting of the minds of the people who need and are privy to the information.

There can be communication breakdowns because, as part of the project planning and control process, the project manager has not identified informational requirements. It is possible that informational needs are known but the project manager has not provided for a system to gather relevant data. Another and worse situation is where the informational requirements are known by the project manager and the information is available but the project manager fails to disseminate the information to concerned activities. This type of oversight or omission is not uncommon; it is indicative of poor management and is bound to affect the morale and effectiveness of the project organization.

There is also the possibility that communication failures can be contrived rather than accidental. Information is a valuable operational commodity. It can be politically used to facilitate the accomplishment of objectives or to undermine a program or project. If there are detrimental organizational politics and information is used for operational leverage, it behooves the project manager to recognize the situation and plan project activities to minimize possible disruptions caused by communication problems.

Time

Time is another common problem associated with project management. Time problems are twofold: related to the accomplishment of project objectives and the effective personal use of time.

The project is invariably under some time constraints to meet its objectives. Establishing realistic schedules for accomplishment and meeting these schedules may result in problems. There often is a question as to how realistic the proposed schedule is in line with planned accomplishments and technical difficulties that can be anticipated. Have foreseeable and unforeseeable problems been factored into the time commitment? Will resources be available in quantity and quality when needed? How much optimism or pessimism was there in generating schedule estimates? In effect, were improbable schedule commitments made as a consequence of pressure to get the project authorized?

Another dimension of time involves individual effort. How effectively are people using their time? In view of the diverse managerial obligations, is the project manager properly allocating his or her time? It is possible that a person is working hard but not getting results commensurate with the time and effort expended. A common failing is to become bogged down in detail or trivia that could more productively be delegated to subordinates. Working smart means ordering priorities, not letting important activities go to the last minute, and not committing oneself to obligations that have a low probability of being met.

Competing with Subordinates

In line with the preceding paragraph, there is the tendency for technically trained project managers to compete with their subordinates. This is especially true of recently promoted project managers who would, at least early in their new job assignment, feel much more comfortable in their area of technical expertise than in their assumed managerial role.

There is a definite and sharp transition, as has repeatedly been mentioned, in moving from the technical ranks to project management. The significant distinction is a shift in obligation from "doing," often in a reasonably defined operational area, to managing the "doer" in a much broader operational setting. Frictions with subordinates can occur when assuming the responsibilities of being a project manager. Subordinates who probably respected the project manager in their previous technical but nonmanagerial capacity could become very resentful if such a person could not make a graceful transition from technician to manager; an important part of the transitional process is the recognition of the shift in operational obligations.

To make the transition and avoid resentment from subordinates the project manager has to understand what their new job description entails. The project manager should be available for advice, moral support, and even on occasion technical assistance when it is requested. The project manager should studiously avoid the inclination to get their hands dirty by pitching in unless they are specifically requested to do so or unless the direct application of their technical skill is essential for the completion of the project. Doing technical work that should be delegated creates operational problems, in that the people who are assigned to the technical phase of the project can become very resentful about being shoved aside while their work is being done by the boss. A situation as described does not build confidence in subordinates, allow them the opportunity for professional development, or afford them the dignity and self-respect of accomplishment. Not only are the aforementioned problems created, but there is also the probability that, in directing their energies to technical activities, the project manager could neglect managerial duties.

A Transitional Problem

Many technically competent and technically proven professionals are subject to organizational pressures to move into the ranks of management. The technical professional may feel comfortable and prefer technical work to that of management, but may move to management for one or several reasons.

As the technical professional gets older, he or she may find it progressively more difficult to keep up with the technical developments within their professional field. The difficulty in keeping up could stem from immediate job obligations that limit the available time and effort to exposure to new technical developments. It is possible that a professional may be reluctant to spend the time and effort required for professional retreading, even if the opportunity for professional reinforcement does exist.

It may be that the experienced professional cannot technically compete with younger and more recently trained professionals. The movement to management might really be defensive, reflecting a feeling of technical inadequacy or obsolescence.

The movement to management can reflect a personal evaluation of career prospects.[12] The decision to change the career direction can be due to the desire to do something different and take on a new challenge. Moving to management can also reflect a reluctant decision that is directed by perceived opportunity. The professional may be of the opinion that better opportunity for recognition and reward exists in the managerial ranks than in the technical area. Another reason for moving into management could stem from organizational pressures. There may be an operational philosophy of "up or out" or a senior person may organizationally be needed to fill a management slot. Still another factor can be that a relatively high salary has been derived over a period of time and justification for high organizational income level can be predicated on assuming additional responsibilities that can include managerial activities.

Some technicians can make a relatively easy and successful transition to management. There are instances where the transition is not so easy but the newly appointed project manager approaches the new position with an open mind and crosses over the bridge from technician to manager after a reasonable learning process. Too often, however, the change is approached in a cavalier fashion. The technician minimizes the skills essential to be an effective manager, having not been extensively exposed to or trained in management. The aforementioned shortcoming can either be due to poor management practice in preparing people for promotion to new activities or an unwillingness on the part of the promoted individual to go through an educational process that would enhance the prospects for success in the new undertaking. And with some people the transition from technician to manager is impossible because they just might not have the aptitude to become a good manager.

Scope of Operational Problems

The project manager operates in an extremely difficult environment. As a technician, the operational sphere is relatively limited. Activity and decision are focused and directed to a relatively tight technical area. As a manager, the decisions required cover a much broader spectrum, involving not only technical directions but managerial considerations as well. The decisional knowledge requirements may be beyond the range of the project manager, who is frequently forced to rely on staff or subordinates for decisional inputs. As a technician, the decision was often made on the basis of direct knowledge and experience with some, little, or no reliance on outside support.

As has been stated several times, the project manager has project responsibility but probably does not control all the resources needed to implement the project. The project manager could be responsible for one project or several technically related projects. The more complex the operational responsibilities, the greater the problems in delegation and coordination.

If the project manager has broad operational responsibilities, it could be difficult to honestly evaluate the project manager's performance. Such difficulty stems from the fact that many activities outside the direct control of the project manager can be influential on the project.[13] To what extent is the ultimate project success or failure attributable to the project manager, considering the extent of dependence on support outside the immediate project domain?

The project manager operates in a high-stress environment. There are constant operational pressures associated with achieving project objectives. There are also stresses attendant to being a project manager. Once the organizational level of project manager has been achieved, there is a natural inclination to perpetuate such an organization position. But the project manager is constantly confronted with the prospect of working himself or herself out of a job when the project is completed. Being a project manager in most project-centered environments is being in a position with little operational continuity and facing the constant specter of transfer, reassignment, or unemployment. A project manager normally has little job security. The probability of job security is further diminished if the manager is coming off an unsuccessful project. A person who desires a job with predictable operational requirements, functional continuity, and a reasonable degree of job security should not become a project manager.

Burn-Out

Despite the admonition in the preceding section, there are and will be unqualified people who move into project management. Some people are more adaptable than others. Some people thrive, within reason, in being placed in a stress situation. Some people cannot cope or function where there is an undue amount of pressure. Stress or, the other extreme, boredom can lead to burn-out. The concept of human burn-out is a relatively recently recognized phenomenon. Burn-out affects the individual's attitude, their interface with other people, and their ability to satisfactorily perform on the job.

Burn-out could well be an occupational hazard and problem associated with project management. Some of the symptoms that might indicate an individual is suffering occupational burn-out are lack of energy, boredom, detachment, cynicism, emotional instability, paranoia, a persecution complex, disorientation, depression, frequent job absence, excessive sick leave, and coming to work late and/or leaving early.

Attitudes

Some of the problems associated with project management have been discussed. Many of these problems come with the territory. The capable project manager will learn to adjust to and cope with the operational problems that are inherently part of the job. The experienced project manager should have learned how to deal with project management problems and be able to anticipate or minimize many of the operationally related difficulties. The neophyte project manager would probably have a higher degree of reliance on people directly assigned to the project and those functions or activities necessary for support but outside the project manager's operational jurisdiction. The extent of support and assistance for either the experienced project manager or the recently promoted project manager might well reflect his or her attitude in dealing with the different constituencies.

Fraenkel, in an excellent article,[14] indicates attitudinal approaches that can lead to unsuccessful management. He says, "This advice is presented here in the form of what might be termed the ten uncommandments of management"[15]:

1. Project the impression that you know more than anybody around you.
2. Use excessive controls to monitor the activities of your subordinates.
3. Frequently check on what people are doing and their work progress.
4. Underutilize people assigned to you.
5. Keep people in jobs they do well—don't give them other professional exposures or the opportunity for personal growth.
6. Build interface barriers between your technical staff and other organizational segments including the commercial side of operations.
7. Limit training opportunities for employees to their immediate technical assignment. Don't expose them to educationally broadening experiences.
8. Minimize interpersonal relations. Take an aloof posture.
9. Do not communicate or enlighten subordinates relative to the financial aspects of their assignment or the project.
10. Be the exclusive representative and spokesperson for the project. Keep subordinates in a subjugated position and minimize their contribution.

Profile of a Good Project Manager

Personal Characteristics

Kerzner aptly points out that the selection of a project manager is not a simple procedure, given the nature and range of activities involved. As a consequence, men or women who are selected to be project managers are more often chosen on the basis of their personal characteristics than whether they fit a specific job description.[16]

Archibald indicates some of the personal characteristics needed for efficient project management[17]:

Flexibility and adaptability
Preference for significant initiative and leadership
Aggressiveness, confidence, persuasiveness, verbal fluency
Ambition, activity, forcefulness
Effectiveness as a communicator and integrator
Broad scope of personal interests
Poise, enthusiasm, imagination, spontaneity
Able to balance technical solutions with time, cost, and human factors
Well organized and disciplined
A generalist rather than a specialist
Able and willing to devote more of his or her time to planning and controlling
Able to identify problems
Willing to make decisions
Able to maintain proper balance in the use of time

Augmenting the aforementioned, Kerzner adds the following[18]:

He must know what he is supposed to do, preferably in terms of an end product.
He must have a clear understanding of what his authority is, and of its limits.
He must know what his relationship with other people is.
He should know what constitutes a job well done in terms of specific results.
He should know when and what he is doing exceptionally well.
He must be shown concrete evidence that there are just rewards for work well done and for work exceptionally well done.
He should know where and when he is falling short.
He must be made aware of what can and should be done to correct unsatisfactory results.
He must feel that his superior has an interest in him as an individual.
He must feel that his superior believes in him and is anxious for him to succeed and progress.

Another look at desirable characteristics for a project manager is the profile of an outstanding leader found in the Hughes Aircraft Company publication on *R&D Productivity*[19]:

Sets a particularly positive example as a person.

Takes a dynamic approach to activities.

Brings out the best in people.

Demonstrates great skill in directing day to day operations.

Facing Reality

There is no single managerial template that can universally be adapted to ensure good project management. By the same token, even if there is concensus as to the critical character ingredients needed to be a successful project manager, the intensity and range of human skill requirements would undoubtedly vary owing to the type of project and operational environment. Furthermore, it would take an extraordinary person to have all the requisite characteristics. A more probable situation and a more practical approach would center on the determination of the critical skills needed for a particular project and select a person who is considered to have these strategic skills. As part of the project organizational process, the project manager can be reinforced by the assignment of people who have essential and complementary abilities but that are not considered as strategic to the project's success as those characteristics of the person who has been selected to be the project manager.

What Can Be Done to Improve Project Management

Awareness of Transitional Problems

Project managers have a variegated spectrum of skills to master to do their job proficiently. As has been noted, promotion to the position of project manager is usually based on technical competence, but the management role has administrative skill requirements that are sharply distinct from technical abilities.

The manager's responsibilities require an extroverted approach. It is not easy for the organizationally compartmentalized professional to shift his or her viewpoint to that of the organizationally involved manager. This very transition in outlook can demand considerable effort. Managerial proficiency does require inclination as well as training, sensitivity as well as exposure; but talent in managing cannot be picked up off the cuff as a simple adjunct to technical competence.

Training the Project Manager

Professional employees who aspire to administrative responsibilities should take adequate steps to prepare themselves to perform these functions properly. They will need to exercise their innate affinity for dealing with people and situations; they will need also to practice their ability to use sophisticated concepts and tools and to innovate applicable techniques that can be used to help them manage their projects. It is very difficult in a complex environment for the manager to achieve objectives merely on the basis of an acute intuitive approach. In many project situations the project manager, to perform effectively, must have dual skills, the ability to technically oversee and guide the project and the administrative ability to plan, control, and coordinate project activities.

Two methods are suggested for handling the requirement that the project manager have double competence: First, the project management system can be reorganized to provide dual management, technical and administrative. This practice is frequently followed in government and military project organizations. A second and perhaps in some operational situations more feasible solution is to educate technically oriented people for management.

The first possibility presents problems of internal coordination, communication, and agreement, and violates the principle of vesting responsibility in only one superior. These problems can be circumvented to a degree by dividing authority between the project manager and a deputy. In practice, the nontechnical manager usually does not have equal authority and frequently is put in a subservient position. For example, the subterfuge of divided authority is used where the project manager has an "administrative assistant." Too often this position deteriorates into a high-level clerical job.

The second alternative appears more practical. Many methods of teaching management skills can be used. In-house training programs are quite common. An internal education program can concentrate on the special knowledge deemed relevant to manage projects in a particular operational environment. The components of a managerial training program can be tailored to the needs of the organization and address the specific managerial weaknesses of the project manager. The project manager may also undertake self-education by exploring the literature in the field of management. But self-study requires considerable personal discipline, can be limited by selectivity, and in itself provides no opportunity for discussion and the exchange of ideas.

There are professional associations in which the project manager can be exposed to a variety of ideas, situations, and people as part of his or her training. The value of this approach is avoiding the danger of being limited to only those concepts that exist within the immediate organization. Outside exposure can give added perspective. Are the managerial problems we encounter unique to our organization? Do other organizations have similar problems? How do they handle or avoid these problems?

University work, of course, is valuable, and it is quite common in graduate schools of business, economics, or government to find that a significant percentage of the students have a degree in one of the sciences. Traditional management education is a start in the right direction, but it often fails to identify and structure the problems encountered in project management. Also, when it is impossible for a professional to take time off from the job to follow a full curriculum leading to a degree, the best approach could be to take selected short courses or seminars in management that are offered by universities and professional organizations.

A Mentor System

Another practical suggestion is to use the mentor system. Too often, as has been repeatedly stated, technically proven professionals are thrown into the managerial arena with little or no applicable experience. The mentor system can be used in several ways; two specific approaches are suggested.

It is assumed that the mentor would be an established and recognized competent project manager. As part of career progression and job assignments, technical professionals could serve full- or part-time as administrative assistants to project managers. It could be determined within the organization at what level of career development the assignment would take effect and the duration of such an assignment. Some of the technical professionals after this exposure might opt to move on to more assignments that emphasize managerial activities. After such an exposure some individuals might decide that management is not for them and their best career prospects lie in the technical direction.

This approach could be a testing ground to determine aptitude and inclination. In some instances it could readily be determined that the assignee has neither the flair nor the inclination to be a manager. In such instances where the individual is a valued professional, it would be better to give them future opportunities to hone their technical skills and provide commensurate career opportunities. Regardless of the outcome as to the career direction to pursue, both the individual and the organization should benefit. It would help, as indicated, to determine individual aptitude and the prospects for the most productive career path. An important ancillary benefit would be a heightened awareness by the technical professional of the managerial sphere of activities. An appreciation and understanding of project management problems by the technician, who is often sheltered from such areas, would encourage better management–technician working relationships.

Another possibility, using the mentor approach, is to establish an operational hierarchy in which an individual is obligated to serve as a deputy project manager before becoming a project manager. This would be tantamount to serving an apprenticeship. Setting such a job requirement as a prelude to assuming the responsibilities of being a project manager would encourage an orderly transition. Under this concept people who aspire to be project managers and people who show promise for such an assignment can benefit from on-the-job training. The difference between the first

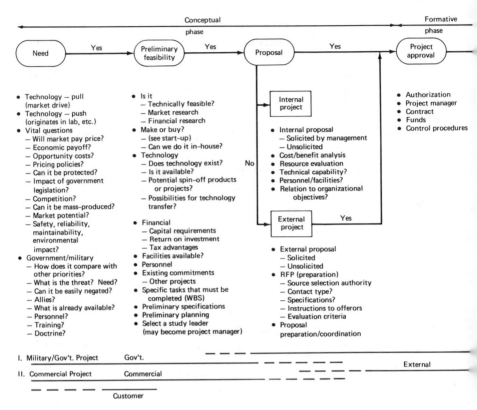

Figure 15-1. Project life cycle. Modified from and developed by F. Cardile and D. Sabatini, Project Management Seminar, The George Washington University, Fall 1982.

approach and this approach is the degree of involvement. A deputy project manager would be assigned to an experienced project manager who could delegate some of the project activities directly to the deputy. The project manager would, in addition, serve as a teacher or trainer. This assignment would require a full-time effort and is based on the assumption that the deputy project manager has made a career decision to move toward management.

In some instances a person could move into a project manager's position after a single exposure as a deputy project manager. On other occasions, more exposure, training, and actual experience might be needed before the individual is considered qualified to move into a project manager's slot. It is also possible that, if a person is considered project management material, they can be moved into such a position starting with relatively simple projects and progress to more important and involved projects as they demonstrate their ability.

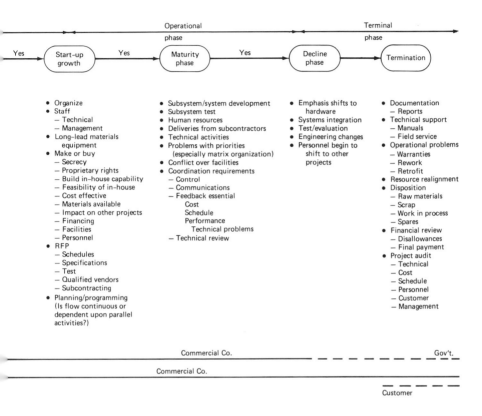

To Minimize Transitional Difficulties

This section has indicated a few ideas that could possibly smooth the transition from technician to manager. Again, the nature of the project operations, the types of technical skills involved, and upper-level managerial philosophy would determine how and when people move into the role of project manager. The central theme of this section has been to heighten sensitivity to the fact that the transition from technician to manager is not a simple or naturally evolutionary process.

Project Management Synthesis

Providing Some Perspective

Figure 15-1 is an attempt to synthesize much of the material covered in this book. This chart depicts the various phases of the project life cycle and many of the activities or decisional factors that might be considered as part of the project management process.

Endnotes Chapter Fifteen

1. R. D. Archibald, *Managing High-Technology Programs and Projects,* New York, Wiley, 1975, p. 35.

2. H. Kerzner, *Project Management A Systems Approach to Planning, Scheduling, and Controlling,* New York, Van Nostrand Reinhold, 1979, pp. 94–95.

3. *Project Manager's Guide,*Technical Document 108, 1st ed., Naval Ocean Systems Center, San Diego, 1 June 1977, pp. 1–3; also see T. Moranian, *The R&D Engineer as Manager,* New York, Holt, Rinehart, & Winston, 1963, p. 2.

4. Archibald, *op. cit.,* pp. 35–36.

5. Archibald also addresses the importance of conflict resolution but treats this as a separate project activity (*ibid.,* pp. 46–54).

6. Kerzner, *op. cit.,* pp. 95–96.

7. L. W. Steele, *Innovation In Big Business,* New York, Elsevier, 1975, pp. 175–182.

8. *Ibid.,* pp. 183–187.

9. See P. O. Gaddis, "The Project Manager," in *Handbook of Industrial Research Management,* C. Heyel (ed.), New York, Reinhold, 1960, p. 95; *Project Manager's Guide, op. cit.,* pp. 1–4.

10. "Honeywell Advanced Technology Report No. 7," Minneapolis, Honeywell, brochure.

11. Steele, *op. cit.,* p. 171.

12. B. Twiss, *Managing Technological Innovation,* London, Longman, 1974, pp. 207–208.

13. Archibald, *op. cit.,* p. 57.

14. S. J. Fraenkel, "How Not to Succeed as an R&D Manager," *Research Management,* Vol. 23, No. 3, May, pp. 35–37, 1980.

15. *Ibid.,* p. 35.

16. Kerzner, *op. cit.,* p. 98.

17. Archibald, *op. cit.,* p. 55.

18. Kerzner, *op. cit.,* p. 99.

19. *R&D Productivity,* 2nd ed., Culver City, Hughes Aircraft, 1978, pp. 100–102.

Index